GLOBALIZATION AND INDIA'S ECONOMIC INTEGRATION

SOUTH ASIA IN WORLD AFFAIRS SERIES
T. V. Paul, Series Editor

TITLES IN THE SERIES

Afghan Endgames: Strategy and Policy Choices for America's Longest War
Hy Rothstein and John Arquilla, Editors

The Engagement of India: Strategies and Responses
Ian Hall, Editor

Globalization and India's Economic Integration
Baldev Raj Nayar

Pakistan's Counterterrorism Challenge
Moeed Yusuf, Editor

Vying for Allah's Vote: Understanding Islamic Parties, Political Violence, and Extremism in Pakistan
Haroon K. Ullah

GLOBALIZATION AND INDIA'S ECONOMIC INTEGRATION

Baldev Raj Nayar

GEORGETOWN UNIVERSITY PRESS
Washington, D.C.

FOUNDATION
BOOKS

FOUNDATION
BOOKS

Foundation Books is an imprint of Cambridge University Press, India.

Cambridge House, 4381/4 Ansari Road, Daryaganj, New Delhi 110 002

www.cambridgeindia.org

First South Asia edition 2015

Printed in India at Bhavish Graphics, Chennai

ISBN 978-93-84463-44-1 Hardback

CONTENTS

IV. SUMMING UP

LIST OF FIGURES AND TABLES

Figures

Tables

PREFACE

Globalization has been the elemental economic force across the globe since at least the last quarter of the twentieth century and, as a consequence, has also become the overarching paradigm in the study of human affairs in the contemporary world. By the same token, all kinds of both ills and blessings have been ascribed to it. The subject may have lost some of its luster in the wake of the global meltdown in 2008, but despite the consequent enormous turmoil, the striking feature of that event has been the lack of resort by nation-states to reverse the onward march of globalization through protectionism. Once the world economy recovers from the aftermath of the meltdown, the omens therefore seem propitious for globalization to resume its course.

The present study on India's political economy deals with but one aspect of the manifold critique about the malign effects of globalization—that is, its alleged impact by way of segmentation of the national economy, leading inexorably, as it were, to economic and even national disintegration. This study, however, takes an agnostic view of the critique, with the principal reservation being that it ignores the role of the state in managing—poorly or effectively—the impact of globalization, even as its understanding of the impact of markets is partial or incomplete. While there exists a strong temptation to ascribe mankind's multifarious ills to globalization, it cannot be stressed enough that globalization is not a single-variable process but a metasocial phenomenon that harbors many trends and countertrends. Globalization has both negative and positive consequences for the national economy, and the challenge for decision makers is to minimize the former and maximize the latter. There is thus no predestination foretold in globalization about the final outcome on economic integration and disintegration.

The critique of globalization and some of the reservations about it are elaborated in chapter 1. Subsequently, the study systematically weighs the critique's position on several aspects of economic integration against the empirical evidence on India. Chapter 2 discusses India's perceptions of globalization in the belief that perceptions have an important bearing on policy. The broad theme that runs through this chapter is that performance of the economy in a given phase fundamentally influences perceptions, which then lead to policy change in a subsequent phase. In contemporary India, a broad centrist consensus on globalization is apparent, not only at the level of the elites but also of the general public; however, besides favoring a prudent openness to the world economy, that consensus also emphatically mandates softening the edges of globalization through stressing "inclusiveness." The contemporary posture on globalization overall is in striking contrast with the earlier preference for economic autarky. Chapter 3 looks at the institutional design of the postcolonial leadership in which, instead of the market, it was the state—through the mechanisms of economic planning, the public sector, and the system of licensing and controls, all instituted as a means to achieving a self-reliant socialism—that served as the dominant instrument for accomplishing economic and national integration, at least until the landmark departure in economic policy by way of economic liberalization in 1991. These three chapters together constitute part I of the study as a backdrop for parts II and III, which examine, respectively, the role both of state policies and market processes in relation to economic integration subsequent to economic liberalization.

Part II of the study consists of three chapters that examine policy change in three different areas of central importance. Chapter 4 deals with economic planning, which many critics had feared would come to an end with the turn to the market when the policy of economic liberalization was launched. It is true that economic planning does not have the same salience today that it once had, say, at the time of the *Second Five Year Plan* or the *Third Five Year Plan*, but then it had already lost such salience following the agricultural and food crisis after the end of the Third Plan. Still, the Planning Commission largely continues to perform the same functions that it did prior to economic liberalization. True, those functions have undergone some change, as ought to be expected given the increased role of the market, but the Planning Commission has shown considerable flexibility in addressing contemporary postliberalization challenges. The chapter delineates three possible futures for the Planning Commission and endorses its continuance, particularly since it performs an essential integrative function for India's continental-size economy.

Alongside the Planning Commission, the Finance Commission is another critical integrative institution in India's federal system. Chapter 5 discusses the remarkable capacity of the Finance Commission to cope with postliberalization challenges. Particularly noteworthy are its taking on the new function of determining the road map to assure fiscal consolidation throughout the federation—making that now the new core task of the commission—besides rationalizing and modernizing the vertical and horizontal distribution of national revenues that earlier constituted its core function. This chapter constitutes an extensive but critical case study of fiscal federalism, which lies at the heart of the relations between the center and states in India's political structure.

Chapter 6, as the last chapter in part II, examines the paradox of how globalization has, instead of segmenting the economy, generated the policy thrust to make India truly a common market through a drastic reform of the indirect tax system at the center and in the states. Considerable though incomplete advance has already taken place in this direction, but the project as a whole still remains a work in progress, waiting on political elites to arrive at a final consensus. This chapter, too, constitutes a compelling case study on the intricacies of fiscal federalism, and illustrates how monumental a task it really is to enact reform in the Indian federal system. Taken as a whole, part II demonstrates both the continued relevance of the state as a key actor in the effort to assure economic integration and also the presence of integration-enabling impulses within globalization itself.

Part III, with its four chapters, is devoted to an examination primarily of the role of market processes in economic segmentation and economic integration. Chapter 7 is concerned with the area of trade, which has seen considerable expansion in the postliberalization period, both externally and internally. Whether the expansion of internal trade is largely a function of domestic growth or merely a reflection of the advance in external trade cannot be proven incontrovertibly for the simple reason that there are no separate data for purely internal trade. By using a proxy variable, however, the chapter shows that expanded postliberalization internal trade tends to advance economic integration rather than segmentation. It also demonstrates that flows of trade, along with those of investment and labor, tend to favor diffusion of economic growth across states rather than economic polarization. At the same time, it also underlines the strong, state-made impediments—in the form of the relative neglect of infrastructure and of excessive regulatory controls—to increased market-driven trade integration.

Chapter 8, dealing with flows of capital, focuses primarily on the diffusion of industry across the states. While much of the literature emphasizes the widening of industrial disparities between the states, this study raises some doubts about that proposition based on more recent data on industrial growth during 1999–2010, even as it questions (based on the same data) the proposition about the coastal states being the principal beneficiaries of postliberalization industrial growth. Contrary to the position of the critics of globalization, the evidence suggests diffusion in relation to industrial location.

Chapter 9, which examines the social composition of the capitalist class in India, argues that, contrary to the assumption of an exclusive domination of the business arena by the traditional business communities, there has been considerable diffusion of entrepreneurship beyond these communities. It underlines that, despite the continued disproportionate presence of traditional business communities, the capitalist system in India has been one that is open, not closed—undoubtedly, a factor favorable to economic integration. Besides, by virtue of its own economic interests and its pan-Indian organization, the capitalist class is a powerful force in favor of India's economic and political unity. Chapter 10, on flows of people or labor, maintains that interstate migration tends to both alleviate poverty and reduce disparities between backward and advanced states, thus contributing to economic integration.

Chapter 11, the sole chapter in part IV, provides a summary of the main findings of the study. From these results, it is fair to conclude that globalization both offers benefits and involves costs (such as external shocks). However, the overall experience since the opening up of the national economy to the world economy with the policy of economic liberalization suggests that, rather than being a victim as the critics posit, India has been a beneficiary of the process with respect to the issue of economic segmentation versus economic integration.

ACKNOWLEDGMENTS

In the course of the research for this study, I have accumulated many debts. Dr. M. Govinda Rao, former director of the National Institute of Public Finance and Policy (NIPFP), provided me with affiliation to the institute, without which this study would not have been possible. I thank him for that privilege and for sharing his views with me on the issues considered in the study. Dr. Pronab Sen and Dr. Saumitra Chaudhuri have been generous with their time over many years in instructing me on the political economy of India, and I truly regard them as my teachers; their insights have been most rewarding for me. Dr. Arun Maira, Dr. Shankar Acharya, and Dr. Sharat Kumar also have been very kind to share their thinking with me on issues of economic policy. My colleague and friend, Jagdish Handa, has kept a stream of commentary and critique flowing on everything I have written during the past four and a half decades. I am grateful as well to my longtime friends C. P. Bhambhri and Dipankar Gupta for their hospitality and many other kindnesses; their generosity and support has been exemplary. I am indebted to Atul Kohli for encouraging me to stay involved with research after retirement.

I have benefited enormously from meeting and corresponding with innumerable academicians and officials during the course of my research; I am indebted to them all for allowing me the opportunity to learn from them. In particular, I would like to express my gratitude to the following people, all of whom have been extraordinarily kind to help me with my work in various ways: in Mumbai, Professor R. Nagaraj at the Indira Gandhi Institute of Development Research (IGIDR) and Professor R. B. Bhagat at the International Institute for Population Sciences (IIPS); in Chennai, Dr. D. K. Srivastava and Dr. K. R. Shanmugam, former and present directors, respectively, of the Madras School of Economics, and Harish Damodaran of the *Hindu Business Line*; in Gujarat, Professor Ravindra H. Dholakia and his colleagues, particularly Ankur Sarin, Navdeep Mathur, and Prem Pangotra at the Indian Institute of Management (IIM) Ahmedabad, and Professor Jaya Prakash Pradhan at the Central University of Gujarat; and in Kolkata, Professor Anindya Sen at IIM and Professor Ajitava Raychaudhuri at Jadavpur University. In New Delhi, I wish to thank Dhiraj Nayyar, formerly of

Indian Express and *India Today*; Dr. Rajiv Kumar and Dr. Arvind Virmani, both former directors of the Indian Council for Research in International Economic Relations (ICRIER); Dr. E. Sridharan at the University of Pennsylvania Institute for the Advanced Study of India (UPIASI); and Anshuman Khanna at the Federation of Indian Chambers of Commerce and Industry (FICCI).

I would also like to thank the following students for invaluable research assistance: Chelsea Moore and Murtaza Shambhoora (both of McGill University), and Vikash Vaibhav at IGIDR. I am profoundly thankful to Professor Joan DeBardeleben, chancellor's professor at Carleton University in Ottawa, for facilitating my use of Carleton's library facilities. I most sincerely appreciate the administrative help of Prachi Kaul and Meenakshi Malhotra at the Shastri Indo-Canadian Institute, New Delhi. No words are adequate to express my gratitude to the Social Sciences and Humanities Research Council of Canada for its generous financial support spanning more than four decades.

I want to thank Taylor & Francis for permission to draw on two articles of mine for chapters 4 and 6: "Economic Planning as an Integrative Mechanism in India: Changes and Challenges after Economic Liberalization," *India Review* 11, no. 4 (October–December 2012): 226–28; and "Globalization, the State, and India's Halting March to the Common Market: The Political Economy of Tax Reform under Federalism," *India Review* 10, no. 3 (July–September 2011), 201–45. Thanks are due also to the Madras School of Economics for allowing me to reproduce in chapter 5 portions of a monograph I wrote for them in 2012, *Globalization and India's Fiscal Federalism: Finance Commission's Adaptation to New Challenges.* I also thank Professors Amitabh Kundu and Lopamudra Ray Saraswati and the *Economic and Political Weekly* for permission to use in chapter 10 parts of three tables published by them. I appreciate, too, the permission by the Food and Agriculture Organization of the United Nations to use figure 7.1 in chapter 7.

Two external referees gave the manuscript a thorough examination; their comments and criticisms were most helpful in revising the manuscript for publication. For sagely advice, incredible expeditiousness in decision making, and incomparable encouragement and support on the manuscript, I would like to express my gratitude to Professor T. V. Paul, series editor for South Asia in World Affairs, and Donald Jacobs, acquisitions editor, at Georgetown University Press.

Most of all, I am indebted to my wife for her steadfast devotion to family and research during our partnership of more than half a century.

Baldev Raj Nayar

ABBREVIATIONS

AIADMK	All India Anna Dravida Munnetra Kazhagam
ASI	Annual Survey of Industries
Assocham	Associated Chambers of Commerce and Industry of India
BJP	Bharatiya Janata Party
BPL	below poverty line
BPO	business process outsourcing
CC	correlation coefficient
Cenvat	central value added tax
CII	Confederation of Indian Industry
CMIE	Center for Monitoring Indian Economy
CPI	Communist Party of India
CPI(M)	Communist Party of India (Marxist)
CPI(Maoist)	Communist Party of India (Maoist)
CPI(ML)	Communist Party of India (Marxist-Leninist)
CSO	Central Statistical Office [or Organization]
CST	central sales tax
CV	coefficient of variation
DICCI	Dalit Indian Chamber of Commerce and Industry
EC	Empowered Committee of State Finance Ministers
FAO	Food and Agriculture Organization
FC	Finance Commission
FICCI	Federation of Indian Chambers of Commerce and Industry
FM	finance minister
FMCG	fast-moving consumer goods
FSC	full-service carrier
GDP	gross domestic product

GoI	government of India
GSDP	gross state domestic product
GST	goods and services tax
HDI	Human Development Index
HT	*Hindustan Times*
ICRIER	Indian Council for Research in International Economic Relations
IDRA	Industrial Development and Regulation Act
IGIDR	Indira Gandhi Institute of Development Research
IIM	Indian Institute of Management
IIPS	International Institute for Population Sciences
IMF	International Monetary Fund
ISI	import substitution industrialization
IT	information technology
LCC	low-cost carrier
MGNREGA	Mahatma Gandhi National Rural Employment Guarantee Act
Modvat	modified value added tax
MoF	Ministry of Finance
NDA	National Democratic Alliance
NDC	National Development Council
NIPFP	National Institute of Public Finance and Policy
NSDP	net state domestic product
NVA	net value added
OECD	Organization for Economic Cooperation and Development
OICA	Organization Internationale des Constructeurs d'Automobiles [International Organization of Motor Vehicle Manufacturers]
PC	Planning Commission
PM	prime minister
PPP	private public partnership
PSE	public sector enterprise
SAIL	Steel Authority of India Limited
SEZ	special export zone
TFC	Tenth Finance Commission
ThFC	Thirteenth Finance Commission
TwFC	Twelfth Finance Commission
UP	Uttar Pradesh
VAT	value added tax

I

INTRODUCTION

Chapter 1

ECONOMIC GLOBALIZATION, SEGMENTATION, AND INTEGRATION

THE economic meltdown, or the Great Recession, which struck the United States in 2008 and then enveloped the world, understandably brought into question the dominant economic paradigm of economic globalization as social process and the associated concept of economic liberalization as state policy. The vulnerability of globalized national economies to external shocks made manifest by the financial crisis seemed to vindicate the long-standing case made by critics of globalization. Vulnerability to external shocks was not the only arrow in their quiver, however. Rather, the radical critique of globalization has been comprehensive from the very beginning, positing economic destabilization, stagnation, deindustrialization, and increased impoverishment as its inevitable consequences. In this critique, then, the consequences of globalization for national economies were malign, not benign. The various aspects of the radical critique have received considerable attention in the literature.[1] Of particular interest in the present study, however, is one specific though still broad aspect of the critique—the consequences of globalization for the nation-state itself via the domestic economy.

There are two general orientations to the issue of the implications of globalization specifically for the state, often appearing in the form of grand statements. One such orientation is represented by Marxist economist Prabhat Patnaik, who forthrightly argues: "The era of 'globalization,' paradoxically, therefore witnesses an acute accentuation of local antagonisms. The third world gets reduced to the position of a ghetto, characterized by poverty, hunger, disease, crime, and conflicts. These conflicts, once they cross a certain threshold, generate demands for secession and give rise to wars." He further maintains that "'globalization' necessarily involves a fracturing of the economic integrity of the nation. . . . Secessionism is simply the outcome of this fracturing."[2] The causal connection between economic globalization and state breakup could not have been expressed with any greater clarity and directness than in this statement. Another Marxist economist, Jayati Ghosh, similarly believes: "The tensions and insecurities brought about by these widening inequalities cause people to seek refuge in particularities: political separation, regionalist demands, revanchist cultural movements, and so on."[3] It is noteworthy that this contemporary critique of globalization had been presaged in an earlier theoretical formulation—dependency theory in the 1970s—which, taking a global view then of the expansion of capitalism across the world, succinctly underlined that international economic integration leads to national disintegration.[4]

Some mainstream economists also share this critique. Thus, the eminent economist Dani Rodrik underlines the pitfalls of globalization, warning against its potential for "domestic social disintegration."[5] Again, while recognizing the contribution of globalization to high levels of prosperity, he nonetheless wants a halt to the current "hyperglobalization" in favor of democratic nation-states safeguarding the social security of their citizens.[6] More pointedly, Paul Streeten makes this critique central to his review of the paradoxes of globalization, with a major section of his chapter in *New Thinking in Macroeconomics* devoted to a comprehensive discussion of "International Integration and National Disintegration." A subsection of it discusses "National Breakup and 'Retribalization,'" proclaiming, in part, that "global integration has provoked national disintegration."[7] The conventional proposition among the critics of globalization, then, has been: if globalization, then national disintegration. The wide range of ills ascribed to globalization and the line of causality in the radical thesis can be somewhat simplified and represented in broad strokes as:

> globalization and economic liberalization → economic stagnation, deindustrialization, and economic segmentation → social impoverishment, polarization, and conflict → regional antagonisms, secessionist movements, and national disintegration.[8]

The *focus* in this study is on the issue of *economic segmentation* as a necessary consequence of globalization and economic liberalization, though some attention is given, where indicated, to the other aspects as well.

In the social sciences, such overly broad positions as manifest in the "globalization-disintegration" thesis rarely go uncontested. There is an alternative orientation that takes a more benign view of the impact of globalization on national integration. Richard Rosecrance, Etel Solingen, and Arthur A. Stein argue that, while economic globalization undoubtedly weakens all states, "it has made things especially difficult" for prospective new states.[9] Given the diversity among states, the authors do not consider states as constituting an undifferentiated category. In that context, they see globalization as having differential effects on states, especially in relation to external shocks. For them, the size of states makes a substantial difference since trade in the world economy is not entirely free: "But the pattern of globalization favors bigger players, with a greater supply of cash. Trade is less free than capital movements whose outflow can penalize a country without deep pockets. In addition, provincial units receiving benefits and subsidies from the center can do better inside than they might as independent units exposed to sudden economic shifts." Moreover, globalization provides states with greater resources. This consequence is an illustration of what others have called the state-enabling or state-empowering impact of globalization.[10] As a result, states can buy off disaffected or disadvantaged regions with subsidies and income transfers. Importantly, the international community—especially the great powers—is averse to disturbing the world economy and tends to discourage movements that would unravel states. Consequently, for Rosecrance and his associates, "independence for such regions is becoming less and less likely," a position that manifestly runs counter to that of the critics of globalization.

Paradoxically, some otherwise negative aspects of increased international integration may even have positive repercussions by way of countering the disintegrative potential within nation-states. For example, the prospect of higher economic volatility from external shocks may serve to bind regions to the state as an insurance against risk and uncertainty.[11] Globalization and national integration thus need not necessarily be seen in a zero-sum relationship. By breaking down barriers to commerce (not only externally but, by extension, also internally), globalization may indeed be considered "nationalizing" in the sense of enhancing intrastate commerce.

TWO ALTERNATIVE PERSPECTIVES

Interestingly, several social scientists have meanwhile gone beyond the making of grand statements and have carried out more systematic research to assess the impact of globalization on national integration. The existing empirical literature offers two very different perspectives. One is typically associated with the work of economists that, employing economic modeling and econometrics, forcefully supports the conventional proposition that economic globalization (independent variable) makes for national disintegration (dependent variable).[12] Building on earlier work, Alberto Alesina and his associates advance, test, and find supporting evidence for the hypothesis that "trade openness and political separatism go hand in hand: economic integration leads to political 'disintegration.'" They posit that, "as the process of economic 'globalization' will progress, political separatism will continue to be alive and well."[13]

While the various contributions by economists on the issue are outstanding, they suffer, however, from a fundamental lacuna. They are remarkably free from the presence of the state as a dynamic actor. The state appears only as an object; the notion of the state as an active subject—that reacts to the pressures of globalization and that acts in the protection and furtherance of its interests—seems foreign to them. Here there is only *structure* in the shape of a pervasive and inexorable globalization, with the state itself treated as if it were a helpless object, without *agency*. It is as if the active state, as the elephant in the room, is missing from the analysis. This perspective thus tends to overdetermine the potency of globalization and to underdetermine the state's ability to cope with the challenges posed by globalization.

This lacuna of the missing state as a dynamic actor is what the second perspective—articulated essentially by political scientists for whom the state as an active agent is central—attempts to overcome. This perspective does not take globalization to be an inexorable social force; rather, it considers its effects to be variant among states, depending on the latter's institutions and policies. In this view, states have a range of choices in coping with the challenges of globalization. With such a perspective, several political scientists—through their cross-national quantitative studies of different aspects of the issue—have taken a deeply skeptical view of the globalization-disintegration thesis advanced in the first perspective.[14]

Theoretically, this second perspective accords with the view that nation-states, individually and especially in interaction with other states through the mechanism of geopolitics, are embedded in a separate and distinct political logic—one of power and legitimacy—that is different from the economic logic of markets, that of profit and efficiency.[15] In this view, in their endeavor to acquire and maintain legitimacy even as they engage in geopolitical competition, states adopt policies that are responsive to the interests of their domestic constituencies because that is essential for the political survival of state elites. Such policies then end up altering ultimate outcomes emergent from the interaction between states and economic globalization. Thus, the relationship between globalization and states is not simply a one-way, subject–object relationship. Rather, states as dynamic actors work both to facilitate globalization to enhance benefits they receive from it, and also to limit its negative impact through public policy. Balancing the gains and losses from globalization through public policy is therefore a principal challenge for states. Policy is, then, key in the consideration of the impact of globalization.

As such, the important issue is not simply the potential of international economic integration to generate disintegrative pressures at the national level. Rather, it is also how states and their elites perceive the threats that arise from economic globalization, how they cope with them through the adoption of appropriate policies, and what the impact is of such policies. It is a fundamental presumption in political science that once states are created—no matter for what reason, which is rarely economic—they are not passive spectators in the face of threats to their existence, but tend to fight to maintain it. The disintegration of a state is therefore an extraordinary event. No doubt, states at times have disintegrated, but such an event is often not the function of globalization but of geopolitics and egregious domestic policies. In this light, the conventional proposition mentioned earlier, which makes globalization the independent variable and national disintegration the dependent variable, needs to be modified through the insertion of the state—with its institutions and decision makers and their particular perceptions and policies—as an intervening variable in the equation. At the same time, such an insertion of the state likely renders the end result more indeterminate than that which is manifest in the conventional understanding. The end result is likely to vary among states, depending on their geographical location and standing, the kinds of institutions they have, the condition of those institutions, the particular public policies that the state elites adopt, and the effectiveness with which they implement such policies.

SITUATING ECONOMIC SEGMENTATION IN A LARGER CONTEXT

While some of the studies cited above limit themselves to specific aspects of the national economy that are affected by globalization, the very notion of disintegration as a consequence of globalization can be—and has been—interpreted to cover a wide area. Taking a rather broad view of the notion, Streeten discusses under its rubric such diverse matters as downward pressure on wages, reduction of social services, elites opting out of commitment to the nation, and nations breaking up into "smaller, ethnic groups."[16] Therefore, in order to lend some clarity to the discussion, "national disintegration" can be considered as having several distinct components:

1. *Economic.* In the economic arena, disintegration can be understood to mean segmentation of the national market. That market no longer remains a national whole, as it was presumably under an earlier, inward-oriented economic regime. Rather, some parts of the national economy become more intensely linked to the world economy than others and see their future as lying outside rather than within the national unit. Besides the market segmentation, different political jurisdictions within the nation-state may press for and obtain different tax systems, thus splintering the nation in the economic arena. Such jurisdictions may also clamor for increasingly more financial largesse from the center, even as they threaten to destabilize the state. They may also make it difficult for the economy to function as a single entity.
2. *Societal.* The disintegrative potential in the economic arena may be aggravated by globalization giving rise to sharp inequalities in society. These inequalities can be of two kinds, which may overlap—*spatial* or regional, where certain regions advance more rapidly than others; and *social* or group-based, where certain groups lag behind while others emerge as winners. The balance in noneconomic transactions, such as communications, may further reinforce such inequalities in society. Regional inequalities may enhance the potential for disintegration; regions that

emerge as winners may strive to delink themselves from the nation-state for fear of being held back by the poorer regions, while regions that fall behind may see a better future in secession. Similarly, social groups that have benefited from the existing regime may want to forsake their less-fortunate compatriots, while disadvantaged groups may increase disintegrative pressures through extremist activity.

3. *Political.* The segmentation of the economy and the rise of inequalities in society may, in turn, lead to political segmentation and generate tensions and disturbances between groups, between regions, and between the nation-state and domestic regions. They may also engender "sons of the soil" movements with disintegrative potential and, indeed, lead eventually to civil strife and breakup.

It is apparent that the notion of disintegration is not descriptive of some single event or element but encompasses a variety of effects that may range along a considerable continuum from the relatively innocuous to the more virulent in form. However, consistent with the state-oriented perspective expressed earlier, there is no inexorability to the process; some concessions to autonomy demands may well serve as an inflection point and halt the process rather than be simply a way station to some inevitable teleological destiny. There also may be considerable ambiguity to both the process and the means to counter it. Thus, decentralization from a unitary to a federal system may be considered by some to be a sign of a disintegrative process at work, while others may regard it as an effective strategy to ensure national integration by arriving at a more stable balance between the state and the regions. Any conclusion in this regard rests, therefore, on a considered judgment about the various forces at work rather than simply being read off from some obvious empirical indicators.

Figure 1.1 summarily lists the various aspects of pressures on national integration ascribed to globalization. It also specifies and thus underlines the importance of possible perceptions of state elites of globalization, the kinds of constraints under which they perhaps function, and the range of policies that may be open for them to meet the various pressures. Briefly, the overall argument may be summarized as follows: (1) Globalization tends—presumably, perhaps, only in the eyes of some—to economically generate the segmentation of the economic unity of the nation-state; it further tends to segment society through giving rise to spatial and social inequalities; and, finally, it tends to foster political segmentation and disintegrative pressures. However, (2) the outcome of these various tendencies will depend significantly on the nature and capacity of the state's political institutions and on the particular strategies (for example, whether or not they are adaptive, accommodative, inclusive, or ameliorative) adopted by state elites to counter such tendencies.[17] Figure 1.1 is set out here only for heuristic purposes; it is not the intention of this study to investigate all of the various aspects it mentions regarding the impact of globalization since that would, in any

Figure 1.1. Globalization Pressures, State Responses, and Possible Outcomes

Independent Variable	*Intervening Variable*	*Dependent Variable*
1	*2*	*3*
Globalization	The State and State Elites	Outcome
Pressures of globalization in terms of: a. Economic Segmentation — breaking up of national markets, with some parts more intensely linked to the world economy — diverse taxation systems b. Societal Segmentation — sharp rise in inequalities i. spatial/regional ii. social/group c. Political Segmentation — generation of tensions and disturbances between i. social groups ii. regions iii. the state, groups, and regions — rise of "sons of soil" and separatist movements — civil strife	a. Perceptions of threats and opportunities — globalization as benign/malign b. State institutions — Capacity: strong/weak i. functional capacity (coercive power, administrative capacity, legitimacy) ii. cohesion — Openness: inclusive/exclusive — Orientation: exploitative/ameliorative c. Policies/Strategies i. External: constraints on openness (extensive/limited) ii. Internal adaptive/recalcitrant accommodative/coercive inclusive/exclusive ameliorative/exploitative	Success or failure in overcoming segmentation

Sources: Developed eclectically from concepts in Paul Streeten, "Paradoxes of Globalization," in *New Thinking in Macroeconomics: Social, Institutional, and Environmental Perspectives*, ed. Jonathan M. Harris and Neva R. Goodwin (Cheltenham, UK: Edward Elgar, 2003); Peter B. Evans, Dietrich Rueschemeyer, and Theda Skocpol, eds., *Bringing the State Back In* (Cambridge: Cambridge University Press, 1985); Joel Migdal, *Strong Societies and Weak States: State-Society Relations and State Capabilities in the Third World* (Princeton, NJ: Princeton University Press, 1988); and Colin H. Kahl, *States, Scarcity and Civil Strife in the Developing World* (Princeton, NJ: Princeton University Press, 2006).

case, be a daunting task for a single researcher. For reasons of feasibility, *attention is therefore directed principally to the challenge of economic segmentation*, some selected state policies on countering such segmentation, and the actual processes at work in the market in relation to segmentation and integration.

In assessing the challenges arising from globalization and the state responses to them, it is worth remembering that most developing countries did not exist in some idyllic stage prior to globalization. Poverty and deep-rooted inequalities, ethnic conflicts, venal corruption, political breakdowns, institutional decay, authoritarian rule, violent uprisings, and secessionist movements were the lot of much of the developing world for decades before the term "globalization" came into common usage. Just because some of these phenomena now occur chronologically in the era of globalization does not mean that they can be causally attributed to globalization. By the same token, it would be remiss to condemn globalization for failing to suddenly and all by itself erase these features from the economic and political landscape. No doubt the market, too, has some internal impulses that push toward economic integration. However, no market exists by itself without the cover and support of the state; therefore, for the market to perform its integrative function adequately, it must receive proper guidance and direction from the state and state elites. As such, domestic reform, both economic and political, would seem to be a prerequisite to avail of the benign aspects and to avoid the malign aspects of globalization.

It bears underlining that most of the various consequences for national integration that are attributed to globalization would in all probability manifest themselves even in the context merely of modernization and development, including especially industrialization. Thus, for example, increasing inequality had been envisaged as a consequence of industrialization under national auspices even before the rise of contemporary globalization. Similarly, it had been established earlier in the social science literature that modernization and development lead to increased social mobilization, which then spurs demands on state and society for political participation and equality and identity politics, leading to multiple and overlapping development crises.[18] Prognoses about the potential disintegration of states in the developing world had thus been made long before the contemporary era of globalization. What can perhaps be said, then, about the distinctive impact of globalization is that it tends to speed up the processes of modernization and development and, therefore, of their consequences.

ECONOMIC INTEGRATION IN DEVELOPED AND DEVELOPING AREAS

If the basic thrust of the radical argument is that globalization leads to economic segmentation, it would equally seem to be the case that the nation-state in developing areas, no less than in developed areas, has as its central concern the preservation and advancement of economic integration, which can be taken to be the opposite of economic segmentation. The *Concise Oxford English Dictionary* defines integration as "the action or process of integrating" and, in turn, says that to integrate means to "combine or be combined to form a whole." Broadly, then, economic integration refers to the action or process of linking different economic entities closer together to constitute a single entity, or of binding closer together parts of an already existing single but insufficiently coherent entity. As Robert Ash and Y. Y. Kueh express it, "economic integration is essentially a process of unification—the means whereby coherence is imposed upon previously separate, even disparate, geographical regions. It may be pursued as a domestic or international goal."[19]

The fundamental aim in economic integration is often welfare enhancement, which is assumed to ensue from the consequent reduction of transaction costs and the increased access to the benefits of economies of scale and division of labor by virtue of the enlargement and expansion of the market that accompany such integration. The motive for economic integration, however, may not necessarily be limited to welfare enhancement alone, but may also involve issues of national security and political destiny; indeed, Andre Sapir underlines that the term economic integration "covers two very different types of situation each with a different objective: one driven mainly or entirely by commercial motives and the other that is not simply commercially motivated but also politically driven."[20]

Achieving economic integration entails the reduction or removal of constraints to economic linkages by way of flows of products and factors of production between different economic entities or different parts of the same entity, thus facilitating or strengthening such linkages. As Yu Chen, Fung Kwan, and Guang-Zhen Sun describe it, "the most obvious real linkage is trading between economies, or different parts/regions of the same economy."[21] Basically, economic integration revolves around flows of three elements—goods and services (trade), capital (investment), and labor (migration)—and the economic linkages that facilitate such flows. The linkage mechanisms include not only transportation networks but also the development of capital and credit markets and regulatory institutions.

The process of economic integration can be illustrated by the evolution of the European Union (EU), which developed from small beginnings as a *free trade area* in 1958 and incrementally progressed through the stages of completion of a *customs union* in 1968, creation of a European *monetary union* in 1979, completion of a *common market* in 1993, and transformation into a *single currency area* (the euro) in 1999.[22] Two stages—*fiscal union* and *political union*—still need to be attained in order to culminate in *complete economic integration*. Although the process toward economic integration may not be irreversible, some maintain that once initiated it may have a built-in momentum, for technological and other reasons, to advance to a fuller integration.[23] This certainly has not proven to be the case, however, with respect to several attempts at economic integration in Africa, which ended in dissolution.

While the case of the EU is instructive, it should be noted that it basically concerns already industrialized countries, though they may vary in their level of industrial development and well-being. In enlarging the common economic space through a gradual process of economic integration among already existing sovereign states, the fathers of the EU had in mind not only the economic aim of benefiting from the welfare-enhancing effects of a larger economic unit but also the strategic aim of overcoming the heritage of interstate rivalries and periodic wars that had proven to be so devastating during the twentieth century.

However, the situation of the developing countries was entirely different as they began to emerge politically from under the weight of colonialism around the middle of the twentieth century. These countries were, first, predominantly agricultural and backward, with impoverished economies; second, they were not simply poor but economically dependent, being tied in a core–periphery relationship with the metropolitan country or countries; and, third, they suffered from multiple internal cleavages, both social and economic. In brief, they were economically segmented at birth—long before the rise of the contemporary post–Bretton Woods economic globalization—as a consequence of both their internal social structure and the legacy of colonialism. That legacy only highlights the enormous challenge that confronts states and state elites in the less developed areas in their effort to assure the economic integration of their countries in the face of the potential threat of economic segmentation from globalization.

GLOBALIZATION, THE STATE, AND THE MARKET IN INDIA

India provides an ideal case for studying the interaction between globalization, the state, and the market for several reasons. First, India is a megastate with a population of about 1.25 billion; it represents more than 17 percent of humanity and, therefore, what happens in and to it is a matter of some consequence from the viewpoint of sheer numbers. With a vast population such as that, India is also a microcosm of the world, at least of the developing world. Second, both much of the world and most Indians today see India as an emerging major power, a perception that was fueled by the swerve to economic liberalization as policy and the ensuing growth acceleration, particularly during the first decade of the 2000s. Third, a principal characteristic of India is its established heterogeneity, which makes it a prime candidate for the kinds of disintegrative pressures that the critics of globalization have underlined.

Finally, another salient characteristic of India is what critics have referred to—since Gunnar Myrdal published his *Asian Drama* in 1968—as a "soft state." This political syndrome has perhaps been aggravated in recent years by policy stalemates at the national level because of the transformation of an earlier "one party dominant" political system, led by the Congress Party until the late 1960s, to a fragmented party system that necessitated coalition governments, especially since the late 1980s. For many, it raises the important question as to how such a political system can make decisions at all to meet the challenges emergent from increasing integration into the world economy. In his masterly study relating state types to prospects for industrialization, Atul Kohli, too, focuses on India's modest state capacity for development with his characterization of it as a "fragmented-multiclass state," in contrast to Korea's "cohesive-capitalist state" presiding over rapid industrialization.[24]

The present case study is eclectic in its methodology, combining quantitative data and qualitative analysis, along with the use of historical materials and contemporary data. It focuses on both the state and market in relation to the challenges from globalization.

SUMMARY

This chapter has set out the larger theoretical context for studying the problem of economic integration in India in view of the prognosis about the malign impact of globalization and economic liberalization by way of economic segmentation and, eventually, disintegration. The present study departs from this prognosis in two ways: First, it assumes globalization to be a more ambiguous and complex process, featuring trends and countertrends and many crosscurrents rather than being a single-variable force trending in only one direction—that of segmentation and disintegration. It is taken to contain both segmenting and integrating tendencies, and therefore compels agnosticism rather than predestination with respect to the final consequences. Second, the study does not take the state to be a helpless and passive object in the face of the challenges thrown up by globalization, but rather to be an active and dynamic subject with agency. Therefore, state policies demand serious consideration in any analysis of the issue of economic segmentation and economic integration.

The study consists of four parts, which are described in somewhat more detail in the preface. Part I includes two other chapters besides the present one, with chapter 2 looking at elite perspectives on globalization and economic policy and chapter 3 discussing the postcolonial institutional design for economic integration. Part II comprises chapters 4 to 6, which are concerned with the state's policy responses after economic liberalization in the areas of economic planning, revenue transfers from the center to the states, and reforms in the indirect tax system. Chapters 7 to 10 in part III, which deals with the market's role in economic integration, look at trends with respect to trade, investment and business groups, and migration. Chapter 11, the sole chapter in part IV, provides the summary and conclusions of the study. Overall, in contradistinction to the globalization-disintegration thesis of the critics, this study takes a more benign view of globalization, particularly with the backdrop of the performance of the economic regime that preceded it.

NOTES

1. See Jagdish Bhagwati, *In Defense of Globalization* (New York: Oxford University Press, 2004), and Martin Wolf, *Why Globalization Works* (New Haven, CT: Yale University Press, 2004). For a critical examination of these claims in relation to India, see Baldev Raj Nayar, *India's Globalization: Evaluating the Economic Consequences* (Washington,

DC: East-West Center, 2006), and *The Myth of the Shrinking State: Globalization and the State in India* (New Delhi: Oxford University Press, 2009).

2. Prabhat Patnaik, *The Retreat to Unfreedom: Essays on the Emerging World Order* (New Delhi: Tulika Books, 2003), 42–43. Patnaik is the dean of Marxist scholars in India and a key adviser to the Communist Party of India (Marxist). During his long tenure at Jawaharlal Nehru University, he was influential in training and mentoring a generation of Marxist economists.

3. Jayati Ghosh, "Economic Globalization, Cultural Identity and Social Conflict," in *India in the Age of Globalization: Contemporary Discourses and Texts*, ed. Suman Gupta, Tapan Basu, and Subarno Chattarji (New Delhi: Nehru Memorial Museum and Library, 2004), 1–33.

4. Osvaldo Sunkel, "Capitalismo transnacional y desintegracion nacional en la America Latina," *Trimestre Economico* 63, no. 250 (April–June 1996): 525–85; William G. Tyler and J. Peter Wogart, "Economic Dependence and Marginalization: Some Empirical Evidence," *Journal of Inter-American Studies and World Affairs* 15, no.1 (1973): 36–45.

5. Dani Rodrik, *Has Globalization Gone Too Far?* (Washington, DC: Institute for International Economics, 1997), 2–3, 70, 73, 84.

6. Dani Rodrik, *The Globalization Paradox: Democracy and the Future of the World Economy* (New York: W.W. Norton, 2011), xvi–xix.

7. Paul Streeten, "Paradoxes of Globalization," in *New Thinking in Macroeconomics: Social, Institutional, and Environmental Perspectives*, ed. Jonathan M. Harris and Neva R. Goodwin (Cheltenham, UK: Edward Elgar, 2003), 53–78.

8. Although this summary formulation of the causal chain is mine, *all* its ingredients are present in Patnaik, *Retreat to Unfreedom*, 12–15, 26–28, 42–43, 63, 98, 102, 160–66, 190–95, 289.

9. Richard N. Rosecrance, Etel Solingen, and Arthur A. Stein, "Globalization and Its Effects: Introduction and Overview," in *No More States? Globalization, National Self-Determination, and Terrorism*, ed. Richard N. Rosecrance and Arthur A. Stein (Lanham, MD: Rowman & Littlefield, 2006), 3–21.

10. Linda Weiss, ed., *States in the Global Economy: Bringing Domestic Institutions Back In* (New York: Cambridge University Press, 2003).

11. Geoffrey Garrett and Jonathan Rodden, "Globalization and Fiscal Decentralization," in *Governance in a Global Economy: Political Authority in Transition*, ed. Miles Kahler and David A. Lake (Princeton, NJ: Princeton University Press, 2003), 87–109.

12. Alberto Alesina, Enrico Spolaore, and Romain Wacziarg, "Economic Integration and Political Disintegration," *American Economic Review* 90, no. 3 (December 2000): 1276–96. See also Alberto Alesina and Enrico Spolaore, "On the Number and Size of Nations," *Quarterly Journal of Economics* 112, no. 4 (November 1997): 1027–56; Patrick Bolton and Gerard Roland, "The Breakup of Nations: A Political Economy Analysis," *Quarterly Journal of Economics* 112, no. 4 (November 1997): 1057–90.

13. Alesina, Spolaore, and Wacziarg, "Economic Integration," 1276–96.

14. See Kahler and Lake, *Governance in a Global Economy*, in particular the contributions by Michael J. Hiscox, Geoffrey Garrett, Jonathan Rodden, and Peter Van Houten.

15. Baldev Raj Nayar, *The Geopolitics of Globalization* (New Delhi: Oxford University Press, 2005), 16, 261.

16. Streeten, "Paradoxes of Globalization," 53–78.

17. Since the publication of Peter B. Evans, Dietrich Rueschemeyer, and Theda Skocpol, *Bringing the State Back In* (Cambridge: Cambridge University Press, 1985), state capacity has been a key concern of social scientists working on the developing countries. See, for example, Joel Migdal, *Strong Societies and Weak States: State-Society Relations and State Capabilities in the Third World* (Princeton, NJ: Princeton University Press, 1988), and Colin H. Kahl, *States, Scarcity and Civil Strife in the Developing World* (Princeton, NJ: Princeton University Press, 2006).

18. These areas were explored in several volumes on political development in the 1960s before the ascendancy of dependency theory and globalization studies; see Howard J. Wiarda, "Rethinking Political Development: A Look Backward over Thirty Years, and a Look Ahead," *Studies in Comparative International Development* 24, no. 4 (Winter 1989–90): 65–82.

19. Robert F. Ash and Y. Y. Kueh, "Economic Integration within Greater China: Trade and Investment Flows between China, Hong Kong and Taiwan," *China Quarterly* 136 (1993): 711–45.

20. Andre Sapir, "European Integration at the Crossroads: A Review Essay on the 50th Anniversary of Bela Balassa's *Theory of Economic Integration*," *Journal of Economic Literature* 49, no. 4 (2011): 1200–229.

21. Yu Chen, Fung Kwan, and Guang-Zhen Sun, "Economic Integration and Development of the Chinese Economy: An Introduction," *Journal of the Asia Pacific Economy* 15, no. 4 (November 2010): 337–40.

22. Sapir, "European Integration," 1205.

23. Ibid., 1219. Sapir notes: "According to Balassa, once market integration is achieved there will be a need for coordinating monetary and fiscal policies to avoid negative spillovers between union members, which in turn would necessitate, as a minimum requirement, 'instituting an intergovernmental body whose decisions do not require unanimity yet are binding for the member states . . . necessitates adopting a supra-national approach that is associated with political unification, possibly in the form of a federation of states.'"

24. Atul Kohli, *State-Directed Development: Political Power and Industrialization in the Global Periphery* (Cambridge: Cambridge University Press, 2004), 1–23.

Chapter 2

INDIA AND GLOBALIZATION

Performance, Perceptions, and Policy

GLOBALIZATION is not a single-variable phenomenon; it is a metasocial process that encompasses many cross-currents, even contradictions. It is not a single-time, uniform phenomenon; its form and content have varied over its long and sometimes interrupted existence, and so have the challenges it has posed for nation-states. Nor is it a recent phenomenon, even though many contemporary accounts of globalization tend to take it as a particularly postwar occurrence, seeing it as emerging either around 1990 at the end of the Cold War, or perhaps earlier, after the collapse of the Bretton Woods fixed exchange rate regime in the early 1970s. However, most serious scholarship recognizes globalization to have been a longtime historical process, coeval with European expansion, if not of earlier origin.[1]

This study agrees with the last view, but importantly, it recognizes that India has been joined at the hip with this long, historical process from the very beginning. India's experience with globalization is not a late twentieth-century phenomenon, but one that goes back to the eighteenth century, when globalization itself roughly began to take shape. Undoubtedly, India today bears the burden of its earlier globalization legacy, whether good or bad. Indeed, contemporary India has been powerfully influenced by globalization over this long period and, in a sense, fundamentally molded by it, albeit in an imbalanced manner. The sheer length of India's encounter with globalization therefore requires a *diachronic* approach to understanding its impact rather than simply a *synchronic* one. The overall proposition that informs the following discussion is that successive phases of India's relationship with globalization have been influential in the formation of its changing worldviews and, consequently, in the shifts in economic policy.

This chapter, which serves as a summary background for the study, consists of several parts. The first part discusses the preindependence legacy of globalization, including the clash between imperialism and nationalism, and demonstrates how it gave rise to a postindependence economic policy that sought to overcome that legacy. The second part examines the thrust of the fairly long postindependence policy favoring autarkic socialism, and also its reversal in the shape of *economic liberalization*, albeit limited. The third part discusses the subsequent modification of liberalization by supplementing it conceptually and practically with *inclusiveness*. The final part outlines alternative policy paths that are offered in opposition to contemporary policy.

THE PAST AS PROLOGUE

Until about the sixteenth and seventeenth centuries, rather than a single, integrated world economy, only regional economies existed on the planet.[2] Europe, however, proved to be a more dynamic economic system from around the eighteenth century, and it expanded to physically encompass the entire globe into a single world economy.[3] The long period during which Europe economically transformed the world can be seen to consist of two phases: extensive and intensive.

The Extensive and Intensive Phases of Globalization

The *extensive* phase of globalization did not occur as a strictly economic process, however; rather, this expansion across the globe was spearheaded by geopolitics in the form of imperialist conquest and coercive diplomacy. Europe had come to acquire a comparative advantage over the rest of the world in war making because of the earlier internecine competition and conflict among its many principalities.[4] Subsequently, industrialization and technological advancement vastly expanded European military capabilities. In this situation of uneven power development between Europe and the rest of the world, war became the historic instrument for forcibly converting the regional economies into a world economy over which Europe held sway by the force of arms during several centuries. Violence and coercion was thus an integral handmaiden of globalization in its extensive phase. In the process, earlier regional economic networks were destroyed or supplanted in order to link the local economies to the metropolitan centers of the imperial powers in a subordinate position, primarily to serve imperial economic interests. Dependency theory, including world systems theory, have long regarded the subsequent "underdevelopment" of the underdeveloped countries as having been directly and causally related to the "development" of the developed world.[5]

In due course, the extensive phase of globalization gave way to *intensive* globalization—resting on flows of trade, capital, and people—the first incarnation of which prevailed from around 1870 to 1914. Still, while the world had become economically integrated during this period, such integration was *shallow* compared to its contemporary *deep* version. In any case, World War I brought an end to this first incarnation, and a long period of economic protectionism ensued, with nations pursuing beggar-thy-neighbor policies. The world finally emerged from this deglobalized state at the end of World War II. Meanwhile, the end of that war saw the beginning of the decolonization process, first in Asia and then in Africa. However, up to around 1970, restrictions on movements of capital, people, and trade continued even as a large part of the world was under economic autarky or semiautarky (the Soviet bloc, China, India, and much of the underdeveloped world). Only with the breakdown of the Bretton Woods fixed exchange rate regime in 1971 can the second incarnation of *intensive* globalization be said to have manifested itself, about 1975. This second incarnation has been marked by *deep* integration, evident partly in the much higher magnitude of the share of exports in gross domestic product (GDP) and the predominant share of exports in trade.[6]

Globalization suffered a setback, however, with the financial crisis in 2008 that triggered a worldwide economic recession, although massive intervention by governments throughout the world helped forestall it from developing into a great depression. Even though the immediate crisis proved to be short-lived, a full recovery eluded the world for several years.

Imperialism and Nationalism: Implications for Postindependence Economic Policy

Because it involved the domination of a modern industrial society over a traditional agricultural society, imperialism had a profound impact on India in many spheres—cultural, economic, and political. The wrenching experience of defeat and conquest was a forceful challenge to the Indians, who sought thereafter to figure out the source of power—ideological and material—that had enabled a small European island to subdue a vast, if divided, subcontinent. On the defensive, local groups came up with several different responses to the new dispensation—rejection, revitalization, reformist adaptation, and assimilation. The dominant response that has endured in India has been reformist adaptation.

At the cultural level, the most critical impact of British rule, with far-reaching consequences for the subcontinent, was the imposition by fiat in the 1830s of the English language as the medium of instruction for higher education, and of Western knowledge—instead of traditional learning—as the content of that education. The purpose of this measure was, in the words of Lord Macaulay, the author of the initiative, to create "a class of persons, Indian in blood and color, but English in taste, in opinions, in morals, and in intellect." In this aim, he succeeded admirably. The modern elites of India emerged in diverse fields from the Macaulay-ordained educational system and soon became the Indian heirs of European Enlightenment, favoring modernity over tradition.[7] Some of these elites willingly offered themselves to man the colonial apparatus for the imperialist rulers. Others, however, eventually became the bearers of the initial stirrings of political ambition to play a greater role in governance. When thwarted in that ambition, they transformed the urge for greater political participation into a nationalist movement that ultimately mobilized the masses to achieve independence from colonial rule.

In governance, the impact of British imperialism was twofold. On the one hand, the British united (if only partially) the subcontinent—previously consisting of many, often warring kingdoms—under a single hegemonic power. On the other hand, as conquerors and colonizers invariably do, they followed a conscious and deliberate policy to divide and rule, though Indians were already divided enough. The intensification of sectarian differences eventually led to the partition of the subcontinent into Pakistan and India. As befits imperialist rulers, the British installed an authoritarian-bureaucratic state, ultimately responsible only to London. That state was manned by an efficient and incorruptible civil service, regarded as "the steel frame" that held together a vast empire in India. Under the pressure of the nationalist movement in the overall context of the weakening of British power under the impact of the two world wars, the British made concessions within the overarching bureaucratic-authoritarian system to local political participation. These included federalism, allocation of limited powers to provincial governments elected on the basis of a narrow franchise, and some legislative voice at the central level. The nationalist platform, however, demanded full independence, democracy, universal franchise, and responsible parliamentary government at the provincial and central levels. With independence in 1947, the nationalist elites set about installing precisely such a state.

In the economic sphere, capitalism under a conquering imperialism resulted in massive dislocation as well as partial commercialization and some limited industrialization. Fundamentally, there are two opposing schools of thought on colonialism's economic impact during its rule over two centuries. The imperialist or neocolonial school, which emphasizes the beneficial effects of colonialism, can be said to have been inaugurated by Karl Marx and was further elaborated by a succession of defenders of the empire, both official and nonofficial. Some aspects of British rule that receive emphasis in this positive view are: the political unification of the subcontinent, thus laying the basis for a potential national market; the installation of the railway network; the integration of the economy with the world under a laissez-faire regime; and the establishment of three major ports, two of which became substantial industrial centers.[8]

The other school of thought, referred to at times as "left-nationalist," or simply nationalist,[9] can be regarded as a precocious indigenous, independently developed formulation of what postwar Western scholarship described as "dependency theory." There are several important elements in the nationalist charge sheet against colonialism. First and foremost among these is the deindustrialization and pauperization of India. The starting point in this indictment is the assumption that India and Britain were at about the same economic level at the beginning of the British conquest of India. Yet by the time of the British departure, a stark disparity had developed between the two interrelated economies—the subcontinent had been turned into a pauperized, underdeveloped area, while Britain emerged in the nineteenth century as the world's foremost industrial power and exporter. The entire structure of colonial policy, fundamentally designed to serve British economic interests, resulted in the expropriation and transfer of vast economic wealth from India—referred to as the "drain theory of wealth"—which caused the development of Great Britain but underdevelopment of India (that is, stunted and distorted development).

The integration of India with the world economy could have aided India's development, but since India lacked political control over its economic destiny, the result was the destruction of a once large and flourishing component of the domestic economy and export trade in the shape of textile production—albeit of the artisanal, preindustrial variety—without it being replaced for many decades by a local modern textile industry. This led to a sort of "deindustrialization" of India—a central part of the critique by the nationalist school—and the consequent "ruralization" of the Indian economy, putting great population pressure on land. The long-term British policy of laissez-faire (which is often the "mercantilist" policy of the strong), its opposition to government intervention to protect Indian interests, and its persistence with an overvalued rupee were all regarded as inimical to India's economic growth.

Even when measures that promoted development were undertaken, such as the railway network, they were structured to promote British industry, thus depriving India of their spin-off effects. Under these circumstances, there was only the growth of some industrial enclaves rather than the development of a modern national economy.[10] The consequent lack of a domestic capital goods industry prevented India from exploiting the opportunity to advance industrialization provided by delinkage from the world economy during the two world wars and the Great Depression. It is not surprising that economic stagnation stalked the land during the first half of the twentieth century—that is, the last half century of colonial rule.[11] Tirthankar Roy recognizes the strong appeal of the left-nationalist school, even as his exaggerated sense of scholarly rigor and his neglect of the earlier period of British imperialism—on the plea of lack of adequate data—prevent him from agreeing with it. Importantly, he does acknowledge that the school's tenets spoke to what the masses instinctively felt about the colonial impact: "The experience, on the one hand, of mass poverty and deprivation, and on the other, of colonialism and lack of political freedom, are overpowering ones. The former tends to make the study of economic history of India a diagnostic exercise—a relentless search for causes of underdevelopment. The latter induces the belief that colonialism must have been responsible, somehow, for the underdevelopment. This second belief in particular is not confined to history textbooks—*it underlies the average Indian's sense of history*."[12]

Other historians may disagree with the left-nationalist paradigm, as Roy often does. Yet the perceptions of what had occurred under colonial rule more or less determined the lines of subsequent policy after independence—generally, *the opposite of what seemed to have existed under colonial rule*. Thus, there was anticolonialism and independence instead of colonialism; autarky and self-reliance instead of integration with the world economy; economic planning and rapid industrialization through massive import substitution instead of laissez-faire; a big push for capital goods and heavy industry instead of an expansion of the consumer goods industry; aggressive promotion of the public sector instead of expansion of the private sector; and, more broadly, socialism instead of capitalism. The concept of globalization as such may not have existed at the time, but it is immediately manifest that this substitute ensemble of policies was, at its core, the very antithesis of globalization.

The foremost proponent and exponent of this alternative set of policies before and after independence was Jawaharlal Nehru (1889–1964), inarguably the most popular leader after Mahatma Gandhi. After the mid-1920s, Nehru had shifted from being simply a freedom fighter to a self-declared socialist, and he openly expressed his admiration for the Soviet Union, its economic model, and its economic accomplishments. During the 1930s, Nehru came to occupy a decisive position in the Congress Party in formulating its policies on economic issues. Just before World War II, he presided over the party's newly created National Planning Committee, which provided him the impetus to think more concretely about solving India's economic problems and to develop a socialist model specifically for India. Despite the committee representing many viewpoints, Nehru believed: "Our plan, as it developed, was inevitably leading us towards establishing some of the fundamentals of the socialist structure."[13] His experience with the committee proved to be consequential for postindependence economic policy. Nehru came to his task as the chief economic planner for independent India with ideas rather fully formed before independence.[14] When independence arrived in 1947, Nehru emerged as the prime minister and was thus strategically placed to implement his economic vision for India that had been worked out during the freedom struggle.

THE POSTINDEPENDENCE THRUST FOR AUTARKIC SOCIALISM AND ITS REVERSAL

At birth, independent India faced enormous challenges arising from the partition of the subcontinent. Political and economic consolidation took about a decade, only after which the Congress Party under Nehru's leadership seriously undertook the task of restructuring the Indian economy and its relationship with the world economy. Although the nationalist movement had encompassed diverse and divergent views on the mode of economic development, it was Nehru's vision of the desired goals for the new state that eventually emerged triumphant over rival positions, owing primarily to his strategic position as both prime minister and supreme leader of the Congress Party.

In line with Nehru's vision—which had been developed during the preindependence years, but was now provided with theoretical scaffolding by economic planners—in 1956, under the auspices of the *Second Five Year Plan (1956–1961)*, the Indian state undertook an autarkic economic strategy based on a gigantic import substitution program, centrally focused on heavy industry.[15] The theoretical rationale or rationalization for the heavy industry strategy was the promotion of machine-making industries in order to advance economic growth over the long term, but an understated (if not entirely unstated) underlying aim was *economic independence* and strategic autonomy through building *national power.*[16] Importantly, the heavy industry strategy was to be carried out principally through the public sector, for Nehru saw the public sector—as it progressively expanded and turned the private sector into a mere appendage—as India's particular route to socialism instead of a more radical, perhaps violent, economic restructuring.[17]

Despite the serious implementation problems encountered by the heavy industry strategy, it was repeated in the *Third Five Year Plan (1961–1966)*, but Nehru died in 1964, before the plan's completion. His heavy industry strategy soon collapsed during the mid-1960s amid war-generated inflation, unprecedented successive droughts, humiliating food dependence on the United States, and the political turmoil that followed a short-lived experiment in economic liberalization—including currency devaluation—under foreign pressure. As the Congress Party suffered heavy electoral losses in the 1967 elections, Nehru's daughter, Mrs. Indira Gandhi, who had become prime minister in 1966, launched the government on an even more radical path than her father's, exemplified by the sudden nationalization of the major banks in 1969. After her victory in the 1971 elections, she carried nationalization even further, with the government taking over the coal and copper sectors and a substantial part of the textile industry. She also drastically limited the economic space for foreign investors, and imposed very high, almost confiscatory taxation and stringent restrictions on the corporate sector. These policies only served to prolong the economic and industrial stagnation that had begun in the mid-1960s. The stagnation, however, eventually precipitated a reversal in economic course.

The Long Road to Economic Liberalization

In the historiography of India's postindependence economic policy, 1991 occupies a hallowed place, marking a rupture with the earlier economic strategy. The "paradigm shift" that took place then, from a regime of socialist or dirigiste economic planning since the mid-1950s to a regime of economic liberalization—both with respect to decompression of the private sector and to integration with the world economy—was a noteworthy event, indeed. However, there had been a long build-up toward this seemingly sudden policy shift and it was preceded by considerable gradual change. Fundamental to the paradigm shift and the gradual change were revised elite *perceptions* about desirable policy that stemmed from the leadership's dissatisfaction with the *performance* of the economy and therefore its search for an alternative policy framework.[18]

The first opening to liberalization after about a decade of implementation of the heavy industry strategy had occurred in the mid-1960s, but that effort proved abortive because of the ensuing economic and political turmoil, particularly since it was associated with foreign imposition. Instead, there was a sharp turn to the left in economic policy. However, India was face-to-face with an enormous economic crisis by the mid-1970s, following a decade of economic stagnation that witnessed an average growth rate of only about 2.5 percent a year. The situation had been further compounded by high inflation, following droughts and oil price hikes in the early 1970s. The economic crisis soon transformed into a political crisis, as opposition parties mounted a powerful mass movement to oust Mrs. Gandhi from office.

The sobering experience of the economic stagnation—which had followed Mrs. Gandhi's turn to radical economic policy—and the resultant economic-political crisis led her to reassess economic policy around 1975. Fundamentally, the reality of economic *performance* over the previous decade forced a change in perceptions about the appropriateness of the economic policy that she had pursued thus far. Mrs. Gandhi therefore decided to reverse course and start the process of economic liberalization—undoubtedly in an inchoate and hesitant fashion—in terms of reintegrating the domestic economy with the world economy and relaxing the restrictions on the private sector. That was a turning point in India's postindependence economic history.[19]

Initially, the change in perceptions may have been confined to Mrs. Gandhi and her close advisers. But the quick improvement in the economy following the resort to economic orthodoxy emboldened the successor government under the Janata Party, combined with the ideological predilections of that party, to continue the reform process, albeit in a gradual manner, during its brief tenure from 1977 to 1979. By the time Mrs. Gandhi returned to power again in 1980, she had shed both her socialist inclinations and socialist colleagues in favor of pragmatism and economic efficiency. Mrs. Gandhi was assassinated in 1984; her son, Rajiv Gandhi, who succeeded her dynastically, held out the promise of a more muscular liberalization. Some important initiatives to liberalize the economy were indeed implemented, but the larger promise was thwarted by the votaries of the ancien régime within his party.

When India faced an economic and financial crisis in 1990 and 1991, which threatened its solvency, the previously existing process of *incremental liberalization* was transformed into a paradigm shift under the unexpectedly bold leadership of Prime Minister P. V. Narasimha Rao, assisted by Finance Minister

Manmohan Singh, thus jettisoning the socialist regime, both internally and externally. No doubt, there was much opposition to the shift in policy, both inside and outside the ruling party, but there was enormous support for it, too, particularly among the middle classes. The circle of those holding to the new perceptions about the appropriate economic strategy for India had widened; the earlier mind-set had undergone considerable change. This shift in perceptions, too, was fundamentally related to *performance*, not only negatively in respect of the socialist regime but also more positively with regard to incremental liberalization, under which the economy had performed better, thus persuading policymakers to move from incremental reform to more-radical reform.

In a wide-ranging interview in 2000 with the Public Broadcasting Service (PBS) network of the United States, Manmohan Singh attributed the jettisoning of the socialist regime in favor of liberalization to that regime's failure to advance economic growth and welfare adequately, particularly when compared to the outward-oriented economies of East Asia (a matter with serious geopolitical implications for India). He believed that the failures of centralized planning—which lacked an effective incentive system—had "become far too big a burden to bear." He adjudged that the controls that went with such planning "became instruments of corruption," delay, and uncertainty, rendering the economy directionless. For Singh, "persistence on that path would have led to more misery, more unemployment." Accordingly, as the then finance minister, he instead took to an alternative path that "got government off the backs of the people of India, particularly off the backs of Indian entrepreneurs," thus releasing the "entrepreneurial spirits" and more competition. He further saw economic restructuring as essential if India was to emerge as "a major global power" without poverty, ignorance, and disease.[20]

Admittedly, the paradigm shift in 1991 did mark a rupture in the socialist and autarkic economic strategy. The extent of policy change it generated should not be underestimated, but neither should it be exaggerated. The legacy of the economic ancien régime continues to substantially inform the era subsequent to the launch of liberalization, given the enormous government presence in and control over the economy and equally of the government's penchant for discretionary intervention in the economy. As is often remarked, exerting government control over the economy is part of the DNA of India's ruling class. Indeed, India is said to have been only a "hesitant and reluctant" reformer,[21] not out of conviction, and it moved to economic liberalization only under the compulsion of circumstances.

Regardless of its limitations, economic liberalization as a state policy that had been launched by the Congress Party eventually became consolidated—after that party's electoral defeat in 1996—when successor governments sustained the new policy and even advanced it further during the next decade. Particularly noteworthy was the promotion of several reform measures by the National Democratic Alliance (NDA), led by the nationalist Bharatiya Janata Party (BJP) over the period 1998–2004. Despite the fact that the initial turn to economic liberalization and integration with the world economy had been a sharp move to the right, reversing the earlier strategy promoting socialism and national self-sufficiency, the new policy seemingly became the established centrist approach to economic policy.

MODIFYING ECONOMIC LIBERALIZATION: FROM ECONOMIC RESTRUCTURING TO INCLUSIVENESS

Even if economic liberalization had now become the established policy framework, changing perceptions about its implications for electoral performance soon substantially modified the posture toward it. To begin with, trepidation over how a public that was weaned on slogans of socialism would receive the policy reversal led to its introduction largely (as has often been charged, perhaps exaggeratedly) by stealth.[22] Regardless, after about a couple years of active promotion of liberalization, the losses that the ruling Congress Party suffered in some state elections resulted suddenly in loss of appetite for further reform. Subsequently, the party's loss of power at the national level in 1996 and its absence from power for eight years led to reticence about reform in the future. Indeed, its changed perception about the value of reform in political terms was reinforced by the unexpected 2004 electoral defeat of its political archrival, the BJP, which had run its election campaign on the premature celebratory reformist theme of "India Shining."

Chastened by these developments, the Congress Party was wary of proclaiming support to economic liberalization (except when compelled by circumstances) after its return to power in 2004 at the head of a multiparty coalition, significantly named United Progressive Alliance (UPA), which was supported by the two major communist parties. In the profound belief that the rival NDA had suffered electoral defeat on account of its enthusiasm for reform, which was now perceived as favoring the rich, the Congress-led UPA government modified economic liberalization to accord with its new perception by making "inclusiveness" the centerpiece of its economic program through which it would address the concerns of the rural unemployed, indebted farmers, backward classes, and minorities.

The Congress Party's triumphant return to power was attributed to the leadership of the left-oriented Mrs. Sonia Gandhi, the Italian-born widow of the slain former prime minister, Rajiv Gandhi. Fearing political turmoil over her possibly becoming prime minister given her foreign origins, in an act of apparent renunciation, Sonia Gandhi instead chose Manmohan Singh for that position, while she exercised real power as supreme chief of the party. Under her guidance, the government enacted several important measures with a popular appeal to the lower and backward classes, such as loan waivers for farmers and a massive India-wide rural employment guarantee program. Renewed success in the 2009 elections convinced Sonia Gandhi that her welfare-oriented approach was correct, and there followed entitlements for the poor, such as the right to education and the right to food.

A remarkable ambivalence can be seen in the Congress Party's approach to globalization and liberalization. At times, the party is eager to take credit for having launched economic reform through liberalization of the economy, but at other times, it is reticent about being associated with its initiation. Thus, the party's 2009 election manifesto contains little discussion of globalization as such; it evidences extreme parsimony on the subject. At the same time, the manifesto does claim, quite legitimately in accord with its centrist role in the polity, that "balance—or the middle path—has always been the hallmark of the policies of the Indian National Congress" and that one manifestation of "it is a balance between taking advantage of globalization and ensuring that these benefits flow to local communities." Alongside that statement, another of the manifesto's overarching themes is "inclusiveness," specifically asserting that "economic growth and social justice are two sides of the same coin and must always go hand-in-hand."[23]

There is, then, a clear temporal demarcation in the posture of the Congress Party toward liberalization between the 1991–96 period, when structural adjustment and economic restructuring with the objective of improving economic efficiency dominated policy, and the period after 2004, when "inclusiveness" became the major motif. Prime Minister Manmohan Singh himself retrospectively distinguished the policy thrust of the two periods. On the first period, he commented: "In 1991, we unleashed the entrepreneurial energies of our people by dismantling the license-permit raj. This released individual creative energies to produce the wealth that we need for fulfilling our responsibility of offering a life of equal opportunity and dignity to our citizens." On the second period, he remarked: "The policies of the Government in recent times have sought to remake the democratic state of India, to make processes of social and economic change more inclusive and thereby empowering over a billion people, one sixth of humanity."[24] Broadly, then, India today is a votary of "inclusive liberalization" or "inclusive globalization."

Interestingly, the Congress Party's commitment to inclusiveness is rooted in its understanding of its political necessity in a democratic system, where a majority of the population looks up to the state to solve problems in such areas as health, education, and housing, in spite of their poor opinion of government performance. On the basis of an India-wide survey of 7,500 citizens for a project on "Globalization and the State in India"—funded by the Ford Foundation—political scientist Neera Chandhoke maintains:

> The irony is manifest. Despite the poor performance of the Indian state in the social sector, despite the fact that scholars and activists have been disillusioned

by the non-performance of the state, across the board, citizens continue to have high expectations of the state.

> Indians across economic strata, religions, regions, and gender continue to believe that [the] state is the *only* capable and reliable agency for ensuring vital social goods such as education, health, housing, food security, and employment. . . . On the other hand neither market nor non-governmental agencies have been able to earn much allegiance from them.[25]

Notwithstanding the Congress Party's modification of economic liberalization by supplementing it with inclusiveness, it has not overturned the basic thrust of globalization and liberalization. This is visible in its government's relentless pursuit of integration with the world economy, not only through the progressive lowering of tariffs but also through several Free Trade Area (FTA) agreements. Again, during the global financial crisis in 2008 and 2009, India desisted from taking recourse to protectionist policies, despite continuously facing huge deficits in its current account balance.

ALTERNATIVE POLICY PATHS

In the future, the shape of economic policy will, of course, depend on the configuration of political parties that come into power. Four major political formations that function within the democratic framework of India's constitution can be distinguished. First, there is the "center," basically represented by the Congress Party, which has been discussed. Second, there is the "right," the primary representative of which is the BJP, a group that is known for its aggressive nationalist (majoritarian) posture. Third, there is the "left," consisting primarily of the two major communist parties—the Communist Party of India (Marxist) and the Communist Party of India, often referred to as simply the CPI(M) and CPI, respectively—and a clutch of minor groups. The two communist parties were political adversaries at one time, particularly in the years after their split in 1964, but they have been in alliance now for a considerable period, with the more prominent and powerful CPI(M) as the senior partner. A key base for these parties has been West Bengal, where they held power for more than thirty years but were overthrown in 2011 by a state-based party. The political declarations of these parties bristle with traditional Marxist rhetoric. Their front organizations among labor groups in strategic sectors of the economy, particularly in the public sector, provide them with considerable political leverage.

Also increasingly important is the Communist Party of India (Maoist), which, however, rejects the parliamentary path to power and—claiming to be explicitly following the Chinese model—instead believes entirely in the revolutionary seizure of power through protracted armed struggle. This organization of left-wing extremism aims to overthrow the present political system through establishing rural bases as a step toward encircling the cities. Over the years, the CPI(Maoist) has acquired considerable strength in the tribal areas of the Mineral Belt across several states in central India, covering some one-third of India's administrative districts. Its armed cadres—the estimates of whose numbers vary between ten and fifty thousand—seem well-endowed with weaponry and extorted money and run almost a parallel government in the affected districts, which the state's security forces have been unable to defeat or weaken.

Finally, there is an assortment of regional or state-based parties. Some of these are centrist and identity-based; others claim to be socialist but are really confined to the intermediate castes. Governments in several important states are headed by state-based parties, for example, as the following were in 2013: Bihar, Jammu and Kashmir, Odisha, Tamil Nadu, Uttar Pradesh, and West Bengal. Such parties have become increasingly influential players at the central level since the end of the 1980s, but they often tend to go along in economic policy with the lead given by the dominant national party in any government coalition. The following discussion is limited to the national parties.

The BJP had occupied the rightist position in the political spectrum in India until 1998, when it came into power for the first time at the national level. Committed to a muscular (Hindu sectarian, in most eyes) nationalism, its defining characteristic was a commitment to India's national interest and the working out of an Indian model of development based on authentic Indian values that centered on economic nationalism and self-sufficiency. For a long time, it rejected both communism and capitalism, and opposed the excessive state intervention in the economy that was identified with the Nehru model. After the Congress government's shift to economic liberalization, the BJP favored calibrating the liberalization so as to give protection to Indian business against foreign multinationals. Once in office, however, the BJP jettisoned its protectionist plank and, facing down the protectionist groups inside it, wholeheartedly adopted the globalization and liberalization paradigm. Indeed, in office, it turned out to be remarkably proreform, especially in privatizing parts of the public sector, rapidly expanding telecommunications within India, and opening sectors of the economy to foreign enterprise.[26] Briefly, in economic matters, there was little to distinguish between the BJP and the Congress Party, but after the BJP's loss of power at the center in 2004, it resorted to opposing any government initiative on reform.

For its part, the CPI(M) accuses both the Congress Party and the BJP of being committed to the neoliberal path. It sees globalization as largely an American plot to dominate and exploit the developing countries. The party's political resolution of its 19th Congress in 2008 opens with the assertion that, besides employing coercion for the purpose, the United States seeks "to expand and maintain its hegemonic drive" by "the imposition of neoliberal policies through imperialist globalization."[27] Four years later, the 20th Congress described the global economic meltdown in 2008 as "the unfolding of the biggest economic crisis in the capitalist world since the Great Depression of the 1930s. This crisis is a direct outcome of the neoliberal capitalist trajectory driven by international finance capital. This prolonged crisis points to the unsustainability of finance capital-driven globalization."[28]

The CPI(M) sees the consequences of globalization to be all negative, and it paints a somber picture of the economic and social conditions generated in India by globalization. It accuses the Congress Party of having fostered increased inequalities through following the neoliberal path, which has benefited only the business class and urban elites: "This period has witnessed the further widening of inequalities in income and wealth distribution, increased regional and social disparities. Prosperity for the upper classes on the one hand and deprivation for the majority of the working people on the other has become the hallmark of the neo-liberal regime in India."[29] The CPI(M) attacks the Congress Party for obdurately clinging to the neoliberal path, which has resulted in "distorted growth" and therefore has been "discredited worldwide."[30] Instead, it offers the alternative path of "a people's democratic revolution," under which there will be instituted land reforms as well as "a self-reliant economic system and path of development which will develop the productive forces, maximize employment and reduce economic and social disparities," and assure planned development and social justice.[31] A particular emphasis of the CPI(M) as well as of the CPI is a dominant role for the state as a producer; both parties want to strengthen and expand the public sector. Party spokesmen often cite Joseph Stiglitz in support of their position on globalization.

Basically, the CPI(M), the CPI, and their smaller allies have made the Nehruvian economic model sacred at the national level and want a wholesale return to it, especially in the matter of the public sector. However, while the national leadership of the CPI(M) is rather inflexible ideologically on these issues, in the states in which the party has been in power, such as West Bengal and Kerala, the state-level leadership has pragmatically accommodated itself to parts of the liberalization project; indeed, critics have underlined the contradiction between theory and practice in the CPI(M)'s posture.[32] It is noteworthy that the leftist position is not altogether completely monopolized by the left; certainly, important elements within the Congress Party also subscribe to it, since that position is, after all, identified with the national icon Nehru. Indeed, in considerable part because of the experience with imperialism, a large section of the population is also generally suspicious of capitalism, the profit motive, and the United States.

The CPI is equally, if not more, vociferous than the CPI(M) in its condemnation of globalization and in highlighting its malign consequences. The political resolution at its 20th Congress characterizes globalization as being the current phase of imperialism, which is marked by the domination of finance capital.[33] The party's manifesto for the 2009 national elections opens with the declaration that "the country faces serious threat to its economic and political independence due to rightward shift in economic policies under the garb of economic neo-liberalism and pro-imperialist tilt in the foreign policy." The CPI further accuses the Congress-led government of "shamelessly pushing forward the policies of economic neo-liberalism dictated by international finance capital in the name of globalization, liberalization and privatization." It paints the government coalitions with the same brush, whether led by the Congress Party or the BJP, and sees both of them as committed to the neoliberal path, which, in its eyes, has led to a disastrous situation in the country.[34]

The political resolution maintains that neoliberal globalization has given rise to "crony capitalism," under which the upper section of the corporate bourgeoisie has "accumulated unprecedented wealth and come to wield tremendous economic power" and "in its ruthless quest for super profits aims to spread its tentacles to other spheres of the economy."[35] Further, India's corporate houses are said to have meanwhile entered into alliances with foreign multinationals that have established bases in the country following liberalization. With the added "economic and financial clout they are able to influence policies not only in the economic but also in the political and other fields." In the CPI's view, globalization and liberalization have generated nothing but pernicious consequences for the population: "Unemployment has been on the rise, regional disparities are widening and inequalities of income, wealth and consumption are fast increasing."[36] The CPI intends to reverse these baleful trends through an alternative strategy that defends India's independence and sovereignty, fosters agrarian reforms to protect the interests of farmers and agricultural laborers, and adopts policies that generate employment, eradicate poverty, and remove gross disparities.

Unlike the two major communist parties, which participate in the democratic process and are therefore sometimes referred to as "social democratic," the CPI(Maoist) aims to entirely overthrow the existing political and economic edifice. Its violent activities have made the party the most dreaded domestic threat to national security. The CPI(Maoist) was formed as recently as 2004, through the merger of two guerrilla organizations, but it has already proven to be an extremely tough security challenge to the state.

The CPI(Maoist) takes the origins of globalization to lie in the general crisis of capitalism, particularly the phase starting in the mid-1970s, which called forth "the neo-liberal economics or monetarist theory." Subsequently, "a new offensive on the world's people through globalization, privatization and liberalization was brought forth after the mid-1980s as the solution to the crisis."[37] In the party's view, India's independence is a fake one, since the British colonialists merely transferred power to their faithful agent, the Congress Party, which represents the comprador bureaucratic capitalist and big landlord classes. The Maoists consider India to be a semicolonial and semifeudal country, whose entire political and economic structure needs to be torn down and replaced by people's democracy of Mao Zedong's design.[38]

SUMMARY AND CONCLUSION

During the course of the twentieth century, three different worldviews about India's relationship with the world economy and about the organization of the domestic economy have predominated at different points in time. First, of course, there was the position taken by the colonial rulers, which held that India must remain open to the world economy and that the colonial government basically keep to a laissez-faire policy domestically; this position was particularly self-serving for Great Britain since it was the pioneer and most advanced industrial power of the time. Subsequent postcolonial positions seem to have been a function largely of India's actual experience with the outcome of colonial policy, and these were highly consequential for public policy in India and led to profound changes in economic policy.

Although there have been many defenders of imperialism, the leaders of India's freedom struggle and the informed general public subscribed to the nationalist school of historiography, which held economic policy under imperialism to have been the chief culprit in the country's economic downfall and stagnation and the resulting mass poverty and deprivation. In particular, they regarded the openness of the economy and the laissez-faire orientation of the colonial rulers to have thwarted India's economic growth. Understandably, then, after independence, these perceptions led the new national government under Nehru to shift to an economic strategy that was in essence the antithesis of colonial policy; in accord with Nehru's vision, India chose to move toward autarky and socialism. The socialist trend was further intensified by the government under Mrs. Indira Gandhi in the late 1960s and early 1970s, after a short-lived, foreign-inspired experiment with economic liberalization.

The economic stagnation, food shortages, and high inflation in the first half of the 1970s, however, fed into a major opposition movement against Mrs. Gandhi. This led her to reappraise her earlier radicalization of economic policy, which had not been functional for either growth or stability—economic or political. Around 1975, she changed course, though hesitantly and partially, this time in a more orthodox economic direction, jettisoning her nationalization drive, relaxing her restrictions on the private sector, and opening up the economy somewhat. This move inaugurated a long period of "incremental" economic liberalization that lasted until the end of the 1980s.

Finally, in 1991, in the midst of an economic crisis, India went in for a more radical economic reform by way of the emphatic "paradigm shift" from the socialist ancien régime to a more comprehensive economic liberalization. This move was based on a mix of perceptions, including that autarkic and socialist policies had constrained economic growth; the interim period of incremental liberalization had shown that liberal policies worked to aid growth; and the East Asian countries, particularly China, were leaving India far behind with their outward-oriented economic policies. This shift in economic policy during the subsequent two decades has been consolidated in that coalition governments of different political persuasions have not reversed it, in large part because of the growth acceleration and the greater access to resources that it has given to the state.

At the same time, there has been increasing realization that the higher inequalities generated by globalization and liberalization, together with the public awareness of them, mandate *inclusiveness* with a strong thrust for social equity—indeed, that globalization and liberalization both facilitate and require "inclusiveness" since the neglect of social equity can be costly, both socially and politically. This perception of the centrist elites matches that of the public's and, in an electorally competitive system, is reinforced by the challenges thrown up by the dissident alternatives offered by the left, particularly in view of the hold of its extremist section over a substantial portion of the tribal population. The emphasis on inclusiveness poses its own challenges, for massive welfare expenditures not only augment expectations but also place tremendous pressures on the treasury, especially when the economy faces external shocks, as with the global financial meltdown in 2008.

NOTES

1. See the contributions by Jeffrey G. Williamson, Angus Maddison, Deepak Nayyar, and Amartya Sen, in *Globalization and Politics in India*, ed. Baldev Raj Nayar (New Delhi: Oxford University Press, 2007).

2. Immanuel Wallerstein, *World-Systems Analysis: An Introduction* (Durham, NC: Duke University Press, 2004).

3. Angus Maddison, "Why and When Did the West Get Rich?" in Nayar, *Globalization*, 76–89.

4. Charles Tilly, "Reflections on the History of European State-Making," in *The Formation of National States in Western Europe*, ed. Charles Tilly (Princeton, NJ: Princeton University Press, 1975), 3–85.

5. Gabriel Palma, "Dependency: A Formal Theory of Underdevelopment or a Methodology for the Analysis of Concrete Situations?" *World Development* 6 (July–December 1978): 881–922.

6. Baldev Raj Nayar, *The Geopolitics of Globalization* (New Delhi: Oxford University Press, 2005), 26–28.

7. Partha Chatterjee, *The Nation and Its Fragments: Colonial and Postcolonial Histories* (Princeton, NJ: Princeton University Press, 1993).

8. See Tirthankar Roy, *The Economic History of India, 1857–1947* (New Delhi: Oxford University Press, 2000). Roy repeatedly bends over backward to give the benefit of the doubt to the beneficial school on the ground that the claims of the opposing school are either too general, or that data are unavailable to make an adequate assessment of them. The Achilles' heel of his work, however, is that it neglects precisely the earlier violent and nakedly exploitative period of colonial rule, which—having already structured

the colonial economy before the generation of quantitative data began—is quite critical to the case of the left-nationalist school.

9. On the left-nationalist school, see Amiya Kumar Bagchi, *Colonialism and Indian Economy* (New Delhi: Oxford University Press, 2010), xvi–xvii, xl–xli, l–li, who forcefully documents the exploitation and the underpinning coercive and racial "structural adjustment" policies of the colonial state and its predecessor, the East India Company; he is particularly scathing in his criticism of Tirthankar Roy's work, which he characterizes as one where neocolonial historiography "reached its acme (or nadir)." See also Sumit Sarkar, *Modern India, 1885–1947* (Delhi: Macmillan, 1983).

10. Dietmar Rothermund, *An Economic History of India: From Pre-Colonial Times to 1991* (London: Routledge, 1993), 33, 58–65.

11. See Angus Maddison, *Class Structure and Economic Growth: India and Pakistan since the Moghuls* (London: George Allen and Unwin, 1971), 76, who estimated that during the period 1900–1946, India's national income grew at the rate of 0.7 percent a year while population grew at the rate of 0.8 percent.

12. Roy, *Economic History of India*, 18 (emphasis added).

13. Jawaharlal Nehru, *The Discovery of India* (New York: John Day, 1946), 404.

14. The evolution of Nehru's ideas on socialism and economic development is discussed in Baldev Raj Nayar, *India's Mixed Economy: The Role of Ideology and Interest in Its Development* (Bombay: Popular Prakashan, 1989), chaps. 4–5.

15. The economic strategy is discussed in Baldev Raj Nayar, *Globalization and Nationalism: The Changing Balance in India's Economic Policy, 1950–2000* (New Delhi: Sage, 2001), chap. 2.

16. The goals of economic independence and national power (including military) in economic planning are discussed in Baldev Raj Nayar, "Political Mainsprings of Economic Planning in the New Nations: The Modernization Imperative versus Social Mobilization," *Comparative Politics* 6, no. 3 (April 1974), and, more thoroughly, in Nayar, *The Modernization Imperative and Indian Planning* (New Delhi: Vikas, 1972).

17. From this account, it should be obvious that poverty removal as such was not a salient goal, let alone the single goal, of the economic strategy except perhaps over the very long run. It is important to underline this point in view of the position taken by eminent economist T. N. Srinivasan that: "In India, eradicating mass poverty has long been the single, intrinsic, and overarching objective of national development." See T. N. Srinivasan, *Growth, Sustainability, and Economic Reforms* (New Delhi: Oxford University Press, 2011), 3, 27, 68. Even when expressed explicitly, poverty eradication often was not the actual, or at least immediate, goal.

18. Of three possible explanations for the policy change—ideational diffusion of a global neoliberal consensus, foreign influence and coercion over policy, and economic performance—I prefer the last one because change initiation preceded the global consensus in time and it was domestically generated.

19. The measures undertaken in the course of this policy change are discussed in Baldev Raj Nayar, "When Did the 'Hindu' Rate of Growth End?" *Economic and Political Weekly* 41, no. 19 (May 13, 2006): 1885–90. This interpretation of change in perceptions and policy as originating in 1975 departs from other interpretations that take 1980 or

1985 as the beginning point: Dani Rodrik and Arvind Subramanian, "From 'Hindu Growth' to Productivity Surge: The Mystery of the Indian Growth Transition," IMF Working Paper 04/77, IMF, Washington, DC, 2004; Arvind Virmani, "India's Economic Growth: From Socialist Rate of Growth to Bharatiya Rate of Growth," Working Paper No. 122, Indian Council for Research on International Economic Relations, New Delhi, 2004; and Arvind Panagariya, "Growth and Reforms during 1980s and 1990s," *Economic and Political Weekly* 39, no. 25 (June 19, 2004): 2581–94.

20. Manmohan Singh, "Commanding Heights," Public Broadcasting Service (PBS) Interview, 2000. Available at www.pbs.org/wgbh/commandingheights/shared/minitext/int_manmohansingh.html.

21. T. N. Srinivasan, "The Costs of Hesitant and Reluctant Globalization: India," *Indian Economic Review* 38, no. 2 (2003): 131–55.

22. Rob Jenkins, *Democratic Politics and Economic Reform in India* (Cambridge: Cambridge University Press, 1999).

23. Indian National Congress, *Lok Sabha Election: Manifesto of the Indian National Congress* (New Delhi: INC, 2009), 1, 5, 9, 31.

24. Manmohan Singh, "PM's Key-note Address at the India-Today Conclave," New Delhi, March 18, 2011, emphasis added. Available at http://pmindia.nic.in/.

25. The first paragraph is from Neera Chandhoke, "Putting Civil Society in Its Place," *Economic and Political Weekly* 44, no. 7 (February 14, 2009): 15; and the second is from her chapter "Globality, State, and Collective Imagination: The Indian Experience," in *Facing Globality: Politics of Resistance, Relocation, and Reinvention in India*, ed. Bhupinder Brar and Pampa Mukherjee (New Delhi: Oxford University Press, 2012), 94–110; emphasis in the original. The percentages favoring state provisioning of services were: education, 92.4; housing, 34.6; employment and care for the underprivileged, 77.2; and food security, 83.0. The survey was conducted by the economics research firm Indicus Analytics.

26. See Baldev Raj Nayar, "BJP's Economic Nationalism in Theory and Practice," in *India and the Politics of Developing Countries: Essays in Memory of Myron Weiner*, ed. Ashutosh Varshney (New Delhi: Sage, 2004), chap. 10. See also Ashok Malik, "The BJP, the RSS Family, and Globalization in India," in Nayar, *Globalization*, chap. 14.

27. CPI(M), "Political Resolution Adopted at the XIX Congress of the Communist Party of India (Marxist), March 29 to April 3, 2008, Coimbatore," para. 1.1. The resolution is available at http://cpim.org/documents/19%20Congress.Political.Resolution.pdf.

28. CPI(M), *Documents of the 20th Congress of the Communist Party of India (Marxist) (Kozhikode, Kerala, April 4–9, 2012)* (New Delhi: CPI(M), 1912), 1.

29. Ibid., 24.

30. CPI(M), *Manifesto for the 15th Lok Sabha Elections, 2009* (New Delhi: CPI(M), 2009), 4; the document is available at www.cpim.org/.

31. CPI(M), "Political Resolution," paras. 2.6, 2.103, and 2.104.

32. Partha Pratim Basu, "The CPI(M) and Globalization: Anatomy of Ambivalence," in Brar and Mukherjee, *Facing Globality*, chap. 6.

33. CPI, "Political Resolution," XX Congress, available at https://sites.google.com/a/communistparty.in/cpi/xx-congress-1/political-resolution.

34. CPI, "CPI Election Manifesto—2009," available at http://allindiapeoplesmanifesto.files.wordpress.com/2009/04/cpi-manifesto-20091.pdf.

35. CPI, "Political Resolution," sec. 11.

36. Ibid.

37. CPI(Maoist), Central Committee, "Political Resolution" (Draft, September 2004), 14. The document is available at www.bannedthought.net.

38. CPI(Maoist), Central Committee (Provisional), "Party Program" (September 21, 2004). The document is available at www.bannedthought.net. For a CPI(M) perspective on the party, see Prasenjit Bose, ed., *Maoism: A Critique from the Left* (New Delhi: Left-Word Books, 2010).

Chapter 3

ECONOMIC INTEGRATION PRIOR TO LIBERALIZATION

At independence, economic integration and, more broadly, national integration were at the center of the concerns of the national leadership. Accordingly, this chapter examines such apprehensions, as well as the institutional design developed by that leadership to overcome economic segmentation and to advance economic integration. In the process, it analyzes the colonial legacy on economic segmentation, the "grand bargain" by way of the constitutional settlement on integration after independence, and the mode of economic integration during the socialist regime, roughly from 1956 to 1991. The broad message of the chapter is that, notwithstanding the best intentions of the constitution makers and the vaunted legal provisions, the institutional design for integration was, for all intents and purposes, flawed in assuring effective economic and political integration, a fact that remained masked under the socialist regime only to become manifest subsequently.

THE COLONIAL LEGACY ON ECONOMIC SEGMENTATION

Economic integration is essentially a feature of the modern industrial economy, for it is industrialization that makes the various parts of a nation's economy truly interdependent through specialization and division of labor. Significantly, Karl Marx had underlined that, unlike an agricultural society, which resembled "a sack of potatoes" and lacked economic unity, the development of modern industry under capitalism had not only made for agglomeration of population and centralization of the means of production but also "*political centralization*. Independent or but loosely connected provinces with separate interests, laws, governments and systems of taxation, became lumped together into *one nation, with one government, one code of laws, one national class interest, one frontier and one customs tariff*."[1]

Given this requirement of an industrial economy for integration in general, colonialism's legacy in India was profoundly unpropitious for prospects of economic integration. Apart from the horrific partition of the subcontinent, that legacy was twofold: a largely agricultural economy and economic impoverishment of the populace—features that are extremely adverse for economic integration. Notwithstanding the growth of some industry in two major urban enclaves, to the very end of British rule, "the economy of India remained poor, basically agricultural and colonial."[2] Factory production at independence hardly amounted to 6 percent of national income, while factory employment constituted less than 2 percent of the labor force.[3] India was particularly deficient with respect to capacity for capital goods production, with manufacturing basically confined to cotton and jute textiles. Because India's economy thus remained unindustrialized, it was therefore largely unintegrated at independence.

In the eyes of the nationalist school of historiography, colonial rule first fostered the "deindustrialization" of India's economy through trade policy and the expropriation of its economic surplus. Later, it impeded the growth of modern industry in India by its hostility to such development, beholden as it was to industrial interests in Britain. Most of what industry developed was concentrated in the seaports of Bombay and Calcutta in a dumbbell formation at the western and eastern ends of the subcontinent. India under colonial rule was, for the nationalist school, an excellent illustration of an "enclave economy" that was disarticulated and lacked internal linkages. India, as the economic "periphery," was linked in a subordinate position to Britain, the economic "center," in order to serve metropolitan interests, and therefore lacked an internal growth dynamic.[4] The economic delinkage or disassociation of India from Britain during the two world wars provided some impetus for industrial development, but the lack of a domestic capital goods industry proved to be a serious constraint on growth. Besides, the pauperized state of the masses provided little demand stimulus for growth. To be sure, the colonial state did foster the railways and the telegraph network and built some irrigation systems, but for the nationalist school, the governing motive in such activity was military security and British economic interests, not India's economic development. Consequently, "the Indian market, which developed in the course of the nineteenth century, was a *fragmented* one."[5] It is not surprising that the colonial state was not a developmental state and that the Indian economy consequently experienced underdevelopment, of which economic segmentation and disarticulation were an integral part.

While the nationalist school's indictment is strong, it would seem, however, that the colonial legacy rested, in turn, on precolonial foundations that were also hardly propitious for autochthonous development and integration. Frequent foreign invasions had been India's lot over the ages. Following the political decay of the Mughal Empire in the eighteenth century, India rapidly degenerated into its traditional pattern of a congeries of independent kingdoms that were constantly engaged in mutual warfare and thus vulnerable to renewed conquest. Besides this political segmentation, India was economically segmented, which was largely a function of its preindustrial stage in economic evolution.

There is no doubt that India was a leading partner in the flourishing international trading system centered on the Indian Ocean, and it contained substantial towns that were centers of administration, pilgrimage, and commerce. Various trading communities managed foreign and domestic trade, and they demonstrated considerable sophistication in developing and managing the financial instruments necessary for such trade.[6] Despite all this, the dominant feature of the land was monsoon-dependent agriculture, carried out in hundreds of thousands of largely self-sufficient villages. Transportation linkages were scarce and weak, based almost entirely on animate energy, and the threat of robbery and violence also inhibited travel. On top of all this, there was immense social segmentation, born out of not only linguistic and regional cleavages but also a rather rigid hierarchical stratification rooted in religious notions of purity and inequality. If India itself was a mere geographic description, then economic integration also was very tenuous and weak. It was into this scene of extreme segmentation—and, in large part, aided by it—that the British inserted themselves and, starting in the mid-eighteenth century, carried out a century-long process of conquest of the vast Indian subcontinent.

In light of the precolonial legacy, it is noteworthy that over its long duration, colonial rule did actually leave behind considerable assets. Among other things, these included an extensive railway and communications network; a large textile industry with the potential to serve, if properly exploited, as the foundation for exports and further industrialization of the country; and a substantial steel industry. In addition, among the assets, there was an authoritative (indeed, an authoritarian) system of governance—admittedly, there were some viable institutions like the central bank—and a common official language for the entire country.

THE CONSTITUTIONAL SETTLEMENT

Economic integration is really premised on some measure of political integration, with the latter a prerequisite for the former. Understandably, therefore, the first task of the new governing leadership at independence was to establish a constitutional framework for achieving an integrated polity. National unity and integrity were central to the concerns and intentions of the leadership from the very beginning. Given the tragedy of the partition of the subcontinent, the threat of possible further disintegration in the future was an enduring concern for the leaders of the new nation-state.

Besides the partition, there were several other reasons for the centrality of national unity and integrity, all pertaining to the leadership's assessment of the contemporaneous present, the past, and the future. When the national leaders set themselves the task of developing a constitution immediately after independence, they did so in the context of a country confronted with a sea of overwhelming problems, including: the outbreak of widespread violence and breakdown of the machinery of law and order all across northern India; the influx of more than five million refugees from Pakistan; and the war with Pakistan. These momentous events had a tremendous impact on the leaders, whether national or regional, in working out the constitutional settlement.

The leaders were therefore fiercely determined to see that nothing should be done in developing the constitution that would harm the nation's unity and integrity. Consequently, while they opted for a dual-level political structure for the country in view of its vastness and diversity, they opted for a strong center in the constitution, which came into force in 1950. In their vision, India was to be—avoiding the term "federation"—a Union of states that could be converted into a unitary political entity, depending on need and circumstance. Moved fundamentally by the larger interests of the future republic, they chose wisely, for India continues to be besieged by threats.

It was not only the present but also the past that had weighed with the constitution makers. Many a leader took recourse to "the lessons of history" argument, which linked the past lack of a strong central government in a divided subcontinent to the long series of military defeats at the hands of foreign conquerors. For some, the collective mind of the constitution makers was "almost Hobbesian in spirit," while the provision of a strong center signified a "race memory." Quite a few reminded the constituent assembly that "the supreme fact in Indian history" was that "the most tragic days were when the central authority in the country was dismembered by the provinces trying to resist it," or that "history undoubtedly proves that whenever there has been no centralization in this country it has been overrun by foreigners."[7] Such sentiments did not even need to be explicitly expressed, for they were widely shared among the leadership and the general public. Interestingly, a postglobalization assessment of India's constitution making points out that, even as the country's social diversity provoked "a fear in its centrifugal potential, 'Hobbes may be the largely unacknowledged mentor of Indian constitutionalism.'"[8]

Finally, the future also had a bearing in favoring a strong center, particularly for Prime Minister Jawaharlal Nehru, the most eminent and prominent among the national leaders and constitution makers. Nehru was determined to have India take a socialist path in accord with his long-held vision for India's development. In his mind, that task could be accomplished only through a considered program of economic planning organized by the center for all of India, not haphazardly or separately by a dozen or more states. For that reason, "economic and social planning" was included in the concurrent list of powers. That item was potentially broad enough to make the center supreme in economic matters. That choice was deliberate, not the result of happenstance.

Scholars have differed over how to characterize the polity in India resulting from the constitutional settlement.[9] The classical writer on the subject of federalism, K. C. Wheare, was reluctant to acknowledge it as a genuine federal state, describing the Indian constitution instead as a unitary one with subsidiary federal features, rather than a federal one with subsidiary unitary features.[10] In actuality, however, there is no inherent prescriptive content to the idea of federalism in relation to the distribution of powers other than that there be two or more levels of government with some defined spheres of jurisdiction. The world's federations vary widely in the distribution of powers among their levels of government, having worked out the distribution that best fit with the preferences of their leaders and publics. In that sense, every federation is sui generis, as the Indian one surely is.[11] The dominant feature of the latter—given the founders' perception of the need for national unity and integrity—is certainly a strong center with the legal capacity to transform the polity into a unitary system when circumstances demand it.

The strong center is manifest, among other things, in the abundance of powers assigned to it in the distribution of powers; the Union list contains ninety-seven items, including the usual principal ones of defense, foreign affairs, and communications. Importantly, the constitution sets up no absolute barrier between the center and the states in the exercise of powers. To begin with, there is a long Concurrent list (forty-seven items), where the center's statutes supersede those of the states in case of conflict. Further, the center can legislate even on items in the State list (sixty-six items) if authorized by the upper house of parliament. Besides, the residuary powers rest with the center. More crucially, the emergency powers enable the center to convert the political system into a unitary one in case of war, financial emergency, or breakdown of the constitutional machinery in one or more states. In addition, the center has the power to issue directions to any state in case of internal disturbance.

India's unity and integrity were further sought to be strengthened by the constitution providing for certain common institutions for both the center and the states. The more important of these are: a single integrated judicial system and several law codes; a number of all-India services that are shared by the center and states, particularly the important Indian Administrative Service and Indian Police Service; and the agencies for the recruitment and training of these services.

Despite the plenitude of powers with the center, it would be mistaken to characterize India as not being a federal state, as some have done. In the normal course of affairs, the states exercise substantial autonomy in the areas of agriculture, internal security (maintenance of law and order) and the management of the social sectors, such as education and health; the State list has more than sixty entries. In addition, the states are responsible for executing the laws of both the center and the states, since the center generally depends on the states for the implementation of its policies and laws; the center is mostly staff and not line. Indeed, an American expert on public administration, Paul Appleby, had long ago pointed out that, of all the federations in the world, the center in India had the least capacity to implement its own policies and was dependent on the states for their execution.[12] More crucially, the states are largely ethnically based. As such, they are both the primary focus of the loyalty of their inhabitants and the locus of mobilization in politics. They have therefore considerable political leverage to be assertive toward the center. Several scholars have pointed out how in reality, notwithstanding the legal distribution of powers, several states have been able to undercut the implementation of central policies or even to defy the center.[13]

While this chapter is limited to developments before economic liberalization, it is pertinent to take note of some subsequent events. In the ultimate analysis, in affairs of the state, it is the balance of political forces that is often decisive in outcomes rather than constitutional stipulations. To put the claims about the superior powers of the center in perspective, it seems that there is merit in the proposition that the actual evolution of politics before and after economic liberalization has, in fact, overturned the intent of the constitution makers on political and economic integration.

Since the mid-1990s, all governments at the center have been multiparty coalitions in which regional parties from the states are not only influential and often veto players but also at times have been able to hold the center to ransom in the pursuit of their regional interests, even at the cost of the larger national interest. The practice of coalitions at the center, which weakened the center, began before the opening to globalization. However, since liberalization, which incidentally widened the powers of the states considerably, the states have often blocked important policies that are essential in a rapidly changing world on such issues as terrorism or economic reform, claiming that they impinged on state autonomy. At times, the states have attempted to coerce the center, even on issues of foreign policy. The fact of the matter is that, despite the vaunted provisions of the constitution, the center is now at the mercy of the states because of its dependence on coalitions, of which regional parties are essential components. In the process, it is the autonomy of the center that has been invaded, and that too by the states. The constitution makers, who endeavored to build a strong center, could never have imagined the possibility of such a threat to the autonomy of the center at the hands of the states.

The situation has come to this because the constitutional design suffers from a fundamental flaw insofar as it does not provide for the direct election of the center's executive by the nation as a single constituency—unmediated by the states and their regional parties—as is the case in the United States. Of course, this is potentially a highly controversial issue since it implies shifting to a presidential system, and it is difficult to see a possible constituency that would push for it, especially since change would mean stepping into unknown territory and it would also require approval of the very states that have succeeded to such power over the center. In any case, the issue underlines how constitutional provisions can also be profoundly consequential and can generate path-dependency outcomes that run counter to the larger intent of constitution makers.

Constitutional Provisions on Economic Integration

For the founding fathers of the constitution, India's economic integration was no less a concern than was political integration. Overcoming economic segmentation was part and parcel of their larger aim of assuring national unity and integrity. Here, as elsewhere in the constitution, however, they had to balance the desirability of building a single integrated national economy with the demands for regional economic autonomy. At the same time, the nature of the economic and financial tools available in that era limited the satisfactory resolution of all the problems they faced. The different provisions of the constitution that they developed with respect to economic integration can be examined in terms of (1) freedom of movement and settlement for citizens, (2) market integration, and (3) division and sharing of tax revenues.

1. Freedom of Movement and Settlement. The constitution provides a single citizenship for all Indians; unlike the United States, there is no separate citizenship for the individual states. Article 19 guarantees the right of freedom to all citizens to move freely and to reside and settle in any part of India. This guarantee is, however, subject to reasonable restrictions in the public interest.[14] In reality, notwithstanding the legal right, chauvinist sons-of-the-soil movements and groups can and sometimes do undermine that right in some regions. They do so not only through political campaigns of intimidation but also with violent, at times murderous, agitations against "foreigners" from other states on the ground that the latter not only impinge on the job prospects of local citizens but are also a threat to the local culture. Also, while states do not have separate citizenship, they can and do impose domicile and language requirements on recruitment for public employment.

In practice, then, the legal right to freedom of movement is modified in significant ways. The right is likely to come under greater pressure in the future as urbanization increases and there is acceleration in the movement of persons across regional borders.

2. Market Integration. The constitution's founding fathers were highly cognizant of the need to assure a common national market for India. They even provided a separate section in the constitution on interstate commerce. Article 301 states that "trade, commerce and [commercial] intercourse throughout the territory of India shall be free."[15] In delivering the majority opinion in one Supreme Court decision, Justice P. B. Gajendragadkar observed that this article was essential to India's economy, to advancing the living standards of its people, and to the economic unity of the country, which was in turn necessary for strengthening political unity.[16]

This emphatic endorsement of unhindered interstate commerce notwithstanding, Article 301 is riddled with reservations and qualifications that, in practice, make for segmentation of the economy. Some of the restrictions are necessary, of course, such as preventing the spread of disease. However, states were allowed to impose restrictions on the movement of goods across their borders more broadly in the name of public interest. This permission has been used especially with respect to "essential" commodities.[17] Whenever there is the possibility of outflow of such commodities from a state on a scale that would cause local shortages or price increases, the state government is likely to quickly impose restrictions on the outflow. Commerce is thus not unhindered within India. In the presence of such segmentation of the market, especially in agricultural commodities, or its ever-present potential, it is difficult to speak of a common market as such in India.[18]

3. The Division and Sharing of Tax Revenues. Nothing better illustrates the intentions of the constitution makers to reject the classical formulations on federalism and to work out arrangements that would be appropriate for India than the provisions on the distribution of powers of taxation. In Wheare's understanding of federalism, "both general and regional governments must each have under its own independent control financial resources significant to perform its exclusive functions." Instead, Granville Austin points out that "the Assembly's approach to the framing of these portions of the Constitution, as well as the financial provisions themselves, exemplify Birch's description of *cooperative federalism*."[19]

In so doing, the constitution makers instituted a complicated division of taxation powers and sharing of revenues in which center and states are tied together in intricate ways rather than set against each other. There is no doubt that the states then, as now, wanted the maximum of resources, but they made little effort at that time to assert a right to entirely separate independent sources of revenue; for the most part, they instead readily agreed to let the union collect the revenues and share them with the states. Austin notes: "This could hardly be called a traditional defence of provincial autonomy," that is, competitive federalism.[20] The underlying reason for their stance was the diverse, perhaps incompatible interests of the different states, depending on whether they were more or less developed, or more or less populous. In the circumstance, they trusted the center more than they did each other for a fair distribution.

Besides the important item of sales tax, the states were given jurisdiction over land revenue and agricultural income tax, as well as over excise duties on alcohol and opium products. In addition, they could levy taxes on professions and trades, vehicles, travelers by road and inland waterways, luxuries, and entertainment.[21]

The allocation of taxation powers to the center was somewhat more complex. Such powers fell into essentially four types: (1) taxes that are levied and collected by the center, the proceeds of which are also retained by the center (such as corporation tax and customs duties); (2) taxes that are levied and collected by the center, but the proceeds of which are shared between the center and states (such as income tax and excise duties); (3) taxes that are levied and collected by the center, but the entire proceeds of which are allocated to the states (such as estate duties); and (4) taxes that are levied by the center but are collected and retained by the states (such as stamp duties).[22] The constitution limits the borrowing power of the states, which can exercise it only within India and subject to approval by the center.

It is evident that the distribution of taxation powers is quite complicated. The multiplicity of arrangements with respect to levying, collecting, and assigning taxes was decidedly not conducive to economic efficiency. More important, despite the significant role conceded to the center regarding taxation, the distribution of taxation powers left India remarkably segmented economically. In particular, allocating the levying and collection of sales tax to the states meant the creation of multiple tax systems. In fact, the problem of such multiplicity was worse than that. In addition to sales tax, states and local governments within them imposed *octroi*, or entry taxes. All this was inimical to economic integration. Undoubtedly, integration would have been aided by a single sales tax throughout India, the proceeds of which also could have been shared among the states. However, this did not happen, and the compromise reached between the center and the provinces during the making of the constitution was adverse for interstate commerce and economic efficiency; it was, in Austin's view, "one of the Assembly's few conspicuous failures."[23]

ECONOMIC INTEGRATION UNDER THE SOCIALIST REGIME

The constitutional settlement was a notable achievement in the developing world. However, as is evident regarding barriers to interstate commerce and multiple sales tax systems, it suffered from serious shortcomings with respect to facilitating the development of a common market. As serious as these deficiencies were, they did not attract the state's attention for rectification after the constitution came into force, for the fundamental reason that the leadership was preoccupied with much weightier tasks and also because of much grander economic initiatives that eclipsed them in importance. Indeed, under the leadership of Jawaharlal Nehru as prime minister (1947–64), the center soon designed an overall architecture for the economy with such powerful integrative elements that it reduced the significance of the shortcomings.

In Nehru's socialist vision for India, economic integration of the country's subcontinental economy would be a function primarily of an interventionist state from above, not an affair of the market from below, and that, too, not just in its regulatory role but, crucially, in its roles as comprehensive economic planner, entrepreneur, owner, and manager. The economy would thus be integrated under the direction of the state, both through economic policy and through some specific state institutions.

Economic Policy and Its Integrative Implications

Despite the turmoil in the wake of the partition and factional strife within the Congress Party, which impeded the initiation of a considered economic policy, Nehru was able to start the process by establishing the Planning Commission in 1950. However, it was not until the mid-1950s, after Nehru had consolidated his power in both government and party, that India under his direction could make a sharp break with the inherited colonial economic policy. That break in economic policy revolved around moving India to replace capitalism, laissez-faire and open economy with socialism, economic planning, and autarky. There was no revolutionary rupture, but Nehru launched India on a gradual but steady course in the direction of achieving these ends, a course that his daughter, Mrs. Indira Gandhi, subsequently intensified during her first tenure as prime minister (1966–77).

At the heart of Nehru's socialist vision, which he had developed during the later stages of the nationalist movement, was a bold and ambitious economic strategy for the rapid industrialization of India. The principal focus of the strategy was the erection of a vast complex of heavy industries under the auspices of the public sector as part of a gigantic "Big Push" inward-oriented import substitution program. The heavy industries were intended to enable India, over the longer run, to become master of its own industrial destiny through building the capacity to set up plants and factories. The economic strategy, modeled clearly after the Soviet experience, was launched with the *Second Five Year Plan (1956–1961)* and was repeated in the *Third Five Year Plan (1961–1965)*.[24] It was sought to be repeated again in the *Fourth Five Year Plan*, which was, however, aborted before it could be finalized as a result of economic and political crises.

It is particularly noteworthy that the heavy industry strategy as an integrative mechanism was designed to encompass the whole of India's economy. While the center directly took on the task of building and managing the heavy industries across India, the strategy in a way also structured economic policy for the entire nation, as it was designed for the development of the national economy as an integral whole. The economic policies and plans of the individual states consequently had to dovetail with the center's overall policy and plans (developed with the concurrence of the states after discussions). Nehru was undoubtedly committed to democracy and pluralism, but at times he tended to assume, at least verbally, as if India were a unitary system insofar as planning was concerned.

What facilitated the adoption of the socialist vision and the heavy industry strategy for all of India was the fact that the Congress Party with Nehru as its supreme leader exercised power at the time not only at the center but in almost all the states. It was the era of the "single party dominant" system. The heavy industry strategy as a component of Nehru's socialist vision was perfectly acceptable to the Congress leaders from the states as a developmental add-on that could be beneficial for many, if not all, of the states. But that was not necessarily true of other components of the socialist vision that were of a redistributive nature, particularly land reform and agricultural cooperatives. As a result, Nehru would be only partially successful in pursuing his socialist vision.

The integrative implications of the heavy industry strategy—carried out principally through the mechanism of a progressively expanding public sector under a regime of comprehensive economic planning—extended beyond establishing a single overarching framework of economic policy for the entire polity, including the different states. This aspect had to do with the strategy's relationship to the world economy. One of the strategy's key aims, if not its principal aim, was to establish a regime of economic autarky in India. The formal rationale for the heavy industry strategy, as expressed in the economic model developed by Nehru's chief economic adviser at the time, P. C. Mahalanobis, was to overcome a potential capital goods constraint on economic growth. Behind the technical rationale, however, there lay a more profound aim, to achieve *economic independence* for India, as explicitly acknowledged by Mahalanobis himself, whose economic model was, in any case, that of a closed economy.[25] Interestingly, while Mahalanobis had provided the technical framework for the heavy industry strategy, the strategy as such and the aim of economic independence or self-sufficiency were presaged in Nehru's thinking before independence. Furthermore, in Nehru's mind, the aim of economic independence was quite self-consciously conjoined with—and regarded as the foundation of—political independence and sovereignty insofar as heavy industry was geopolitically essential for *national power*, in particular, military capabilities.[26] In this respect, the motives for the heavy industry strategy were the same as they were in the Soviet economic model. The goals of socialism, economic nationalism, and strategic independence were all combined in the Indian economic model as developed by Nehru and his planners. They entailed insulating India from the turbulence and turmoil of the capitalist world economy and protecting it from imperialism and power politics. Economic autarky under socialism would thus function to facilitate the eventual development of a single integrated national economy.

State Institutions

It is evident that during the regime of socialism in India, from 1956 to 1991, it was the state led by the center that was the visible instrument of economic integration, rather than the invisible hand of the market. This was so not only with respect to economic policy but also to the establishment of some powerful institutions that were organized to achieve the ends of that policy. Of particular importance were those pertaining to the three areas of economic planning, the public sector, and the system of licensing and controls.

Economic Planning. The key institution for economic planning was the high-powered Planning Commission at the center, which had been established in 1950. Normally consisting of experts backed up by a considerable bureaucracy, the commission regularly developed five-year plans, except for some occasional breaks due to economic exigencies.[27] Its power and eminence in India's governmental system derived from the fact that from the very beginning it had the prime minister as its chairman, even though the functioning head of the organization was the deputy chairman. Remarkably, with its highly professional staff, the commission soon "acquired an influence on national policy making almost equal to that of the Central Cabinet."[28]

The Planning Commission supplemented its major function of producing a five-year plan by issuing annual plans, which set out the financial outlays for the year. The procedure for the formulation of the five-year plan involved developing and publishing for public and official discussion a paper on the overall strategy or framework for the relevant period, usually called the "Approach Paper." The paper would set out the desirable sectoral thrust, growth rate, and size of the plan. After obtaining official approval for the Approach Paper from the appropriate authorities, the Planning Commission prepared a draft plan, which indicated the proposed outlays for the various sectors and, after its approval, published the final version.

The significant point about the integrative implications of economic planning is that such planning was done for all of India, not just the center. To begin with, this is apparent in the very process of planning, in which both the center and states were involved in what can be regarded as a demonstration of cooperative federalism. Early on, to lend the imprimatur of national legitimacy to planning, a higher political body was set up in the form of the National Development Council (NDC). Consisting of the chief ministers of the states as well as the cabinet ministers at the center heading portfolios that had a connection with planning, the NDC was the authoritative body that approved the Approach Paper and the five-year plan; however, given its size, it tended to be more a debating rather than a policymaking body.

The interaction of the Planning Commission with the states extended much beyond the consultative process over obtaining NDC approval for the overall national plans, however. The commission played a continuously active role in the five-year plans of the states. This was a consequence of several factors. To begin with, the national five-year plan was an overall plan for the entire country, of which the states were a part. The commission played a coordinating role and attempted to make sure that the plans of the states fit in with the overall national plan. It was able to play this role because of two important reasons. First, the commission had financial leverage since the allocation of taxing powers under the constitution endowed the center with greater resources. The Planning Commission held discussions individually with each state and approved the overall plan outlay for the states and assessed what was needed from the center to supplement each state's own resources through central grants-in-aid to fulfill the objectives of the plan.[29]

The second reason for the continued important role of the Planning Commission in the development of state plans was the higher quality of its staff compared to that of the states. Regardless, the process of consultation between the center and the states over the years became quite regularized. The Planning Commission turned into a site of hectic activity at the time of the preparation and finalization of state plans, with state delegation after state delegation, often headed by the chief minister, arriving for discussions with the commission.

Overall, then, institutions related to economic planning, such as the Planning Commission and the NDC, served as important instruments for economic integration under the regime of socialism. But economic planning, as a mechanism for achieving industrialization and other societal goals, also carried certain other elements that were also enabling for economic integration. Such elements included establishing a national vision, fostering élan around the articulation of a national destiny, and encompassing the entire economy and polity in a common endeavor.

Besides this integrative *function* that may have been an incidental accompaniment of economic planning, the process of planning and its implementation also seem to have had economic and political integration as an explicit *purpose*. When economic planners specifically articulated the goal of removing or reducing disparities—whether among India's various social groups or its many regions—they were consciously seeking the goal of economic and national integration. In his preface to India's *Sixth Five Year Plan*, the Planning Commission's then deputy chairman Manmohan Singh gave a more comprehensive expression to this goal: "The planning process . . . provides a framework of time and space that *binds sectors, regions and States together* and relates each year's effort to the succeeding years. By *strengthening the social and economic fabric of the country as a whole and of the different regions and States*, it makes a powerful contribution to the goal of *national integration*. The planning process has contributed a great deal to evolving a broad national consensus regarding the basic objectives, strategies and design of our developmental policies."[30]

The Public Sector. A vast, far-flung public sector, the creation of which was the direct consequence of the pursuit of socialism, was itself an integrative factor in India's national economy. Nehru envisaged an expanding public sector as India's particular route to achieving his vision of socialism. To begin with, through the public sector owning the principal means of production, Nehru aimed to have the state assume control of the "commanding heights" of the entire economy. Moreover, his economic planning was directed at expanding the public sector rapidly, not simply in absolute terms but especially relative to the private sector, so as to reduce the private sector to a mere appendage of the national economy. Although Nehru nationalized the airlines, the life insurance companies, and the largest bank in India, generally, he thought that the private sector with its obsolescent and obsolescing technology was not worth wasting resources on its nationalization; to his mind, simply restricting its growth while rapidly expanding the public sector would be adequate for the transition to socialism.[31]

The center under Nehru reserved a vast area of the economy for development by the public sector. Consistent with the Congress Party's turn to socialism from mid-1954 onward—its specifically Indian character expressed in the term "the socialistic pattern of society"—the center devised the Industrial Policy Resolution of 1956 to demarcate the fields open to the public and private sectors. The resolution classified industries into three categories, with the first including seventeen industries that were of basic and strategic importance, the future development of which was made "the exclusive responsibility" of the state. Four of these industries (railways, air transport, arms and ammunition, and atomic energy) were required to be monopolies of the center. Among the other items in this category were: iron and steel, heavy plant and machinery, heavy electrical equipment, mining of coal and other ores, mineral oils, manufacture of aircraft and ships, telephones, and electric power. The second category's twelve industries were intended to be "progressively State-owned," with the state normally taking the initiative in starting new establishments; among others, these included: aluminum, machine tools, basic and intermediate chemicals, antibiotics and essential drugs, fertilizers, synthetic rubber, and road and sea transport.[32] Clearly, except when the state decided otherwise, the private sector was excluded from the areas that were significant for contemporary industrialization.

The private sector could enter industries that lay outside these two categories, but even in this third category, the state reserved the right "to start any industry." Further expressive of the government's attitude toward the corporate sector was the resolution's declaration about the high importance it attached to the growth of cottage, village, and small-scale industries, and its intent to assist them "by restricting the volume of production in the large scale sector by differential taxation, or by direct subsidies." Significantly, the *Second Five Year Plan*'s economic strategy envisaged heavy industries to be the responsibility of the state, while relying largely on small-scale industries for consumer goods in order to save resources for investment and to prevent concentration of wealth.[33] Thus squeezed between the heavy industries of the public sector and the cottage industries, the corporate private sector, while not altogether excluded, was not left with a substantial role in economic development. The state reserved for itself the role of being the driver of India's industrialization. Subsequently, Mrs. Indira Gandhi further tightened the screws on the private sector with a more restrictive regime and by supplementing the state's entrepreneurial role through large-scale nationalization of private industry, starting with bank nationalization in 1969.[34]

The significance of the public sector under the ownership and control of the center for economic integration lay, in the first place, in its very size. The cumulative result of the entrepreneurial role of the state initiated by Nehru and carried forward by his successors, and of the aggressive nationalization undertaken by Mrs. Indira Gandhi, was to make the public sector hegemonic in the Indian economy, dwarfing the organized private sector. The public sector at the center consisted of two parts—*departmental enterprises* that were owned and managed by departments of the government (railways being the prime example), and *non-departmental enterprises,* normally referred to as public sector enterprises (PSEs). The PSEs were state owned, but were supposed to follow the model of private sector companies and function as autonomous business enterprises (at least in form, though not in practice). The center's PSEs, to which the present discussion is limited, soon came to constitute an economic leviathan during the socialist era.

If we consider the one hundred largest companies by sales income in the mid-1980s (about a half decade before the paradigm shift in economic policy), the hegemonic status of the public sector is made immediately evident in the fact that half of these firms were with it.[35] That fact does not, however, provide an adequate measure of the public sector's economic power. First, the list only accounts for PSEs and does not include the vast network of railways, airlines, posts and telegraphs, general and life insurance companies, the nuclear and space organizations, and radio and television (all of which were state monopolies at the time), besides most of the banking and military ordnance factories. Second, even if only the fifty PSEs are taken into consideration, their economic clout is colossal; together, they accounted for 93 percent, 80 percent, and 77 percent of the total paid-up capital, net assets, and sales income of the total, respectively. Still more impressive is the sheer size of the individual PSEs. One PSE alone, Steel Authority of India Limited (SAIL), had three times the paid-up capital of all the fifty private sector firms put together. The hegemonic position of the public sector is again driven home by the fact that twenty of the top twenty-five companies in India in 1986–87 were PSEs, as were the first nine.[36]

The massive size of the center's public sector led to the consequence that there were strong linkages within the sector itself. In 1989–90, on the eve of economic liberalization, there were 233 central PSEs, spread all over India.[37] These enterprises were strongly interrelated among themselves, as a result of which the public sector existed almost as if it were a parallel national economy, bypassing the organized private sector. The public sector was integrated within itself and, because it was hegemonic in the economy, it was a substantial factor in India's economic integration.

Industrial Licensing and Controls. The third key institution under planning with integrative implications related to the system of industrial licensing and controls, which received considerable notoriety as "license, quota, permit

Raj." Wartime controls and rationing under colonial rule provided the foundation for India's complex machinery of physical controls. Economic planning with its socialist aims in the context of an economy of generalized scarcity, which it partially generated, provided the new rationale for the postindependence intensification and elaboration of the system. The scarcity pertained not just to food but also to capital goods and foreign exchange, while socialist aims encompassed, among other things, serving the public good, prevention of monopolies and concentration of wealth, and location of industries in backward areas. Economic planning raised the complexity and pervasiveness of physical controls to new heights, dispensing with the price mechanism in all but name. Such controls came to govern not just the world of private business but economic and social life in general.

The Industries (Development and Regulation) Act, 1951 (IDRA) had set the ball rolling on controls over production and investment in the private sector. Although IDRA formally concerned industrial enterprises that employed at least fifty workers using power or at least one hundred workers not using power, it actually came to apply to all industrial enterprises.[38] In order to develop and regulate industrial production and investment, IDRA required that all existing industrial enterprises register with the *central government*. Further, no new industrial enterprise could be established and no existing industrial capacity expanded without obtaining a license beforehand from the same government.[39] Meanwhile, with the *Second Five Year Plan*, planning became very detailed, going down to the product level, specifying what was to be produced, how much of it, and in what sector.

Under government regulations, industrial enterprises were required to submit an application to an interministerial licensing committee to obtain a license for new or additional capacity. But that was not the end of the matter in terms of government's physical controls. If import of capital goods was necessary to create or add capacity, the enterprise had to apply for a license to the capital goods licensing committee. If the project entailed a foreign collaboration, it had to get additional approval from the foreign agreements committee.[40]

In addition to the regulatory controls on industry, the Essential Commodities Act of 1955, building on wartime and subsequent measures, empowered the government to dominate economic life through distribution and price controls. These controls allowed the government to control the market for most products. Even small-scale industry, while exempt from some of the licensing requirements, could not entirely escape the web of controls. Precisely because it was a sector favored by the government, small enterprise needed to approach the government in order to benefit from the various supportive programs.

The system of industrial licensing and controls had significant implications for economic integration. The striking feature of the system of licensing and controls was its centralized nature, with New Delhi as the nerve center. The system undoubtedly reinforced the traditional "mai-baap" (mother-father) orientation of the public toward government as savior, with all public expectations directed toward the government. As for the private sector, all roads led to New Delhi. The major industrial houses set up their own "embassies" in New Delhi to prod the labyrinthine bureaucracy to push their files along to a successful conclusion. At the same time, the high and mighty of India's business class from all over the country often waited as supplicants outside the doors of ministers and bureaucrats in the corridors of power (in what was often referred to as the *neta-babu* [minister-bureaucrat] nexus), since they had the legal authority to decisively make or mar business fortunes. Unsurprisingly, enormous rent seeking followed as a matter of course in a system where a mere signature on a piece of paper provided industrialists the license to mint untold profits in a highly protected autarkic economy.

SUMMARY AND CONCLUSION

At independence, India inherited from the colonial rulers a rather segmented economy by sheer virtue of its underdeveloped and overwhelmingly rural condition, regardless of the fact that colonial rule at the same time had been the historic instrument for the violent introduction of modernity and capitalism into the country. The new leadership took its first task to be the establishment of a new constitutional order, which it met by setting up a fairly centralized polity, even as it provided the constituent states with a considerable measure of autonomy. Its schema for the economic integration of the country, however, suffered from several weaknesses, particularly with regard to limitations on interstate commerce and also taxation, where it made for a multiplicity of taxation systems, thus constraining the development of a common market. These weaknesses were soon rendered less significant in 1956, when India turned to replace the colonially inherited capitalism with socialism. Several aspects of the socialist regime—such as economic planning; autarky; a vast, far-flung, and rapidly expanding public sector; and industrial licensing and controls—were instrumental in providing India with a strong measure of economic integration, albeit all under the direct auspices of the state.

During the long stretch of the socialist (or dirigiste) regime from 1956 to 1991, India made considerable advances in industry, particularly in creating a diversified industrial base. Although India did not match the industrial performance of the Asian tigers, it was industrially precocious in that—despite its low levels of per capita income and of the share of industry in gross domestic product (GDP)—it had the capacity to produce capital goods and manage sophisticated technology. Some suggest that this industrial advance had already assured India's economic integration. There is certainly some merit in the argument, considering the size and India-wide spread of industry in the public sector. Still, about half of India's population remains dependent on agriculture for livelihood, while about a quarter of it is illiterate. Moreover, given the immense social diversity of the country, integration must remain a foremost concern for the national leadership. As Ernst Renan once proclaimed, nationalism—that is, national integration—is a daily referendum.

In any case, around 1975, in the midst of an economic-political crisis, the socialist regime came under question because of the very slow pace of economic growth. A gradual policy change then began to loosen some of the rigidities of the socialist system, which was incrementally widened until it escalated into the paradigm shift to economic liberalization in 1991. The consequent end to autarky and the erosion of economic planning, along with a halt to the relentless expansion of the public sector and the dismantlement of much of the system of controls, raised anew the issue of challenges to economic integration. Radical critics posited that malign consequences for economic integration would inevitably follow the exposure to the forces of globalization. To what extent have such consequences by way of economic segmentation transpired?

NOTES

1. Karl Marx and Frederick Engels, *Manifesto of the Communist Party* (Moscow: Progress, 1975), 44–48; emphasis added.
2. Amiya Kumar Bagchi, *Private Investment in India, 1900–1939* (Cambridge: Cambridge University Press, 1972), 442.
3. Ibid., 88; Dharma Kumar, ed., *The Cambridge Economic History of India*, vol. 2 (Cambridge: Cambridge University Press, 1983), 642.
4. On the center–periphery relationship, see Samir Amin, *Accumulation on a World Scale: A Critique of the Theory of Underdevelopment* (New York: Monthly Review Press, 1974); and Andre Gunder Frank, *Dependent Accumulation and Underdevelopment* (New York: Monthly Review Press, 1979).
5. Dietmar Rothermund, *An Economic History of India: From Pre-Colonial Times to 1991* (London: Routledge, 1993), 64–65; emphasis added.
6. Claude Markovits, *Merchants, Traders, Entrepreneurs: Indian Business in the Colonial Era* (Houndmills, Basingstoke, Hampshire, UK: Palgrave Macmillan, 2008), chap. 8.
7. Mohit Bhattacharya, "The Mind of the Founding Fathers," in *Federalism in India: Origins and Development*, ed. Nirmal Mukarji and Balveer Arora (New Delhi: Vikas, 1992), 87–104.
8. Uday S. Mehta, "Constitutionalism," in *The Oxford Companion to Politics in India*, ed. Niraja Gopal Jayal and Pratap Bhanu Mehta (New Delhi: Oxford University Press, 2012), 14–27.
9. For diverse perspectives on India's constitution, see Verinder Grover, ed., *Political System in India: Volume 4, Federal System, State Autonomy and Center–State Relations* (New Delhi: Deep and Deep, 1989).
10. See R. B. Jain, "Federalism in India: Emerging Pattern and Public Policy," in Grover, *Political System in India*, 440–55; and Pradeep Kumar, *Studies in Indian Federalism* (New Delhi: Deep and Deep, 1988), 14–16.
11. See the classic work by Granville Austin, *The Indian Constitution: Cornerstone of a Nation* (Oxford: Clarendon Press, 1966), 186–87; see also R. S. Gae, "Administrative Relations between the Union and the States," in Grover, *Political System in India*, 384–423.
12. See Austin, *Indian Constitution*, 234.

13. See the discussion in Bhawani Singh, "Federalism and State Autonomy in India: The Paradigm and the Paradox," in Grover, *Political System in India*, 97–107; and Kumar, *Studies in Indian Federalism*, 20–22, 48.

14. H. M. Seervai, *Constitutional Law of India: A Critical Commentary*, 3rd ed. (Bombay: N. M. Tripathi, 1984), vol. 1, A-8.

15. Durga Das Basu, *Introduction to the Constitution of India*, 13th ed. (New Delhi: Prentice-Hall of India, 1991), 315.

16. Seervai, *Constitutional Law of India*, vol. 2, 2155–56.

17. Arvind Panagariya, *India: The Emerging Giant* (New York: Oxford University Press, 2008), 313–14.

18. See Seervai, *Constitutional Law of India*, vol. 2, 2153.

19. Austin, *Indian Constitution*, 217; emphasis added.

20. Ibid., 187.

21. Ibid., 219; and M. V. Pylee, *Constitutional Government in India* (Bombay: Asia Publishing, 1965), chap. 40.

22. Austin, *Indian Constitution*, 219.

23. Ibid., 230.

24. The debates surrounding the strategy of the *Second Five Year Plan* are analyzed in Baldev Raj Nayar, *The Modernization Imperative and Indian Planning* (New Delhi: Vikas, 1972), chap. 2, and *Globalization and Nationalism: The Changing Balance in India's Economic Policy, 1950–2000* (New Delhi: Sage, 2001), chap. 2.

25. Nayar, *Globalization and Nationalism*, 64–65.

26. Ibid., 63–73. A fuller documentation on this point is provided in Nayar, *Modernization Imperative*, chap. 3.

27. Panagariya, *India*; Sukhamoy Chakravarty, *Development Planning: The Indian Experience* (Oxford: Clarendon Press, 1987); Nayar, *Globalization and Nationalism*; Jagdish N. Bhagwati and Padma Desai, *India: Planning for Industrialization* (London: Oxford University Press, 1970); Pulapre Balakrishnan, *Economic Growth in India: History and Prospect* (New Delhi: Oxford University Press, 2010).

28. K. S. Krishnaswamy, I. S. Gulati, and A. Vaidyanathan, "Economic Aspects of Federalism in India," in Mukarji and Arora, *Federalism in India*, 186.

29. These plan grants were different from the statutory grants-in-aid to the states that came under the auspices of the Finance Commission and also from the discretionary grants-in-aid that were made by the central ministries.

30. Government of India (GoI), *Seventh Five Year Plan (1985–1990)* (New Delhi: Planning Commission, 1985), preface; emphasis added. This and other plans are available at http://planningcommission.nic.in.

31. On the theme, see Baldev Raj Nayar, *India's Mixed Economy: The Role of Ideology and Interest in Its Development* (Bombay: Popular Prakashan, 1989), 202–6.

32. GoI, *Second Five Year Plan* (New Delhi: Planning Commission, 1956), 43–50.

33. Ibid.

34. Some scholars tend to set Nehru and his daughter Indira Gandhi, both heroic figures, against each other, with the former pictured as a moderate, responsible statesman and the latter as a more radical risk taker (see, for example, Panagariya, *India*, chaps. 2 and 3). But the reality is more complex, and it can be argued that Nehru with his socialist

project set in motion economic and political forces—as manifest in the Bhuvaneshwar resolution of January 1964 (ostensibly, his last political testament) and subsequent political events—that tilted the scales in favor of radicalism. Considered thus, despite Mrs. Gandhi's capriciousness and authoritarianism, her policies constituted an evolution of the path set by Nehru, not a contradiction of it. See Nayar, *India's Mixed Economy*, 250–51.

35. Indian Institute of Public Opinion, *Quarterly of Public Opinion*, nos. 124–25 (July–December 1988): 5.

36. Baldev Raj Nayar, *The Myth of the Shrinking State: Globalization and the State in India* (New Delhi: Oxford University Press, 2009), 33–37.

37. GoI, *Public Enterprises Survey, 1989–90* (New Delhi: Bureau of Public Enterprises, 1991), 18.

38. Panagariya, *India*, 34.

39. Ibid., 34–35; Bhagwati and Desai, *India*, 250.

40. Bhagwati and Desai, *India*, 252.

II

THE STATE AFTER ECONOMIC LIBERALIZATION

Chapter 4

CONTINUITY AND CHANGE IN ECONOMIC PLANNING

THE paradigm shift in policy to economic liberalization was a momentous event, celebrated by some and regretted by others. Its consequences reverberated in many areas of the economy and polity, and threw up policy challenges for the leadership. Part II of this study, consisting of three chapters, examines liberalization's impact on economic integration in three areas: economic planning (this chapter), fiscal federalism (chapter 5), and reform of the indirect tax system (chapter 6). This chapter comprises two major sections. The first one deals with the postliberalization relationship between planning and integration, and analyzes the continuities with the previous dispensation and the changes in it. The second section discusses the contemporary challenges to economic planning and their bearing on economic integration. The summary conclusion is that economic planning continues to perform a significant integrative function, though not in the same measure as before, and that it has continuing utility.

PLANNING AND INTEGRATION AFTER ECONOMIC LIBERALIZATION

Economic liberalization marked a serious rupture with the earlier regime of economic planning since the hallmark of that regime had been the subordination of the market to the state, whereas the intent of the economic reform was to liberate the market from the control of the state. In most eyes, economic planning was precisely the target of economic liberalization—that is, reform aimed to release the market from the grip of economic planning, from the hegemony of the public sector, and from the system of discretionary controls.

In actuality, however, despite the appearance of a sudden rupture, considerable ambivalence and ambiguity surrounded the official turn to liberalization, for the then prime minister P. V. Narasimha Rao favored both economic liberalization *and* economic planning. Rao undoubtedly wanted removal of unnecessary controls and regulations for the sake of national advance, but he also believed that "the growth and development of the country cannot be left entirely to the market mechanism" since the market basically responded to existing purchasing power and not need. Consequently, for him: "Planning is necessary to overcome such limitations of the market mechanism. Planning is essential for macro-economic management, for taking care of the poor and the downtrodden, who are mostly outside the market system and have little asset endowment." Rao therefore opted for both the market mechanism *and* planning, asking in effect that the two be dovetailed.[1] The break with the previous economic regime was therefore not as comprehensive and thoroughgoing as it appeared at the time or as its opponents painted it to be.

The state, with its particular leadership, was thus critical to the kind of economic liberalization that was acceptable. There are therefore elements of both continuity and discontinuity with the previous regime after economic liberalization. Those who had favored Nehru's socialist project thought that the 1991 reforms would mean the end of economic planning. In fact, however, the entire apparatus of planning that had existed before liberalization, though much reduced in importance, has continued to be an essential part of government operations. The two decades after liberalization have seen the launching and completion of four five-year plans (*Eighth*, *Ninth*, *Tenth*, and *Eleventh*), and the start of the *Twelfth Five Year Plan (2012–2017)*. The fact that economic planning persists as an essential feature of government functioning suggests that there is no inevitability to the consequences attributed to liberalization; instead, public policy is key.

India's economy had earlier been proclaimed to be a "mixed economy," and it still can be regarded as such, for little privatization has occurred after liberalization while a vast public sector continues to exist. At that level of generality, then, not much appears to have changed. Continuity with the past is therefore one aspect that is apparent with respect to the question of the impact of liberalization. At the same time, there can be no denying that economic liberalization did mark a sharp shift in the relations between state and market, and could not leave planning unaffected. The pertinent issue is, then, what has changed and how much has changed with respect to economic planning?

At its base, economic planning is a political and administrative mechanism of the nation-state to develop a consensus over the essential economic tasks for the center, the states, and the market for a finite period of time (say, five or fifteen years), and it is equally also a site where these three forces intersect and interact. Four changes in planning are striking with regard to the relationship between the center, the states, and the market.

1. From Comprehensive Planning to Indicative Planning

While not as thoroughgoing as it was in the Soviet Union, planning in India was comprehensive insofar as it covered the entire economy and its various sectors.[2] It was detailed with meticulous multisector models employed to work out input-output balances with some degree of internal consistency for a largely closed economy. It was also prescriptive, particularly for the public sector, with the plans serving as an allocation mechanism. In great measure, it was prescriptive for the private sector, too, with the state using policy instruments like licensing and controls to implement plans. Occupying "the commanding heights" of the economy, the state was able to exert control over the entire economy through its vast and far-flung public sector, its regulatory framework for the private sector, and its hold over private sector savings in the nationalized banking and insurance industries.

With the dismantling of a substantial part of the licensing and controls system and the opening up of vast areas of the economy to the private sector after economic liberalization, economic planning could no longer be comprehensive. Also, with the economy opening up internationally, input-output balances were no longer of much relevance since foreign trade could serve as a balancing mechanism. Detailed planning could continue, though, for the nontradable sector, primarily in the area of infrastructure, which was largely the responsibility of the public sector.[3] However, with the increased empowerment of the private sector, planning could no longer be prescriptive for much of that sector. In this fashion, comprehensive planning was transformed into *indicative* planning, particularly in relation to the private sector.

However, economic planning as a focused activity of the state has continued into the postliberalization period and, contrary to popular perception, it is not limited to the public sector. As it did earlier, planning encompasses the entire economy within its scope, determining the overall strategy, the desired or acceptable rate of growth, and the thrust areas and priorities. The Planning Commission (PC) establishes and approves *allocations* for the public sector, while it expects *policy* to provide the enabling environment or incentives to accomplish what is desired in the private sector. But that is precisely what it did before liberalization.[4] The decisive difference with the period prior to economic liberalization is that the state no longer wields discretionary controls in most areas of concern to the private sector. Rather, the state is now conceptualized, ideally at least, as a *facilitator*, while the market is the arena where the private sector competes and carries the national economy forward. In practice, however, besides its influence through the regulatory agencies headed by current or former bureaucrats, the state continues to exercise considerable discretionary controls over the private sector in important areas, such as telecommunications licenses, space allocations in special export zones, land acquisition for entrepreneurs, mining licenses, and especially environmental clearances. It is not surprising that in all these areas, there is an abundance of rent-seeking behavior, leading in recent years to widespread corruption and multiple and massive scams amid charges of crony capitalism.

The change from comprehensive planning to indicative planning was heralded by the *Eighth Five Year Plan (1992–1997)*, which saw itself as marking and facilitating the transition from the former to the latter. Declaring that it had redefined the PC's role, the plan announced that "*from a highly centralized planning system, we are gradually moving towards indicative planning.*"[5] This shift, though, did not mean an end to the use of formal economic modeling for planning, which the PC has continued to employ. While economic planning no longer establishes sector-wise targets as in the past, modeling is seen as useful since it provides, according to former PC member Kirit Parikh, "a broad picture of the economy, its likely direction and pace, a consistent macro-picture, the plans for the development of infrastructure and the provision of public goods and services. All these help private entrepreneurs in their decisions." More broadly, economic planning is seen as having a continuing importance: "Even in a market economy governments continue to spend substantial amounts, and inclusive development requires government programs and projects to deliver public goods and services to all peoples and regions."[6]

In sum, then, the PC continues to perform its role of articulating an economic vision for the country, developing the overall economic strategy for a period of five years at a time, charting out the thrust areas over that period, laying out the roles of the public and private sectors, and specifying the policy instruments to accomplish the goals of a given five-year plan. To the extent that there is thus a substantial continuity in economic planning into the postliberalization period, it follows that the integrative implications of such planning also continue to hold in substantial measure after liberalization. The future role of planning, however, undoubtedly remains a strongly contested terrain.

2. From Planning for State Hegemony to Adapting to Private Sector Expansion

India had a mixed economy before economic liberalization and it continues to have one afterward, but the balance between the public sector and the private sector in the mixed economy has decisively changed. With economic liberalization, the public sector has seen a relative decline in the pace of its expansion and therefore in its presence in economic planning, which was precisely the intent of the shift. But the halt to the relentless expansion of the public sector was profoundly consequential for the PC since the latter had derived its drive and energy earlier from planning for the public sector.

The decline of the public sector as an arena of investment is reflected in the comparative data on public investment as a share of gross domestic product (GDP) (see table 4.1). Two things are noteworthy. First, *total investment* as a percentage of GDP has seen a major expansion in the postliberalization period, marking a significant structural change in the economy. Total investment was 24.4 percent during the *Eighth Five Year Plan (1992–1997)*, but it rose dramatically to 32.1 percent during the *Tenth Five Year Plan (2002–2007)* and was projected to go up to 36.7 percent during the *Eleventh Five Year Plan (2007–2012)*. What is especially significant is that this steep rise took place on a much-

Table 4.1. Share of Public Sector in Total Investment (%)

	Planned %	*Realized* %	*Total Investment as % of GDP*	*Public Investment as % of Total Investment*
Fifth Five Year Plan (1974–79)	57.6	43.3	—	—
Sixth Five Year Plan (1980–85)	52.9	47.8	—	—
Seventh Five Year Plan (1985–90)	47.8	45.7	—	—
Eighth Five Year Plan (1992–97)	45.2	34.3	24.4	34.7
Ninth Five Year Plan (1997–2002)	—	—	24.3	29.0
Tenth Five Year Plan (2002–7)	—	—	32.1	22.0
Eleventh Five Year Plan (2007–12)	—	—	36.7	21.9

Sources: GoI, *Ninth Five Year Plan (1997–2002)* (New Delhi: Planning Commission, 1997), table 2.2; GoI, *Eleventh Five Year Plan (2007–2012): Inclusive Growth* (New Delhi: Oxford University Press, 2008) I, 28. Figures for the *Eleventh Five Year Plan* are projections.

expanded GDP base because of the postliberalization acceleration in economic growth, particularly during the first decade of the twenty-first century.

Second, another "important structural change" has been the shift in the share of *public investment* in total investment.[7] During the *Fifth*, *Sixth*, and *Seventh Five Year Plans*—all of which were prior to liberalization—actual public investment was around 45 percent. Since then, such investment has seen a precipitous fall; it now stands at around 22 percent. Thus, most of the investment, amounting to nearly 80 percent, now comes from the private sector, indicating a remarkable change from the preliberalization period.

Despite the reduction in the extent of public investment *relative* to private investment, there has been no significant diminution in the role of the *existing* public sector as such in India's economy. That role continues to be immense; indeed, it is overwhelming and, paradoxically, it has been expanding in *absolute* terms in the postliberalization period. First, there has been little privatization of the public sector after liberalization. Only a handful of public sector firms were sold off to the private sector, chiefly the Indian Petrochemicals Corporation, Bharat Aluminium, and Maruti Udyog. Thus, there has been no hollowing out of the public sector as had been feared by the critics of liberalization. Some disinvestment has taken place through listing public sector firms on the stock exchanges and selling part of their equity to the public, in large part because of the government's need to cover budget deficits; the government, however, has steadfastly retained management control.

Second, the public sector has counterintuitively seen a huge expansion after liberalization. Taking into account only the national level, the departmental enterprises—such as railways, banking and insurance, and nuclear energy—have been consistently expanding, but so have the nondepartmental enterprises, comprising about 250 public sector enterprises (PSEs) or firms. The expansion of the PSE component since liberalization is evident in table 4.2. In the eighteen

Table 4.2. Central Public Sector Enterprises after Liberalization (Rs. Billion)

Year	*Number of PSEs*		*Capital*				
	Making Profits	*Losses*	*Employed*	*Turnover*	*Profits*	*Losses*	*WPI*
1992–1993	131	106	1,401.10	1,472.66	73.84	41.13	92.3
1993–1994	121	116	1,598.36	1,580.49	97.68	52.23	100.0
1994–1995	130	109	1,624.51	1,873.55	120.70	48.83	112.6
1995–1996	132	102	1,739.48	2,269.19	147.63	51.88	121.6
1996–1997	129	104	2,311.78	2,607.35	161.25	59.39	127.2
1997–1998	134	100	2,498.55	2,760.02	202.79	66.97	132.8
1998–1999	126	107	2,650.93	3,101.79	225.08	93.05	140.7
1999–2000	126	105	3,029.47	3,891.99	246.33	103.02	145.3
2000–2001	123	110	3,313.72	4,582.37	284.94	128.41	155.7
2001–2002	120	109	3,899.34	4,787.31	364.32	104.54	161.3
2002–2003	119	105	4,171.60	5,728.33	433.16	109.72	166.8
2003–2004	139	89	4,523.36	6,307.04	616.06	85.22	175.9
2004–2005	143	73	5,044.07	7,443.07	744.32	90.03	187.2
2005–2006	160	63	5,854.84	8,372.95	763.82	68.45	195.4
2006–2007	154	61	6,613.38	9,648.90	895.81	85.26	208.2
2007–2008	160	54	7,240.09	10,963.08	915.77	103.03	218.1
2008–2009	158	55	7,922.32	12,715.29	984.88	146.21	235.7
2009–2010	158	59	9,088.42	12,350.60	1,084.35	158.42	244.1

Sources: GoI, *Public Enterprises Survey 2001–2002* (New Delhi: Department of Public Enterprises, 2002), vol. 1, 25; GoI, *Public Enterprises Survey 2009–2010* (New Delhi: Department of Public Enterprises, 2011), vol. 1, 3. Figures for WPI are from GoI, *Economic Survey 2006–2007* (New Delhi: Ministry of Finance, 2007), S-60; and *Economic Survey 2010–2011* (New Delhi: Ministry of Finance, 2011), A-62.

Notes: WPI = Wholesale Price Index

1. The total number of public sector enterprises (PSEs) for any one year is the sum of profit-making and loss-making PSEs plus an additional one or two that made neither profit nor loss.

2. WPI figures are on the basis of 1993–94 series up to 2004–5, while the subsequent figures are based on the 2004–5 series but have been recalculated to obtain a continuous set of figures.

years after liberalization, the PSEs saw their turnover multiply 8.39 times and their profits multiply about 15 times, even as the wholesale price index (WPI) increased only 2.64 times. Economic liberalization seemingly had a reinvigorating impact on the public sector—known earlier for its inefficiency and unprofitability—because it provided the sector with a far more expanded and expanding market and also with the stimulus of greater competition.[8]

The impact of liberalization becomes particularly visible with the sharper acceleration of economic growth after 2001–2. Turnover and profits climbed higher by 258 percent and 298 percent, respectively, in the subsequent eight years up to 2009–10; WPI was, meanwhile, higher by 151 percent. Note also that the number of profit-making PSEs jumped dramatically from about 120 in 2002–3 to about 160 in 2009–10, while that of loss-making PSEs fell correspondingly from 105 to 59.[9]

The continued importance of the public sector in India's economy also can be seen in its monopoly of railway transportation and nuclear energy and its oligopolistic dominance of banking and insurance and some other areas of the economy. The PSEs have a predominant share in domestic output of some important sectors, such as coal (about 80 percent), thermal power (38 percent), telephone landlines (85 percent), and refineries throughput (70 percent).[10] Indicative of the persistent heft of the public sector is the fact that five of the top six listed companies in India are state owned.[11]

In summary, it is patent that there has been a substantial decline in the share of public investment in India's total investment since economic liberalization. That said, however, the continued massive presence of the public sector as an inheritance from the past and, especially, its reinvigoration and expansion after liberalization suggest that India remains a mixed economy in which the state is not only a major economic actor but a dominant one. As such, the public sector continues to perform the same functions for India's economic integration subsequent to liberalization as it did before, primarily knitting India together economically. True, there has been a decline quantitatively in its relative share of the economy, but qualitatively it has improved its efficiency and profitability, in considerable part in response to the challenge of economic liberalization. Given the massive presence of the public sector in the national economy and its ongoing expansion, detailed and prescriptive economic planning in relation to it would seem to be of continued relevance.

3. From Planning for a Producer State to Planning for a Quasi-Welfare State

Prior to 1991, economic planning was largely geared toward building a self-reliant (read autarkic) socialist economy. As part of that aim, the planners had focused on promoting the role of the state as an entrepreneur and producer. Economic liberalization certainly interrupted the ever-expanding role of the state as producer by removing most constraints on private producers to install and expand capacity. Since the state now relied on the private sector for economic growth, there was thus a decline in the role of the public sector as a producer, though only relatively and not absolutely. Supporters of the socialist regime had feared the shrinking of the state's role as producer—and thus as economic planner—and had therefore opposed liberalization.

Despite the relative diminution of the role of the state as *producer*, in actual fact, there has been no shrinking of the *overall* economic role of the state. Indeed, the postliberalization period has seen an expansion of that role. That fact is manifest in the data on total government (center and states) expenditure (see table 4.3). At first sight, total expenditure as a share of GDP seems relatively stable at around a quarter of GDP (column 6). However, this apparent stability is deceptive;

Table 4.3. Total Government Expenditure (Center and States)

Year	Rs. Billion	% Increase over Previous Year	Inflation: WPI	Inflation: % Increase	Share of GDP
1990–91	1,526	—	—	—	26.8
1995–96	2,875	—	121.6	—	24.2
1996–97	3,199	11.3	127.2	4.6	23.4
1997–98	3,678	14.9	132.8	4.4	24.2
1998–99	4,428	20.4	140.7	5.9	25.4
1999–2000	5,139	16.1	145.3	3.3	26.5
2000–2001	5,448	6.0	155.7	7.2	25.9
2001–2	6,048	11.0	161.3	3.6	26.6
2002–3	6,564	8.5	166.8	3.4	26.7
2003–4	7,458	13.6	175.9	5.5	27.1
2004–5	8,211	10.1	187.2	6.4	25.3
2005–6	9,292	13.2	195.4	4.4	25.2
2006–7	10,842	16.7	208.2	6.6	25.3
2007–8	12,392	14.3	218.1	4.8	24.9
2008–9	15,071	21.6	235.7	8.1	27.0
2009–10 (RE)	18,309	21.5	244.1	3.6	28.0
Average		14.2		5.1	

Sources: GoI, *Indian Public Finance Statistics 2004–05* (New Delhi: Ministry of Finance, 2005), 16, and *Indian Public Finance Statistics 2010–11* (New Delhi: Ministry of Finance, 2011), 16. GoI, *Economic Survey 2001–2002* (New Delhi: Ministry of Finance, 2002), table 5.1, and *Economic Survey 2010–11* (New Delhi: Ministry of Finance, 2011), A62. WPI figures from 1995–96 to 2004–5 are based on the 1993–94 series, while the WPI figures for the subsequent years have been recalculated to get a continuous set of figures.

Note: WPI = Wholesale Price Index, RE = Revised Estimates

it masks the consistently higher rise in expenditures in absolute terms since these have been expanding on average at a rate much greater (14.2 percent) than that of inflation (5.1 percent). The explanation for the paradox of stability in expenditure as a share of GDP and yet a rapid rise in absolute terms lies in the growth acceleration in the postliberalization period, particularly during much of the first decade of the twenty-first century. Rapid growth allowed the absolute expansion of government expenditures even as their proportion in the GDP remained stable.

There has thus been no shrinking or erosion of the state in the economy and society. But it is equally manifest that at the same time there has been a decline in the relative role of the state as a producer of private goods. This indicates that there has been a shift in the concerns of the state. Most notably, there is an apparent tilt away from the producer state to a quasi-welfare state, where the resources at the command of the state have been increasingly directed toward the social sectors, particularly for programs that provide some minimum recompense for economic deprivation. This trend is made abundantly obvious in table 4.4, where the expenditures on social services have gone up from 16 percent in the *Seventh*

Table 4.4. Pattern of Plan Outlays in the Public Sector (% Distribution): Select Items

	Seventh (1985–90)	*Eighth (1992–97)*	*Ninth (1997–2002)*	*Tenth (2002–7)*	*Eleventh (2007–12)*
1. Agriculture	5.8	5.2	4.9	3.9	3.7
2. Rural Development	7.0	7.9	8.7	8.0	8.3
3. Special Areas	1.6	1.6	0.4	1.4	0.7
5. Energy	28.2	26.6	25.9	26.5	23.4
6. Industry and Minerals	13.4	10.8	7.6	3.9	4.2
7. Transport	13.5	12.9	13.9	14.8	15.7
10. Social Services	16.0	18.2	21.3	22.8	30.2
a. Education	3.5	4.5			
b. Health	1.7	1.7			
c. Family Welfare	1.4	1.5			
d. Housing	1.2	1.2			
e. Urban Develop.	1.0	1.2			
f. Other	7.1	8.0			

Sources: GoI, *Economic Survey 2010–11* (New Delhi: Ministry of Finance, 2011), A42–A46, and *Economic Survey 2012–13* (New Delhi: Ministry of Finance, 2013), A45; GoI, *Indian Public Finance Statistics 2010–11* (New Delhi: Ministry of Finance, 2011), 55.

Notes:

1. The figures for the *Eleventh Five Year Plan* are *projections*; the figures for the other plans are *actuals*. Significantly, however, Social Services formed 32.2 percent, 33.3 percent, 30.1 percent, and 32.9 percent of *actual* expenditures of the first four annual plans of the *Eleventh Five Year Plan*, respectively.

2. Breakdown for "Social Services" for *Ninth*, *Tenth*, and *Eleventh Five Year Plans* not yet available.

3. Sectors not deemed relevant and therefore not included in the table are: (4) Irrigation and Flood Control; (8) Communications, and Information and Broadcasting; and (9) Science and Technology.

Five Year Plan (prior to liberalization) to 30.2 percent in the *Eleventh Five Year Plan (2007–2012)*. Indeed, social services attracted by far the highest allocation in the *Eleventh Five Year Plan*. To get a truer reflection of the provision for social services, one would perhaps need to augment it with the allocations for rural development and for special areas programs.

The shift to welfare in state expenditures is not a result of happenstance but of consciously thought out state policy, and it has become more pronounced with time. The conceptual change on the role of the state was best expressed by the PC in its Approach Paper for the *Eleventh Five Year Plan*, with its focus on socially inclusive growth. The paper rejected apprehensions about economic policy "moving in a direction that involves *a dismantling or erosion of the role of the state* in the development process." Instead, for growth acceleration and greater inclusiveness, it envisioned "*a very active, and in many respects, expanded role for the state* in some areas," but with that role restructured by directing it to sectors that could not be left to market forces.[12] Of course, as with most things regarding planning in India, the concern for inclusive growth—and thus for the welfare state—is not entirely new, but the postliberalization period does represent its intensification.

However, it was growth acceleration, a significant consequence of economic liberalization, that transformed the change in the balance into a more qualitative one with respect to the welfare state. India has seen significant growth acceleration since liberalization, particularly after 2002. Postindependence India had not earlier witnessed as long a period as the one stretching for seventeen years, from 1992 to 2010, with as high a growth rate as 6.92 percent on average, despite the several crises both India and the world economy had to endure. Particularly striking is the growth rate of 8.5 percent during the eight-year period from 2003 to 2010.[13]

The significance of the outlays for the welfare state is therefore not fully conveyed by the change in the relative ratios of outlays for social services and rural development in table 4.4. India's GDP expanded rapidly from less than half a trillion U.S. dollars (current) in 2001 to almost two trillion dollars a decade later in 2011. The growth acceleration on an expanded GDP base generated the revenues that allowed the state to spend more liberally on the social sectors and welfare programs. Given the expanded GDP base, the scale of effort for social services in reality therefore goes far beyond the changes in the relative ratios in outlays. There is, however, an important qualification that needs to be made to this assessment: expenditures do not necessarily add up to effective delivery, a department in which India has shown decided weakness, marked by enormous leakages.

The relative shift to the welfare state in planning is fundamental to India's economic and social integration. It is indicative of the intent of the political leadership to build an economically and socially cohesive nation-state. At a minimum, such an endeavor requires the alleviation, if not the removal, of the existing sharp social and economic disparities, particularly with respect to those living below the poverty line. Earlier, the meeting of this requirement may have been covered by the notion of "growth with social justice," but today, in its more intensified form, it is encompassed under the term "inclusive growth."

To enhance inclusiveness and reduce poverty, the economic planners have instituted a plethora of programs. Table 4.5 on thirteen "flagship programs" gives an idea of the activities undertaken for the purpose. Clearly, the M. G. National Rural Employment Guarantee Act (MGNREGA), the first on the list, is today the showpiece of programs for inclusive growth since it provides some measure of employment security to rural households "below the poverty line" (BPL) by assuring each such household one hundred days of employment at minimum wages as a matter of right.[14] In addition, the National Social Assistance Program provides a pension to BPL individuals aged sixty and over. Other significant programs include midday meals for children in schools and health insurance for workers in the unorganized sector. Additionally, in order to reduce interstate and intrastate disparities, there are special programs for development

Table 4.5. Flagship Programs for Inclusiveness (Rs. Billion)

Program	*Expenditure under Eleventh Five Year Plan*
1. M. G. National Rural Employment Guarantee Act (MGNREGA)	1,563.01
2. Indira Awas Yojana [Indira Housing Plan]	414.86
3. National Social Assistance Program	235.36
4. Pradhan Mantri Gram Sadak Yojana [P. M. Village Roads Plan]	650.02
5. National Rural Health Mission	692.14
6. Integrated Child Development Scheme	389.80
7 Mid Day Meal Scheme	386.02
8. Sarva Shiksha Abhiyan [Universal Education Campaign]	775.76
9. J. N. National Urban Renewal Mission	484.85
10. Accelerated Irrigation Benefit Program	466.22
11. R. G. Gramin Viduyatikaran Yojana (Rural Electrification Plan)	259.13
12. R. G. Drinking Water Mission and Total Sanitation Campaign	467.22
13. Rashtriya Krishi Vikas Yojana [National Farmers Uplift Plan]	185.50
Total	6,919.76

Source: GoI, *Faster, Sustainable and More Inclusive Growth*—Draft (New Delhi: Planning Commission, 2011), 6–7.

of backward regions, border areas, hill areas, and areas affected by left-wing extremism.

Under the pressure of social activist groups, some with considerable support from key political leaders, such as Congress president Sonia Gandhi, a major drive has been under way to provide the population, particularly the less privileged, with a stream of entitlements, such as the right to education and the right to food, even as the state has lacked adequate revenues to fund them. This drive is fueled, on the one hand, by genuine concern for the poor and malnourished and, on the other, by the motivation to mobilize electoral support. Others within the government, such as the Prime Minister's Economic Advisory Council (PMEAC), have advised caution and fiscal prudence against hasty extension of entitlements. Many critics fear a fiscal collapse from such profligacy. There are also serious questions about the actual capacity of the state to effectively and efficiently deliver public services that the various programs promise.

There are two major issues relating to the impact of economic planning after liberalization that have given rise to a virtual growth industry in scholarship. One pertains to the issue of poverty, and the other to the matter of interstate disparities. Briefly, regarding poverty, if the same criteria are used for measuring it, then it can be asserted with some certainty that poverty has seen a considerable decline after liberalization, even though neither the pace of poverty reduction nor the absolute level at which poverty is defined may be acceptable to most. In terms of the earlier poverty criteria, the percentage of the population below the poverty line came down from 36.0 percent in 1993–94 to 27.5 percent in 2004–5.

The poverty level was then officially reworked upward with the new Tendulkar methodology, and the percentages were revised to 45.3 and 37.2 percent, respectively. By 2011–12, however, the population below the poverty line had seen a dramatic decline to 21.9 percent.[15] The annual rate of decline was 2.18 percent for the seven years from 2004–5 to 2011–12, compared to 0.74 percent for the eleven years from 1993–94 to 2004–5, with analysts differing over whether the explanation for the dramatic change lay in the general growth acceleration or the specific antipoverty programs.

Interstate disparities had existed before economic planning. The economic planners did not attack the problem with any seriousness or consistency, as they had been more focused on growth. Not surprisingly, "over time, the poor states became poorer and the rich richer."[16] After liberalization, the disparities increased during the 1990s, as the states with better infrastructure pulled further ahead while the poor states continued to lag behind. However, the earlier laggard states also participated in the growth acceleration during the first decade of the twenty-first century, with some of them displaying a strong performance. Despite the surge in their growth, though, some hold that the advance was not sufficient enough to generate convergence among the states, and "divergence in the growth performance across states continues."[17] Others, however, demur and advance evidence to demonstrate that there has indeed been convergence over the period 2001–10.[18] Still others, arguing from the perspective of human development indicators, also see convergence at work.[19] This study subsequently shows that there is considerable evidence in favor of a broad pattern of diffusion of growth and convergence among the states, to which there are some exceptions.

There is a large consensus that social inequality has increased sharply with the greater concentration of wealth at the upper end of income distribution. Therefore, despite the reduction in poverty and the advance toward the welfare state through planning, there is serious concern among many that the rise in such inequality may threaten both India's higher growth rate of recent years (as had happened in Latin America at one time after a spurt of high growth) and its social and economic integration.[20]

4. From Centralization to Coordination in Planning

Economic liberalization resulted in significant and substantial change in economic planning with regard to the relationship between state and market. But it also resulted in change in planning in terms of the relationship between the center and the states. If a command-and-control relationship between the state and market had prevailed earlier, prior to liberalization, shades of a somewhat similar relationship can be said to have existed between the center and states in India's polity. This relationship was not entirely a function of the centralized nature of India's federal setup, but was in considerable part a consequence of the particular configuration of the party system at the time.

Economic planning in India began in the context of the "single party dominant system," in which the Congress Party was in power at the center and in almost all the states. Despite the powerful position of that party, the extent of the center's influence in the states need not be exaggerated. If the center was headed by a charismatic political hero from 1947 to 1964, the chief ministers of the states were also highly respected stalwarts of the nationalist movement. Significantly, the most intense debates on plan strategy in the history of India's economic planning took place in the mid-1950s during the *Second Five Year Plan*'s formulation, and the state chief ministers took an active part in that debate, quite a few times in opposition to the official line at the center.[21] Moreover, even then, the chief ministers would often agree with the center in New Delhi on policy matters and then do pretty much what they wanted to after getting back to their state capitals, particularly with regard to land reform and rural cooperatives.

After Nehru's death in 1964, the one-party-dominant system began to decay, and it suffered a major blow in the 1967 elections, as a result of which most of north India came under the rule of non-Congress governments. Thereafter, even when the Congress Party recovered its strength at the center during the 1971–77 and 1980–89 periods, it had to contend with a considerable number of states that were periodically under non-Congress parties, often confined to and appealing only to the populace of a given state or region. The trend toward fragmentation of the national party system and regionalization of politics cannot be attributed to economic liberalization since it had already become consolidated before economic liberalization entered the scene in 1991. Indeed, the phenomenon underlines a larger analytical point: the nature of the state and polity often stands on its own and cannot always be ascribed to liberalization or globalization.

Subsequent to liberalization, the political pattern at the center has been one of coalition governments, with regional parties playing an influential and sometimes critical role in them. Indeed, governments at the center are in some sense now simply shifting "coalitions of the regions," after the rise of regional parties reduced the political space open to national parties. Further, since the stability of coalition governments can often crucially depend on the support of regional parties, the latter can exercise a veto over national policy and bend the center to the interests of one or more states. However, the flow of political influence is not just one way from the states to the center since the core of coalition governments at the center has mostly been constituted by one or another national party. As such, the political system manifests considerable complexity compared to the simplicity of the one-party-dominant system, and it is in this more complex situation that economic planning has to take place.

The states, especially the better endowed among them, were the principal beneficiaries of the dismantlement of many of the controls following liberalization, as the authority to attract private industry and investment now vested in them. In this sense, liberalization can be said to have reinforced the greater devolution of power to the states that had ensued from the regionalization of politics.

However, liberalization's impact is double-edged, and not one-dimensional. Economic liberalization has two aspects—an internal one and an external one. The former revolves around the relaxation or removal of controls by the state over the market. The latter, involving the integration of the national economy with the international economy, carries benefits, but it also confronts the nation-state with new challenges by increasing the exposure to external shocks; individual regions of the nation-state do not remain immune from their destabilizing effects. External shocks necessitate national measures by the center, both remedial and preventive, to cope with them.

Such measures have implications for the states, particularly in the area of fiscal discipline, just as the conduct of fiscal affairs in the states has implications for the center's macroeconomic management. In the circumstance, there can be no escape under globalization from cooperation between the center and states in coping with such challenges. "Cooperative federalism" is therefore not a choice but a necessity for both center and states; the center needs the cooperation of the states in order to cope with challenges from the world economy, and the states need the support of the center to mitigate the malign aspects of such challenges. Paradoxically, then, globalization also carries "nationalizing" or centralizing aspects, not simply segmenting effects, as is made evident in chapter 5. The increased exposure to external shocks in globalization has implications, however, not only for managing economic emergencies but also for longer-term economic planning.

The Planning Commission is a key agency, among several at the center, which has responsibility for managing economic affairs between the center and the states. Although it formulates a five-year plan on the basis of economic parameters for the nation as a whole, it also scrutinizes similar plans of the states, discusses them with state representatives, determines in consultation with each state the size of its plan in light of the state's available and potential resources, tentatively agrees to the level of support it can provide to each state, and integrates the various states' plans within the overall national plan. Since the flow of funds to any state from the center for implementing its plan programs depends on the size of its plan, the state has an incentive to aim for a large plan, and it usually pleads with the commission to approve it. At the same time, the commission's role in the allocation of funds for states' plans provides it leverage with the states in integrating or accommodating their state plans into the overall national plan. That leverage is critical to national planning.

As an economic agency at the center, the PC interacts extensively with the states and is in continual contact with them on issues of development. Perhaps because it consists of technical experts, principally economists, it commands considerable credibility with the states despite being a part of the center. The states regard it as an agency that is somewhat more independent-minded, not a subordinate wing of the central government, insofar as states' development interests are concerned. As a former commission member noted: "The Planning

Commission is the only organization which the state governments saw as a somewhat neutral body, free of the political bias of the ruling party at the center. . . . It is perhaps the one institution which the state governments still trust to be fair."[22] Still, as a manager of public funds, the PC exercises its professional judgment on the feasibility of what can be conceded to the states. This is important since the primary aim of all subnational governments is to extract as much as possible from the center without being subject to discipline about program performance or matching requirements from their own resources.

For its part, the PC is a self-reflective organization and, as such, it has been responsive to shifts in the balance of power between the center and states and to changes in the economic regime. In the changed environment after liberalization and the regionalization of politics, it places greater emphasis on coordination, rather than on command, in which reliance on persuasion occupies center space. In a sense, it has had to do this because of the devolution of power to the states, the greater role accorded to the private sector, and also the absence of a towering leadership at the center. Interestingly, in 2009, the PC inducted a new member from the private sector, Arun Maira, who presumably had the qualities to help the commission navigate the rough waters of planning in the new context. The very induction of such a member is an index of the PC's flexibility and openness to new ideas.

The PC is a key integrative mechanism in India. In India's turbulent politics and amid the global economic turmoil, it must toil constantly to stay relevant. The changes in India's economic planning reviewed earlier underline the endeavor of the planners to remain alert to India's key concerns in the context of economic and political volatility. Such changes have not, however, been sufficient to satisfy the commission's critics.

CONTEMPORARY CHALLENGES TO INDIAN PLANNING

Notwithstanding its effort to reorient the nature of economic planning in India in light of changes in the economy and polity, the PC as India's planning agency remains the target of strong criticism and it faces serious attempts to reduce its traditional role in government decision making. Some critics, no doubt, see a continued need for economic planning even after economic liberalization. For example, the late Dr. Amaresh Bagchi, a renowned public finance expert, had underlined the validity of such a need on two essential grounds. One, given the context of resource scarcity, a well-designed plan was necessary as "a guide to action," not only for the public sector but also for the private sector. Two, the state needed to play a critical role in providing basic infrastructure. Over and above these reasons, the state had also to play "a redistributive role" in view of the existing economic disparities. Accordingly, a planning agency was necessary for harmonization and coordination of plans.[23] Some other experts would tend to agree; Hiten Bhaya, a former PC member, has argued: "The logic for having an institution like the Planning Commission is inescapable in a country like ours with limited resources, a vast backlog of basic development, millions at the margin of living and great inequalities of incomes and assets between regions and classes. There has to be a body of inspired and dedicated professionals who can look beyond governments into the future of the nation. . . . 'the Planning Commission is a lobby for development.'"[24]

Despite such endorsement, there are strong questions as to whether or not the PC should continue. Essentially, there are three positions on the future of the existing commission—that it be abolished altogether, that it be converted into a think tank, or that it be allowed to continue but with its financial leverage withdrawn. None of these positions are entirely new; they all have antecedents in the period before liberalization and their origins partly lie in the dynamics of bureaucratic conflict and federal politics. Economic liberalization has perhaps generated a more hospitable environment to put the future of the PC under question, however.

Abolishing the Planning Commission

At one extreme, there is the view that the PC should simply be abolished since it is not necessary because it allegedly duplicates functions that are performed elsewhere in the government. This view goes back to the time of the very origin of the PC, when its establishment provoked the then finance minister, John Matthai, to resign on the grounds that it would become a rival cabinet. Subsequent critics have seen the commission with its large bureaucracy as a mere replica of the national government. Importantly, some find it objectionable that the PC combines both staff and line functions since it not only renders advice to government on planning but also actively participates in approving allocations of funds and scrutinizing specific programs and projects.

Omens of the extreme position to abolish the PC have been apparent for long in discontent on the part of the rival institution of the Finance Commission, which makes recommendations on the sharing of revenues between the center and the states. The two agencies have seemingly different and rather contradictory orientations stemming from their respective mandates: "The Finance Commission strives to ensure the financial autonomy of the states so that they may fulfill satisfactorily the functions assigned to them by the constitution. On the other hand, the Planning Commission strives to bring the states into a national plan frame."[25] The concrete bone of contention here really is that the existence of the PC reduces the Finance Commission's domain since it constitutes an additional channel of funds from the center's revenues to the states. With the PC presiding over the allocation of plan outlays to the states, the Finance Commission is precluded from having a say on them and is limited to deciding only on nonplan funding.

This exclusion has been a source of resentment to several finance commissions from early on. In the early 1960s, the Third Finance Commission was dubious about the soundness of the distinction between plan and nonplan expenditures, whereas Hanson, in his classic study on Indian planning, believed that "the Finance Commission just did not like the Planning Commission."[26] The Ninth Finance Commission, the last one prior to liberalization, pointedly questioned the rationale of a nonstatutory body like the PC allocating public funds.[27] The argument against such allocation proceeds on the basis of high principles as to what is essential for sound public finance in a federal system, since it seemingly thwarts the Finance Commission from adequately discharging its function of effectively adjudicating on the funding needs of the center and states by preventing it from taking a holistic view of India's public finances. Others see merit in the plan and nonplan bifurcation, however, "insofar as it focuses attention on development expenses, as distinct from consumption."[28]

While the objection to the segmentation of channels for fiscal transfers from the center to the states has been a cause of considerable heartburn to several finance commissions, the Eleventh Finance Commission regarded it as a key institutional infirmity at the center. Interestingly, in a separate note, one of its members recommended merging the PC into the Finance Commission.[29] There may have been sound accounting or public finance reasons for this stance, but the differences also had the semblance of a turf war within the government. Hanson saw these differences as an attempt at empire building and "usurpation of the planning function."[30] Interestingly, in 2011, one analyst argued that the Ministry of Finance (MoF), already containing separate divisions for the budget, the plan, and the economy, was equipped to manage it all, declaring: "The rationale for continuing the Planning Commission as a separate organization outside the Finance Ministry is doubtful."[31] Perhaps such a position has support in that ministry since finance commissions, after all, lie within the jurisdiction of the MoF, while the PC began its life in the shadow of the resignation of Finance Minister Matthai in protest.

Converting the Planning Commission into a Think Tank

A growing body of opinion believes that the PC ought to be turned into a think tank of economic specialists that would function largely independent from the government and would not involve itself with day-to-day operations of the government. With this change, the PC would simply employ its expertise to develop alternative economic scenarios and offer policy advice, leaving it to the government to decide which path to take and what policy to implement.

In the mid-1980s, the reform-minded prime minister Rajiv Gandhi had apparently envisioned such a think tank role for the PC.[32] Newspaper commentators also have occasionally advocated a think tank role for the commission.[33] In recent years, the keenest advocate within the PC for the think tank role has been

Arun Maira. In a 2011 lecture on "A Vision for Planning," he agreed with the view that, as hardwired as it is to function according to the requirements of a different era, the PC is unable to contribute significantly to national advance in the new context in which "the country had changed" and "was more decentralized politically and administratively." His own preference was for the South African think tank model for planning that offers alternative scenarios to the leadership with little or no bureaucracy. He endorsed transforming the PC "to lift itself out of the rut of allocating funds and approving proposals and play a much more strategic role in helping to shape the future." That is, it should become "a strategic group that, like a radar, could sense the forces that were causing change to happen and that could provide governments in the center and in the states, and private industry, with insights into the forces shaping the future."[34] In the absence of funds to allocate and the power to approve projects, the new PC, and the larger leadership as well, would apparently then depend on its powers of persuasion to coordinate planning with the private sector and the states.

While the idea of the PC as a think tank has a contemporary ring to it, it had been articulated early on in India's planning experience. In the 1950s, the Lok Sabha's Estimates Committee favored the think tank model,[35] while one of India's foremost economists of the time, D. R. Gadgil, forcefully supported it. Characterizing the PC as a "total failure" in 1958, and criticizing it for having become an arm of the government through its participation in policymaking, Gadgil wanted the commission to shed *all* ministers from its membership and truly become a body of experts who would exercise no executive functions and would "not be mixed up with the essentially political process of final policymaking."[36] Hanson, however, appreciated the Indian planning model, particularly in light of the experience of other developing countries, where planning bodies tended "more likely to be too weak than too strong." He thought: "What the Indian system, with all its faults, avoids is the situation, so dismal to the serious planner, in which the experts sit isolated and neglected in small back rooms, drawing up projects of economic development and making policy recommendations which few of the politicians read and none feel committed to. . . . The cardinal virtue of the Indian system is that it has put political teeth into planning."[37]

It would seem that the idea of the PC as a think tank that is totally removed from government and politics misconceives the relationship between planning and power. An economic planning that is untouched by politics is a myth. Economists are not like physicists whose personal values or preferences have little relevance to the subject matter of their specialization. Quite the contrary, the subject matter in which economists specialize is quite prone to the manifestation of personal values and preferences, especially when public affairs and issues are at stake. That is one reason for the abundance of groups into which economists are divided. There can therefore be no such thing as morally and politically neutral advice from any group of economists on matters of the state (especially a democratic state) that can be noncontroversially adopted by a political leadership.

In a modern democratic state, any plan that aims to be sustainable has to meet the requirement of its political acceptability to the populace or its representatives. In a democratic system, economic planning cannot function in a political vacuum. A host of political considerations enter into determining the size, growth rate, and thrust of a given five-year plan. No political leadership can abdicate decisions on these issues to a group of economists. Besides domestic political pressures, there are geopolitical factors that need to be taken into account. An economic plan worked out by economists in a political vacuum would not carry much weight with the political leadership. More likely, the planning function will shift to where power resides. A planning unrelated to politics is simply a will-o'-the-wisp in an otherwise politically charged democracy.

In this light, it is precisely the frequent interaction between technical experts and political leaders that makes India's planning relevant to its economy. Despite its multitude of shortcomings, planning in India has derived its energy from its involvement with political leadership. Indeed, the vision of the leadership emergent from the political process provided the major thrusts to economic policy over successive decades—the big push to industry, economic self-reliance, the green revolution, growth with social justice, poverty alleviation, removing infrastructural bottlenecks, economic liberalization, and inclusive growth. None of these landmark policy thrusts were merely a matter of technical calculus.

Regardless of the earlier overrepresentation of political leaders, the PC has actually evolved into essentially an economic think tank for its normal working, but one that is also connected to the political leadership at critical points in the planning process. As presently constituted, the PC consists of a *core* team of about eight technical experts led by the deputy chairman, usually an economist or a public figure of high caliber, who is the executive head of the commission and presides over it in this core form. For major decisions, the *full* PC meets in its larger configuration that includes, besides the core team, some ten key members of the cabinet with the prime minister as the chairman.

The advantage of the current composition, comprising a core group and the full membership, is that it allows going beyond a simple, one-time presentation of scenarios from which the political leadership chooses one for implementation. In particular, it permits interaction between the core team and the political leadership on a more sustained basis. The deputy chairman is the linchpin of such interaction. Holding cabinet rank, he is aware of the entire spectrum of economic and political challenges facing the country and the full range of opinions about them within the government by virtue of his attendance at cabinet meetings. In addition, depending on personal equations, the present system keeps open the possibility of more frequent consultation between the deputy chairman and the prime minister as chairman.

Moreover, the planning process as currently structured provides for even wider consultation between the technical team and the political leadership when the full PC meets at several stages in any five-year plan's formulation. For example, the full commission meets to discuss the kind of thrust that the Approach Paper should accord to the economy during the next plan, and subsequently gathers to discuss the Approach Paper after it has been drafted. After the Approach Paper has been finalized, an even broader consultation takes place in the National Development Council (NDC), which consists of several economy-related cabinet ministers at the center and all the chief ministers. After the approval of the Approach Paper by the NDC, the PC proceeds to work out a five-year plan, which is subsequently considered by the full PC and later by the NDC.

This process of sustained interaction between the technical team and the political leadership is the unique strength of the Indian model of plan formulation for a vast and diverse country. The same process underlines the integrative aspect of economic planning twice over—it involves the political leadership of the national government that has been placed in office through an electoral process that covers the entire country, and also the political leadership of the states from all across India that has been elected to office by the specific electorate of each and every state. Politics plays a key role in planning, as it must in a democracy, which by the same token implies that not all the nation's economic ills can be laid at the doors of the PC.

In the context of rising expectations, spurred by growth acceleration, there is increasing impatience with all institutions. But it is difficult to see how the avoidance of politics through the think tank model in as political a process as economic planning can really be an improvement over the existing system. To be sure, institutions are susceptible to inertia and sclerosis once they are established, but India's planning mechanism has shown considerable flexibility to change when an essential need for it has arisen.

Divesting the Planning Commission of Financial Leverage

It is evident that there is a considerable consensus among analysts about the continuing need for economic planning in India, and that consensus includes even critics of planning as presently structured, such as Bagchi. It could not be otherwise, given resource scarcity, the state of global and domestic turmoil, and the urgency of traversing the challenge of development in a diverse and underdeveloped country.

If there is recognition of the need for economic planning in the contemporary nation-state, then it follows that to be worth anything it has to be national planning. It would be meaningless to talk of national development if the planning for it is not national and does not encompass the entire nation within its scope. In turn, as long as planning is considered important for the economy and polity, the PC must work as effectively as possible. One of the commission's functions is to coordinate the plans of the center and the states in order to have them constitute an integrated national plan. It cannot be national planning if the commission is just a bystander to the creation of an agglomeration of thirty-five or so separate plans. It is understandable that state leaders must use the rhetoric of state autonomy and pass on the blame to the center for their own failings, for that is a matter of bread and butter for them in order to get elected. But the founders of the republic very self-consciously described their choice of the polity as a union of states—and not a federation, let alone a confederation—in view of the country's divergent pulls, and they endowed the center with a plenitude of powers to ensure its unity and integrity. The founders made "economic and social planning" a concurrent subject, which makes the center's powers overriding in that sphere, and they endowed the center with the power to make grants to states. At the same time, they erected an institutional and legal structure that made imperative what later came to be termed "cooperative federalism" (as opposed to "competitive federalism"); as Chief Minister Ramakrishna Hegde once observed: "The web of relationship as worked into our constitution is so complex that the only atmosphere in which the center and the states must work is one of cooperation and not competition."[38]

If planning is both essential and constitutional, then it is important for it to have adequate financial teeth to perform its functions. Admittedly, employing persuasion in the conduct of human affairs is a great virtue, but the feasibility of its practice depends on the existence of a common interest (like higher production ought to be, as between industry and labor). In a world of competing interests, however, persuasion alone is unlikely to suffice; indeed, it is utopian to expect that it would. That is why in the cause of higher purposes, nation-states provide for constitutions, laws, and incentives to draw out desired behavior from social groups.

Interestingly, while advocating a reduced role for the PC in accord with his own state autonomist predilections, Bagchi nonetheless indirectly recognized that the commission's ability to coordinate planning among the ministries and between center and states rested on its control of financial largesse. He pointed out that the PC "derives its sway over ministries and states, not so much from the mathematical models as from its authority to disburse large sums—center's support for the plan called Gross Budgetary Support (GBS)—to help them implement projects/schemes under the plan."[39] Bhaya, too, underlined the same point: "The real source of authority of the Planning Commission lies in its role as allocator of plan funds and approver of the plan size and projects, both for the central ministries and states."[40]

Some believe it is precisely this leverage that the PC had exercised for some six decades that is threatened by the 2011 recommendations of the high-level committee headed by Dr. C. Rangarajan. Mandated to improve public expenditure management, particularly to enable linking of expenditures to outputs and outcomes rather than merely inputs, the committee recommended that the distinction between plan and nonplan "*should be*" dispensed with in favor of taking "a holistic view" of budget making and public expenditure.[41] Stated in this stark manner, the recommendation struck supporters of a continued prominent role for the PC as spelling the death knell of planning as it has been known in India since it would pass decisive power to the MoF in budget making, whether plan or nonplan. Perhaps there is exaggeration in the fear that the recommendation will be seized by opponents of planning to now scuttle it. As with many committees, however, there is some ambiguity about the Rangarajan committee's real or full intent. It is not clear what shape the relationship between the PC and the MoF will assume after the government takes a decision, not only on the plan/nonplan distinction but on the entire range of the committee's views on PC/MoF consultation on budget preparation. Perhaps the committee's recommendations, on balance, favor a more decisive role for the MoF, but they also do seem to envision some continued role for the PC.

Importantly, the committee also seemed to weaken the role of the PC in plan coordination in the federal framework. In relation to the states, the committee asked that they "assist Planning Commission in preparing overall FYP (Five Year Plan) and plans for various Sectors and Services in accordance with priorities approved by Planning Commission," to "prepare respective State Plan in accordance with national and State priorities," and also to provide information to the PC on various budgetary and planning matters. Crucially, however, the committee no longer saw the need for the PC to approve state plans, as is the current practice,[42] thus eliminating a key link between the PC and the states. Obviously, a clearer picture on the future role of the PC can emerge only after the central government takes a decision on the committee's recommendations.

SUMMARY AND CONCLUSION

Directly and indirectly, economic planning under the auspices of the state as a nation-building enterprise has played an enormous role in economic integration. The socialist regime accomplished such integration through adopting an India-wide economic strategy and by establishing a set of important institutions prior to economic liberalization. The key national strategy revolved around "the big push" to industrialization, while the key institutions were a high-powered Planning Commission that oversaw economic planning for the entire nation, a hegemonic public sector all across India, and a bureaucratic system of licensing and controls over economic activity.

Economic liberalization, undertaken in 1991 to accelerate the pace of economic growth, resulted in the substantial relaxation and dismantlement of economic controls and consequently posed serious challenges to the planning mechanism that was long accustomed to operating through a command-and-control economic regime. However, contrary to the fears of the supporters of planning, the liberalizers did not dismantle the basic planning mechanism, which has continued into the postliberalization period for more than two decades and has adjusted itself to operating in the new environment of a largely market-driven economy and a looser federal polity. Perhaps this adjustment was eased by the fact that the two major features of the earlier economic regime were, in form if not in spirit, the mixed economy and "cooperative federalism," and these two features have for the most part continued into the postliberalization period, though the internal balance within each has changed. In any case, the continuity of planning would, at first blush, seem to demonstrate that the impact of liberalization was not as severe as originally feared. This outcome is the direct consequence of the state's decision that continuity of planning was essential to the integrity and welfare of the nation.

At the same time, however, by altering the balance in favor of the market as against the state in the economic sphere, liberalization has generated considerable change in the planning system. This change is evident in four aspects of planning, which have seen a shift during the subsequent two decades: (1) from comprehensive planning to indicative planning; (2) from planning for state hegemony over the economy to adapting to private sector expansion; (3) from planning for a hegemonic producer state to planning for a quasi-welfare state, with the latter becoming, as it were, the centerpiece of planning; and (4) from centralization in planning to coordination in planning within a system of cooperative federalism.

Not all the shifts can be attributed directly to economic liberalization, but the first two and, in part, the third certainly can be. The shift to indicative planning and the rise of the private sector are clearly a consequence of liberalization. The turn to the welfare state through the emphasis on "inclusiveness" in planning is largely a function over time of the higher social mobilization of the population—which liberalization and the accompanying growth acceleration have advanced—and of the democratic nature of the political system, which dictates responsiveness to the electorate, much of it being poor and deprived. The fourth shift undoubtedly stems from the reduced role of public investment, but additionally flows from domestic political tendencies over a longer period, such as the decline of the one-party-dominant system, the regionalization of politics, and government formation on the basis of coalitions, all of which predate liberalization.

These shifts, on the one hand, testify to the adaptability of the planning mechanism to the new environment engendered by liberalization. On the other hand, despite the changes, the future role of the planning mechanism remains under question as it confronts serious challenges. There is no doubt that the decline in public investment—a direct consequence of liberalization—has weakened the influence of the planning organization, with that weakness being accentuated by the decline of the one-party-dominant system and the rise of regionalization of politics. It is yet to be seen whether the shift to "inclusiveness" and the focus on the quasi-welfare state will be sufficient to compensate for the loss of influence stemming from the reduced role of public investment.

Whether by design or otherwise, planning has served as an influential integrative mechanism for the economy and the nation for some six decades. Despite its many shortcomings, during that long stretch, it did foster economic growth and industrialization and thus created a substantial structural base for economic integration. On the face of it, rapid economic growth and industrialization will continue to be critical goals for India, given its poverty and its position as a manufacturing laggard in Asia. In the postliberalization period, the emphasis on inclusiveness in planning is also an important contribution to social and national integration. A fuller transition to an industrial society and the welfare state will also mean a socially and economically integrated nation. Whether planning will continue to contribute to accomplishing economic growth and welfare, and consequently social and economic integration, will depend crucially on decisions by the state, and not simply on market forces. Prudence would likely demand that decision makers be alert to Hippocrates's advice to "first, do no harm," and therefore seek to preserve and strengthen, not weaken, the links that planning provides between the center and states in an otherwise fragile federation under many centrifugal pressures.

NOTES

1. Government of India (GoI), foreword to *Eighth Five Year Plan (1992–1997)* (New Delhi: Planning Commission, 1992).
2. See Alec Nove, "Planned Economy," in *The New Palgrave: A Dictionary of Economics*, ed. John Eatwell, Murray Milgate, and Peter Newman (London: Macmillan, 1987), 3:879–85; and Klaus Nielsen, "Indicative Planning," in *The New Palgrave Dictionary of Economics* (2008), available at www.dictionaryofeconomics.com.
3. GoI, *Eleventh Five Year Plan*, vol. 1, para. 2.6.
4. GoI, *Seventh Five Year Plan*, vol.1, paras. 6.1–6.2.
5. GoI, preface to *Eighth Five Year Plan (1992–1997)*, vol. 1, para. 5; emphasis added.
6. Kirit S. Parikh, "The Role of Planning," *Business Standard*, July 21, 2007.
7. GoI, *Eleventh Five Year Plan (2007–2012): Inclusive Growth* (New Delhi: Oxford University Press, 2008), vol. 1, 28.
8. However, not all public sector enterprises (PSEs) were able to rise to the challenge of competition, for example, the telecommunications firm Bharat Sanchar Nigam Limited (BSNL) and the airlines.
9. The loss-making enterprises are a considerable drain on India's treasury, the most egregious cases being the public sector airlines and fertilizer companies.
10. GoI, *Public Enterprises Survey 2009–2010* (New Delhi: Department of Public Enterprises, 2011), vol. 1, 11.
11. *Economic Times*, "ET 500," October 2010.
12. GoI, *Towards Faster and More Inclusive Growth: An Approach to the 11th Five Year Plan* (New Delhi: Planning Commission, 2006), 95–96; emphasis added.
13. Growth rates tabulated from data in *World Bank Indicators 2011*, available at http://databank.worldbank.org/data/views/variableSelection/selectvariables.aspx?source=world-development-indicators, accessed September 16, 2011.

14. Reetika Khera, ed., *The Battle for Employment Guarantee* (New Delhi: Oxford University Press, 2011), offers a collection on the achievements and shortcomings of the program from the perspective of social activists.

15. GoI, "Press Note on Poverty Estimates, 2011–12" (New Delhi: Planning Commission, July 2013).

16. S. P. Gupta, *Planning and Development in India* (New Delhi: Allied, 1989), 247–48.

17. Utsav Kumar and Arvind Subramanian, "Growth in India's States in the First Decade of the 21st Century: Four Facts," *Economic and Political Weekly* 47, no. 3 (January 21, 2012): 48–57.

18. Swati Raju, "Growth across States in the 2000s: Evidence of Convergence," *Economic and Political Weekly* 47, no. 23 (June 9, 2012): 76–79.

19. Santosh Mehrotra and Ankita Gandhi, "India's Human Development in the 2000s: Towards Social Inclusion," *Economic and Political Weekly* 47, no. 14 (April 7, 2012): 59–64.

20. Asian Development Bank, *India 2039: An Affluent Society in One Generation* (Manila: Asian Development Bank, 2009).

21. Baldev Raj Nayar, *The Modernization Imperative and Indian Planning* (New Delhi: Vikas, 1972), chap. 2.

22. Hiten Bhaya, ed., *Indian Planning: Search for Change* (New Delhi: Asian Institute of Transport Development, 1997), 121.

23. Amaresh Bagchi, "Role of Planning and the Planning Commission: Case for a Review," *Economic and Political Weekly* 42, no. 44 (November 3, 2007): 92–100.

24. Bhaya, *Indian Planning*, 99, 107.

25. V. M. Dandekar, "Planning: What and How," in Bhaya, *Indian Planning*, 136.

26. A. H. Hanson, *The Process of Planning: A Study of India's Five-Year Plans, 1950–1964* (London: Oxford University Press, 1966), 342–43.

27. Bhaya, *Indian Planning*, 93.

28. Ibid.

29. GoI, *Report of the Eleventh Finance Commission on the Additional Term of Reference (for 2000–2005)* (New Delhi: Finance Commission, August 2000), 13–14; and GoI, *Report of the Eleventh Finance Commission (for 2000–2005)* (New Delhi: Finance Commission, June 2000), 118–20.

30. Hanson, *Process of Planning*, 342, 344.

31. A. Rangachari, "Role and Relevance of Planning Commission," *Hindu*, September 18, 2011; available at www.thehindu.com.

32. Bhaya, *Indian Planning*, 97.

33. "Plan for Change," *Hindu Business Line*, editorial, April 25, 2011; P. Vaidyanathan Iyer, "A Four-Year Plan?" *Indian Express*, January 5, 2010.

34. Arun Maira, "A New Vision for Planning: 15th Dr. Rajendra Prasad Memorial Lecture, New Delhi, 9th December 2011," typescript, New Delhi, 2011. Under Maira's direction, the Planning Commission has developed such scenarios for India; see GoI, "Scenarios: Shaping India's Future" (New Delhi: Planning Commission, 2012), available at http://planningcommission.nic.in/reports/genrep/scenarios_v10712.pdf.

35. Hanson, *Process of Planning*, 70.

36. D. R. Gadgil, *Planning and Economic Policy in India* (Poona, India: Gokhale Institute of Politics and Economics, 1961), 150–72.

37. Hanson, *Process of Planning*, 72–73.

38. Cited in D. K. Srivastava and Bhujanga C. Rao, "Fiscal Relations between the Center and the States: Dependence of States on Devolution of Funds," in *Commission on Center–State Relations: Supplementary Volume-II: Research Study* (New Delhi: GoI Commission on Center–State Relations, March 2010), 3.

39. Bagchi, "Role of Planning," 94.

40. Bhaya, *Indian Planning*, 93.

41. GoI, *Report of the High Level Expert Committee on Efficient Management of Public Expenditure* (New Delhi: Planning Commission, July 2011), iii, xv, xxiv, 7; emphasis added.

42. Ibid., 11, 13.

Chapter 5

FISCAL FEDERALISM

Finance Commission's Adaptation to New Challenges

FISCAL federalism has to do with fiscal relations between the center and the states; in India, it has been principally concerned with the sharing of national revenues between the two entities. The key integrative institution of the nation-state in India in this regard, among others, is the constitutionally mandated Finance Commission, which is appointed every five years. Since 1950, thirteen such commissions have submitted their reports; the fourteenth one was appointed in January 2013. The appointment of the Finance Commission is constitutionally a prerogative of the national government, as are the setting out of the terms of reference for the conduct of its work.

Consisting of highly reputed professionals and public figures, the Finance Commission, as a largely independent body, has the responsibility for making recommendations on the transfer of revenues from the center to the states ("devolution") and on distributing the states' share among the various states ("distribution"). The very institution of the Finance Commission as a constitutional authority apportioning shares to the states from central revenues serves as an integrative device in India's largely ethnically configured political system, where the states are at different levels of development and vary in their revenue potential.

The commission's integrative role lies in the fact that it travels all across India and receives representations from the national government and the states as well as interest groups, and exchanges views with them. After making a considered assessment of all the issues brought before it, the commission sets out its broad approach to devolution and distribution in one or more reports, and then makes specific recommendations on them for the ensuing five-year period.[1] Such revenue sharing is extremely important to the states since it increases their own revenue receipts by about 45 percent.[2] Because of the very thorough and judicious manner with which finance commissions have conducted their business, their recommendations have commanded considerable authority and, barring occasional exceptions, it is a convention with the national government to accept them as if they constituted an award.

A vast literature exists on fiscal federalism and also on the Finance Commission. The core question for distinctive consideration in this chapter, however, is the narrower one of the impact of globalization on fiscal federalism and the response of the state and the state-appointed Finance Commission to the new challenges after economic liberalization. The analysis of these issues is divided into several parts: the first part analyzes the impact of globalization on fiscal federalism more generally; the second part examines the challenge of the new task of fiscal consolidation and fiscal discipline at the national and state levels; the third part investigates the issue of rationalization and modernization of "devolution" and "distribution"; and the final part provides the conclusions. Taken together, the analysis shows that, despite the deep-rooted nature of India's fiscal problems and the oft-manifest general lack of state capacity to achieve national goals, India's state institutions can rise to the occasion at times to accomplish such goals. Indeed, when so motivated or compelled, the Indian state can display exemplary initiative, creativity, and fortitude to accomplish the set tasks, thus demonstrating the critical importance of the state as an intervening variable between globalization and economic integration.

FISCAL FEDERALISM AND THE GLOBALIZATION-INDUCED IMPERATIVE OF EFFICIENCY

Under the new economic dispensation after the shift to liberalization in 1991, as India opened up its economy through drastically reducing customs tariffs, it now faced the heightened challenge of economic competition from the world economy. This challenge required India to become competitive in producing goods and services, not only to pay for its essential imports but also to prevent its own productive structure from being overwhelmed by foreign firms and imports. The requirement of competitiveness under a regime of economic liberalization thus made *economic efficiency* an imperative. Indeed, the then finance minister Manmohan Singh declared economic efficiency to be the central aim of economic reform in his very first budget speech in 1991: "The thrust of the reform process would be to increase the *efficiency* and international competitiveness of industrial production."[3]

The turn to economic efficiency, though not in full measure, demanded that India refashion its internal economic and financial order. This was especially necessary since the decade preceding economic liberalization had seen a serious deterioration in public finances because of fiscal profligacy, considerably stimulated by the heightened political competition after the decline of the single dominant party system and the regionalization of politics. Importantly, persistent and rising fiscal deficits and current account deficits had been the principal trigger in shifting to economic liberalization. Fiscal correction and consolidation were thus fundamental to the healthy functioning of the national economy.

Fiscal correction and consolidation, however, required reforming fiscal federalism, since the public finances of the center and states were inextricably linked. In this fashion, the quest for economic efficiency in a causal chain, as it were, necessitated harmonization between center and states in fiscal federalism, just as it also required attention to issues of accountability and transparency, as well as of system design and appropriate incentives. In these distinctive ways, the impact of economic liberalization stretched into the arena of fiscal federalism. Change in fiscal federalism was not altogether absent prior to economic liberalization, but such change was episodic or insubstantial. In contrast, the change in fiscal federalism after liberalization has been sustained and comprehensive, though stretched over a considerable period.

Fundamentally, the changes in fiscal federalism following economic liberalization were designed to meet the challenge of fiscal stress faced by the polity, including the states. Three elements entered into the adoption of the changes. The first element pertained to the greater sensitivity of decision makers, as a result of economic liberalization, to the *threat* that lack of fiscal prudence created for domestic firms in their quest for international competitiveness. The second element was that of *emulation*, which economic liberalization encouraged among decision makers through greater exposure to the outside world. This aspect is certainly manifest in the new inclination among decision makers to adopt "best international practices." Finally, the third element concerned the *facilitative* role that economic liberalization played through the growth acceleration that it engendered; this made it easier for the government to initiate, adopt, or accept modifications or innovations in policy than would have been possible otherwise.

The Revenue Sharing Process in India

Revenue sharing between the national government and the states in India takes place through three different channels—the Planning Commission; different ministries of the national government; and the Finance Commission. The last channel is the focus of the analysis here in examining the impact of globalization on fiscal federalism.

There are important reasons of both efficiency and equity for establishing a body like the Finance Commission in a federation to decide or advise on revenue sharing. To begin with, federations often face the problem of "vertical imbalance" between the center and the states, with the former having access to more abundant and buoyant revenues than the states. Apparently, this favorable position of the center is built into modern public finance in federations. The different constituent states often have varying revenue potential, and equity demands that certain revenue sources be assigned to the center since assigning them to the states would reinforce the disadvantage of the weaker states. Besides equity, efficiency considerations may also favor assignment of certain taxes to the center, such as those referred to as "mobile" taxes that can move from one jurisdiction to another. Since such assignment of tax powers increases the revenues of the center, it becomes necessary to create an institutional mechanism to decide or advise on the criteria for revenue sharing in order to assure a proper fiscal balance between the center and the states, taking into consideration the revenue needs of both.

Besides the vertical imbalance, there is also the issue of "horizontal imbalance." Since economic disparities, and therefore differences in revenue potential, often exist among the various constituent states of any federation, *equity* considerations require that the economically weaker units not be unduly disadvantaged in providing essential public goods and services to citizens resident in their jurisdiction. Maintaining some semblance of balance across the units in offering essential public services is precisely the responsibility of the center. This progressive function is one of two that the eminent authority on public finance, Richard Musgrave, reserves for the national government—stabilization and redistribution.[4] In India, the Finance Commission aids in discharging this redistributive function by providing advice to the center.

While India is not unusual with regard to the national government having to share revenues with the constituent units, it is decisively different from federations like Australia and Canada in two major respects. One, unlike the other two, India is not an advanced industrial economy with high standards of living. Rather, its national government is charged with and aims to perform the historic task of transforming an agricultural and poor economy into an industrial and advanced one. As such, a key function of the national leadership is to provide and implement a *national vision* of economic transformation for the entire nation.[5] The national government therefore has multiple economic and political objectives, not the single one of sharing revenues with the constituent units, and it necessarily has to make trade-offs among them.

Two, set within enormous social diversity and a continent-sized civilization-state, India's political unity is fragile; as M. Govinda Rao and Nirvikar Singh underline, "the 'idea of India' is still contested."[6] Consequently, nation building remains a historic task of the leadership of the nation-state in India. Contemporary national decision makers therefore have to be constantly sensitive to a multiplicity of internal and external threats to achieving that task, and in particular to any weakening of the national government as the key guardian of the republic. According to the Thirteenth Finance Commission: "The federalist developmental State is a domain for evolutionary policymaking, *responsive to internal and external policy imperatives such as political integration and globalization*, with sovereign powers to fulfill its mandate."[7] Considerations of national integration are likely to have priority with national decision makers over those of solely applying textbook theories of public finance. The requirements of politics—

sometimes noble, other times base—may therefore at times trump arguments based solely on grounds of efficiency.

Globalization's Impact on Revenue Sharing

Earlier, this chapter has shown more broadly how the imperative of economic efficiency arising out of globalization reverberated widely through the economy, including the arena of fiscal federalism. A more specific question relates to how globalization as social process or economic liberalization as policy has affected the functions and functioning of the Finance Commission. Economic liberalization could not help but have a significant impact on such functioning because it initially aggravated the existing situation of fiscal stress. The sharp cuts in customs duties and income taxes, on top of the earlier cumulative fiscal stress, adversely affected national finances. The institutional response on the part of the national government and finance commissions to this serious situation reveals change in two particular areas.

The single most important effect of economic liberalization has been the expansion of the jurisdiction of the Finance Commission to encompass the completely new task of *fiscal consolidation*, rightly so given the situation of extreme fiscal stress. The new task vastly expanded the scope of the commission's work beyond the usual tasks of *devolution* and *distribution* in revenue sharing. Following liberalization, the commission gradually assumed the role of monitoring performance in select areas of management of public finances and to make specific recommendations on the restructuring and consolidation of public finance in those areas across the federation.

This role expansion stemmed from the heightened realization that the health of public finances could no longer be treated in separate compartments of the national government and state governments. A comprehensive view needed to be taken on the state of public finances at both levels and on the corrective action necessary to set it right. Overseeing harmonization and coordination between center and states on issues pertaining to fiscal federalism thus became a regular function of the commission. Fiscal correction, fiscal consolidation, and fiscal sustainability were urgent requirements since there had to be adequate revenues first before they could be shared and distributed, and there had to be some assurance that such revenues would be productively deployed for their intended purposes. Inaction in the face of fiscal stress could only generate more fiscal crises.

Another significant effect of economic liberalization on fiscal federalism lies in the area of *rationalization and modernization* in the processes concerning the traditional business of the Finance Commission about devolution and distribution of revenues. Thus, there was greater emphasis placed on economic rationality, simplicity in system design, transparency and accountability, reliance on incentives for the different stakeholders, and avoidance of perverse incentives and moral hazards.

However, the impact of economic liberalization on fiscal federalism in the two areas of fiscal consolidation and rationalization of devolution and distribution did not occur in one sudden move or by fiat. Rather, it evolved through sustained and persistent effort during the long tenure of four successive (the Tenth through Thirteenth) Finance Commissions after liberalization.

THE NEW THRUST OF PAN-INDIAN FISCAL CONSOLIDATION

Historically, the "core" or primary task of the Finance Commission has been to make recommendations on the *devolution* of revenues from the union to the states and on the *distribution* of such revenues among the states. That is its constitutionally mandated task (Article 280). But the commission does not do as it pleases in an economic and political vacuum. The national government is authorized by the constitution to refer to it "any other matter . . . in the interests of sound finance." The commission thus functions within a frame of reference established by the democratically elected national government. Its terms of reference have often "reflected some of the dominant concerns in the area of Center–State relations and the emerging issues in national public finance."[8]

Tenth Finance Commission (1995–2000): Laying the Groundwork

The Tenth Finance Commission was appointed in 1992. Its work was pathbreaking and it issued directly out of its terms of references, which asked the commission, in making its recommendations, to consider "the objective of not only balancing the receipts and expenditure on revenue account of both the States and the Central Government, but also generating surplus for capital investment and *reducing fiscal deficit*."[9] It was recognized at the time that this was an innovation, but one necessitated by the grim and daunting economic and fiscal situation facing the country.[10] The commission's report attested to that: "Our approach has been guided by the paramount need to restore fiscal equilibrium in the economy." The commission was in utter dismay over the dire straits into which the economy had been driven by fiscal profligacy, bemoaning that "the principal factor underlying the fiscal imbalance is the unbridled growth of government expenditure . . . borrowings are financing such revenue expenditure."[11] The fiscal position of the states was equally bad, exhibiting "a similar picture of increasing revenue deficits" since 1987–88.[12]

In the commission's view, the reason for India coming to this pass was that the central and state governments had not made an adequate effort to exploit the potential for mobilizing resources, even as they had allowed expenditures to keep rising. Even though recommending action on fiscal consolidation in a situation of fiscal disequilibrium was not in the commission's mandate—which was only to take the fiscal situation into account in making its recommendations on devolution and distribution—the commission had abundant advice for the national and state governments on fiscal discipline, most of which had to do with cutting expenditure, eliminating or reducing subsidies, and selectively privatizing the public sector.

The commission's excursion into macro fiscal deterioration had the function of establishing the point that the business of devolution and distribution had to take into account the larger fiscal condition of the republic and that it could no longer be done in a vacuum. This stance would provide an opening for both the government and future commissions in requiring stricter fiscal discipline on the part of the states.

The Tenth Finance Commission's report on fiscal consolidation was not entirely limited to giving stern advice, however. It offered debt relief to the states but, unlike the past, it linked the relief to fiscal performance. This latter step was deemed essential since debt relief in the past provided a perverse incentive to fiscal profligacy. Besides, the center complained that debt relief to the states would not leave the center unaffected, and that debt relief measures offered by past commissions indeed "have at least partly been responsible for the rise in Central debt and consequently the burden of increased interest payments."[13] Thus, the center and states did not exist in separate silos with regard to the fiscal situation; they were, instead, interrelated.

The commission did not call its linking of debt relief to fiscal performance a "conditionality," but that is what it was (if only in a minor way); this step would, again, provide an opening for more substantial "conditioning" by subsequent commissions. Besides performance-linked debt relief, the Tenth Finance Commission also encouraged states to retire part of their debt through the sale of their equity in government-owned firms.[14] One distinguished administrator thought that these were all "interesting innovations," marked by "a touch of sophistication" and "an invocation to the virtues of self-help on the part of the states."[15] Meanwhile, the opening pointed by the Tenth Finance Commission by way of employing the conditionality mechanism was carried forward further by the Eleventh Finance Commission.

Eleventh Finance Commission (2000–2005): A Valiant Effort at Fiscal Restructuring

When the Eleventh Finance Commission was appointed in July 1998, the central government entrusted it also with new responsibilities. What was really novel among the additional tasks and unheard of in the annals of the preceding ten finance commissions—"a striking departure from the past"—was the government's explicit instruction to the commission to go beyond the usual assessment of the state of finances of both the union and the states and "suggest ways and means by which the governments, collectively and severally, may bring about a *restructuring of the public finances* so as to restore budgetary balance and maintain macroeconomic stability."[16]

The seriousness with which the government now viewed the issue of fiscal consolidation was made abundantly evident by its subsequent but belated action to ask the commission, when it was almost finished with its final report, to not confine itself merely to suggestions on fiscal restructuring but also to draw up "a *monitorable fiscal reforms program* aimed at reduction of revenue deficit of the States and recommend the manner in which the grants to States to cover the assessed deficit . . . may be linked to progress in implementing the program."[17] The central government thus explicitly opened up the issue of a quantifiable fiscal reforms program for the states, which may be accompanied by "conditionalities" that would include incentives and penalties to encourage implementation.

Fiscal Restructuring. While the task for economic restructuring had been instituted by the national government, the Eleventh Finance Commission was easily persuaded of its necessity by the patent fiscal deterioration. Its narration of the condition of India's public finances constitutes one long tale of fiscal woes, remarking that "the fiscal profile of the country was, perhaps, worse than ever before." It thought that "in this disturbing scenario, growing worse and worse over time . . . without major structural reform no improvement was going to be possible" and that "breakthrough recommendations" were therefore necessary.[18]

In the commission's assessment, the causes of the fiscal imbalances were "predominantly structural," reflecting decline in the tax-GDP ratio and stagnation in nontax income on the revenue side and, on the expenditure side, periodic higher wage packages for government employees, higher interest payments, and "burgeoning subsidies" as a consequence of "competitive populism."[19] In its view, several institutional infirmities lay behind the structural weaknesses that had resulted in fiscal imbalances. The commission highlighted three key deficiencies in the area of fiscal transfers from center to states that had evolved over half a century. Interestingly, its account of these deficiencies followed the line of argumentation developed by what may be called "the NIPFP school"—after the center-funded National Institute of Public Finance and Policy in New Delhi—with its economics-centered and state-autonomist critique of India's fiscal federalism. The commission's prescriptions to rectify these deficiencies were also in line with those of the school. Perhaps this coincidence was a function of one of the commission members being a prominent representative of that school—Dr. A. K. Bagchi, a former director of the NIPFP (1985–95); significantly, one authority maintains: "In 1998–2000, he was the specialist Member and guiding light of the Eleventh Finance Commission."[20]

The deficiency that was of most concern to the commission was the segmentation of fiscal transfers from the center to the states, since there were three different institutions dealing separately with parts of these transfers: the Finance

Commission, Planning Commission, and central ministries. The multiple channels of fiscal transfers had resulted in promoting competitive inflation of expenditures by the states, in relaxing the hard budget constraint, and in excessive borrowing under various subterfuges. The second deficiency pertained to the design of devolution and distribution, where a "normative approach" had not been strictly followed in the past in applying objective norms in assessing need and capacity across the board in distribution. The third deficiency related to the weakness, indeed the absence, of institutional arrangements for the center and states to consult with each other and coordinate policy, which resulted in tax competition and tax exportation among states. The commission's strategy for fiscal restructuring was precisely to rectify these three deficiencies.[21]

The key aim in the commission's scheme of things in relation to restructuring of public finances was the restoration of budgetary balance over the medium term. It sought to do this through recommending a reduction in the fiscal deficit from 9.84 percent of GDP in 1999–2000 to 6.5 percent by 2004–5 (center 4.5 percent, states 2.5 percent) and the near elimination of the revenue deficit (center 1.0 percent, states 0.0 percent). These changes were to be accomplished through increasing revenues and reducing expenditures.[22]

The commission's restructuring plan to achieve the budgetary targets called for reforms in several areas. First, it asked the center to widen the tax base and to incorporate services more fully in the tax base through a comprehensive Value Added Tax (VAT) system for goods and services, and to effectively impose user charges for goods and services supplied by the center and states. Second, it wanted governments to cut expenditures on administration and subsidies.[23]

Third, it recommended restructuring of public sector enterprises (PSEs), particularly at the state level, where they should be sold off or shut down since they were perpetually in loss and a "chronic drain on state budgets."[24] Fourth, the commission placed high importance on institutional reform as a prerequisite for sustainable budgetary balance, and it offered some radical proposals in this regard. One such proposal was for reduction in the vertical imbalance in fiscal federalism to the largest extent possible through a reassignment of tax powers in the constitution so as to give the states greater access to revenues, thus reducing their dependence on the center. Another proposal was to impose stricter controls on incurring debt, if necessary through constitutional changes.[25]

It is clear that the commission's analysis of fiscal federalism was thoroughgoing and comprehensive, leaving few aspects of the center's and states' public finances untouched. This was the first time that a finance commission had carried out an examination of such wide scope. It would not be far-fetched to say that, especially with respect to the states in India, the commission had assumed a role that paralleled that of the International Monetary Fund (IMF) in relation to the world's nation-states, particularly those that were faced with a financial crisis. In that respect, it was a homegrown surrogate IMF.[26] Experts may differ over whether or not India's shift to economic liberalization in 1991 was the cause of this development, but it is noteworthy that the package of reforms recommended by the Eleventh Finance Commission—the very term "economic restructuring" is significant—followed the lines of a "structural adjustment program" under IMF auspices, such as imposition of fiscal prudence through compressing expenditure and expanding tax revenues, and in general downsizing the public sector. In that sense, the commission's recommended restructuring was an extension of economic liberalization to the arena of fiscal federalism. Soon, at the center's request, the commission added to this recommendation the element of monitoring the performance of the states on the basis of quantitative indicators.

Toward a Monitorable Fiscal Reforms Program. It was not until near the end of the commission's tenure that the national government asked it to supplement its fiscal restructuring proposals with "a monitorable fiscal reforms program" designed to reduce the fiscal deficit in the states, along with recommendations on linking deficit-covering grants for states to performance in meeting program targets. The commission complied on short order, completing an additional report in four months.[27]

Consistent with its broader analysis of the country's fiscal malaise and the recommended aim of bringing down the states' revenue deficit to zero over the five-year period 2000–2005, the commission developed a quantifiable and measurable program to evaluate performance with respect to (1) growth in revenue receipts (tax and nontax) and (2) reduction in revenue expenditure (salaries, interest, and subsidies), with equal weight assigned to both. It then went on to recommend the establishment of an "incentive fund" amounting to Rs. 106.07 billion for motivating states to reduce their revenue deficit.[28]

In view of the diversity of the country, the commission recommended entrusting the state-specific tasks for enforcing the program to a "monitoring agency" for each state, consisting of representatives from the center and the particular state. It is significant that the monitorable program applied only to the *deficit-covering grants-in-aid*, and absolutely not to the devolution of tax revenues, where the center has been punctilious to a fault in avoiding any suggestion of conditionality.

Dissent on Monitoring and Conditioning. The noteworthy outcome of the supplementary task for the commission was not so much the generation of a monitorable fiscal reforms program, but the exposure of the fault lines in India's fiscal federalism to public view. To begin with, the states questioned the constitutional validity of the additional term of reference, holding that the constitution contained no provision for "any conditionality" on grants-in-aid to the states.[29] More seriously, one of the commission members, Dr. A. K. Bagchi, penned a vigorous note of dissent, in which he held the conditionality on release of revenue deficit grants to be both "unjustifiable" and "contrary to the *spirit* of Article 275 of the constitution which authorizes the Finance Commission to recommend such grants-in-aid." He averred that "a fundamental principle is involved in proposing conditionality to be attached to the release of grants-in-aid to meet revenue deficits." Consistent with the state-autonomist theme that runs through his note of dissent, Bagchi believed that "to require the states to get their fiscal policies reformed according to a plan approved by a monitoring agency heavily dominated by the center detracts from their autonomy in a fundamental way."[30] In his dissent note, Bagchi acknowledged that it can be argued that the constitution allows the center to lay down "any conditionality to grants-in-aid under Article 275," and that there would be support for this argument in judicial decisions. In the event, he appealed to the vague notion of "federalism"—without specifying its content or its empirical referent—in support of his position.

What this posture revealed was that the note by Bagchi reflected an attempt to insert a stance based not on the constitutional position as it existed but founded on personal or political and ideological preferences. It is not surprising, then, that the other four members of the commission found his argument unconvincing and dismissed the note, asserting that the Indian Constitution did, indeed, permit the imposition of conditionalities in relation to the states in this matter. Thus, the Eleventh Finance Commission decisively settled the issue of conditionalities, and future finance commissions were free to apply conditionalities to fiscal transfers, at least to their grants-in-aid component.

The Eleventh Finance Commission played a historic role in the evolution of fiscal federalism in India. It did not merely take an integrated view of the nation's fiscal federalism, in which fiscal performance at the center and in the states was treated as linked. Rather, it definitively settled the issue that establishing "conditionalities" in fiscal transfers from the center to the states, at least in terms of grants-in-aid, was a legitimate and constitutionally legal function of the Finance Commission and, by extension, of the national government. Henceforth, the application of conditionalities to grants would be treated as normal by finance commissions. The commission could be faulted, however, for the insufficiency of its material incentives to overcome the fiscal predicament of the states.

Twelfth Finance Commission (2005–2010): Radical Breakthrough in Fiscal Restructuring

If there had ever been the hope that the Eleventh Finance Commission's monitorable fiscal reforms program would overcome the challenges facing fiscal federalism in India over a single five-year period, that hope was soon belied, for the budgetary balances quickly worsened. The Eleventh Finance Commission could hardly be blamed for the outcome. For one thing, hefty wage and pension packages for public employees and a considerable economic slowdown intervened to wreck the budgetary balances, particularly of the states. As the Twelfth Finance Commission pointed out in retrospect, "the six years from 1997–98 to 2002–3 have been the worst in the history of state finances."[31] Besides, the Eleventh

Finance Commission's restructuring program had provided little incentive for fiscal discipline by the states.[32]

Under the circumstance, the task of providing a solution to the worsened budgetary balances was passed on to the Twelfth Finance Commission, which was appointed in November 2002. For its part, the new commission offered some radical proposals to set India's federal fiscal house in order; as Bagchi opined, the commission "has broken new ground in several key areas and made recommendations which, if fully implemented, will have a far-reaching impact on the finances and functioning of government in the country at all levels."[33]

The terms of reference of the Twelfth Finance Commission were largely similar to that of the previous commission, but there was another, still newer task for it, which required attention to "debt reduction along with equitable growth."[34] The priority task for the Twelfth Finance Commission was rescuing the center and the states from the parlous fiscal condition in which they were placed as a consequence of the persistence of revenue and fiscal deficits. In this respect, the commission saw some promise for fiscal reform in the advance already made in the institutional environment through the national government's 2003 enactment of the Fiscal Responsibility and Budget Management (FRBM) Act. That act sought to bring down the center's fiscal deficit to 3 percent. This legislation soon became the fulcrum for a more generalized fiscal restructuring across the states.

Attacking Public Debt. In view of the serious fiscal imbalances, the commission focused centrally on public debt since that had serious consequences for public finance. It was struck by the acceleration of growth in the debt–GDP ratio since 1996–97, with the ratio jumping in a matter of six years from 56.3 percent in 1995–96 to 76 percent in 2002–3. In the commission's own understanding, a more accurate figure would be 85 percent. The villain of the piece here was persistent fiscal deficits, but the result nonetheless was a vicious cycle in public finance with fiscal deficits leading to rising debt, which in turn ended up in persistent fiscal deficits.[35] Consequently, the commission needed to attack the issue of debt sustainability. Its key recommendation in this regard required the center and the states to bring down, in equal proportions, the combined debt to 56 percent and the fiscal deficit to GDP ratio to 6 percent.

In its multipronged strategy for fiscal restructuring, the commission recommended reforming the taxation system, imposing adequate user charges, rationalizing subsidies, reducing the role of the public sector, reforming the planning process, and increasing the role of the third tier of government in the delivery of public goods. In terms of fiscal federalism, it was particularly important to target two areas for reform: (1) economic planning, so as to remove the center's role as a lender while at the same time enforcing a hard budget constraint, and (2) public debt of the states, so as to restructure it in order to reduce the states' fiscal burden.

A New Borrowing Regime. Under economic planning, the center extended aid to the states for the mutually agreed five-year and annual outlays in the form of grants and loans. The loan component was borrowed by the center from the market and then passed on to the states at an interest rate that was at times 300–400 basis points higher than the borrowing cost. However, with states unable to abide by their debt obligations and the center unwilling to interrupt the planning process, the states were able to borrow increasingly more funds from the center just to keep going.

The Twelfth Finance Commission now advanced a radical solution to resolve the states' debt problem. It required that, in the future, the center should terminate its role as an intermediary between the market and the states, and the states should be encouraged to rely directly on the market for their borrowing needs at market interest rates. Along with this change, which linked the states directly to the market and its discipline, the hard budget constraint would be enforced in order to induce fiscal discipline among the states and to attenuate moral hazard.[36]

Debt Restructuring. Even with the installation of this new "borrowing regime" for the states, the issue of the overhang of past accumulated debt still remained. Here, the commission offered a debt restructuring plan, which consisted of two parts. One part involved a debt swap under which the debt owed by any state to the center would be consolidated and then rescheduled for a new period of twenty years at an interest rate of 7.5 percent (compared to the contemporaneous average of 10.5 percent). This package of consolidation and rescheduling of debt would save the states Rs. 212.76 billion on interest payments and Rs. 119.29 billion on repayments of the principal.[37] The commission sought to use this facility as leverage for fiscal reform in the states, and therefore made it dependent on compliance with an explicit conditionality, which required that states adopt fiscal responsibility legislation on the pattern of the center's FRBM Act that would commit them to phasing out the revenue deficit entirely by 2008–9. At the same time, such legislation would lay down annual targets for reducing revenue and fiscal deficits.[38]

The other part of the debt restructuring plan was much bolder, and it involved debt write-offs. Under it, repayment write-offs were linked directly to fiscal performance; they were made dependent on the quantum of annual reduction of the revenue deficit. Eligibility for the scheme was limited to states that contained their fiscal deficits to at least the level of 2004–5. As with debt consolidation, debt write-offs also required fiscal responsibility legislation as a prerequisite. If all states abided by these requirements, the total amount to be written off would be a staggering Rs. 322 billion by 2008–9.[39] Observers considered the commission's recommendations to be both sagacious and generous. Interestingly, Bagchi, who had earlier strongly protested against conditionalities, was quite appreciative of the Twelfth Finance Commission's work and raised no objection to the new conditionalities on the states.

For the Finance Commission as an institution, the encounter with the task of fiscal consolidation was a novel experience. Understandably, an adequate policy to cope with the challenge of fiscal deterioration and fiscal stress did not emerge suddenly in response. Rather, the institution worked out such a policy through an evolutionary process of learning by doing over the course of three commissions, from the tenth to the twelfth. The Tenth Finance Commission had started the process with a sharp analysis of the fiscal deterioration, and linked its debt relief scheme to fiscal performance. The Eleventh Finance Commission carried it forward further, supplementing it with conditionalities, but only weak incentives for effective implementation. Finally, a substantial fiscal reform program that was linked to adequate incentives emerged with the Twelfth Finance Commission, and it had a significant impact.

Thirteenth Finance Commission (2010–2015): Sustaining Fiscal Consolidation and Economic Growth

When the Thirteenth Finance Commission was appointed in November 2007, India's fiscal situation had vastly improved, perhaps principally because of the growth acceleration after 2002–3. While other factors may have been at work, not least the fiscal correction measures recommended by the Twelfth Finance Commission, the buoyant economy had been instrumental in restoring fiscal health at the center and in the states, essentially by boosting revenues. Fiscal deficit, revenue deficit, and public debt at the center as a share of GDP had dropped from 4.48, 3.57, and 43.12 percent, respectively, in 2003–4, to 2.69 (that is, less than 3.00), 1.11, and 40.66 percent in 2007–8. The fiscal performance of the states was even better; their aggregate fiscal deficit and revenue deficit as a share of GDP came down from 3.40 and 1.25 percent, respectively, in 2004–5, to 1.51 and minus 0.94 percent in 2007–8; similarly, their public debt as a proportion of the aggregate GSDP (gross state domestic product) fell from 40.49 to 35.28 percent.[40] India thus seemed well on its way to accomplishing its goal of fiscal consolidation.

Expanded Agenda for Finance Commission. That happy prospect did not materialize, however, as the fiscal consolidation could not be sustained. First, there were domestic shocks resulting from hefty wage hikes for the bureaucracy, a massive waiver of farm loans by the center, and the launching of major welfare measures. Second, there were external shocks by way of the global spiraling of commodity prices, which added to the center's subsidy bill for fuel and fertilizer, and then the global financial meltdown in 2008, which necessitated a stimulus program that added to revenue and fiscal deficits. The center hurried to add another item to the Thirteenth Finance Commission's already heavy and complex agenda, asking it "to review the roadmap for fiscal adjustment and suggest a suitably revised roadmap with a view to maintaining the gains of fiscal consolidation."[41]

A New Road Map for Fiscal Consolidation. In charting out a new road map, the commission was clear-eyed on what its central aim ought to be—not merely to get back to the path of fiscal adjustment, but to sustain the economy's growth dynamism. For the commission, growth was key. There was a two-way logic in the relationship between fiscal consolidation and a rapidly growing economy in its strategy of "expansionary fiscal consolidation": fiscal consolidation engendered higher economic growth since it made possible increased investment, while higher growth was enabling for fiscal stability because of the increased revenues it brought in to the government. Sustaining the resultant virtuous cycle was not, however, simply a matter of reducing deficits and debts, but one that required to be supplemented by structural reform through enhancing the productivity of public expenditure, advancing the economy's competitiveness, "and above all better governance at all levels of government through increased transparency and accountability."[42]

Strictly in terms of resuming the path of fiscal consolidation, the commission emphasized the need to bring down public debt sharply in view of "the imperative of creating an environment favorable to private investment in the Indian economy."[43] The commission laid down the target for debt at 68 percent by 2014–15 (center, 45 percent; states, less than 25 percent), which was slightly more ambitious than the Twelfth Finance Commission's earlier target of 75 percent. The Thirteenth Finance Commission's consolidation path for the center in terms of revenue and fiscal deficits, however, was similar to that of the Twelfth Finance Commission. It required progressive reduction and final elimination of the revenue deficit by 2013–14, and thereafter instituting a permanent policy of no more revenue deficit in line with the "golden rule" of no borrowing for consumption purposes. Similarly, it asked for the fiscal deficit to be reduced to 3 percent by 2013–14.[44] None of this came to pass, however, since the economy entered into a crisis around 2012, not only as an aftermath of the worldwide financial meltdown but also because of economic mismanagement by, and policy paralysis in, the government.

As for fiscal consolidation at the state level, the Thirteenth Finance Commission was evidently pleased with the performance of the states following the adoption of fiscal responsibility legislation by twenty-six of the twenty-eight states (Sikkim and West Bengal being the only two exceptions). The states had met the revenue and fiscal deficit targets ahead of schedule; even their debt at less than 30 percent of GDP was quite close to the target of 28 percent; besides, all general category states and three special category states no longer had postdevolution nonplan revenue deficits.[45]

In the circumstance, the Thirteenth Finance Commission encouraged the states to continue doing what they had been doing in following the golden rule of zero revenue deficit and, indeed, to make it "a long term and permanent target." The commission also asked the states to amend their fiscal responsibility legislation to set the targets for revenue deficit at 0 percent or less and for fiscal deficit at 3 percent. As an incentive for the states to do so, it made the release of all state-specific grants conditional on such amendments. At the same time, it asked that the center prescribe borrowing limits for each state on the basis of that state's performance with respect to the fiscal deficit road map as determined by the commission; these borrowing limits were to serve as "an enforcement mechanism for the fiscal correction by states."[46]

The Thirteenth Finance Commission was apparently sensitive to objections about such conditionalities. However, its posture on the issue seemingly flowed naturally out of the imperative concern for macroeconomic stability. In modern economies, macroeconomic stability is uniquely and inescapably the responsibility of the central government. However, fiscal consolidation of the nation-state is inextricably linked with the fiscal behavior of the constituent states; the two cannot be compartmentalized, nor can either in isolation be shielded from the impact of international economic forces, especially in a sharply more integrated world economy. Conditionalities at the states' level thus issue out of these fundamental facts of contemporary economic existence. The commission's overall approach in this context was: "We have also carried forward the practice, introduced by FC-XII [Twelfth Finance Commission], of incentivizing fiscal consolidation by states. The intent is not to restrict the discretionary latitude of states with respect to their fiscal domain, but to secure commitment by all states to the national fiscal consolidation required for achievement of macroeconomic stability."[47]

In summary, with the Twelfth Finance Commission having shown the way of what could be accomplished through effective incentives, the Thirteenth Finance Commission could take a more relaxed view of fiscal consolidation in the states. Meanwhile, it was undoubtedly helped in this view by the realization on the part of the states, too, that conditionalities had been helpful to their own fiscal recovery and contributed more to their fiscal autonomy in substantive terms by giving them control over larger resources than any rhetoric about such autonomy would have done.

RATIONALIZATION AND MODERNIZATION OF DEVOLUTION AND DISTRIBUTION

Contemporary economic thinking on public finance places considerable emphasis on issues of system design, sound incentives, avoiding perverse incentives, simplification of procedures, and transparency and accountability. Advancing this element of rationalization and modernization is certainly evident in the work of postliberalization finance commissions with regard to fiscal transfers in the areas of both devolution and distribution, which had constituted the principal function of past commissions.

Tenth Finance Commission: Pathbreaking Innovations

While the venerable civil servant S. Guhan had certainly appreciated the Tenth Finance Commission's initiatives in the area of fiscal consolidation, he thought that "conceptually, the most interesting part" of its work related to its alternative scheme on fiscal devolution and distribution.[48] Looking at devolution first, the Tenth Finance Commission dealt with the issue in two different ways—the conventional and the novel (or radical). Realizing that shifting to the novel procedure would require a time-consuming constitutional amendment, by deliberate choice, the commission worked out a formula within the conventional approach in which the final outcome in terms of devolution to the states would be the same as in its radical proposal. Thoughtfully, it did this in order to facilitate the transition from the conventional mode to the novel one. In both cases, with fiscal stress as the backdrop, it was guided by considerations of efficiency and equity, eager to provide incentives to greater tax effort in relation to the former and to not disturb the share of the states with respect to the latter.

Radical Change in Vertical Devolution. Constitutionally and traditionally, fiscal transfers from the center to the states through the Finance Commission had been tax-specific, revolving around the "net" proceeds from two taxes—income tax and excise duties—each dealt separately, using different criteria. The share of the states had climbed incrementally from 55 percent of net revenues from income tax with the First Finance Commission to as high as 85 percent with the Seventh, Eighth, and Ninth Finance Commissions, leaving little incentive to the national government to be efficient in collecting this particular tax. Interestingly, however, some states clamored for even more, asking that it be raised to 95 or 100 percent. As in the case of income tax, the share of the states in excise duties, which began modestly at 40 percent with regard to only three commodities with the First Finance Commission, had expanded over time to 45 percent for *all* commodities. Again, the states wanted this share increased to 55 or 60 percent.

The Tenth Finance Commission, however, decided to reduce the share of the states in income tax from 85.0 percent to 77.5 percent in order to provide the center greater incentive in tax collection. At the same time, to compensate the states by an equivalent amount for the loss from income tax, the commission raised the share of the states in excise duties to 47.5 percent.[49] Importantly, the Tenth Finance Commission dispensed with the application of separate criteria to the distribution of revenues from income tax and excise duties. Instead, it used the same criteria for both taxes. Guhan believed that this "adoption of an identical formula, predominantly based on population and the distance criterion [in terms of per capita income], is a reform that is sound and progressive in its logic."[50]

Far more interesting than these changes in the traditional approach, however, was the radical step that the commission recommended on an "alternative devolution scheme," the essence of which was to get away from limiting devolution to the states from the center to just income tax and excise duties. Under this new scheme, any future finance commission would have under its mandate the entire corpus of *gross* proceeds of *all* taxes of the center (except surcharges and cesses), with the commission then allocating a certain share to the states from this combined or "divisible" pool. This was a sharp change from the constitutionally dictated practice and a giant leap forward to simplicity in fiscal transfers. The Tenth Finance Commission saw merit in the new move since "it would make the vertical sharing simple and transparent." The commission felt: "In the context of the current economic reforms, this new arrangement is likely to have distinct advantages over the present system." More specifically, the new scheme would allow the states to share in the overall buoyancy of the central taxes, even though they would feel "the impact of the fluctuations" as well. The scheme would also give the national government the freedom to determine its tax policy in an integrated manner, uninhibited by concerns over not getting an adequate share of the tax proceeds. Importantly, it would additionally remove suspicions on the part of states about the center being selective in its application of efficiency in collecting specific taxes.[51] In Guhan's view, the alternative scheme "may prove to be a historic contribution if it stimulates thought and action on a rational restructuring of federal fiscal transfers."[52]

The idea of this alternative pattern of devolution was not original to the Tenth Finance Commission; the Tax Reforms Committee under Raja Chelliah had broached it in 1991. Indeed, the Ministry of Finance itself had suggested to the Tenth Finance Commission that it may want to examine the desirability of shifting to a pattern of tax sharing based on the center's entire tax pool. It had favored placing the share for the states at 22–23 percent for a fixed period of twenty years.[53] Apparently, it was only with economic liberalization that the idea was first mooted and became a matter for serious consideration. The Tenth Finance Commission made a formal recommendation for its adoption, allocating a share to the states from the total divisible pool, but one that was much larger than what the Ministry of Finance had contemplated—26 percent plus an additional 3 percent, in a fifteen-year arrangement.[54]

The Tenth Finance Commission's bold move on vertical devolution demonstrated the self-correcting and self-steering capacity of the state in India at the time, though it required the pressure of fiscal distress and the general thrust of economic liberalization to persuade it to act.

Horizontal Distribution. In relation to horizontal distribution among the states, too, the commission's proposals were "a significant step forward in terms of logic, simplicity and equity," as they applied uniform criteria with respect to distribution for *both* income tax and excise duties. The origins of this seminal change, though unacknowledged, actually lay in a note of dissent that the late Dr. Raj Krishna had given in 1978 to the Seventh Finance Commission.[55]

The hallmark of horizontal distribution is supposed to be progressiveness, but ironically, several past commissions had at one time advantaged the richer states by using, even if only in part, the criterion of state contributions to the central collections of income tax. The Tenth Finance Commission's own common criteria for distribution of both income tax and excise duties were based on population, 20 percent; per capita income distance (or disadvantage relative to the top three states), 60 percent; tax effort, 10 percent; area, 5 percent; and infrastructure weakness, 5 percent. Conceptually, population and income distance represented *need*; area (dispersed territory) and infrastructure weakness reflected *cost disability*; and tax effort as also fiscal discipline depicted *fiscal efficiency*.[56] If one takes income distance and infrastructure weakness as representing economic backwardness, the Tenth Finance Commission's total weight of 65 percent for it symbolized its readiness to be helpful to the disadvantaged states.

Overall, the Tenth Finance Commission's work on devolution and distribution was truly pathbreaking and established the mold for the functioning of subsequent finance commissions.

Eleventh Finance Commission: Tweaking the Numbers, but Questioning Tax Assignments

The predominant concern of the Eleventh Finance Commission was the situation of extreme fiscal stress and how to promote fiscal correction. In the circumstance, it did not invest too much effort on the nuts and bolts of the task of devolution and distribution, though its concern with fiscal correction did not leave that task entirely unaffected.

The center's memorandum to the Eleventh Finance Commission had underlined that a key reason for the high fiscal deficit at the center was the high magnitude of revenue transfers to the states. However, the commission made little change with respect to devolution of tax revenues; it merely tweaked the ratio of 29.0 percent of the center's *net* tax revenues for devolution to states by raising it to 29.5 percent. At the same time, it took a more comprehensive view of resource transfers in order to protect the interests of both the center and the states. In this endeavor, it now placed an "indicative limit" or ceiling on total transfers to the states (including transfers by the Planning Commission and central ministries) at 37.5 percent of the center's gross revenues, regardless of the channels under which they were transmitted.[57]

With little change in the devolution of tax revenues, the commission sought to accomplish its goal of reducing fiscal and revenue deficits through "providing a structure of incentives which is designed to reward fiscal prudence and discourage fiscal profligacy." It did this directly by adding fiscal discipline (7.5

percent) to the criteria for distribution of revenue shares among the states—population, 10.0 percent; income distance, 62.5 percent; area, 7.5 percent; infrastructure weakness, 7.5 percent; and tax effort, 5.0 percent. The commission also attempted to aid fiscal consolidation indirectly by strengthening the "normative principle" or "normative approach" through applying it more systematically in assessing the needs and resources of the states.[58]

"Vertical Imbalance" and Reassignment of Tax Powers. Although the Eleventh Finance Commission may not have elaborated much on the nuts and bolts of devolution and distribution, it raised a more fundamental issue about the assignment of tax powers that demands a deeper analysis. It pointed out in its report that a "vertical imbalance" existed between the center and states with regard to revenues because of the constitutional assignment of tax powers, and it went on to prescribe reassignment of these powers: "A major source of fiscal instability is the vertical imbalance that necessitates transfer of revenues from the Center to the States. The first step towards achieving fiscal stability and accountability is to reduce this vertical imbalance as much as possible so that the governments at all levels are able to raise the resources they require, keeping the need for transfers at a minimum. This in turn calls for a review of the scheme of assignment of tax powers and functions between the Center and the States in our Constitution."[59] This position of the commission corresponds closely with Bagchi's own view that "the new India's constitution built into it provisions that invested the center with a position of dominance. These detracted from its character as a *true federation*. . . . In several respects, *the unitary elements clearly overshadowed the federal attribute*."[60] By extension, apparently the same imbalance between the center and the states manifested itself more specifically in the fiscal arena as well. Similarly, Govinda Rao holds that "the constitution exhibits a clear *centripetal* bias in the distribution of tax and regulatory powers," and he also refers to "the centralization inherent in the constitutional assignment of powers . . . a high degree of fiscal centralization and vertical fiscal imbalance."[61]

Interestingly, both Bagchi and Rao attribute the center's dominance or centralization to the fact of the constitution being framed in the wake of the traumatic experience of partition, which for Bagchi provoked fears among decision makers about further breakup of the country while for Rao it removed a political obstacle to a strong center.[62] While there may be merit in this attribution (albeit not novel) of the overall domination of the center or its centripetal character to the historical fact of partition and secessionist threats, Bagchi and Rao err fundamentally in assuming that the same argument can be extended to the assignment of tax powers and, thus, to the "vertical imbalance." There is likely an "ecological fallacy" at work here, according to which what is true of the whole is necessarily true of all its parts. Quite the contrary, the vertical imbalance in federal finance does not flow at all from some hidden attempt by the center at independence to grab excessive tax powers at the cost of the states in a grand endeavor at centralization. Indeed, it is absolutely mistaken to set the center against the states on the particular issue of vertical imbalance.

Fundamentally, the vertical imbalance flows directly out of the "horizontal imbalance" that actually exists in the country—the fact of unequal development among the states, where the states were and are at different levels of development and, therefore, of wealth. Simply put, if there had been no horizontal imbalance, there would likely have been no vertical imbalance, except perhaps that which was dictated by considerations of efficiency in tax collection. There were certainly plenty of political stalwarts from the regions to fight for the rights of the provinces (states) in the Constituent Assembly, incidentally, a body elected indirectly by provincial legislatures. Despite that, the provinces agreed to the distribution of financial powers in the constitution that made the center the custodian of the more lucrative taxes. Why?

The paramount reason that the provinces agreed to the particular distribution of financial powers was the division among them, then as now, between the rich and the poor provinces. That made equity considerations elemental. The basic question then was, as it would be now if the issue would be reopened: What would happen to the poor provinces if a larger area of tax powers was left with the provinces? The poor provinces of the time were interested more in resources or revenues than in tax powers as such. The redistribution that they wanted on the basis of need could not take place among the provinces if they were left to manage them alone. They, therefore, chose to let the center have the tax powers and distribute the revenues. It is thus the division between the rich and poor provinces—not the partition or the fear of secession—that is responsible for the particular vertical fiscal imbalance. Granville Austin's testimony in his classic work on the Indian Constitution is decisive on this point:

> The logical result of these views was increased Union authority. With the provinces—or at least seven out of the nine of them, not counting the former Princely States—in favor of sharing revenues *on the basis of need*, there had to be an agency to fulfill this coordinating role, to collect the revenues of the richer provinces and to distribute them among the poorer. Certainly revenues could not be effectively divided by province-to-province negotiations. The inevitable third party between the wealthy and the poorer provinces was the Union Government—whose part as dispenser of bounty would be watched over by the Finance Commissions.[63]

No doubt, the states wanted a greater share of the revenues, but for the states as a whole, the distribution of which would be determined by a body appointed by the center. Furthermore, while every state wanted a greater share, it was to meet its social responsibilities and absolutely not "from any dream of 'provincial autonomy,'" as Austin underlined.[64]

In retrospect, perhaps the poor states have not benefited sufficiently from the mechanism for distribution of tax revenues in the constitution as they thought they would. It is well-known that interstate disparities have continued and, in some respects, increased over the decades. There may be many causes for the persistence or the increase of regional disparities, such as initial conditions, nature of governance, and economies of agglomeration. However, such persistence or increase cannot necessarily be attributed to the failure of finance commissions to single-handedly mitigate regional disparities.

Whatever may have been the failure earlier in this respect, since the Eighth Finance Commission, considerable weight has been accorded to economic backwardness in the recommendations by finance commissions.[65] In the schema of the Tenth Finance Commission for distribution of revenues among the states, the weights were: population, 20 percent; per capita income distance (that is, disadvantage), 60 percent; infrastructure weakness, 5 percent; and others, 15 percent. The Eleventh Finance Commission marginally improved the progressive elements: population, 10.0 percent; per capita income distance, 62.5 percent; infrastructure weakness, 7.5 percent; and others, 20.0 percent. It is striking, however, that the Eleventh Finance Commission's report was followed by an uproar on the part of the nonpoor states, led by the then Andhra Pradesh chief minister Chandrababu Naidu, over the commission having allegedly discriminated against them in favoring equity over superior and prudent fiscal management.[66] The moral of this episode is quite clear—the poor states could not really expect social justice from their richer fellow states, but only from the center and its institutions (regardless of their many imperfections), and that their ancestors had chosen wisely in determining the assignment of tax powers. In this light, it would seem that the approach of the Eleventh Finance Commission and of the NIPFP school on reassignment of tax powers to rectify the vertical imbalance was really a regressive one and, in objective terms, meant siding with the richer states even if it may not have been so intended.

Twelfth Finance Commission: Further Modernizing Devolution and Distribution

At first sight, any superficial review of the recommendations of the Twelfth Finance Commission is likely to suggest that the commission merely tweaked the numbers inherited from the previous commission—undoubtedly, to the benefit of the states—by increasing the share of the states in the net proceeds of the center's shareable taxes from 29.5 to 30.5 percent and by similarly increasing the "indicative limit" of all central transfers to the states from 37.5 to 38.0 percent.[67]

Indeed, it may further seem that the commission had grievously erred—perhaps in an attempt to preempt protests from the better-off states—in reversing the progressive trend in the distribution among the states by downgrading the role of equity. Such a reversal may be seen in the commission drastically reducing the weight given to the criterion of per capita income distance (to 50.0 percent from the Eleventh Finance Commission's 62.5 percent) and eliminating altogether the criterion of infrastructure weakness, while upgrading the role of efficiency by increasing the weight for tax effort from 5.0 percent to 7.5 percent and retaining that of fiscal discipline at 7.5 percent.[68] Such a reading of the commission's intent would, however, not only misrepresent the commission's thinking but also be the very opposite of the direction that the commission wanted fiscal federalism to take.

An indication of what was central to the thinking of the commission in terms of equity among the states is the importance it gave to the concept of "equalization" as a guiding principle in fiscal transfers in view of its potential contribution to both equity and efficiency.[69] The aim of such equalization in fiscal transfers is to insure that all citizens, regardless of the state in which they may be located, have the same access to certain basic public goods and services. The concept itself is not new to finance commissions in India. Interestingly, it was first articulated by the First Finance Commission (1952–57), which stated that "an important purpose of grants-in-aid is to help in equalizing standards of basic social services."[70]

While equalization funds can compensate the states in this manner for any deficiency in fiscal capacity, at the same time, it is also important that such funding does not undermine the states' own revenue effort, a point that makes intelligible the commission's emphasis on tax effort and fiscal discipline among the criteria for the horizontal distribution of shareable taxes. In this respect, the Twelfth Finance Commission reemphasized the importance of the "normative" approach in order to neutralize any adverse incentives. At the same time, it was appreciative of the application of the equalization principle in Canada and Australia, both of which the commission visited. No doubt the commission was constrained by the weight of past practice in India's fiscal federalism from making a clean break in favor of applying the principle on a larger, if not full, scale, but Bagchi gave it "credit for at least trying to carry the logic of equalization further than any FC [Finance Commission] in the past."[71]

A key mechanism in the explicit introduction—partial, no doubt, at this stage—of the equalization principle by the Twelfth Finance Commission was the considerable change it recommended from the recent past about the division of fiscal transfers from the center as between tax devolution and grants-in-aid. Traditionally, the fiscal transfers under the auspices of finance commissions have accounted for about two-thirds of the total fiscal transfers from the center to the states (the remainder being managed through economic planning and the central ministries). For their part, finance commissions have employed two routes to further distribute this part to the states—tax devolution (which states prefer since it is without conditions and is regarded as flowing from a constitutional entitlement) and grants-in-aid (which may be either "unconditional and general purpose or conditional and purpose-specific"). For its part, the Twelfth Finance

Commission saw the grants-in-aid as a superior instrument for purposes of redistribution and, accordingly, "allowed a greater role for grants in overall finance commission transfers."[72] It is noteworthy that, in the case of the five finance commissions prior to the Twelfth Finance Commission, grants had a share on the average of less than 10.0 percent as compared to tax devolution, which was apportioned a little more than 90.0 percent; even the 10.0 percent share is an exaggeration since the average is boosted by the unusual figure of 13.47 percent for the Eleventh Finance Commission. In any case, as against this average, the Twelfth Finance Commission raised the share of grants to 18.87 percent in an effort to advance equalization.[73]

With the extra leverage of a larger share for grants, the Twelfth Finance Commission decided to contribute to equalization among the states, even if only in a limited manner at this time, through focusing on two social sectors, that of education and health.[74] The amounts allocated were strictly an addition, intended to supplement what was currently being spent by either the state or the center in these areas. In this fashion, the commission sought to enhance the progressive element in fiscal transfers to the states.

Thirteenth Finance Commission: Refining and Elaborating Devolution and Distribution

The Twelfth Finance Commission had made equalization a key objective in its handling of the issue of devolution and distribution. Perhaps continuity with that objective over a substantial period would have made for stability in policy over time and thus enabled analysts to assess its consequences. However, the Thirteenth Finance Commission chose to replace it with an idiom that had greater resonance with contemporaneous policymaking—"inclusiveness."[75]

As the necessary initial step to horizontal distribution, the commission increased the share of the states in the divisible pool of net tax proceeds of the center from the Twelfth Finance Commission's 30.5 percent to 32.0 percent, and raised the "indicative ceiling on all revenue account transfers" (including those from the Finance Commission, Planning Commission, and central ministries) from the Twelfth Finance Commission's 38.0 percent to 39.5 percent. The increase seems to be indicative of a fashionable trend, with every successor commission proceeding as if invariably it has to incrementally raise the share of the states established by its predecessor.

In the distribution of fiscal transfers among the states, recent commissions have used both equity and efficiency as the guiding principles in their choice of criteria and the weights assigned to them. Table 5.1 displays the criteria and the weights from the Tenth to the Thirteenth Finance Commissions. It is apparent that the Thirteenth Finance Commission has further simplified the distribution by reducing the number of criteria to four from the six of the Eleventh Finance Commission and five of the Twelfth Finance Commission. But it has also added

Table 5.1. Fiscal Transfers to States by Finance Commissions: Criteria and Weights (%)

Criterion	*Tenth*	*Eleventh*	*Twelfth*	*Thirteenth*
Population	20.0	10.0	25.0	25.0
Area	5.0	7.5	10.0	10.0
Income Distance/Fiscal Capacity Distance	60.0	62.5	50.0	47.5
Infrastructure Weakness	5.0	7.5	—	—
Fiscal Discipline	—	7.5	7.5	17.5
Tax Effort	10.0	5.0	7.5	—

Sources: Reports of the various finance commissions; see also D. K. Srivastava, "Vertical Sharing and Horizontal Distribution of Resources: The Equity and Efficiency Trade-Off," *Economic and Political Weekly* 45, no. 48 (November 27, 2010): 64–70.

to complexity by changing the simple criterion of per capita income distance as a proxy for tax capacity (or, interpreted differently, need) to a more complicated one of "fiscal capacity distance," worked out on the basis of three-year averages of state GSDP. Public finance experts, however, did not see much merit in this particular innovation.[76]

Regardless, what is striking is the decline in the element of progressiveness or equity as reflected in the shrinking weight of the distance criterion from the Eleventh Finance Commission (70.0 percent, as a combined figure for distance and infrastructure) to the Twelfth Finance Commission (50.0 percent) and then again to the Thirteenth Finance Commission (47.5 percent). Correspondingly, there is a consistent rise in the weight of fiscal discipline from the Eleventh Finance Commission (12.5 percent, as a combined figure for fiscal discipline and tax effort) to the Twelfth Finance Commission (15.0 percent) and to the Thirteenth Finance Commission (17.5 percent). It is interesting to note that the protests mounted by the better-off states against the Eleventh Finance Commission's report were not evident after the Twelfth and Thirteenth Finance Commissions submitted their reports. Perhaps the inference is unjustified, but reducing the weight of the distance criterion and boosting the weight of fiscal discipline may have been an attempt to appease the better-off states; interestingly, two authors (a former chairman and a member of the Twelfth Finance Commission, respectively) state: "A large part of equalization should be delivered through grants rather than devolution. This will create the possibility of reducing the weight attached to the distance formula a little more and arrest the fall in the share of high income and middle income states."[77]

Impact of Distribution on Equalization. A critical question relates to the impact of fiscal transfers from the center to the states under the auspices of the Finance Commission, both by way of tax devolution and grants-in-aid. Despite the various criticisms leveled from time to time against the Finance Commission's schema of fiscal transfers, it can still be maintained that the commission does a fairly reasonable job in providing for equalization. Important insight into this aspect is provided by an ingenious analysis by Dr. D. K. Srivastava, a senior authority on public finance, in which he investigates the impact of fiscal transfers by the Thirteenth Finance Commission.

Srivastava takes fiscal transfers to a state as consisting of three components: (1) a "vertical component," which is an amount equal to that received by the highest per capita income state, on the understanding that all the other states will receive an amount that is higher than that because of the additional transfers to them from the other two components; (2) an "equalizing component," which reflects compensation for the weakness in fiscal capacity; and (3) a "residual component" that covers special needs and incentive allocations. Srivastava's analysis demonstrated that the "vertical component" in fiscal transfers to all the states amounted to 54 percent of total transfers, with the rest belonging to the other two components. The "residual component" covering special needs and incentives was less than 10 percent of total transfers. The remainder of about 36 percent thus belonged to the "equalizing component," and Srivastava concluded that it would "be able to achieve 90.5% of the needed equalization. This is commendable."[78] In another analysis with respect to the Twelfth Finance Commission, Rangarajan and Srivastava maintain that "the degree of equalization achieved was nearly 88 percent."[79]

SUMMARY AND CONCLUSION

As the key institution of the state in the area of fiscal federalism, the Finance Commission is by its very nature an integrative mechanism. As a sort of pan-Indian institution, it promotes integration through its very engagement in an active process of consultation on an India-wide basis with all the major stakeholders in the fiscal federal process—center, states, and interest groups—before rendering its award-like recommendations on the extent and mode of fiscal transfers from the center to the states. It has worked under a variety of political dispensations and, consisting of highly qualified professional authorities, it has shown a considerable degree of independence.

Both the Finance Commission and the state of which it is a part have demonstrated remarkable adaptive capacity in dealing with the challenges to fiscal federalism emergent from economic liberalization, directly or indirectly. In the process, the Finance Commission itself has undergone substantial change in its management of fiscal transfers. The direct and indirect impact of economic liberalization on the functioning of the Finance Commission is evident in two important areas. First, the Finance Commission has vastly expanded the scope of its work after being entrusted with the entirely novel task of assessing the country's fiscal condition and making recommendations on fiscal correction and consolidation both at the center and, especially, in the states. Through a process of learning by doing over the course of several successive appointments, the

Finance Commission finally figured out the right mix of policies, incorporating financial incentives and conditionalities, to encourage fiscal reform in the states with a view to fostering fiscal consolidation. Second, the Finance Commission has rationalized and modernized the process of devolution and distribution of fiscal transfers, bringing in greater simplicity and transparency to the process. Further, it attempted with reasonable success to juggle the competing claims of equity and efficiency in the distribution of fiscal transfers among the states with varying fiscal needs and capacity.

Fiscal consolidation, with its conditionalities, may have been initially resented by the states, but it was made palatable—indeed, profitable—for them through the accompanying financial accommodation in the form of debt consolidation and debt write-offs, the burden of which the Finance Commission placed on the center. With the hindsight of experience, the states, too, realized that the conditionalities had widened their fiscal space by enabling them to put their public finances on a more solid basis. Through the combination of *firmness* (conditionalities for fiscal reform) and *accommodation* (additional resources), the commission and the center were able to cope with the challenges to fiscal federalism after economic liberalization. Ironically, insofar as the process of fiscal consolidation on a national basis was inspired or aided by liberalization and globalization since such consolidation is central to these efficiency-driven processes, it seems that globalization and liberalization also have been "nationalizing" for India rather than simply segmenting it economically, as assumed by the critics.

The fiscal accommodation extended by the Finance Commission and the center to the states is evident, not only in consolidating the states' debt and the debt relief accorded to them but also in the overall fiscal comfort provided to them with more generous fiscal transfers from the center. These fiscal transfers to the states demonstrate a slight rising trend over the recent *medium* term. Table 5.2 provides data on the share of the center and states in their *combined* revenue receipts. It shows that the share of the states has tended to rise after Finance Commission transfers (and also after total transfers) while, conversely, the share of the center has tended to decline over the period since the Eighth Finance Commission (1984–89), which largely coincides with the postliberalization period. Any conception of the center as having been niggardly toward the states is thus shown decidedly to be a myth. Note that the share of the states in the total revenue receipts of the nation (center and states combined) is almost two-thirds under the Eleventh and Twelfth Finance Commissions, while that of the center is only about a third—that is, the share of the states is about twice that of the center in India's total revenues. Note, too—in view of the criticism about the multiplicity of channels in fiscal transfers—that the bulk of transfers have taken place under the auspices of the rule-based institution of the Finance Commission, particularly during the periods of the Tenth, Eleventh, and Twelfth Finance Commissions.

Table 5.2. Share of the Center and States in Combined Revenue Receipts (%)

Average for Commission Periods	*Share of Center*			*Share of States*		
	Before Transfers	*After FC Transfers*	*After Total Transfers*	*Before Transfers*	*After FC Transfers*	*After Total Transfers*
Eighth	65.4	49.1	38.7	34.6	50.9	61.3
Ninth	62.8	45.6	35.3	37.2	54.4	64.7
Tenth	60.8	44.1	36.3	39.2	55.9	63.7
Eleventh	58.5	40.4	33.3	41.5	59.6	66.7
Twelfth*	62.6	42.4	35.7	37.4	57.6	64.3

Source: Adapted from GoI, Thirteenth Finance Commission, *Report* (New Delhi: December 2009), 61.
Note: *Average for first three years.

Statistical data can at times make for differing interpretations, especially over the short or medium term. But the considerable change in favor of the states in resource transfers from the center is made tellingly manifest by data *over the long term*. An analysis by Rangarajan and Srivastava demonstrates a wide divergence between the fiscal transfers by the first three and the tenth to twelfth commissions. Whereas the fiscal transfers to the states as a share of the center's gross revenue receipts (and as a share of GDP) during the period of the first three commissions stood at 23.9, 30.7, and 25.1 percent (and 1.2, 2.0, and 2.3 percent), respectively, the figures were 35.6, 35.9, and 40.8 percent (and 4.1, 4.2, and 5.2 percent) during the period of the tenth to twelfth commissions, respectively.[80]

To be sure, states are likely to continue to manifest "voice" (complain) against the center, since that provides them with greater leverage in bargaining for increasingly more revenues. However, the Organization for Economic Cooperation and Development (OECD) has conclusively shown how extraordinary India is in the generous apportionment of revenues to the states, indeed unmatched by any other OECD federation. States' revenues as a share of total revenues in 2002 were 67.3 percent in India, compared to 38.8 percent in Australia, 47.7 percent in Canada, and 35.2 percent in the United States.[81] Indeed, even Bagchi, a strong critic of India's fiscal federalism, had perforce to acknowledge in 2003 that: "Judged by the share of the states in aggregate government expenditure the allegation about centrist bias would not appear to be valid. Of the total government expenditures in India the states have consistently accounted for more than 50 percent, and the proportion now stands at nearly 58 percent . . . as compared to no more than 40 percent in USA (including the expenditure of local governments) and 45 percent in Australia."[82]

The pattern of distribution of revenues *before* transfers undoubtedly shows a vertical imbalance as between center and states (table 5.2), but that is a function of the horizontal imbalance in fiscal capacity among the states, in turn related to the state of development. Remarkably, the poorer states seem to trust the center more with the assignment of larger tax powers than they do their fellow richer states. While economic disparities may have increased, the Finance Commission still provides a considerable degree of equalization in revenue sharing.

Overall, it is manifest that the Indian state has managed quite reasonably well the challenge of economic segmentation that the critics of globalization had underlined. This has been done not only through fiscal transfers under the auspices of the Finance Commission but also through other mechanisms such as tax reform, which is discussed in chapter 6.

As for fiscal consolidation, the Finance Commission has had a fair amount of success at the level of the states. Success at the center has been more problematic, in large part because running a transitional country under a democratic framework tends to push political elites toward intermittent bouts of competitive populism and thus toward fiscal profligacy. But that is less a function of globalization and economic liberalization, and more of the internal nature of society and polity.

NOTES

1. See D. K. Srivastava and Bhujanga C. Rao, "Fiscal Relations between the Center and the States: Dependence of States on Devolution of Funds," in GoI, *Commission on Center–State Relations: Supplementary Volume-II: Research Studies* (New Delhi: Commission on Center–State Relations, March 2010), 1–78.

2. Calculated from data in GoI, Thirteenth Finance Commission, 2010–2015, *Volume I: Report* (New Delhi: Finance Commission, December 2009), 61; hereafter cited as GoI, Thirteenth Finance Commission, *Report*. Total transfers from the center to the states, including transfers under the auspices of the Finance Commission, are even more massive; they increase the states' own revenue receipts by 60 percent to more than 75 percent.

3. GoI, *Finance Ministers' Budget Speeches, 1947 to 1996* (New Delhi: Lok Sabha Secretariat, 1996), 2:1294; emphasis added.

4. See Amaresh Bagchi, "Evaluating India's Fiscal Federalism: Some Reflections on Past Half Century," in *Fiscal Federalism in India*, ed. P. K. Chaubey (New Delhi: Deep and Deep, 2003), 86–103. The third in Musgrave's trilogy of fiscal functions of government is "resource allocation," which would obviously be shared in a federal polity.

5. Ha-Joon Chang, *Globalization, Economic Development and the Role of the State* (London: Zed Books, 2003), chaps. 2–3.

6. M. Govinda Rao and Nirvikar Singh, *The Political Economy of Federalism* (New Delhi: Oxford University Press, 2005), vii.

7. GoI, Thirteenth Finance Commission, *Report*, 22; emphasis added.

8. GoI, Tenth Finance Commission, *Report for 1995–2000* (New Delhi: Finance Commission, 1994), 4.

9. Ibid., 1; emphasis added.

10. Raja J. Chelliah, M. Govinda Rao, and Tapas Kumar Sen, "Issues before Tenth Finance Commission," *Economic and Political Weekly* 27, no. 47 (November 21, 1992): 2539–50.

11. GoI, Tenth Finance Commission, *Report*, 4–5.

12. Ibid., 5.

13. Ibid., 54–55. This would seem to contradict the position of Rao and Singh, *Political Economy*, 355, which seems to cast the blame on the center for fiscal deficits in the states.

14. GoI, Tenth Finance Commission, *Report*, 56–58, app. 6.

15. S. Guhan, "Report of Tenth Finance Commission," *Economic and Political Weekly* 30, no. 16 (April 22, 1995): 884.

16. GoI, *Report of the Eleventh Finance Commission (For 2000–2005)* (New Delhi: Finance Commission, June 2000), 1, 6, 24; emphasis added; hereafter GoI, Eleventh Finance Commission, *Report* (Main).

17. GoI, *Report of the Eleventh Finance Commission on the Additional Term of Reference (for 2000–2005)* (New Delhi: Finance Commission, August 2000), 1; hereafter referred to as GoI, Eleventh Finance Commission, *Report* (Additional).

18. GoI, Eleventh Finance Commission, *Report* (Main), 110.

19. Ibid., 9–10.

20. Shankar Acharya, "My Friend Amaresh," in *Public Economics: Theory and Policy—Essays in Honor of Amaresh Bagchi*, ed. M. Govinda Rao and Mihir Rakshit (New Delhi: Sage, and NIPFP, 2011), 326–29.

21. GoI, Eleventh Finance Commission, *Report* (Main), 13–14.

22. Ibid., 25, 110. There may have been an error in the original in relation to the figures on the fiscal deficit.

23. Ibid., 32, 111, 118–20.

24. Ibid., 34.

25. Ibid., 35–36.

26. The use of homegrown conditionality may be more common in India than assumed; see Jason A. Kirk, *India and the World Bank: The Politics of Aid and Influence* (London: Anthem Press, 2010), 109.

27. GoI, Eleventh Finance Commission, *Report* (Additional), 1–8.

28. Ibid., 3–7.

29. Ibid., 1.

30. Ibid., 12.

31. GoI, Twelfth Finance Commission, *Report of the Twelfth Finance Commission (2005–10)* (New Delhi: Finance Commission, November 2004), 37–38.

32. Ibid., 204–5.

33. Amaresh Bagchi, "Symposium on Report of Twelfth Finance Commission: Introduction and Overview," *Economic and Political Weekly* 40, no. 31 (July 30, 2005): 3388.

34. GoI, Twelfth Finance Commission, *Report*, 2, 22, 271.

35. Ibid., 65.

36. Ibid., 82–83.

37. Ibid., 84, 225.

38. Ibid., 227.

39. Ibid., 228, 231.

40. The data on the fiscal indicators are from GoI, Thirteenth Finance Commission, *Report*, chap. 4 (tables 4.1, 4.3, 4.7, 4.12).

41. Ibid., 13–14.
42. Ibid., 141.
43. Ibid., 126.
44. Ibid., 131 (table 9.3).
45. Ibid., 126.
46. Ibid., 138, 140, 148.
47. Ibid., 26.
48. Guhan, "Report of Tenth Finance Commission," 884.
49. GoI, Tenth Finance Commission, *Report*, 22.
50. Guhan, "Report of Tenth Finance Commission," 886.
51. GoI, Tenth Finance Commission, *Report*, 6, 59–60.
52. Guhan, "Report of Tenth Finance Commission," 886.
53. GoI, Tenth Finance Commission, *Report*, 59–60.
54. Ibid., 67.
55. Guhan, "Report of Tenth Finance Commission," 881.
56. See GoI, *Report of the Twelfth Finance Commission*, 129–30.
57. GoI, Eleventh Finance Commission, *Report* (Main), 111.
58. The normative principle or approach refers to not taking the figures for revenues and expenditures at face value by the Finance Commission in its assessment of finances or allocation of transfers or grants, but to reassess them in the light of the adequacy of tax effort and fiscal discipline. See Srivastava and Rao, "Fiscal Relations," 26–27.
59. GoI, Eleventh Finance Commission, *Report* (Main), 34. As a counterpoint to the stance of the Eleventh Commission, it is significant that the authoritative commission on center–state relations, headed by Justice R. S. Sarkaria, had found in 1988 that the basic schema on distribution of financial powers was "sound" and required "no major modifications." *Sarkaria Commission and Its Recommendations*, para. 10.5.74. Available at http://interstatecouncil.nic.in/CHAPTERX.pdf.
60. Amaresh Bagchi, "'Rethinking Federalism': An Overview of the Current Debates with Some Reflections in the Indian Context," in *Development, Poverty, and Fiscal Policy: Decentralization of Institutions*, ed. M. Govinda Rao (New Delhi: Oxford University Press, 2002), 245; emphasis added.
61. M. Govinda Rao, "India: Intergovernmental Fiscal Relations in a Planned Economy," in *Fiscal Decentralization in Developing Countries*, ed. Richard M. Bird and Francois Vaillancourt (Cambridge: Cambridge University Press, 1998) 79, 85; emphasis added.
62. Bagchi, "'Rethinking Federalism,'" 245; Rao, "India," 79, 89.
63. Granville Austin, *The Indian Constitution: Cornerstone of a Nation* (Oxford: Clarendon Press, 1966), 222–23; emphasis added.
64. Ibid., 217–18.
65. Debes Mukhopadhyay, "Center-State Financial Relations in India: An Account of Major Debates," in *Fiscal Federalism in India*, ed. P. K. Chaubey, 63; GoI, Eleventh Finance Commission, *Report* (Main), 55–58.
66. See Ruddar Dutt, "Eleventh Finance Commission Report—Catch Up Time for Poorer States," *Hindu Business Line*, September 26, 2000; Jairam Ramesh, "Naidu's Wrong: It Is Sad to See a Dynamic Chief Minister Play Partisan Politics and Forget India," *India Today*, September 4, 2000. See also Amaresh Bagchi and Pinaki Chakraborty,

"Towards a Rational System of Center–State Revenue Transfers in India: An Exploration," in *The Dynamics of Fiscal Federalism: Challenges before the Twelfth Finance Commission*, ed. G. C. Srivastava (New Delhi: Taxmann, 2004), 15–16.

67. GoI, Twelfth Finance Commission, *Report*, 261.

68. Ibid., 130–33; the weights for population and area were increased from 10 percent and 7.5 percent to 25 percent and 10 percent, respectively.

69. GoI, Twelfth Finance Commission, *Report*, 10.

70. Cited in Srivastava and Rao, "Fiscal Relations," 25.

71. Bagchi, "Symposium on Report of Twelfth Finance Commission," 3390.

72. GoI, Twelfth Finance Commission, *Report*, 13, 174.

73. Ibid., 175 (table 10.1).

74. Ibid., 178–79.

75. GoI, Thirteenth Finance Commission, *Report*, 22.

76. See M. Govinda Rao, "The 13th Finance Commission's Report: Conundrum in Conditionalities," *Economic and Political Weekly* 45, no. 48 (November 27, 2010): 46–55, and D. K. Srivastava, "Vertical Sharing and Horizontal Distribution of Resources: The Equity and Efficiency Trade-Off," *Economic and Political Weekly* 45, no. 48 (November 27, 2010): 64–70.

77. C. Rangarajan and D. K. Srivastava, *Federalism and Fiscal Transfers in India* (New Delhi: Oxford University Press, 2011), 236.

78. Srivastava, "Vertical Sharing," 69.

79. Rangarajan and Srivastava, *Federalism*, xvi.

80. Ibid., 227.

81. Richard Herd and Willi Leibfritz, "Fiscal Policy in India: Past Reforms and Future Challenges," Economics Department Working Paper 595, OECD, Paris, 2008, 31.

82. Bagchi, "Evaluating India's Fiscal Federalism," 88.

Chapter 6

INDIA'S HALTING MARCH TO COMMON MARKET

Reforming the Indirect Tax System

CONTRARY to the prognostications of the critics, it seems that globalization paradoxically has been instrumental in engendering a process of transforming India's existing highly segmented economy into a genuine common market. In short, globalization and a domestic common market are integrally joined together, with globalization compelling India, as it were, to endeavor to foster a common market. There seems to be a certain inexorable logic that leads globalization to make for the paradoxical result of developing a domestic common market rather than tending toward market segmentation, as the critics believe. Of course, the state, as an institutional variable that sits astride as a gatekeeper between globalization and common market, has a critical role in the final outcome.

In analyzing the paradox of globalization and the moving forward to a national common market, this chapter focuses on one of the crucial elements in promoting a common market—establishing an appropriate system of *indirect taxation* that fosters, rather than hinders, the free flow of goods and services in the domestic market. The chapter examines the issue in several parts: (1) the relationship between globalization and tax reform; (2) the successful postliberalization process of tax reform among India's states as a group; (3) the continuing effort for reform at the pan-Indian level; and (4) the impulses in such tax reform.

GLOBALIZATION, ECONOMIC REFORM, AND TAX REFORM

The key connecting link between globalization and common market is the quest for *economic efficiency*. India had turned to economic liberalization precisely because it had concluded that the socialist autarkic regime was economically inefficient and consequently had retarded economic growth, thus perpetuating poverty and diminishing national capabilities. As indicated in chapter 5, the then finance minister Manmohan Singh had underlined economic efficiency as the central goal of economic reform in his very first budget speech in 1991. This move toward economic efficiency, in turn, demanded that India refashion its internal economic order. The substantial dismantlement of the system of administrative controls over industry was part of the thrust for economic efficiency. But so was the reform of the tax system, albeit still a work in progress. Tax reform was an integral part of economic reform. The almost simultaneous turn to tax reform—though stretched out over an extended period—was organically linked to economic reform. The story of tax reform is long, but one can begin with the constitutional settlement of 1949 and the tax system that was established under the socialist regime.

Constitutional Settlement, Socialist Autarky, and the Tax System

The late Raja Chelliah—widely regarded as the intellectual father of India's post-liberalization tax reform—once characterized the division of taxation powers in India's constitution as "quite antiquated." Subsequently, the socialist regime made its own contribution to the creation of "an unsatisfactory and economically irrational tax system," but Chelliah thought that "most of the blame for [it] must go to the scheme embodied in the Constitution."[1] Notwithstanding the inherent deficiencies of the constitutional provisions on taxation, socialism's own contribution to the irrationalities of the tax system, no matter how well intended, was massive.

Since tax policy follows economic policy, the postindependence leadership's commitment to a regime of socialism and import substitution industrialization (ISI) had profound consequences for tax policy. Apart from the quantitative restrictions on imports to protect and promote local industry, the ISI program entailed high customs tariffs. However, the program required additional huge financial resources for investment in the rapidly expanding public sector. These were obtained through deficit financing—which imposed an arduous burden on the people through its impact on prices—but also through almost confiscatory direct taxation and heavy doses of indirect taxation. The quest for increased resources and the socialist aims concerning equity and progressiveness often trumped considerations of rationality in taxation.[2]

Table 6.1 provides data on tax–GDP ratios for the center under different tax categories for several years. If we take 1990–91 as a proxy for the socialist period, then it is evident that there was heavy dependence on revenues derived from external indirect taxes, that is, customs. That, of course, is quite consistent with the aim of developing a self-reliant or an autarkic economy through delinking it from the world economy. At the same time, there was even greater dependence on do-

Table 6.1. Shares of Different Taxes in the Center's Revenues (as % of GDP)

Tax Category	*1990–91*	*1995–96*	*2001–2*	*2005–6*	*2007–8*	*2010–11*
Direct	1.9	2.8	3.0	4.3	5.9	5.6
Personal	0.9	1.3	1.4	1.5	2.1	1.8
Corporation	0.9	1.4	1.6	2.7	3.9	3.8
Indirect	7.9	6.5	5.1	5.4	5.6	4.4
Customs	3.6	3.0	1.8	1.8	2.1	1.7
Excise	4.3	3.4	3.2	3.0	2.5	1.8
Services	—	0.1	0.1	0.6	1.0	0.9
Total	10.1	9.4	8.2	9.9	11.9	10.2

Sources: GoI, *Economic Survey 2006–07*, 23; GoI, *Economic Survey 2010–11*, 47; and GoI, *Economic Survey 2012–13*, 61.

mestic indirect taxes. Roughly, the ratio between indirect and direct taxes was 8:2; that is, 80 percent of the center's revenues came from indirect taxation.[3] Since indirect taxes are considered less progressive, the high incidence of customs and excise duties clearly meant that socialist industrialization was built on the backs of the people. Incidentally, direct taxes also had a high rate of incidence even though their total contribution to revenues was unimpressive. In 1973–74, the marginal income tax rate (including surcharges) had been raised to the confiscatory level of 97.5 percent.[4]

Notwithstanding the high rates of taxation, the state provided many exemptions in order to direct savings to particular sectors or areas. The result was a chaotic tax system, which was highly discretionary, lacking in transparency, and characterized by great complexity and a multiplicity of rates. For the public, the system was a source of enormous and perpetual bureaucratic harassment, and for the bureaucracy, a perverse incentive to rent-seeking behavior.

The country's federal structure further added to the complexity and irrationality of the system, with each state having its own variant. Under the constitution, the center levied income taxes, both personal and corporate. It also imposed excise duties during the manufacturing stage, that is, at the factory gate but not beyond. The center shared the revenues from personal income tax and excise duties with the states. Conversely, the states imposed sales taxes on goods, which constituted 60 percent of their tax revenues, while local governments levied property and octroi (or entry) taxes.[5] Since there was no concept yet in India of the "value added tax"—with offsets for taxes paid at earlier stages of sales or production—the system entailed "taxes on taxes" at multiple successive stages, leading to immense tax cascading, a high degree of economic inefficiency, and reduced international competitiveness. Chelliah underlined the deficiencies of the system of domestic indirect taxes prior to the economic reforms of the early

1990s: "The domestic indirect tax system in the country represented by the combination of the Central excise and the States sales tax systems remains extremely irrational from the economic point of view. All the drawbacks of a cascading type of tax system—escalation of production costs, distortions, loss of competitiveness, inducement to vertical integration and an uncontrolled pattern of incidences—are the hallmarks of the system. In addition the heterogeneous sales tax systems have led to considerable diversion of trade."[6] The cumulative pressure of the high incidence of taxes and of tax cascading led to massive tax avoidance and tax evasion, besides making the tax system increasingly resistant to providing more revenue.

Economic Liberalization and Tax Reform

The shift to economic liberalization as government policy and the opening up to globalization detonated a radical change in tax policy. The shift meant integration with the world economy and, with it, cutting or whittling down those economic and social features of the earlier regime that kept the country relatively isolated from the world economy. The protectionist wall of quantitative restrictions on foreign trade and high customs tariffs was one such feature of the previous economic regime. Indeed, cutting down tariffs and eliminating quantitative restrictions, even if only gradually, were both an accompaniment and a mark of economic liberalization.

Such cutting down of tariffs, however, has the unwelcome simultaneous effect of sharply reducing externally derived revenues. That reduction in income then compels governments to search for revenues from domestic taxation in compensation. As Richard Bird maintains, "fiscal crisis has been proven to be the mother of tax reform."[7] Since the domestic tax system already seemed recalcitrant to yielding additional income, the need for revenues after economic liberalization added to the urgency of rationalizing and modernizing it. Fundamentally, to that end, India needed to broaden the tax base, to lower the tax rates to more moderate levels, and to reduce the number of rates to a few, even as it needed to eliminate as much as possible administrative discretion in operating the tax system, and to cut down the complexity of the system. That, indeed, has been the broad thrust of the direction in which India proceeded after economic liberalization, even though the work on reform is yet to be completed. In that sense, liberalization has been the fountainhead of revolutionary change in India's tax system.

Although triggered by economic crisis, tax reform has not been ad hoc; rather, it has been based on considerable thought, deliberation, and analysis. Even though the decision makers have willingly and readily learned from practice abroad, tax reform in India has been homegrown.[8] In its reform effort, India has benefited enormously from having a galaxy of stellar, world-class public finance experts, chief among them Raja Chelliah.

Ironically, though such change has meant that the socialist regime's claimed tax progressiveness has had to give way to the introduction of economic rationality in taxation, in reality, there has been a stronger element of genuine systemic progressiveness under the new dispensation. Reform has radically changed the balance between direct and indirect taxes in favor of the former, lowered tax evasion, and reduced tax cascading. Successive doses of tax reform have drastically brought down the rates of customs tariffs and also of direct taxes so that their rates are now quite comparable to those of at least the East Asian economies. The lowering of the rates of income tax (both personal and corporate) did not, however, hurt revenues, which is what the critics had predicted; rather, it has been productive of higher revenues. A likely explanation for this outcome is not only the Laffer Curve (simplistically, moderate rates of taxation are more productive for revenue) but also better tax administration, such as through the "tax deducted at source" (TDS) mechanism in the case of income tax.[9]

Table 6.1 clearly shows that the share of customs tariffs in the center's revenues has come down sharply, as has that of domestic indirect taxes. However, the shares of personal income tax and corporation tax have gone up sharply, particularly with respect to the latter. In contrast with the situation in 1990–91, when the ratio between indirect and direct taxes at the center was roughly 8:2, by 2010–11, the ratio had changed to an average of 4:6, effectively overturning the long-standing regressive situation of domination of indirect over direct taxes. Thus, in systemic terms, the new postliberalization tax dispensation has, in actuality, been more progressive than the earlier socialist one.

As interesting as these broader trends are, of central importance here is the reform of the India-wide domestic indirect tax system of the center and states, but particularly the states, since that system has a critical bearing on the prospects of nationwide economic integration, in particular in promoting a common market. It bears repeating that globalization and the consequent integration of the national economy with the world economy—thus, inarguably bringing into play the need for national firms to compete and to be competitive in global markets—make economic efficiency in the domestic productive process imperative. Indeed, as Chelliah had noted in 1994, the need for international competitiveness sets up the broad agenda for thoroughgoing economic reform, not least in the area of taxation: "Attainment of international competitiveness has become a major policy objective. This requires a thorough overhauling of the economic system, including tax and tariff reform, greater internal competition together with gradual exposure to external competition and, finally, vast improvement in the infrastructure industries."[10]

The earlier complexity of India's tax system as it had evolved during the socialist era and the built-in cascading of taxes, however, were a serious impediment to competitiveness. Nevertheless, the compulsions of international competitiveness demanded tax reform. While the process of tax reform has been slow, remarkable change has nonetheless occurred on the tax front, though the "last mile" still has to be traversed. The center has understandably taken the initiative in pushing reform, but the role of the states has been enormously significant—at times, pushing reform forward with enthusiasm, at other times, impeding and blocking it. Economic experts, administrators, and political leadership all have played a part in this reform. The economists, with their elegant models and austere formulations based on considerations of economic rationality, have made a critical contribution to tax reform. However, political leaders have hammered these models and formulations into actual policy on the anvil of political economy considerations. At the same time, the administrators have insisted that the actual tax policy up for adoption should be feasible, so that final outcomes would correspond to intended goals.

Toward Partial Value Added Tax (VAT) at the Center

There is a strong consensus among public finance experts that the ideal system for domestic indirect taxation in modern states is the one that centers on the value added tax (VAT), since its principal strength is the avoidance of tax cascading.[11] VAT is a consumption tax, the key feature of which is tax offsets for the taxpayer for taxes already paid at preceding stages in the production and distribution of goods and services. There are thus no taxes on taxes paid earlier. The VAT system was started by France in the early 1960s, but was applicable to only a limited number of items, while Brazil instituted it a few years later on a comprehensive scale.[12] The European Union adopted the system in the late 1970s. In India, as part of its liberalization thrust, the Rajiv Gandhi government took the first modest step toward introducing the VAT principle at the center in 1986, through applying it in the matter of excise duties in manufacturing to a very limited number of goods; it was referred to as Modified VAT (Modvat).[13] Although a modest step, Modvat was intended as the first stage in a larger reform process, but it soon "seemed to have stopped in its tracks."[14] In addition, it suffered from "multifarious rates, riddled with total and partial (end use) exemptions, ever changing with notifications."[15]

At the cost of getting a little ahead of the story on tax reform—presently limited to the preliberalization period before 1991—it is noteworthy that the Tax Reforms Committee in 1993 had asked that, in the next three to five years, Modvat should be changed to a "genuine VAT," covering most of manufacturing and services with the multiple rates reduced to three.[16] In subsequent years, the coverage of this tax was expanded gradually to more goods, as Parthasarathi Shome maintains, in "a seemingly deliberate, learning by doing approach." In 2001, there was further reform of Modvat; the number of rates for the center's excise tax was reduced to just two and the tax was given the new name of Central VAT (Cenvat). The system continued to suffer from several shortcomings, however. First, some goods (sugar, tobacco, and textiles) had their own specific statutory authorization and, therefore, had their separate excise rates, which tended to "clutter the overall rate structure." Second and more important, the Cenvat structure was a "truncated" one.[17] Cenvat was not a true consumption tax since it was limited to manufacturing because of the constitutional division of taxing powers. The states had the power to levy sales tax as the consumption tax, thus perpetuating tax cascading. Moreover, they continued with their variant traditional systems, making for a multiplicity of systems of indirect taxation, thus inevitably breaking up the national market into many fragments.

The 1991 Paradigm Shift and the Acceleration of Tax Reform

With the paradigm shift in economic reform in 1991, there was a major step-up in tax reform at the center along a broad front, especially in the area of customs tariffs and income taxes, which were within the center's own jurisdiction. A key role in this reform was played by Dr. Raja Chelliah, who chaired the high-powered Tax Reforms Committee. In its interim report in 1991 and its final report, that committee self-consciously saw its role as setting "the trend for inaugurating a new era in the development of tax policy" through "introducing certain fundamental reforms in the direct tax and indirect tax systems."[18] It then went on to recommend a comprehensive reform package on tax policy and administration at the center. The overall approach of the committee was to set tax rates at a moderate level, to limit the number of tax rates to a few, to broaden the base on which the taxes were levied, and to largely dispense with exemptions, besides simplifying tax regulations and procedures.[19] In the matter of the center's excise duties during the manufacturing stage, as already noted, the committee recommended moving to a genuine VAT system.[20]

Meanwhile, the taxation of services assumed increasing importance. Following the Chelliah committee's recommendations, the center for the first time initiated the taxing of services in 1994, when three items were brought within the tax net. Gradually, the number was expanded to twenty-six by 2001, when the government declared its intent to add another fourteen services. A committee headed by Dr. M. Govinda Rao recommended in 2001 that the center go beyond such a selective approach and implement a comprehensive coverage of the services sector with a view to integrating the tax on services with Cenvat on goods so as "to evolve into a comprehensive levy on goods and services by 2004–5."[21] In the subsequent years, the number of services subject to the service tax was gradually increased from 75 in 2004–5 to 119 in 2011–12. Seeing that the service tax was a lucrative source of revenue, the center made a paradigm shift with its budget of 2012–13 making all services subject to the tax at the higher rate of 12 percent, except for those services that were included in a negative list.[22]

It is evident that economic liberalization had resulted in making tax reform a core part of economic reform. This was unquestionably obvious at the central level in the case of both direct and indirect taxes. With tax reform in the air at the center, the states could not remain unaffected. Since VAT, albeit truncated, already existed and was set to be extended and reformed at the center, the next logical step was to persuade the states to switch to VAT as well.

TOWARD VAT IN THE STATES: COOPERATIVE FEDERALISM AT WORK

VAT at the state level was critical to the common market because the various states' sales tax regimes segmented the national market into some two dozen parts. Tax reform at the state level, however, has proven to be a complex and complicated affair, a fairly prolonged and arduous process that still remains to be completed. It has passed through several stages in which cooperative federalism has been manifest, but not in a uniform manner; rather, center–state cooperation has been present in varying degrees, indeed at times bordering on "competitive federalism."[23] Tax reform in the states therefore constitutes a revealing study on the working of Indian federalism.

Launching the VAT System

The Chelliah committee had been cognizant that the constitutional settlement on the division of tax powers between the center and states was a serious constraint on tax reform, but it still approached the reform project from the perspective of a broad national vision. Taking an encompassing but radical perspective on the tax structure at the center and states together, it averred, remarkably as early as 1991: "It would be ideal if there were *one comprehensive VAT replacing the present system of Central excise, the State sales taxes and other indirect taxes.*" If that were done, then "the proceeds of the tax could be shared between the Center and the States." Henceforth, a single "comprehensive VAT" of the committee's understanding would become a sort of lodestar for tax reform, especially for the center. The committee's attention, however, was for the moment focused on the immediate task at hand of reforming the center's indirect tax structure. Interestingly, in recommending changes in Modvat at the center, the committee nonetheless took pains to see that they "should be consistent with and represent a further move towards *the ultimate goal of a comprehensive value added tax.*"[24]

Of course, besides reforming Modvat to make it a genuine VAT at the center, a single unified VAT system for India required as a prerequisite the transforming of the various sales tax regimes in the states into VAT as a potential base for a possible future merger of the center and state systems. The process of moving toward a VAT system in the states was set rolling politically by Finance Minister Manmohan Singh in a budget speech in 1993, when he declared that "our long term aim should be to move to a Value Added Tax system" and then designated the public finance think tank National Institute of Public Finance and Policy (NIPFP) headed by Dr. A. K. Bagchi to come up with a road map for the purpose.

The Bagchi team's report, submitted the following year, was a seminal document, with all subsequent considerations of tax reform toward VAT, whether on the national or regional scale, being mere variations on the themes that it had set out in considerable detail.[25]

Like the Chelliah committee, the Bagchi team was harsh in its condemnation of the existing sales tax system for the multifarious ill consequences that it had engendered for public finance, the economy, and society. Impressively, it cast the issue against a broad and comprehensive canvas, advocating VAT on a national scale. It examined different options and, while appreciating an otherwise "most attractive" national VAT system, it did not endorse it because it would deprive the states of their "most important tax powers" and increase "their dependence on the center." It also rejected a national VAT run by states, as it would alter the distribution of powers between the center and the states, sharply reduce the center's revenues, and be risky since the states varied in the quality of their tax administration.

Instead, it opted for the radical solution of a dual VAT system in which both the center and states would have "concurrent jurisdiction in taxing goods as well as services going up to the retail or final-point sale. Under such a system, there would be a common base for both Central and State VATs. The States would have the powers to fix the rates but within a harmonized system of narrow rate bands." It is important to note that at this early stage of tax reform, the team incorporated in its coverage both goods *and services*, for it believed that the exclusion of services would narrow the tax base and encourage tax evasion.

As attractive as this option may have been, the team still felt that even "a concurrent VAT would be seen by the States as an invasion into their tax powers." In this situation, the team found "the only feasible option . . . to be a dual system in which the VAT is levied by the two levels of government independently within the existing constitutional framework." In this schema, the center would change Modvat to a full-fledged manufacturing level VAT, eventually with a single rate (around 10 percent) that applied to both goods and services, while the states would convert the sales tax into a VAT covering both goods and services. With that, the team turned to its main task of a state-level VAT; following a thorough examination of all the issues relating to the subject, it laid out an elaborate road map for it, which would be invaluable to any subsequent consideration of state VAT.

Tax reform at the state level was, however, not within the constitutional jurisdiction of the center, even though the latter had been the source of reform ideas and plans. If the center felt that tax reform at the state level was essential, the states had to be sold on the idea. On receipt of the Bagchi team's report, Manmohan Singh appointed an eleven-member committee of state finance ministers (FMs) with Dr. Chelliah as the convener and the NIPFP as the secretariat to coordinate the process of tax reform in the states. To educate the states on the merits of VAT, the committee's members were split into three separate teams to visit six different countries that had instituted VAT successfully. After this field study, the committee set out a road map for implementing VAT in the states.[26]

In 1995, Manmohan Singh called a meeting with the chief ministers (CMs) of the states to discuss the introduction of a state-level VAT in a preliminary fashion.[27] But no big bang development took place on tax reform following the meeting. By this time, the enthusiasm for economic reform on the part of the central government under the Congress Party had in general waned, while the second half of the 1990s saw considerable political instability at the center.

In 1998, the National Democratic Alliance (NDA) led by the Bharatiya Janata Party (BJP) came to power on a plank of opposition to the Congress Party's policies, but ironically it played a momentous role in advancing the cause of state VAT. However, there were enormous hurdles to cross. For one thing, consistent with its nationalist posture, the NDA's first decision was to undertake nuclear tests in May 1998, thus embroiling the government in noisy controversy and hostile reaction from the opposition at home and from the major powers abroad. Despite that, the thread of reforming the indirect tax system at the state level was picked up by the NDA's finance minister, Yashwant Sinha, who went on to play a critical role in furthering it. In his first budget speech, he expressed his determination to push forward with a Cenvat in relation to the center's excise taxes. At the same time, he realized that such reform would not suffice in setting right the indirect tax system as a whole as long as the sales tax system in the states remained unreformed. However, undertaking the latter was a monumental task since unlike tax reform at the center, where the central government was master, installing a uniform tax system across the states in India required cooperation of more than two dozen states at various levels of development. The evolution of policy in this respect and its implementation shed important light on the political economy of policymaking in India's federal system, involving technical experts, administrators, and political leaders.

To move state tax reform forward, Sinha called a meeting of the state CMs the same year, and showed rare statesmanship in limiting his active role to serving as counselor and facilitator rather than trying to dominate the tax reform agenda, as would normally be the wont of central ministers. This was astute action since not only sales tax was constitutionally within state jurisdiction, but also because he realized that the regionalization of politics and the consequent fragmentation of the national party system in recent years had made the states considerably more assertive in relation to the center. Sinha very shrewdly decided to have the states take the initiative, and suggested a committee of state CMs to make recommendations, to be headed by the senior most CM—West Bengal CM Jyoti Basu, belonging to the Communist Party of India (Marxist), or CPI(M). The CMs wholeheartedly endorsed the suggestion.

Appointing Basu was a masterstroke in building trust between the center and states since, if there was one political party for which the BJP was a total anathema, it was the CPI(M). The report of the Basu committee favored moving forward on the issue of tax reform in the states. Sinha then called another meeting of state CMs, where he recommended that, for the smooth achievement of the goal, the CMs establish a committee of state FMs, and that it be headed by West Bengal's FM, Asim Kumar Dasgupta. The CMs accepted his recommendation.[28] From that point on, this committee, soon to be endorsed by the CMs as the "Empowered Committee of State Finance Ministers," took charge of the task of evolving a VAT design for the states, of building administrative and political consensus on it, and of taking it forward right to the implementation stage. Respected for his high intellectual credentials, Dasgupta proved to be a superb consensus builder in the committee.

A major step in the direction of state-level VAT took place in November 1999, when a meeting of all CMs called by Sinha decided to move to a VAT system. To lay a sound foundation for this game-changing development, they also agreed to end tax rate wars among themselves through harmonizing their sales tax regimes by establishing uniform floor rates, and also to discontinue the various tax-based incentives for attracting business and industry. In addition, they delegated the making of decisions on state VAT to the Empowered Committee (EC) of state FMs.[29] In this manner, the states gained ownership of the state tax reform agenda. Sinha provided advice, but he was determined "to remain in the background."[30] Meanwhile, a center-appointed advisory group on the *Tenth Five Year Plan*, headed by the world-renowned tax expert Parthasarathi Shome, offered advice on state VAT design and action on reform of state sales tax preliminary to implementing VAT.[31]

It is significant that within a year and a half of its establishment, the EC had succeeded in achieving a consensus on harmonization of sales tax rates among the states and in ending tax-based incentives to attract industry. Subsequently, after several meetings, the committee developed and built a common VAT design, which struck "a balance between the needed convergence and federal flexibility as well as ground reality." The committee saw enormous benefits from the VAT of its design by way of rationalizing the tax burden, stopping tax rate wars, bringing simplicity and transparency to the tax system, and improving tax compliance.[32] Interestingly, it made no mention of its possible contribution to the potential of a common market. In general, it seems that the states rarely acknowledge the vision of a common market, as if doing so would diminish their bargaining power with the center on fiscal autonomy for the states; the common market is apparently an attribute only of the center, not the units.

Under the common VAT design agreed on by the states, some 550 goods were subject to VAT. Two basic VAT rates were accepted—4.0 percent, largely for basic necessities, and 12.5 percent for other goods—thus ending the existing structure of numerous rates.[33] The introduction of VAT in 2003 was delayed because of some political opposition; meanwhile, a change of government took place at the center after the elections in 2004, when the Congress-led United Progressive Alliance (UPA) replaced the NDA coalition. Despite the radical difference in political orientation between the two coalitions, the new government was just as determined to go forward with a uniform VAT system across India's many states. VAT finally came into effect in the states on April 1, 2005, more than a decade after it had been first proposed. A major milestone was thus reached in India's tax reform. Some states had initially held back, but soon all joined in once the advantages of the new system became evident. The clincher in the states accepting VAT was, in a way, a generous financial package from the center that assured compensation to states that suffered revenue loss as a result of the change—100 percent in the first year, 75 percent in the second year, and 50 percent in the third year.[34] The central leadership showed considerable maturity in handling this aspect of possible revenue loss.

The installation of a uniform VAT design across India's many states was a revolutionary event in overthrowing a deep-rooted traditional system. It was also a monumental accomplishment, as it involved collaboration among twenty-eight states to develop and launch a common new system. As Shome expressed it, the establishment of VAT in the states all across India was "a remarkable achievement of successful federalism after almost a decade of consultation among states and between the center and states under the auspices of an Empowered Committee of state-level finance ministers."[35] The accomplishment of "cooperative federalism" lay in (1) the political process of reaching a consensus among the states and between the center and the states; (2) political innovation demonstrated in creating new institutions, such as the EC; and (3) the center's vital support in assuring compensation in case of any revenue losses to the states. In the process, this episode of tax reform also showed the enormous skills and maturity of India's political leadership.

TOWARD A NATIONWIDE GOODS AND SERVICES TAX (GST): BETWEEN COOPERATIVE AND COMPETITIVE FEDERALISM

Much before the move toward VAT had been concluded, the center had already begun to contemplate moving forward on an even bolder and more arduous undertaking. When the center under the NDA government appointed the Shome advisory group on tax policy, it interestingly asked the latter to make recommendations on "a comprehensive VAT whereby the central and state VAT stand integrated."[36] Thus, the idea planted by the Chelliah committee and supported by the Bagchi team had not been forgotten; it was still very much alive. The Shome advisory group examined the pros and cons of a *single VAT* for the entire country, managed nationally, as against a dual VAT (that is, a parallel or joint VAT), "whereby the VAT is levied by the Center and the states concurrently but independently." The group, however, opted for the easier option of a dual VAT, with Cenvat at the center and VAT in the states coexisting, chiefly because a single national VAT "would grievously erode their [states'] fiscal autonomy."[37] The group also may have simply been deterred from recommending a single national VAT, replacing both Cenvat and sales taxes in the states, by the awesome challenges of overcoming obstacles to revising the constitutional division of taxation powers.

A more radical approach to a comprehensive VAT for the center and states was taken by one of the task forces appointed in 2002 by the Ministry of Finance that was headed by Vijay Kelkar. As one of India's eminent economists, with a strong nationalist outlook, Kelkar has had a profound influence on working out the country's fiscal architecture, with VAT as a key component, under both the NDA and UPA governments. Kelkar chaired three different task forces in the first half decade of the twenty-first century. The first task force was on direct taxes (2002), which is not relevant to the discussion here on VAT. The second was on indirect taxes (2002), which focused more on technical issues of tax administration. Finally, the third task force (2004), which is the object of analysis here, dealt with issues relating to the implementation of the Fiscal Responsibility and Budget Management (FRBM) Act, 2003. Beyond these task forces, in the second half decade, Kelkar presided over India's Thirteenth Finance Commission during 2008–10, which devoted considerable attention to VAT and goods and services tax (GST).

The third task force on the FRBM Act had a very broad scope—nothing less than setting India's fiscal house in order; it was mandated to recommend policies for fiscal consolidation in view of India's high fiscal deficit and high debt–GDP ratio. Its foray into tax reform (for both direct and indirect taxes) arose out of this wide mandate, for it saw tax reform as a means to removing economic distortions, improving economic efficiency and therefore competitiveness, and boosting GDP growth, thus enhancing revenues. In considerable part, the prominence gained by the task force's tax proposals owed precisely to the broad scope of the mandate. In principle, the task force was oriented toward revenue enhancement rather than expenditure reduction, and therefore favored "a revenue-driven strategy for achieving the FRBM targets" on cutting down the fiscal deficit. As part of this strategy, it aimed to increase the tax–GDP ratio through "policies which are compatible with the core economic policy goals of promoting efficiency, equity and high quality growth."[38]

Insofar as indirect taxes were concerned, it offered a new architecture in 2004 that was as remarkable for its elegance and simplicity as it was for its bold vision. In a "paradigm shift" in tax reform thinking, it suggested effectively overturning the constitutional division of powers on domestic indirect taxes. It asked that the center *and* the states arrive at a "grand bargain" to institute a comprehensive VAT system encompassing *a single common base* of all goods *and* services (with some exceptions), with the two parties levying two different sets of rates on this common base; this system would be in replacement of all existing domestic indirect taxes. More specifically, the grand bargain on the GST had ten key components, the more important of which required that (1) the center and states both exercise "*concurrent but independent jurisdiction over common or almost common tax bases*," which would extend over all goods and services up to the final consumer; (2) the center and states replace all their existing indirect taxes by Central-GST and State-GST, each of the modern "value added tax" design; and (3) the center and states both have independent powers to fix rates, with the rates limited to three, of which the standard rate should not exceed 12 percent and 8 percent for Central-GST and State-GST, respectively.[39] It is impressive that this first concrete and detailed plan from an official committee of the central government, in its essential dimensions, endured through ten years of discussion and debate.

The Kelkar task force saw its proposed GST as a powerful means to meet challenges on many fronts in public finance, benefiting many economic and social sectors in the process. First and foremost, it would assist in fiscal consolidation, the problem that the task force had been mandated to address. Importantly, it would establish a world-class fiscal system that would reduce compliance costs and eliminate most distortions in tax-induced economic behavior, which would bolster economic efficiency and thus accelerate GDP growth. The removal of economic distortions would reorient economic actors to focus on productivity and global competitiveness rather than on tax planning, thus boosting manufacturing, investment-led growth, and higher exports. Remarkably, the new system would meet the demands of both efficiency and equity. Since a complex tax system is "inherently regressive," replacing it with a simple system such as the GST would be a strike in favor of equity; indeed, the proposed GST would make for "the most equitable tax system in India's post-independence period."[40]

Pushing the GST Forward

With the Kelkar report, the term GST firmly entered the vocabulary of economics and politics in India. The GST began to be seen as an inevitable end goal of reform of the indirect tax system. However, the task has been extremely demanding. Given the federal nature of the political system, its democratic framework, and its immense social diversity, the policymaking process is quite complex; it is not a simple process in which the center, on the advice of tax experts, can impose reform by fiat. In a sense, the very length of the process and its protracted nature are explained by the complexity of decision making in the system. Examining the evolution of policymaking on the GST sheds important light on that complexity.

Essentially, there have been two streams of inputs into the policy process on tax reform to institute the GST. One is the technocratic stream in which economists and administrators have assessed the issue, largely from a national perspective (but not exclusively so), while taking into account technical considerations such as efficiency and compliance costs. The Kelkar task force discussed earlier is an example of this stream. The other stream is the political one, where the states actually have played an activist role while the center has largely kept a low profile, at least until near the end, when amending the constitution was essential, and even then apparently making considerable—in some eyes, excessive—concessions to the states in order to appease them, which is perhaps a reflection of the changed balance of power in the polity.

In February 2007, Finance Minister P. Chidambaram announced the government's intention to introduce the GST, and he invited the states through their EC to work on a road map for its introduction. In response, the EC organized a joint working group of officials from the center and states in May 2007. This group held discussions with experts and peak business associations, on the basis of which it prepared a report. After extensive deliberations, the EC sent its views in a paper to the center in April 2008.[41] After receiving the center's comments at the end of the year, the EC appointed a working group of state officials, which, in consultation with senior representatives of the center, made detailed recommendations on the structure of the GST. Finally, the EC arrived at a considered position on the GST model and on a road map for its introduction, and published it as a discussion paper.[42]

The EC assessed the earlier VAT installed in the states in 2005 to have been "a major step—an important breakthrough" in tax reform. It had a sound basis for this conclusion, since the growth rate of tax revenues of the states was about twice as much after VAT than for the five-year period prior to its introduction.[43] The EC was now persuaded of the need for a GST by the shortcomings of the existing VAT structure, both at the center and in the states, since many taxes continued to be left outside the VAT framework, thus allowing cascading to continue. More practically, believing the GST to be a positive sum game, the EC saw material gain for the center and states from it through increased revenues from the widening of the tax base. In addition, the EC felt that the GST would benefit business, agriculture, and consumers.

The EC conceptualized the GST in India as a dual structure with the center, on the one hand, and states, on the other, each having its own defined jurisdiction. The GST itself would consist of two components—with the central goods and services tax (CGST) imposed by the center and the state goods and services tax (SGST) imposed by the states—both of which would be applied to all transactions of goods and services. The EC's GST model listed the current taxes that would be subsumed under the GST, but it is interesting that the list for the central taxes was far more extensive than the one for the state taxes, the latter leaving out items such as stamp duties and purchase tax. In a game of "heads I win, tails you lose," it seems the states understandably wanted the maximum benefit from GST by the inclusion of the large and expanding sector of services in the tax base without letting go of all of their own taxes.

The EC model envisaged the center and states as having "concurrent jurisdiction for the entire value chain and for all tax payers." However, it established different thresholds for the center and states for coverage under GST, Rs. 15 million for the center and Rs.1 million for the states. The model set up a dual-rate structure, with a standard rate for most goods and a lower rate for necessities; besides these, there would be a list of exempted items, while precious metals would bear a nominal rate. The EC asked that the center follow the two-rate structure for goods, but stipulated that there could well be a single rate for services. At the same time, exports would have a zero rate while imports will bear a GST on the basis of the destination principle.[44]

To an extent, the EC's discussion paper reflected a larger national consensus, in two senses. First, all parties—center, states, and business—were broadly agreed, though not in all details, on a GST being the best tax option for the country. Second, the states through a long process of consultation had come to an agreement on a specific GST model that settled most issues relating to the subject. Still, both states and the center continued to have concerns on the implementation of the GST. Moreover, there were differences among the states themselves, basically along the division between higher-income and lower-income states.

Regardless, both groups of states cast themselves as prospective losers in relation to the center, suspecting that the GST would worsen the vertical imbalance, already weighted in favor of the center, by the latter somehow pegging the CGST at a higher level and benefiting from a larger consumption base. More crucially, they felt that the stable rate structure, which seemed required for the GST, would erode their fiscal autonomy. At the same time, they were against a single rate structure, holding it to be regressive. The states wanted a number of taxes, which were beneficial to them because of their high incidence, to be excluded from being subsumed under the GST. In addition, they desired only a selective implementation of the GST, with states retaining the option to shift or not to shift to the GST. The center had its own concerns. It was against different thresholds for center and states, wanted "a uniform and limited list" of exemptions for center and states, and opposed excluding taxes that states found lucrative.[45]

The EC's discussion paper—which essentially offered the GST model politically preferred by the states—was followed by two other proposals on a GST from the *technocratic stream*. One of these was a lengthy report, consisting of eleven chapters, from a task force appointed by the Thirteenth Finance Commission (hereafter referred to as the ThFC task force), while the other consisted of a chapter in the report of the commission itself. The ThFC task force, which consisted of administrators and academicians, thought that the EC's proposals in the discussion paper "do not adequately advance the cause of indirect tax reform due to a number of infirmities. The initiative seems to be an amalgam of compromises and continued fear of revenue losses and adverse impact on the low income groups."[46] The task force also regarded that model to be "an extremely diluted form of GST," since it continues with several cascading taxes while the tax base is limited because of the large number of exemptions. In addition, it believed that the EC model's dual GST rate substantially dilutes the nature of the tax and, consequently, erodes the potential benefits to be derived from it.[47]

One senses that the ThFC task force was concerned that the center had let the states, to put it strongly, hijack the process of policy formulation, while the center itself had kept a low posture; it therefore urged the center to be more proactive in policymaking on the GST.[48] The task force was quite tough-minded in its approach to the GST issue, and its stance on the issue was determined by its views regarding the overall economic and political interests of the nation and how they were best served by a GST model that was simple and rigorous. Simplicity and rigor, it thought, would enhance compliance and reduce costs. The task force was strict on the exclusion of exemptions; on the uniformity of the tax base for center and states alike; and, quite distinctively, on subsuming all existing taxes on goods and services, whether at the center or in the states. It did, however, allow the center and states to impose taxes besides the GST rate on some categories. The task force was equally tough in terms of demanding strict controls on implementation because of its apprehension that the states were likely to deviate from rates and conditions that they agree to, given that some of them had already done so with respect to VAT. Holding the GST to be a game changer and the last mile in the indirect tax reform process started in 1986, and insisting on a world-class GST regime, the task force maintained: "The benefits from the switch-over to the GST are contingent upon the purity of the GST design."[49]

The ThFC task force's own model envisaged a dual GST—comprising CGST and SGST, with a common (that is, identical) base—that would be "imposed concurrently by the Center and the States, but independently."[50] A novel element in this respect was—in sharp contrast to the Kelkar task force's triple rate and the EC's dual rate—a single rate for the GST, and quite a low one at that. In its view, 5 percent for CGST and 7 percent for SGST (of which 2 percent was to be assigned to the third tier of local government)—in total, 12 percent—was more than adequate for bringing in the same amount of revenues as was generated by the current taxes ("the revenue neutral rate"); indeed, it calculated that 11 percent would be enough.[51]

While tough-minded overall, the ThFC task force was sensitive to the issue of fiscal autonomy of the states. Its position on the issue had several strands. It acknowledged that once the center and the states come to an agreement on the GST design and structure, neither can exercise independent power to institute changes. Any changes would have to be agreed on by the two tiers of government, which will be represented in a new joint administrative mechanism. The task force felt that "since both levels of Government would be similarly placed, this has no impact on the balance of power." However, it believed that, since the GST will provide concurrent power to both center and states to tax all goods and services, the states will be able to extend their taxing power to the services sector, which constitutes more than half of GDP and is "the fastest growing sector," and thus benefit from the tax buoyancy of that sector. Consequently, the task force concluded: "Since the expansion in the power of the States is significantly larger than the Center, the proposed GST would alter the balance of power in favor of the States, thus reducing the vertical imbalance."[52] It also believed that, since all governments lose autonomy to make changes in the GST system in a federal structure with concurrent jurisdiction on taxing goods and services, the issue needs to be assessed on a wider canvas than just tax autonomy. The task force felt that in India's federal structure "what is relevant is overall fiscal autonomy rather than tax autonomy," and in that respect, it saw "no loss of fiscal autonomy of the states."[53]

Because of its simplicity and rigor, one could call the ThFC task force's model "the dream GST model," as it was focused on the national economy as a whole and based on sheer economic rationality. Yet that model was unrealistic insofar as it failed to factor in the country's immense political diversity, particularly in light of the rise of the states in India's polity and political economy during recent decades.

In its own report, the Thirteenth Finance Commission generally followed the task force's position in its essentials, except that for some unexplained reason, it did not specify either the GST single rate that would be revenue neutral or the rates for CGST and SGST. Significantly, however, to provide an incentive to the states to implement the GST, it recommended that the center make a grant of Rs. 500 billion to the states in the aggregate for the purpose of compensation during a five-year period in case of losses from the switch over to GST.

The Center Finally Surfaces on GST, but Questions Remain

Initially, the GST was intended to become operational on April 1, 2010, but that deadline could not be met because of the global economic crisis in 2008 and 2009, the lack of full accord between the center and states, and the absence of adequate administrative preparedness. Nor is it likely to be operational until perhaps after the 2014 elections. However, after much delay, the center unveiled in July 2010 a three-year road map for rolling out a GST. In typical Indian fashion, it attempted to combine features of the various proposals, but in fact was more accommodative of the states' demands.[54]

The center's plan provided for a dual GST, the rates and revenues of which would be equally split between the center (CGST) and the states (SGST). The first year of the road map would start with a complicated formula with three somewhat high GST rates. However, by the third year, a simple formula of only one GST rate would come into operation at 16 percent. The tax would be levied on a common tax base of all goods and services except for—in a concession to the states—a relatively long exemption list of ninety-nine items. The final tax rate would be about a third higher than the one proposed by the ThFC task force, but it would not have been too far out of line with the rates in Canada (in Quebec, federal 5.0 percent plus provincial 9.975 percent; in Ontario, harmonized sales tax of 13.0 percent).

The center also promised to compensate the states for losses as a result of shifting to the GST. As a further concession to the states, the center kept petroleum products, alcohol, and some other items such as real estate—big revenue earners for the states—outside the GST net. The third tier of government was apparently given a short shrift in the plan; however, the plan allowed local governments to keep the entertainment tax and, more harmfully for the potential common market, the octroi out of the GST system. Notwithstanding the high GST rate and other deficiencies, the organized trade and industry endorsed the center's plan.

Having arrived at what looked like the final and conclusive stage of the GST decision-making process, the project suddenly hit a brick wall. Perhaps the center had made a tactical error in its approach as to how the GST system ought to be regulated after it would come into operation, an approach that to the states seemed overly domineering. Switching over to a GST required amending the constitution since it involved a fundamental reordering of the assignment of taxation powers, with the center being allowed to tax goods beyond the factory gate right to the retail stage and the states being given the power to tax services. In putting forward the amendments to the constitution, the center also proposed a new GST council that would decide on changes in the GST, if and when necessary in the future, and also a dispute settlement mechanism to resolve possible conflicts that may arise under the new tax regime. The proposed GST council was to consist of all state finance ministers with the center's finance minister as chairman; while decisions in the council would be required to be made by majority vote, the chairman was given the veto power under the proposed amendment.

The center, however, obviously had not read the mood of the states right. When the states expressed strong opposition to the arrangement, the center quickly gave up the idea of the veto and suggested that decisions be made on the basis of consensus. Despite the center's capitulation on this point, the episode left the states suspicious about the center's intentions and its possible behavior in the future. It also emboldened the states to make increasingly more audacious demands on the center for concessions. Some of the harshest critics were the finance ministers of the BJP-ruled states. However, more than differences over taxation seemed to be at stake. It had been evident for some time that the two major national political parties leading the opposed coalition groups at the center had come to treat each other not just as political adversaries but as political enemies that have to be pushed beyond the political pale or finished off. With the two parties seeing each other in a zero-sum relationship, all political tactics on any occasion were fair game. In this process, the disputes over the GST proposals may be seen as an expression of deeper political passions rather than a policy matter over which reasonable men and women could differ but still negotiate and bargain in the pursuit of what is in the common interest. "Cooperative federalism" is therefore often difficult to practice in this situation, which partakes more of "competitive federalism."

Resumption of the Discourse on the GST Proves Inconclusive

A long hiatus followed the disputes over the center's 2010 proposals, as the center soon became distracted by other concerns—such as corruption scandals, economic slowdown, high inflation, credit downgrade by rating agencies, and policy paralysis—with the consequence that the GST project was thrown into a limbo. When P. Chidambaram returned as finance minister at the center in August 2012, the markets and the country greeted the event with a sense of relief. Chidambaram took the revival of investor sentiment as his principal task through ending the policy paralysis by actively promoting measures of economic reform, one of which was to give another push to the GST project, even if it may not be ready for implementation before the next general elections.

Meanwhile, the defeat in 2011 of the CPI(M) government in West Bengal, whose finance minister had ably chaired the EC from its very beginning, necessitated the installation of a new chairman; the state finance ministers unanimously elected Sushil Kumar Modi, deputy chief minister of Bihar, for the position. Interestingly, Modi was from the BJP, whose representatives had been strong critics of Pranab Mukherjee's GST proposals, but Modi proved adept at working with Chidambaram. Considerable progress was made but the center and states failed to reach a final consensus on all the pertinent issues, and the matter went into indefinite suspension again, awaiting resolution on the formation of a government with a new mandate. It is nonetheless significant that most stakeholders still regard the GST as a win-win proposition for everyone and hope that it will eventually be implemented.

There is no doubt that the launching of the GST project has been excessively delayed, even though it seems to be in everyone's interest to push it through. However, there is deep irony in the fact that it is a patently internal factor pertaining to the nature of the state and the wider polity—rather than the international factor of globalization that critics proclaim as the one to be dreaded—that has stood in the way of the expeditious adoption of a policy that would mitigate economic segmentation and promote the economic integration of the country. But perhaps the delay is a necessary price to pay for carrying along a vast and complex society and polity. Maybe reason and common sense will ultimately prevail. In the meantime, the march to the common market remains uncompleted. However, the accomplishment meanwhile by way of the shift to VAT separately at the center and in the states—within the constraints of the current distribution of powers in the constitution—should not be underestimated. In this light, a comprehensive GST for both center and states together would be an incremental albeit game-changing improvement, but not an altogether radical one.

THE COMMON MARKET AS UNINTENDED CONSEQUENCE OF GLOBALIZATION

At one level, the advance to the common market in India through tax reform, although not yet fully operational, can be seen to have been the unintended consequence of the adoption of the policy of economic liberalization as part of adapting to globalization. In this interpretation, globalization and economic liberalization can be considered to have necessitated the drastic reduction of customs tariffs in order to integrate with the world economy. That action on customs, however, obviously created a *threat* to India. This threat was of two kinds. One was an immediate challenge to the fiscal stability of the state through the reduction in revenues, which had been excessively dependent on high customs tariffs. In the face of this challenge, the government was necessarily compelled, for reasons of revenue mobilization, to reform an antiquated tax system that featured enormous tax evasion and low and diminishing productivity by way of revenues for the state.

The other type of threat pertained to the low competitiveness of the Indian economy, which had now been additionally exposed to a far more efficient world economy through the drastic reduction in customs tariffs. The challenge in this respect involved reforming, in particular, the system of domestic indirect taxes since the existing one not only evidenced cascading taxes, which made Indian goods less competitive, but its plethora of tax structures across India seriously segmented the internal market. Reform was imperative, as the ThFC task force had underlined in a slightly different context, because it was "critical to the survival of the Indian industry in the face of increasing international competition."[55]

It is precisely the reform of the existing indirect tax system through a GST—which, admittedly, is work that is still in progress, but its direction is nonetheless abundantly manifest—that is set to unify India's many tax structures into a single tax system, thus making for the development of the common market in India. A common market may or may not have been intended in undertaking tax reform, but the sequence of events generated by the turn to globalization and liberalization has led India inexorably in this direction. This sequence can be indicated in a simplified manner as:

> globalization → sharp reduction in customs tariffs and income taxes → anticipated fall in revenues and threat from foreign competition → search for revenues from other sources and for means to enhance economic competitiveness → undertaking reform of tax system through VAT and GST → unification of various indirect tax systems across India → likely reduction of economic

segmentation and consolidation of common market and enhancement of economic competitiveness.

Beyond this interpretation, which grounds the development of the common market in the material need to generate revenues and to enhance economic competitiveness, globalization also provided the stimulus to tax reform from another direction—that of *emulation*. As India began its reintegration into the world economy, it was spurred to become increasingly interested in how other countries had organized and operated their tax systems. Indian decision makers now aspired to establishing a "world class" tax system and to adopting "best international practices." They were increasingly persuaded that modern states necessarily featured VAT and GST as core elements of their indirect tax systems, and India needed perforce to follow their model.

Interestingly, Chelliah characterized the recommendations of the Tax Reforms Committee, which he had chaired, as being in accord with international thinking on these matters and maintained that, if adopted, they would lead to the kind of tax structure that is being built up in several Asian countries.[56] It is noteworthy that not just economists but the government itself at the center was cognizant of the need to adopt the best international practices as part of the economic liberalization project. Indeed, the NDA government's Ministry of Finance appointed a special eleven-member task force in 2002, headed by Kelkar, with the explicit mandate "to bring the indirect tax systems and procedures at par with the best international practices and thus, encourage compliance and reduce transaction costs."[57] The task force's own view of globalization was definitely a positive one, and it set an ambitious goal for both the government and the country. It urged both to embrace globalization wholeheartedly and comprehensively:

> It is the need of the hour to move away from incremental changes, from the policy of taking ad-hoc and half-hearted measures. What is required is a formulation for a macro-jump of the Indian economy so that India is no longer perceived as a nation hesitantly approaching globalization—a strategy that revolutionizes the way things are looked at and causes fundamental changes in the way things are done in indirect tax administration. Only such a strategy would result in a quantum improvement in the administration of indirect tax system in the country. India must be seen as an economy offering the best internationally accepted standards of tax administration and tax payer facilitation—now and for all time to come.[58]

The task force then went on to lay down six guiding principles to serve as the touchstone against which India's tax system should be measured. It is worthy of note that the second of these six principles was the adoption of the best international practices, the others being: trust, simplicity, transparency, stability, and service. Explaining its view, the task force averred: "Having committed ourselves to fully integrate with the world economy we can no longer remain unconcerned about having procedures which are not at par with the best in the world." Bringing the threat element into the argument, it maintained: "It is only by adopting the best international practices that we can hope to compete internationally." The task force recognized that some improvements had taken place in tax administration, but urged: "We must act in a hurry and quickly do much more."[59]

Three years later, another Kelkar task force—on fiscal consolidation—also stressed the emulation factor; it reminded policymakers and the public that a large number of developing countries (including Bangladesh, Indonesia, Korea, Nepal, and Thailand in Asia alone) had undertaken reform with "a simple VAT with a broad base and a few rates, and a simple law." It went on to underline that "India is yet to fully catch up with such reforming countries in its VAT reform at the central level." Significantly, it described its own proposal for a comprehensive VAT system for the center and states as instituting a "world-class tax system."[60] It is evident, then, that globalization, through both its *threat* and *emulation* effects, has indirectly facilitated moving toward the establishment of a common market in India.[61]

SUMMARY AND CONCLUSION

Ideas, interests, and institutions all have been involved in tax reform in India during the period since the paradigm shift in economic policy. While long held as a vision by the national leadership, the common market as an achievable policy goal became a matter of active pursuit only with globalization and economic liberalization, which ended the regime of slow-growth socialist autarky. It is globalization that sharpened the necessity for the national leadership to achieve that goal because of the threat that it created for the national economy even as it facilitated the achievement of the goal, albeit only in slow installments, by opening up wider horizons for the leadership about tax and economic models elsewhere in the world. Globalization, it would appear, is not a single unified social force, but one that incorporates many trends and crosscurrents, some perhaps tending toward market segmentation but others aiding market integration instead.

At the same time, India's actions in response to globalization, whether as threat or as stimulus to emulation, demonstrate that the state is no passive bystander to developments in the world economy. Where the state perceives threats, whether from the world economy or from the interstate system, to the stability of the national economy or to its own integrity, it intervenes directly and proactively to ward them off. This assessment, arising from the particular case of tax reform in India, is reinforced by the massive state interventions in countries across the world in response to the worldwide financial crisis in 2008. Even though the common market has not yet fully arrived in India, impressive strides toward it have been made through tax reform. These strides have occurred during globalization, have been compelled by it, and have been facilitated by it.

The common market, however, does not follow automatically from globalization. The movement toward the common market in India underlines the critical role of the state and political institutions in generating adequate responses to the challenges of globalization. However, like globalization, the state is not a single entity either. While there are some elements in the state, particularly at the center, that have eagerly pursued the building of a common market and have shown considerable statesmanship and political sagacity in building political consensus and innovatively creating new political institutions to foster the common market, there are other elements in the political structure that have resisted reform. It is in the interstices of the relationship between these two opposing sets of elements in the state that the movement toward the common market has taken place.

NOTES

1. Raja J. Chelliah, *Towards Sustainable Growth: Essays in Fiscal and Financial Sector Reforms in India* (Delhi: Oxford University Press, 1996), 147–48.
2. M. Govinda Rao, "Tax System Reform in India: Achievements and Challenges Ahead," paper prepared for the International Symposium on Tax Policy and Reform in Asian Countries, Hitotsubhashi University, Tokyo, Japan, July 1–2, 2005. Available at www.econ.hit-u.ac.jp/~kokyo/sympojuly05/papers/Tax%20System%20Reform-Tokyo(india)2.pdf.
3. See also Government of India (GoI), Tax Reforms Committee, *Interim Report* (New Delhi: Ministry of Finance, 1991), 15.
4. Rao, "Tax System Reform in India," 7.
5. Ibid., 5, 20.
6. Chelliah, *Towards Sustainable Growth*, 148–49.
7. Cited in Rao, "Tax System Reform in India," 19.
8. Ibid., 3, 20.
9. Ibid., 22–23.
10. Chelliah, *Towards Sustainable Growth*, 7.
11. M. Govinda Rao and R. Kavita Rao, "Trends and Issues in Tax Policy and Reform in India," in *The India Policy Forum 2005–06*, ed. Arvind Panagariya and Suman Bery (New Delhi: Sage, 2006), 58–61.
12. Ibid., 118.
13. Rao, "Tax System Reform in India," 9–10.
14. GoI, Tax Reforms Committee, *Interim Report*, 38.
15. GoI, Tax Reforms Committee, *Final Report: Part I* (New Delhi: Ministry of Finance, August 1992), 6.
16. Ibid., 5, 36, 171–72.
17. Parthasarathi Shome, "India: Resource Mobilization through Taxation," in *A Sustainable Fiscal Policy for India: An International Perspective*, ed. Peter S. Heller and M. Govinda Rao (New Delhi: Oxford University Press, 2006), 197–98.

18. GoI, Tax Reforms Committee, *Interim Report*, 1–2, and *Final Report: Part I*, and *Final Report: Part II* (New Delhi: Ministry of Finance, 1993).

19. GoI, Tax Reforms Committee, *Interim Report*, 108, and *Final Report: Part I*, 3.

20. GoI, Tax Reforms Committee, *Final Report*, 36, 172.

21. GoI, "Final Report of the Expert Group on Taxation of Services," typescript, Department of Revenue, Ministry of Finance, New Delhi, 2001, 21, 26.

22. GoI, *Economic Survey, 2012–13* (New Delhi: Ministry of Finance, 2013), 65–66.

23. On the differentiation between the two types of federalism, see M. Govinda Rao and Nirvikar Singh, *The Political Economy of Federalism* (New Delhi: Oxford University Press, 2005), 152.

24. GoI, Tax Reforms Committee, *Interim Report*, 108; emphasis added.

25. This and the following three paragraphs are based on National Institute of Public Finance and Policy, *Reform of Domestic Trade Taxes in India—Issues and Options: Report of a Study Team* (New Delhi: NIPFP, 1994), xx–xxiii, 19.

26. M. Govinda Rao, "Think TIN, Not Just GST," *Business Standard*, March 21, 2010; available at www.business-standard.com.

27. Empowered Committee of State Finance Ministers, *A White Paper on State-Level Value Added Tax* (New Delhi, January 17, 2005), 3; available at www.tinxsys.com.

28. Yashwant Sinha, *Confessions of a Swadeshi Reformer* (New Delhi: Penguin/Viking, 2007), 128–29.

29. Empowered Committee of State Finance Ministers, *A White Paper*, 4.

30. Sinha, *Confessions*, 129.

31. See GoI, *Report of the Advisory Group on Tax Policy and Tax Administration for the Tenth Plan* (New Delhi: Planning Commission, May 2001); available at http://planning commission.nic.in.

32. Empowered Committee of State Finance Ministers, *A White Paper*, 14.

33. Ibid., 13.

34. Ibid., 16.

35. Shome, "India," 211.

36. GoI, *Report of the Advisory Group*, 20, 197.

37. Ibid., 20–21, 197–98.

38. GoI, *Report of the Task Force on Implementation of the Fiscal Responsibility and Budget Management Act, 2003* (New Delhi: Ministry of Finance, July 2004), 44, 48–49; available at http://finmin.nic.in.

39. Ibid., 72–74, 153, 158; emphasis added.

40. Ibid., 153–55, 161.

41. "A Model and Road Map for Goods and Services Tax in India—Views of the Empowered Committee of State Finance Ministers," New Delhi, April 30, 2008, cited in GoI, Thirteenth Finance Commission, *Report of the Task Force on Goods and Services Tax* (New Delhi, December 15, 2009), 3; available at http://fincomindia.nic.in.

42. Empowered Committee of State Finance Ministers, *First Discussion Paper on Goods and Services Tax in India* (New Delhi: Ministry of Finance, November 10, 2009); available at http://finmin.nic.in.

43. Ibid., 8.

44. Ibid., 13–24.

45. GoI, Thirteenth Finance Commission, 2010–2015, *Volume I: Report* (New Delhi: Finance Commission, December 2009), 64–65.

46. GoI, Thirteenth Finance Commission, *Report of the Task Force*, 3.

47. Ibid., 119–20.

48. Ibid., 112–13.

49. Ibid., 3, 114, 120.

50. Ibid., 5.

51. Ibid., 85.

52. Ibid., 103.

53. Ibid., 105.

54. This section draws on news reports in the contemporaneous daily press and individual discussions with officials, academicians, and newspaper columnists during November and December 2010.

55. GoI, Thirteenth Finance Commission, *Report of the Task Force*, 112.

56. Chelliah, *Towards Sustainable Growth*, 89.

57. GoI, *Task Force Report on Indirect Taxes: Final Report on Indirect Taxes* (New Delhi: Ministry of Finance, 2002), para. 1.2. While this report is no longer available on the Internet, the paragraphs cited here are the same as in GoI, *Consultation Paper: Task Force on Indirect Taxes* (New Delhi: Ministry of Finance, October 2002); available at www.gstindiablog.com.

58. GoI, *Task Force Report on Indirect Taxes*, para. 2.3.

59. Ibid., para. 2.7.

60. GoI, *Report of the Task Force on Implementation of the Fiscal Responsibility*, 53–54, 153.

61. Beyond the notion of the common market as an unintended consequence of globalization, it also can be suggested that the advance to the common market has a teleological element in that such advance had a basis in intention since the common market has been a long-held goal of the leadership in India. On this aspect, see Baldev Raj Nayar, "Globalization, the State, and India's Halting March to Common Market: The Political Economy of Tax Reform under Federalism," *India Review* 10, no. 3 (July–September 2011): 234–40. It is remarkable, however, that not much movement took place in this direction before economic liberalization.

III

THE MARKET AFTER ECONOMIC LIBERALIZATION

Chapter 7

TRADE AND ITS INTEGRATIVE IMPACT

PART I of this study provides the background to investigating the issue of the impact of globalization on India's economic integration. Part II analyzes the postliberalization policy responses of *the state* in the cause of advancing economic integration in the three areas of economic planning, fiscal federalism, and the indirect tax system. Part III now turns to examine the role of *the market* in economic integration. A major caveat is essential, however, prior to such an examination—the market does not stand as a separate entity independent of the state or society. The market as a social institution has emerged out of society, its development and form in each society have been deeply influenced by state policy and other social institutions, and it ideally functions within the state-established legal and regulatory parameters. Accordingly, the form and nature of the market vary from state to state. Still, the state and the market have their separate logics and, while the state cannot leave the market alone because its functioning has consequences for state and society, too much intervention by the state can also undermine the performance of the market and thus deprive society of the fruits of its efficient working.[1] This predicament would seem to be especially applicable to India, given the political and administrative legacy of its earlier socialist regime and the fact that the reforms instituted in 1991 and after represent only a case of *limited liberalization*, with substantial areas of the economy still subject to discretionary decision making by the state.

Part III consists of four chapters; three of these deal with the roles of the three linkage mechanisms of trade, investment, and migration in India's economic integration. These mechanisms have to do with flows of three different economic elements—goods and services, capital, and labor, respectively—which serve to link different parts of the economy. The nature of these mechanisms and the factors that influence them provide an indication of the present state and future prospects of integration. The fourth of these chapters supplements the one on investment and deals with the carriers of capital, that is, the capitalist class.

This chapter looks at the role of trade in India's economic integration. It has three sections, the first of which deals briefly with the issue of whether the market makes for polarization or diffusion in economic growth. The second section investigates the question of whether trade has had an integrating or a segmenting effect in India after economic liberalization, while the third section examines the impact of trade and other linkage mechanisms on economic convergence or divergence among India's states. As against the critics' position, the evidence here demonstrates that despite many state-established impediments, trade under globalization and liberalization has aided economic integration rather than segmentation.

THE MARKET AND ECONOMIC INTEGRATION: POLARIZATION VERSUS DIFFUSION

In 1957, Gunnar Myrdal offered the concepts of (1) *backwash effects* and (2) *spread effects* within his larger theory of *circular cumulative causation*. Simply put, his position was that, when in the course of economic activity, development is triggered in a region (core), it can have either a beneficial impact (spread effects) or an adverse impact (backwash effects) in a reinforcing manner in other regions (periphery) through trade, capital movements, and migration. Myrdal believed that the backwash effects tended to be predominant and, strongly pessimistic about the possibilities of self-generated regional or international equality, he favored recourse to public policy in order to assure greater equality.[2] In contrast, Albert Hirschman was more optimistic and thought that economic development, with (1) *trickling down* predominating over (2) *polarization*, would be favorable to greater equality over the long term.[3] Jeffrey Williamson offered a synthesis of the two opposed pessimistic and optimistic orientations by suggesting an "inverted U" pattern to the process, with the backwash effects or polarization dominant in the short term and the spread effects or trickling down more influential over the longer term.[4] Note here may also be taken of the concept advanced by Paul Krugman about *agglomeration economies* that attach to an industrialized "core," as against an agricultural "periphery."[5]

Broadly understood, these various concepts taken together imply that, once triggered, the process of economic growth leads to the development of a core, which, because of the economies that inhere in it, tends to become a magnet for attracting the factors of production. The consequent cumulative expansion of the core can often be at the cost of the periphery, as capital and labor migrate to the core with the result that the periphery is likely to see economic decline—a consequence that can be politically damaging to national integration.[6] This *polarization* process, however, is not everlasting or irreversible, though opinion varies on the imminence of such reversal. As the core cumulatively advances, at a certain stage, it tends to generate diseconomies (say, labor shortages and high wages, or excessive congestion and high land prices, or dense traffic and pollution) that then drive entrepreneurs to other locations and persuade labor to do likewise. In the process, new cores arise, thus contributing to the *diffusion* or spread of economic growth. In this fashion, markets themselves are driven to countering the tendency toward concentration of factors of production in the core and thus, instead, to reducing or moderating disparities between core and periphery. Thus, markets can be said to carry a self-correcting mechanism that may, at least over the longer term, foster economic integration through the diffusion of economic growth across regions.

In the eyes of many, however, especially in democratic contexts, the prospect of diffusion—and thus of economic integration and overcoming of segmentation—under the normal processes of the market extends too far into the future. Understandably, then, there are strong pressures for state intervention to overcome segmentation and to hasten the process of economic integration. In trying to accomplish this end, however, prudence may be necessary, especially where state capacity is weak, in order to have the state work with the market rather than against it, so that public policy supplements the market instead of supplanting it.

TRADE—FOREIGN AND DOMESTIC: INTEGRATING OR SEGMENTING?

Trade is a key stimulus to economic integration, and it can also serve as an important policy instrument to bring about integration. Trade is also an indicator of the state of economic integration. Here, we begin with international trade since it affects domestic trade. Increased international trade symbolizes greater international economic integration (contemporarily, globalization), while a reduction in international trade indicates lesser integration (deglobalization, protectionism) as had occurred during the Great Depression in the 1930s.

India's Reintegration into the World Economy

Prior to economic liberalization, India was poorly integrated with the world economy; its level of international integration was minimal. In 1991, India's merchandise exports were 0.50 percent of world exports; surprisingly, at independence, India's share of world exports was more than four times higher, at 2.17 percent in 1949. Later, it went on a course of consistent decline, reaching 0.48 percent in 1974 and then hovering around the half percentage mark during the subsequent decade and a half.[7] This lack of integration with the world economy was consistent with the inward-oriented autarkic economic strategy of the preliberalization period.

Since economic liberalization, however, there has been a dramatic change in India's integration with the world economy. Foreign trade (exports plus imports) in goods and services as a share of GDP was 12.95 percent in 1976, and after a decade and a half it stood at 15.68 percent in 1990. But in the subsequent two decades it expanded to 46.32 percent, that is, three times the level before liberalization. Indeed, India is now more integrated with the world economy than the United States and Japan. Table 7.1 provides data for 2010 on trade for the top twenty economies of the world (plus the major economies of South Asia). India is at the medium level of international integration or globalization; most of these economies are in the high and above category. While India's foreign trade, as a share of its GDP, expanded threefold between 1990 and 2010, the expansion in constant (2000) U.S. dollars was more than eleven-fold from $38.4 billion in 1990 to $451.2 billion in 2010.[8]

Although India's integration with the world economy lags considerably behind that of the other major economies, for the critics of globalization, even this level of integration is inimical to India's interests. The critics posit *economic stagnation* as one of globalization's consequences for the domestic economy.[9] However, the empirical data do not support this position. Table 7.2, which provides data on GDP growth for the period from 1981 to 2010, establishes this point clearly. Economic liberalization as a more radical incarnation of policy reform may have begun in 1991, but it can be taken to have actually started in a gradual and incremental manner as early as 1975. Regardless, the three decades after 1981 demonstrate a remarkably long period of growth. Contrary to the predictions of economic stagnation, the Indian economy continued to expand during the period of structural adjustment and economic restructuring following the crisis years of 1990 and 1991. The average growth rate from 1992 to 2002 was a healthy 5.8 percent. What stands out, however, is the acceleration of the growth rate to an average of 8.2 percent in the eight years from 2003 to 2010. Subsequently, there was a setback to economic growth, in which both external shocks and domestic policy failures were implicated; the growth rate dropped to 6.9 percent in 2011, and likely even lower to 5.0 percent in 2012. In absolute terms, India's GDP in constant (2000) U.S. dollars increased 3.7 times, from $279.4 billion in 1991 to $1.0 trillion in 2011.[10]

The critics also posit another malign consequence of globalization—*social marginalization*. However, provided we use the same—and not constantly shifting—criteria for defining poverty, the period since liberalization has seen a consistent decline in poverty, particularly during growth acceleration. It is true that the period of high growth has seen a rise in inequality, with the first decile of the population benefiting greatly from it. While such increased inequality may or may not be normatively acceptable, it has not been accompanied by an increase in impoverishment at the lower levels, as is made evident by the decline in the proportion of the population below the poverty line (BPL).

Of course, the very definition of the poverty line has been mired in controversy. In 2010, following the recommendations of a committee headed by a renowned economist, the late Suresh Tendulkar, the government upgraded the definition of the poverty line somewhat, particularly for the rural population.

Table 7.1. Share of Trade in GDP (%) of World's Top 20 (Plus South Asian) Economies in 2010

Low (10–29%)		*Medium (30–49%)*		*High (50–79%)*		*Very High (80–109%)*		*Super High (110% and Higher)*	
Brazil	23.30	Pakistan	32.32	Russia	51.75	Poland	85.76	Netherlands	148.63
United States	28.77	Australia	41.39	Sri Lanka	52.51	Germany	88.18		
Japan	29.29	Bangladesh	43.42	France	53.27	Switzerland	95.76		
		India	46.32	Spain	54.68	S. Korea	101.99		
		Indonesia	47.59	China	55.23				
		Turkey	47.76	Italy	55.33				
				Canada	60.74				
				U.K.	62.29				

Source: World Development Indicators, http://databank.worldbank.org/data/views/variableSelection/selectvariables.aspx?source=world-development-indicators, accessed March 30, 2012; the figure for Australia is for 2008.

Table 7.2. GDP Growth Rate (%): 1981–2010

Year	*Rate*	*Year*	*Rate*	*Year*	*Rate*
1981	6.0	1991	1.1	2001	4.9
1982	3.5	1992	5.5	2002	3.9
1983	7.3	1993	4.8	2003	7.4
1984	3.8	1994	6.7	2004	7.8
1985	5.3	1995	7.6	2005	9.3
Avg.	5.2	Avg.	5.1	Avg.	6.7
1986	4.8	1996	7.5	2006	9.3
1987	4.0	1997	4.0	2007	9.8
1988	9.6	1998	6.2	2008	3.9
1989	5.9	1999	8.5	2009	8.2
1990	5.5	2000	4.0	2010	9.6
Avg.	5.9	Avg.	6.0	Avg.	8.2
				2011	6.9
Average for 1992–2002: 5.8		Average for 2003–10: 8.2			

Source: World Development Indicators, http://databank.worldbank.org/data/views/variableSelection/selectvariables.aspx?source=world-development-indicators, accessed March 30, 2012 and April 10, 2013.

While the new methodology undoubtedly served to drastically increase the proportion of the BPL population, it could not reverse the manifest declining *trend* in poverty after economic liberalization, particularly the increased pace of decline during growth acceleration (see table 7.3). Whereas the annual rate of reduction in poverty was 0.74 percent between the periods 1993–94 and 2004–5, that rate tripled to 2.18 percent between the periods 2004–5 and 2011–12, coinciding with growth acceleration. In the seven years of the latter period, evidently 137.8 million people were lifted above the poverty line.

Understandably, the low level of living standards in general—along with the fact that hundreds of millions continue to live in abysmal poverty and the decline in poverty is slow—evokes great anguish and dismay among the intelligent-

Table 7.3. Decline in Poverty after Economic Liberalization under Tendulkar Method (%)

NSS		*Poverty Level (% of Pop.)*			*Annual Rate of Reduction (%)*			*Nos. Below Poverty Line (Mill.)*		
Round	*Year*	*Rural*	*Urban*	*Total*	*Rural*	*Urban*	*Total*	*Rural*	*Urban*	*Total*
50	1993–94	50.1	31.8	45.3	—	—	—	328.6	74.5	403.7
61	2004–5	41.8	25.7	37.2	0.75	0.55	0.74	326.3	80.8	407.1
68	2011–12	25.7	13.7	21.9	2.32	1.69	2.18	216.5	52.8	269.3

Source: GoI, "Press Note on Poverty Estimates, 2011–12" (New Delhi: Planning Commission, July 2013), 3.

sia. However, that angst does not void the conclusion that globalization has not had the consequence of increasing pauperization that the critics had charged it would. Rather, the period since liberalization has seen a consistent decline in poverty. In any case, the period of socialist autarky prior to economic liberalization was no idyll, and it is really the tremendous backlog of poverty left behind by that period that continues to provide the challenge for the country.

Trade Expansion and Infrastructure Growth

As one would expect, the growth of the economy has been accompanied by considerable trade expansion in the country. Trade had grown steadily year after year over the entire planning period before economic liberalization (except for 1979–80). After liberalization, its growth speeded up considerably. As a share of *net* domestic product, trade now outranks both agriculture and manufacturing and almost rivals financing (see table 7.4). Besides, the trade expansion is certainly reflected in foreign trade. In terms of constant (2000) U.S. dollars, India's exports of goods and services expanded from $21.9 billion in 1992 to $265.9 billion in 2011; similarly, its imports of goods and services increased from $23.3 billion to $304.7 billion over the same period.[11]

The trade expansion has, in turn, been accompanied by a considerable augmentation of the physical infrastructure in the country, even though poor and inadequate infrastructure remains the Achilles' heel of Indian development. Although the route length of the railway network—which, as the fourth largest in the world, crisscrosses the country—has not seen a substantial increase like China's, the numbers of passengers carried by it have vastly expanded, as have the numbers of tonnes of freight transported (see table 7.5). The number of "passengers originating" after economic liberalization grew from 3.86 billion in 1990–91 to 4.83 billion in 2000–2001, with the subsequent nine years seeing particularly hectic growth, as passenger traffic increased to 7.25 billion in 2009–10. The enormous growth in passenger traffic is replicated in freight traffic, which increased by about 50 percent from 318 million tonnes in 1990–91 to 474 million tonnes in 2000–2001 and then about doubled over the subsequent nine years, to 888 million tonnes in 2009–10 (in 2013, India joined the select group of world railways carrying more than one billion tonnes of freight a year).[12] Importantly, in 2009–10, the bulk commodities of coal, iron ore, iron and steel, cement, petroleum and oil, and fertilizers constituted almost 85 percent of the freight traffic, with coal alone at 45 percent. Briefly, economic liberalization has given an immense boost to passenger and freight traffic on the railways.

Unlike the railways, where there has been inadequate expansion and modernization of the network, the road network length has seen an enormous expansion since independence and especially since economic liberalization; it is the third-largest such network in the world, even if much of it is of poor quality. The total length increased from 2.3 million km in 1991 to 3.4 million km in 2001 and

Table 7.4. Trade as a Share of GDP (%)

Sector	*1960–61*	*1970–71*	*1980–81*	*1990–91*	*2000–2001*	*2004–5*	*2008–9*
Trade	8.5	9.5	10.6	12.1	13.1	14.6 (16.1)	15.0 (16.5)
Agriculture	45.4	39.4	34.4	28.7	21.8	15.9 (16.3)	13.2 (13.5)
Manufacturing	10.9	12.6	13.8	14.9	15.3	15.3 (13.4)	15.6 (13.6)
Financing	7.0	6.8	7.5	10.6	13.0	14.7 (15.0)	16.9 (17.5)

Sources: GoI, Central Statistical Organization, Press Releases and Statements: (1) Summary of Macroeconomic Aggregates (1999–2000 Prices), 1950–51 to 2008–9: "Statement 1: Gross Domestic Product by Economic Activity"; and (2) "*New Series of National Accounts Statistics (Base Year 2004–05)*" (New Delhi: March 2010), 94, 98.

Notes:

1. Figures for 1960–61 to 2000–2001 are in 1999–2000 prices, while those for 2004–5 and 2008–9 are in 2004–5 prices.
2. Figures in parentheses are for *net* domestic product.
3. Financing includes banking and insurance, real estate, and business services.

Table 7.5. Transport Infrastructure

	1950–51	*1970–71*	*1990–91*	*2000–2001*	*2009–10*
Railways					
Route km Total	53,596	59,970	63,367	63,028	63,974
Route km Electrified	388	3,706	9,968	14,856	18,927
Passenger Traffic (mill.)	1,284	1,594	3,858	4,833	7,246
Freight Traffic (tonnes mill.)	73	168	318	474	888
Roads					
Length—Total ('000 km)	399	915	2,331	3,374	4,109
Length—Surfaced	157	398	1,091	1,601	2,036
Registered Vehicles					
Total ('000)	306	1,865	21,374	54,991	114,951
Goods Vehicles ('000)	82	343	1,356	2,948	6,041
Buses ('000)	34	94	331	634	1,486

Sources: GoI, Ministry of Railways, *Indian Railways Yearbook 2009–10* (New Delhi: Railway Board, 2010), available at www.indianrailways.gov.in/railwayboard, accessed April 5, 2012; GoI, *Economic Survey 1996–97* (New Delhi: Ministry of Finance, 1997), S-32; and *Economic Survey 2011–12* (New Delhi: Ministry of Finance, 2012), A-30.

Note: The figures under 2009–10 for Roads are for 2007–8, and the figures for Registered Vehicles are for 2008–9.

4.2 million km in 2008 (66,754 km of national highways and 154,522 km of state highways). The expansion of the road network has greatly added to connectivity in India. Indeed, such expansion has had economic and national integration as a specific goal, especially through road-building programs such as the Golden Quadrilateral (linking the four large metropolises) and the North-South/East-West Corridors with four- to six-lane highways. Meanwhile, the number of registered motor vehicles exploded from 21.37 million (1.36 million trucks) in 1990–

91 to 54.99 million (2.95 million trucks) in 2000–2001 and 114.95 million (33.48 million trucks) in 2008–9. Freight haulage by road has expanded rapidly at the expense of the railways, where cross-subsidization of passenger travel by freight carriage has adversely affected railway business. The truckers have been increasingly taking the freight business away from the railways in categories other than bulk commodities. Roads now carry some 60–65 percent of all domestic freight.[13] Despite the vast expansion in railways and road transport, the lagging infrastructure, including power generation, remains a serious constraint on India's economic growth.

The augmentation of the infrastructure—even if not adequate—does not, however, necessarily translate into economic integration of the country. Indeed, it can result in economic segmentation, as the critics suggest. If parts of the national economy are tied up only with world markets while most of it remains outside this linkage, unconnected with those parts or with the world, then surely that is a description of economic segmentation. However, the critics are not the only ones who hold the view that globalization may result in segmentation; so do many among India's political class, though they may not admit it openly. Interestingly, in 2003, a senior government leader, K. C. Pant, then deputy chairman of India's Planning Commission, gave public expression to the fear of segmentation, even though his target was not globalization but regional protectionism within India: "It is ironic that during a period when as a nation we are embracing globalization, we still persist with local protectionism. Unless we reverse this process decisively, a day may come when parts of our country become more closely integrated with the global economy than with their neighboring States. This would place unbearable strain on the unity and integrity of our nation."[14]

This concern with economic segmentation and integration raises an important issue. Has domestic (internal, inland) trade also expanded to keep abreast of—or stay ahead of—foreign trade as a contributor to and indicator of domestic economic integration? Or, has it lagged behind and is subsidiary or even subservient to external trade, thus contributing to economic segmentation? Has domestic trade expanded more during the period of reform (1990s) or the period of growth acceleration (2000s)? A major limitation, however, is noteworthy with regard to studying domestic trade—unlike foreign trade, there is absence of data specifically on domestic trade alone. Perhaps in the future, if a nationwide goods and services tax (GST) system is established, it may be possible to generate separate data on domestic trade, but for now, the lack of such data places serious constraints on drawing firm conclusions on the subject.

Trade Expansion and Economic Integration

There can be no doubt that trade in the country has expanded enormously in the postliberalization period. The point at issue, however, is whether this trade expansion has served merely to segment the economy or to contribute to *domestic* economic integration. True, integration with the international economy has increased substantially, and potentially that can cause economic segmentation if parts of the domestic economy become integrated with the world economy while other parts remain isolated from it. However, international integration per se is not necessarily inconsistent with domestic integration. There is no reason to assume some inevitable zero-sum relationship between national and international integration. It is not inconceivable that both national and international integration can advance at the same time. Such an inference can reasonably be drawn from the conclusions of a 2006 study on market integration—a first of its kind—at the highly reputed economic policy think tank the Indian Council for Research in International Economic Relations (ICRIER) by Arvind Virmani and Surabhi Mittal.[15]

Virmani and Mittal examined consumer price ratios for about two hundred commodities across seventy centers in India in 2004 with a view to determining the extent of market integration. Their study also compared change in market integration between 1994 and 2004 for twenty-four select commodities (since data for all commodities were not available for 1994). In respect of 2004, obviously the law of one price cannot be said to hold for the market in India, since the consumer price ratio varied in the range of 1:1.47. Admittedly, this ratio is too extreme; as the authors acknowledge: "The mean consumer price ratio is 1.10, or 10 percent above the lowest price in the 2004 sample. If we consider West Maharashtra (1.47) as an outlier even then consumers in Rajasthan pay 18 percent higher than the lowest price state Bihar." They find evidence, too, of regional clustering, with the southern states having prices higher by 12 to 14 percent than elsewhere. Interestingly, Virmani and Mittal found that "the manufactured goods market is much more integrated than the primary food market," obviously because of controls imposed by states on movement of agricultural commodities.[16]

The study's conclusion on the comparison between consumer prices in 1994 and 2004 is particularly noteworthy:

> For all commodities the consumer price ratio ranged from 1–1.20 in 1994 and this range has narrowed down to 1–1.06 in 2004. In a decade's time the sample mean has declined from 1.09 to 1.03. If we take CV [coefficient of variation] as *the measure of integration* among states, then, *a high level of integration is visible in [the] last ten years.* The CV of all the commodities was 0.06 in 1994 which declined to 0.02 in 2004. . . . There is very clear evidence that, across India, *states are moving towards one price* . . . in a decade's time [the] commodity markets network has been strengthened. CV has shown uniform decline across all commodities and their subgroups between the two points of time, offering *strong evidence of market integration in India.*[17]

The study demonstrates that, even as India was becoming more integrated with the world economy between 1994 and 2004 under the impact of globalization and liberalization, it was also becoming more integrated internally.

The study by Virmani and Mittal was done just as India entered the period of growth acceleration. Perhaps the growth acceleration further strengthened the market integration. An analysis by Arne Melchior of different scenarios of international integration and their implications for economic growth and for domestic market integration in India concludes that the high growth scenario promotes greater domestic economic integration. In Melchior's estimation, high growth has the same internal integrative effect as economic autarky.[18] It turns out, then, that higher growth promotes not only welfare, poverty reduction, and increased government revenues but also *national* economic integration. In a sense, following Melchior, the postliberalization period in India should not be treated as a single piece but one that should be differentiated between (1) economic reform (1992–2002)—promoting integration with the world economy—and (2) growth acceleration (2003–10), which is expected to have intensified domestic market integration. Thus, economic liberalization can be taken to have promoted economic integration rather than economic segmentation and to have done so through advancing competition and, again, through generating growth acceleration.

Aviation: A Case Study in International and National Integration

Precisely the same point about globalization or economic liberalization not necessarily being opposed to domestic economic integration can be illustrated by using air travel as a proxy for trade in both the national arena and the international arena. Unlike trade, where domestic trade cannot be strictly differentiated from foreign trade, data on aviation allow us the unique opportunity to separate domestic air traffic within India from the country's international air traffic.

According to international aviation law, domestic air traffic is normally restricted to national carriers, and until the early 1990s in India, it was a monopoly of the public sector. International air traffic of a country, however, is usually shared equally between its national air carriers and the air carriers of foreign countries unless the particular country signs away its bilateral rights through design or negligence, neglects to build its national carrying capacity, or mismanages its aviation sector—with all of these characteristics unfortunately featured in India's case, to a greater or lesser extent.

Data on India's international air traffic are not fully available before 1993–94, but they are for the subsequent period. The separate data for domestic air travel and for international air travel (by both Indian and foreign carriers) enable us to examine the consequences of economic liberalization for each. During the second half of the 1980s, the air passenger traffic of India's scheduled carriers was roughly 9.5 million a year for domestic operations and about 2.5 million for international operations (see table 7.6). Interestingly, the initial year (1990–91) of the economic crisis of the early 1990s saw a sudden dip in India's passenger traffic, especially on the domestic scene. India did not recover from this drop in

Table 7.6. Domestic and International Aviation Passenger Traffic ('000) by Scheduled Carriers

		International Traffic: Indian and Foreign Carriers			
Year	*Domestic Traffic*	*Indian*	*Foreign*	*Total*	*Ratio: Domestic to International*
1985	8,825	2,207	N/A	—	—
1986	9,465	2,309	N/A	—	—
1987	9,786	2,547	N/A	—	—
1988	9,720	2,713	N/A	—	—
1989–90	9,529	2,678	N/A	—	—
1990–91	7,912	2,430	N/A	—	—
1991–92	8,919	2,234	N/A	—	—
1992–93	8,205	2,324	N/A	—	—
1993–94	9,938	2,321	5,521	7,842	1:0.79
1994–95	11,057	2,591	5,771	8,362	1:0.76
1995–96	12,188	3,094	6,551	9,645	1:0.79
1996–97	11,700	3,296	7,041	10,337	1:0.88
1997–98	11,545	3,436	7,403	10,839	1:0.94
1998–99	12,025	3,520	7,704	11,224	1:0.93
1999–2000	12,711	3,657	7,994	11,651	1:0.92
2000–2001	13,712	3,828	8,687	12,515	1:0.91
2001–2	12,854	3,698	8,452	12,150	1:0.95
2002–3	13,951	4,201	9,203	13,404	1:0.96
2003–4	15,677	4,493	10,372	14,865	1:0.95
2004–5	19,445	5,326	12,261	17,587	1:0.90
2005–6	25,205	6,547	14,016	20,563	1:0.82
2006–7	35,793	7,561	16,213	23,774	1:0.66
2007–8	44,355	9,108	18,492	27,600	1:0.62
2008–9	39,467	10,049	19,383	29,432	1:0.75
2009–10	45,359	11,611	21,016	32,627	1:0.72

Source: GoI, Directorate General of Civil Aviation, "Air Transport Statistics," various years; available at dgca.nic.in.

traffic until 1993–94, a year that can serve as a benchmark to evaluate the subsequent impact of liberalization on air traffic.

In 1993–94, the ratio between India's domestic traffic and its total international traffic (under both national and foreign carriers) was 1:0.79. This ratio began to change soon afterward in favor of international traffic, and continued to do so, though not always consistently, until it reached the figure of 1:0.96 in 2002–3, thus making the proportions of international traffic and domestic traffic almost equal. That is, during the first phase of liberalization (reform), in terms of air travel, India was becoming increasingly more integrated with the world outside rather than within the nation itself. At that point, however, there was a reversal of the trend. During the second phase of liberalization (growth acceleration), the proportion of domestic traffic to international traffic began to rise, again not always consistently, and reached the high point of 1:0.62 in 2007–8; it declined somewhat in the following two years, but it still remained higher than the starting point in 1993–94.

The basic conclusion suggested by the new trend is that increasing integration with the international economy is no bar to increased internal economic integration, since the density of India's domestic traffic also increased with liberalization. To be sure, India's international traffic increased about fourfold, from less than 8 million in 1993–94 to 32.6 million passengers in 2009–10, which meant higher integration with the world economy. But it is equally impressive that domestic air traffic increased more than four and a half times, from less than 10.0 million to 45.4 million over the same period. Compared to 1993–94, when the difference of domestic traffic over international traffic was only 2.1 million passengers, in 2009–10, the difference was as high as 13.7 million. For the period after this long-term comparison, preliminary data show that domestic passenger traffic grew from 45.3 million in 2009–10 to 54 million during 2010–11, while international traffic grew from 32.1 million to 38 million over the same period, with the difference between domestic and international traffic widening from 13.7 million in the previous year to 16.0 million in the later year.[19]

The integration with the international economy patently, thus, did not block the explosion in domestic air traffic and can indeed be said to have contributed to it. It is noteworthy that the reversal in the trend of the increasing ratio of international traffic to domestic traffic coincided precisely with the growth acceleration in the economy starting in 2003–4. That phenomenon supports Melchior's observation that high growth has integrative implications similar to a policy of economic autarky. Briefly, then, as illustrated by the case of aviation passenger traffic, international economic integration is not necessarily inconsistent with the intensification of domestic economic integration; indeed, it can augment it. The aviation experience also underlines the importance of high growth to economic integration.

However, India has considerable catching up to do in international air traffic. By right, its carriers should be carrying about half of the total international air passenger traffic rather than about a third, which it carries at present. Perhaps the trend will move in that direction, with the state finally having ended in 2012 the monopoly over India's rights in international air traffic that was long held by the egregiously mismanaged state-owned national carrier.

Regional Connectivity. While India's domestic air passenger traffic has evidently expanded enormously and at a faster rate than its international traffic, and globalization has thus not proven to be a block to the intensification of civil aviation as a national integrative mechanism, it may be objected that this conclusion says nothing about air connectivity within the country. In actuality, it is reasonable to assume that if there is a radical expansion of domestic air passenger traffic from 8 million in 1990–91 to 54 million in 2010–11, it could not help but enhance connectivity among the nation's regions, even if it were not evenly spread. Data in support of this point are not available over this long period, but some data for the more recent period underscore the point.

The domestic airline industry in India has undergone a vast churning during the postliberalization period as it transited from a state monopoly to a new aviation regime in 1994 that saw the entry and exit of many new private carriers, followed by mergers and a consolidation into six carriers by 2011. The period saw a remarkable decline in the fortunes of the state carrier, the share of which came down to 14.6 percent in the domestic market while the five private carriers had the rest. Meanwhile, since 2003, the industry has seen internal differentiation with the entry of low-cost carriers (LCCs) in addition to the existing full-service carriers (FSCs), which have also established their own low-cost subsidiaries or services. In 2011, India had three FSCs and three LCCs; in 2011–12, as high as 70 percent of the market was with the LCCs and the low-cost services of the FSCs. Jet Airways (FSC) along with its low-cost arms was the largest domestic carrier with a little more than 26 percent of the market, while IndiGo (LCC) was the second-largest domestic carrier with almost 20 percent of market share.[20]

One way to examine the issue of diffusion or polarization in civil aviation is to look at the state of air connectivity of the northeastern region. Except for a small strip of territory north of Bangladesh that connects India with the region, the northeastern region is largely disconnected geographically from the mainland; even internally, the region is poorly served by road or rail facilities. Besides this region, there are other parts of India, too, which are remote from the country's main economic centers. Table 7.7 demonstrates that air connectivity by way of the number of domestic flights per week increased at a much higher rate in the northeastern region (43 percent) and other remote areas—such as Jammu and Kashmir (72 percent), Andaman and Nicobar Islands (75 percent), and Lakshadweep Islands (67 percent)—during the five years from 2006 to 2011 than it did over the domestic network as a whole (39 percent). The increase in the number of flights need not all be attributed to the wonders of the market, because the hand of the state is very much visible in the outcome. The state has established route dispersal guidelines, which require air carriers to deploy to the remote (thus noneconomical) routes at least 10 percent of the capacity devoted to the intermetropolitan (thus surplus-generating) routes.[21]

In addition, a look at the destination points of the different domestic airlines can provide a broader view of the regional coverage by the airline industry and that industry's contribution to economic integration, even as it can indicate the relative economic and administrative importance of the different destinations and their larger region. Jet Airways has the largest number of domestic destinations—52 (besides 20 international); the figures for the other airlines are: Air India, 49 (26); Spice Jet, 45 (8); IndiGo, 28 (5); and GoAir, 21. However, it would

Table 7.7. Domestic Flights per Week to Northeastern Region and Other Remote Areas

Flights	*2006*	*2007*	*2008*	*2009*	*2010*	*2011*
Total Domestic Network	8,724	10,624	11,048	11,063	11,315	12,107
Northeastern Region	259	285	298	286	347	370
Jammu and Kashmir	104	116	110	113	120	179
Andaman and Nicobar Islands	24	42	42	35	40	42
Lakshadweep Islands	6	13	10	7	13	10

Source: GoI, *Report of Working Group on Civil Aviation Sector: National Transport Development Policy Committee* (New Delhi: Ministry of Civil Aviation, June 2012), 113.

Table 7.8. IndiGo—Number of Daily Flights from Originating Towns in India

Agartala	9	Delhi	105	Jaipur	13	Patna	7
Ahmedabad	26	Dibrugarh	2	Jammu	3	Pune	21
Bengaluru	57	Goa	15	Kochi	13	Raipur	6
Bhubaneshwar	13	Guwahati	13	Kolkata	53	Srinagar	8
Chandigarh	4	Hyderabad	42	Lucknow	19	Trivandrum	10
Chennai	36	Imphal	7	Mumbai	75	Vadodara	6
Coimbatore	5	Indore	7	Nagpur	14	Visakhapatnam	5

Source: Flight information from the IndiGo website, available at http://book.goindigo.in, accessed April 15, 2013.

be arduous to assess the number of flights with respect to destinations for all the airlines; here, the second-largest domestic air carrier with not too excessive a number of destinations—IndiGo—has been selected for analysis. IndiGo is known for its low-cost, hub-and-spoke business model that relies solely on a single type of aircraft, Airbus A320, and also for its on-time service. Table 7.8 shows the number of daily flights across the length and breadth of India.

While IndiGo with its modest number of destinations has quite a wide network, the metropolitan centers of Delhi (105 destinations), Mumbai (75), Bengaluru (57), Kolkata (53), Chennai (36), and Hyderabad (42) stand out in its domestic business. Some of the other airlines have more extensive networks, but the larger pattern of metropolitan dominance would seem to hold for them, too, since it reflects the economic and political power of the metropolitan centers. The metro airports account for 70 percent of all passengers handled at Indian airports. The six metropolitan centers, interestingly, lie at the north, west, south, and east ends of the country; remarkably, south India has three of these centers—Bengaluru, Chennai, and Hyderabad—a testimony to the rising economic power of the south. Not to be underestimated is the economic and administrative attraction of the Delhi-Mumbai sector, which has almost 60 percent of all the metro airports' traffic and about 41 percent of the entire passenger traffic for all the country's airports.[22] The larger conclusion is that, while passenger traffic is concentrated on some routes more than others, no region has been neglected.

The State as Facilitator and Impediment in Trade as Linkage Mechanism

Whether the market works to promote or retard economic integration through the trade mechanism is not just a function of the forces of the market but also of the very visible hand of the state. The state can act as a key facilitator of economic integration through trade by building the necessary physical and social infrastructure that assures greater connectivity between different parts of the economy. To be sure, the state has mounted a considerable effort in this direction, as evidenced by the intensification of freight and passenger movement by the railways and the massive road building undertaken during the first decade of the new century. Despite this activity of the state, however, the poor condition and inadequate nature of the infrastructure remain a serious constraint not only on economic growth but also on market integration. The weakness in infrastructure is, thus, one enormous impediment to more-effective trade and economic integration, for which considerable responsibility lies at the doors of the state.

But there are two other major barriers to trade for which the state is also entirely accountable. One pertains to government controls on the movement of goods and the other to the complex system of taxation of goods in transit. The two together have had seriously adverse consequences for market integration. As one government report observed in 2002: "All this has led to breaking up the vast Indian market into a large number of smaller regional markets. The paperwork involved in complying with the various controls, regulations and licenses, the cost involved in terms of time and resources and the inevitable corruption and malpractices that this leads to have served as [a] big drag on the efficiency of trading operations in the country."[23] Astonishingly, while India has been a single political system for six and a half decades, the degree of market integration in the country is less than in the European Union (EU) with respect to the ease with which goods can move across the borders of the constituent units of the system. As a Food and Agriculture Organization (FAO) study noted in 2005: "In India at present there are no internal customs duties but certain fiscal levies and administrative orders are sometimes applied to restrict or prevent movement of agricultural products from one state to another, which have led to erection of check posts at borders." Consequently, in that study's judgment, while India could be described as being close to a common market, it "has several steps to take to reach what, in EU terminology, would be called a Single Market."[24]

The original fault for this situation lies in India's constitution. While much is made of the center's dominant position in the distribution of powers, the constitution is flawed, as already underlined in this study, when it comes to upholding a common or single market. The constitution formally invokes and endorses the importance of a common market, but in actuality, it tends to foster market fragmentation. Article 301, which provides for free interstate commerce, is in fact riddled with such reservations as to nullify its impact, thus promoting economic segmentation.[25] In effect, the constitution allows the states to impose restrictions on the movement of goods across their borders in the name of public interest.

The key mechanism in the control of trade is the Essential Commodities Act, 1955, which is an umbrella legislation of the central government that enables states to restrict the storage and transport of various types of goods. The justification advanced for the continued existence of such controls is that they are essential to avoid hoarding and speculation in essential goods by traders but, as a government document admits, "they are typically misused by the lower levels of the administration and become an instrument for harassment and corruption."[26] At one time, there were one hundred items on the control list. The act was amended in 2006, when there were fourteen items on the list; the amendment reduced the number of controlled items to seven (drugs, fertilizers, foodstuffs, hank yarn, petroleum and petroleum products, raw jute and jute textiles, and seeds of various kinds); an eighth item, cotton, was added subsequently.[27]

If a state finds, for example, that there is an actual or a looming shortage of wheat, or cotton, or onions, and that this situation is likely to adversely affect the welfare of its populace, it can then place restrictions on the movement of such commodities out of the state. Or, if the state finds that there are shortages of such commodities in other parts of India with the result that there is likely to be a rapid outflow of them from the state, it may impose controls on their movement out of the state. To achieve its objectives, the state can utilize its existing checkpoints at its borders or undertake additional measures to control the movement of such goods. As a result, there are often huge lineups of trucks at border checkpoints, where truck drivers fill in multiple forms and wait for long hours for clearance. Thus, a system of internal "mercantilism" prevails through physical controls in place of customs duties.

Over and above the physical controls on movement of specified goods, there are constraints on trade through fiscal demands on traders and consumers. A complex and elaborate system of taxes acts as a powerful barrier to trade. The key feature of the system is multiple authorities, multiple taxes, multiple tax rates, and multiple checkpoints. As one authoritative study done for the central government pointed out: "The system [of trade taxes] that is operating at present is antiquated, complex—according to knowledgeable experts, the most complex in many ways. . . . Such a system causes incalculable damage to the economy by arbitrarily interfering with the decisions of economic agents. . . . Unless radically reformed, the tax system will impede the growth of the economy and realization of the full potential of the huge common market that the Union of India offers."[28]

No doubt, reform of indirect taxes has been under way since the 1980s, but it has been extremely slow and repeatedly stalled for long intervals. In 2005, the states replaced their multiple and variant sales tax systems with a consumption-based value added tax (VAT) with agreed common rates, but since then, they have started changing the rates so that their tax systems have again begun to diverge and become more complex. Meanwhile, the major piece of indirect tax reform in the shape of the GST still awaits consensus. Presently, the center imposes excise duty on manufactured goods at the factory gate and the states impose VAT on the sale of goods; in addition, the center collects the Central Sales Tax (CST) on interstate trade, which it then distributes among the states. But that is not the end of tax collections; there are also other taxes that traders have to contend with, such as purchase tax, market fees, and so forth. The most pernicious of the local taxes is the octroi, which many cities and municipal corporations levy on the entry of goods. As a consequence, it is not just India as a market that is broken up into regional markets by the states but there are also barriers to trade even within the states.

Take, for example, a truck carrying goods from Punjab's state capital of Chandigarh to its holy city of Amritsar, a distance of about 230 kilometers; during its journey, it will have to pay the octroi tax four times as it proceeds through some cities on the way. An FAO study adds: "More than the fiscal burden, the procedure involves harassment and long delays, sometimes leading to rent-seeking activities as well." No doubt, some states have abolished the octroi, but others have not. In addition, there are other transport constraints stemming from laws covering the trucking industry. These include the Motor Vehicles Act, the Motor Transport Workers Act, and the Carriage of Goods Act. The application of these laws means that "smooth flow of goods carriage is hampered to a great extent by frequent stoppage of vehicles for a variety of reasons. Vehicles are frequently detained for checking essential documents. . . . Besides, there are numerous other reasons under different legal provisions that can detain a vehicle, like check on the movement of essential commodities, food adulteration and hazardous chemicals etc. These checks are generally conducted by respective agencies at separate points, resulting in more than one detention."[29]

Taken together, the various taxes and license fees add to transaction costs, and at times it is cheaper for some of the coastal states to import goods from abroad than to have these transported from other states in India.

Figure 7.1 gives a comprehensive view of the various barriers to trade that exist in the Indian economy. It is apparent that domestic administrative authorities themselves, rather than globalization and economic liberalization, have done quite an effective job in segmenting the economy. The situation therefore calls for active harmonization of laws and practices between center, states, and local authorities so that barriers to internal trade are reduced in order to assure an effective common market.

Figure 7.1. The Regulatory Regime for Interstate Movement of Agricultural Goods

Regulatory Regime: Agricultural Goods

Commodity Specific	<------------------------------>	Location Specific
Restriction on Flow of Commodities	Fiscal Related	Restriction on Flow in Locations
Essential	Customs	National Borders
Hazardous	Excise	State Borders
Adulterated	Sales Tax	District Borders
Licensed	Octroi	Municipal Limits
Forest	Entry Tax	Law and Order
Endangered Species	Toll	Bridges
Others		Others

Enforcement Agencies are different, and a truck may be detained under any criteria

Random Checks
RTO: Road Tax, Payload, Permit
Police: Vehicle Papers
Forest, etc.

Source: Food and Agriculture Organization, "Towards an Indian Common Market: Removal of Restrictions on Internal Trade in Agricultural Commodities," submitted to the National Commission on Farmers, Ministry of Agriculture, Government of India, New Delhi, December 2005; available at www.fao.org/docrep/010/ai566e/ai566e00.htm. Reproduced with permission.

Note: RTO = Regional Transport Officer.

DIFFUSION OR POLARIZATION IN ECONOMIC GROWTH

Trade is a key linkage mechanism between different parts of the economy and is therefore an essential element in economic integration. It serves as a transmission belt between different segments of the economy, carrying impulses of economic growth or stagnation across the economy. As shown earlier, India has seen considerable growth of its economy since 1980. Trade, too, has seen continuous expansion and now forms a share of the GDP that is larger than that of agriculture and manufacturing. Of course, trade is not the only linkage mechanism, since flows of capital (investment) and labor (migration) are equally important to economic integration. In combination, they determine whether the outcome of economic growth in India has been diffusion or polarization, that is, whether growth has been marked by spread or backwash effects.

Though most scholars do not explicitly address this issue in these specific terms, they nonetheless do shed light on it by focusing on the issue of interstate disparities. Have interstate disparities increased or decreased during the course of development? Is there a tendency toward convergence or divergence among the states? Investigating the issue of the impact of economic development on interstate disparities has indeed given rise to a cottage industry, employing more or less sophisticated statistical methodologies. However, because of differences in the data sets chosen, the time periods selected, or the particular methodologies employed, research investigations offer contradictory results.[30] For the period prior to economic liberalization, some of the studies did not find much impact of economic development on existing interstate disparities, while others found disparities to have risen, and still others concluded that there had indeed been a reduction in disparities; some studies saw the emergence of regional congruence. Most studies on the period after economic liberalization have underlined increasing interstate disparities and regional divergence. There are some exceptions to this consensus, however; relying on some measures of well-being, two studies concluded that regional disparities had not worsened after liberalization.[31] One of the latest among the studies on the state of disparities, published in 2012, acknowledged some progress by India's laggard states, but concluded that divergence is alive and well, and saw no evidence of convergence.[32] However, this position was rebutted by another contribution, which provided evidence of convergence.[33] As is apparent, disagreement among scholars is pervasive on the issue.

It is noteworthy that whether economic development, before or after economic liberalization, makes for increasing or decreasing disparities is something that can be easily accommodated in economic theory. Simon Kuznets had shown the way a long time ago, when he stated that development or industrialization, at least in its early stages, generates increase in inequality or disparities; of course, he posited the lessening of inequality or disparities later over the longer run, in the pattern of an inverted "U" curve—the Kuznets Curve—as development advanced and became widespread in the economy. But such an initial increase in inequality or disparities was not the result of stagnation or deindustrialization but an outcome of growth and industrialization. Of course, such a position naturally leads to the question of what defines maturity of development as against its early stages.

Critical of earlier studies on disparities in India—whether they relied on coefficient of variation of per capita Gross State Domestic Product (GSDP) or Gini coefficient of inequality—for being merely descriptive while inattentive to causality, Dholakia took a different approach that is of direct relevance to our present concern. He asked the question of whether the impact of economic advance of the richer states on the poorer states in India was positive or negative, that is, whether there was trickling down or polarization. He divided the then twenty-five states into those with per capita GSDP above the average for all of India (nine states) and those below the average (sixteen states), and then applied the Granger Causality test to the data on the level and growth of GSDP of the two groups of states for the period from 1980–81 to 2006–7. His results supported the proposition that "an increase in the level (and the rate of change) of GSDP of the better-off states would lead to (or cause) an increase in the level (and the rate of change) of the worse-off states in India." Dholakia concluded: "Thus, the Indian regional data over the last 27 years clearly support the hypothesis of spread or trickledown effect rather than the backwash or polarization effect. . . . Economic growth in better off states does spur growth in the worse-off states."[34]

This is a highly significant conclusion on growth diffusion as against polarization but, while it is evidently based on empirical data, it remains at a highly abstract level in which all the states are reduced to two binary groups for the purposes of generalization. Moreover, it does not specifically address the issue of the impact of economic liberalization. The following analysis, however, attempts to add more concrete data, basically in raw form without much statistical transformation; the observer can check the results by mere visual examination.

India today has twenty-eight states and seven union territories, which vary considerably in population, with the largest having more than 200 million and the smallest less than 100,000. Taken into account here are only those states and territories that have more than 10 million people according to the 2011 census (for some, the inclusion of Delhi may be questionable, for even though it has a large population, as the nation's capital, it is basically an urban conglomeration and an outlier in per capita income). These political units (nineteen states and the union territory of Delhi—hereafter referred to as a state) have been divided into two groups on the basis of whether their per capita income (that is, per capita Net State Domestic Product [NSDP]) for 2010–11 (at 2004–5 prices) is above or below the all-India average per capita income; quite accidentally, the states divide into two equal groups of ten each.

The focus here is on the lower-income states, but more particularly on a subset of them, pejoratively referred to as *Bimaru*, which is an acronym for *B*ihar, *Ma*dhya Pradesh, *R*ajasthan and *U*ttar Pradesh. Some would add Odisha (earlier called Orissa) to the acronym, making it *Bimarou*, which leaves the original pronunciation unaffected. The acronym as a word in the vernacular refers to being sick or diseased, perhaps congenitally, with the implication of the particular states being a blight on India, holding it back. In 2000, Chhattisgarh was split off from Madhya Pradesh, Jharkhand from Bihar, and Uttarakhand from Uttar Pradesh, thus making a total now of eight states within the erstwhile acronym, which occupy much of the space and contain much of the population of India. The implicit proposition in the popular representation of the Bimarou states is that they are somehow condemned to remain backward and underdeveloped, even as they drag down the rest of India. The key question is regarding what has happened to economic growth in these states since economic liberalization.

First, it is noteworthy that the period prior to economic liberalization was no paradise of equality with an absence of interstate disparities. Of course, in a country as large as India, disparities are to be expected. But over the long period before liberalization, disparities were a persistent phenomenon. Catriona Purfield's 2006 study for the International Monetary Fund (IMF) showed Punjab at the top and Bihar at the bottom among the fourteen largest states in 1970–74, but twenty years later in 1990–94 the situation had remained unchanged.[35] Her study further pointed out that, in 1970, per capita income in Punjab was 3.4 times that in Bihar. In actual fact, Punjab was still at the top in 1999–2000 (if one ignores Delhi for the moment and takes account only of the major states) and Bihar at the bottom, with the per capita income of the former being 4.4 times the latter's, indicating a worsening of disparity between the two.

Undeniably, while some change had taken place among the states earlier, it would not be hyperbolic to suggest that the first decade of the new century saw a considerable amount of churning among the states, with quite a few of *the lower income states* manifesting miracle rates of economic growth (that is, 7 percent and above), in effect demonstrating growth diffusion, not polarization. To be sure, revolutionary change may not have occurred in the sense of the overthrow or reversal of the older ranking altogether, but there has certainly been no polarization either in the sense of the rich states getting richer and the *poor states poorer.* Instead, there has been growth diffusion, and it has coincided with growth acceleration in the economy as a whole during the first decade of the new century.

Table 7.9 provides data on five-year averages of GSDP growth rates during the period from 1981–82 to 2011. The table is remarkable for the evidence it provides of growth rates of 7 percent and higher during the first decade of the new century; out of forty possible instances of state averages, there are twenty-six instances of such growth rates (sixteen in the upper-income group, and ten in the lower-income group). Among the lower-income states, apart from the ten instances of growth rates of 7 percent and higher, there were another seven instances of respectable growth rates of between 5 and 7 percent. In other words, growth diffusion was pretty much universal among the states.

In contrast, the earlier periods do not demonstrate either such strong growth or such strong consistency. Particularly noteworthy is the performance of the Bimarou states in the latest five-year period; except for Jharkhand, all of the others—including Uttar Pradesh and Bihar at the bottom—performed at the miracle level of 7 percent or more. Indeed, none of the lower-income states had a growth rate of below 6 percent. In other words, growth elsewhere in the economy was not resulting in the immiserization of these states, even if they may not have been performing at the superior level of the upper-income states. Remarkably, the state of Uttarakhand, earlier part of Uttar Pradesh—the latter being consistently the second from the bottom—was in the lower-income group in 1999–2000, ranking 13, but it made a forceful entry subsequently into the upper-income group and ranked 8 in 2010–11.[36] Notably, however, despite the good show put up by them in the latest decade, all the Bimarou states and their offshoots (except Uttarakhand) still remain in the lower-income group. But that status is no longer a bar to rapid growth among them as long as India as a whole accomplishes a high growth rate, for—as is apparent—the empirical evidence convincingly demonstrates growth diffusion.

As far as the upper-income group is concerned, the big loser has been Punjab, which receded from rank 2 in 1999–2000 to rank 7; its per capita income now is

Table 7.9. Gross State Domestic Product (GSDP): Five-Year Averages of Annual Growth Rates (%)

Rank/States	*Per Capita Income (Rs.)*	*1981–86*	*1986–91*	*1991–96*	*1996–2001*	*2001–6*	*2006–11*
Above India's Average Per Capita Income (2010–11)							
1. Delhi	108,876 (1)	7.40	7.68	4.98	10.44	8.05	11.67
2. Maharashtra	62,729 (4)	4.50	7.74	7.92	3.98	8.82	10.41
3. Haryana	59,221 (3)	6.74	6.56	3.44	6.60	7.32	9.69
4. Gujarat	52,708 (7)	5.08	6.78	8.72	4.54	10.19	9.35
5. Tamil Nadu	51,928 (6)	5.84	5.60	6.60	6.30	5.41	9.48
6. Kerala	49,873 (5)	2.14	5.20	6.28	5.04	8.08	8.06
7. Punjab	44,752 (2)	5.90	4.64	4.36	5.02	4.44	7.75
8. Uttarakhand	44,723 (13)				4.28	10.73	12.63
9. Andhra Pradesh	40,366 (10)	5.22	7.64	5.32	6.08	6.73	9.20
10. Karnataka	39,301 (8)	4.12	6.30	6.80	8.66	6.32	8.75
Below India's Average Per Capita Income (2010–11)							
11. West Bengal	32,228 (9)	4.14	4.68	6.48	7.00	6.98	7.47
12. Jammu and Kashmir	27,607 (11)	3.80	3.12	4.60	4.42	5.36	6.05
13. Chhattisgarh	27,156 (16)				1.66	8.03	10.00
14. Rajasthan	26,436 (12)	5.20	10.92	4.52	5.30	7.16	8.48
15. Odisha	25,708 (18)	4.36	2.28	5.60	3.14	7.22	9.36
16. Madhya Pradesh	22,382 (14)	3.64	6.78	4.14	3.78	5.46	8.99
17. Jharkhand	21,734 (17)				5.24	3.62	6.43
18. Assam	21,406 (15)	5.16	3.18	3.16	2.18	5.12	6.10
19. Uttar Pradesh	17,349 (19)	4.08	6.04	3.08	3.98	4.92	7.27
20. Bihar	13,632 (20)	5.24	4.60	−1.62	10.10	2.06	13.03

Source: Tables on "Annual Growth Rate of GSDP at (1980–81) Prices over Previous Year," "Statement: Gross State Domestic Product at 1993–94 Prices," "Gross State Domestic Product at Constant (2004–05) Prices: As on 01-03-2012," and "Statement: Per Capita Net State Domestic Product at Constant (2004–05) Prices"; available at the website of GoI, Ministry of Statistics and Programme Implementation, Central Statistics Office, National Accounts, mospi.nic.in, under "Press Releases and Statements."

Note: The per capita income figures are for the end year 2010–11 (2004–5 prices); the all-India average per capita income in that year was Rs. 35,993. The figures in *parentheses* represent the rank of the state in 1999–2000 on the basis of per capita income (1999–2000 prices); nine states were above the all-India average per capita income.

3.2 times that of Bihar, the bottommost state, which is a figure not only lower than the one in 1999–2000 but also lower than 1970. A big gainer has been Gujarat, which has moved from rank 7 in 1999–2000 to rank 4. Interestingly, all the four southern states are in the upper group; as a result of that status, an image of the north prevails among them today (which they almost equate with the Bimarou states) that pretty much parallels the one held by the west of India as a whole—poor, backward, malnourished, and unsanitary. Regardless, the first decade of the new century clearly demonstrates that rapid advance in per capita incomes among the lower-income states is possible; indeed, there is even greater progress in the narrowing of the gap, that is, there is visible movement toward "convergence" among the states in the matter of social development.[37] What emerges as essential from this analysis is that through appropriate policy and good governance, the national government ought to assure an overall high growth rate for the economy as a whole, which serves not only to improve personal incomes but also to bring in higher revenues to the government that can, in turn, be channeled into investment and social expenditures.

Opinions are likely to continue to vary over whether globalization and economic liberalization are the cause of growth acceleration and growth diffusion. But there can be no question over the fact that these outcomes have occurred during the period of increased openness to the international economy and that they are the opposite of economic stagnation and polarization, which the critics had posited as the consequences of globalization.

SUMMARY AND CONCLUSION

Prior to economic liberalization, economic integration had been a function of economic intervention, planning, and ownership by the state. The turn to the market after economic liberalization raises the question whether the market system can act as a substitute mechanism to assure economic integration in place of the earlier state management of the economy. The answer by the radical critics of globalization is that the turn to market, particularly the opening up of the national economy to the world market, will inevitably engender economic stagnation and economic segmentation, which would lead to economic, and ultimately national, disintegration. The position of the mainstream economists is somewhat more ambivalent on the issue. The more optimistic among them envision growth *diffusion* (spread effects, trickling down) as a necessary consequence of the market, which in turn is likely to make for economic integration rather than segmentation. In contrast, the more pessimistic among them tend to believe that the likely result of the free functioning of the market will be *polarization* (backwash effects) and thus economic segmentation and increased disparities. Some have offered a combined formulation in which the two foregoing positions are accommodated in the manner of an inverted "U" pattern, where polarization may occur at the initial stage, but where at a subsequent stage growth diffusion would tend to predominate over polarization, thus favoring economic integration and reduced disparities. How does the evidence on trade with respect to India correspond to the expectations of the different theoretical positions?

Certainly, with the opening up of the Indian economy to the world economy after economic liberalization, India has rapidly integrated into the international economy. Indeed, India's integration into the world economy through foreign trade today is at a higher level than that of the United States and Japan. This integration, however, has not led to either economic stagnation or decline, but instead has made for, first, a respectable growth rate during the 1990s and, then, growth acceleration during the first decade of the new century.

But has the international integration resulted in segmentation of the national economy? Has it occurred at the cost of domestic integration? There can be little question that trade in general in India as an integrative linkage mechanism has been consistently expanding over time and particularly after economic liberalization, and its share in India's GDP now stands at a higher level than that of either agriculture or manufacturing. However, it is difficult to say how much of this trade expansion is merely a reflection or an afterglow of the country's expanded foreign trade, or to what extent it is principally generated by domestic economic processes. For, while there are data collected on foreign trade, there are no separate data available for what is strictly domestic trade, unrelated to foreign trade. If separate data on domestic trade were available, they would have allowed the discerning of trends about domestic market integration.

We are not, however, without help in being enlightened on the issue. A study by Virmani and Mittal at ICRIER examined price variations of a large number of commodities in markets across India's various regions in order to determine market integration. That study demonstrated greater integration in 2004 compared to 1994. In other words, the period after economic liberalization, which saw increased openness to the world economy, experienced higher domestic market integration rather than segmentation.

The proposition that higher market integration rather than segmentation can accompany increased openness to the world economy is confirmed by the case of aviation, if we take aviation to be a proxy for trade. Unlike trade, there are separate data available for domestic air travel as against foreign air travel. What the data reveal is that increased international integration and the consequent expansion of foreign air passenger traffic have not led to any diminution of domestic air passenger traffic. Quite the contrary, both domestic and international air passenger traffic have seen continued and substantial expansion, with domestic air traffic staying ahead of foreign traffic. Increased domestic air traffic would denote greater domestic market integration. There does not seem to have been any zero-sum relationship in this case between international economic integration and domestic economic integration. Interestingly, while international air traffic increased faster than domestic air traffic in the initial phase of reform during economic liberalization in the 1990s, the subsequent phase of growth acceleration during liberalization saw a reversal of this trend and domestic air traffic expanded at a faster rate than foreign traffic. This pattern of comparative performance seems to confirm the proposition that growth acceleration has domestic integrative effects similar to autarky.

Regarding the impact of trade and other linkage mechanisms on regional disparities, Dholakia demonstrated in his quantitative study of growth data during a twenty-seven-year period that there was growth *diffusion* rather than *polarization* at work between the group of upper-income states and the group of lower-income states. An investigation of more-recent data on growth rates in the Indian states shows that growth acceleration has come with greater growth diffusion to the lower-income states, again confirming the importance of higher growth for economic integration. In the first decade of the new century, the lower-income states have largely grown in rhythm with the higher-income states, even if not at their pace, rather than in the opposite direction. In other words, there is diffusion of growth impulses at miracle levels, even if there is continued divergence among the states.

What emerges from the analysis of trade in India, then, is that the market, including exposure to the international market through globalization and economic liberalization, is no barrier to domestic economic integration. Rather, globalization and liberalization have been helpful to economic growth, to growth diffusion, and to economic integration. Concurrently, however, important state-made barriers to trade continue to exist—in the areas of regulation, fiscal demands, and infrastructure—that act as impediments to domestic market integration and, therefore, require urgent remedial action on the part of the state.

NOTES

1. On the relationship between states and markets, see Robert Gilpin, *The Political Economy of International Relations* (Princeton, NJ: Princeton University Press, 1987), chaps. 1–2; Karl Polanyi, *The Great Transformation* (New York: Rinehart, 1957); Baldev Raj Nayar, *Globalization and Nationalism: The Changing Balance in India's Economic Policy, 1950–2000* (New Delhi: Sage, 2001), chap. 1.

2. Gunnar Myrdal, *Rich Lands and Poor Lands: The Road to World Prosperity* (New York: Harper and Row, 1957).

3. Albert O. Hirschman, *The Strategy of Economic Development* (New Haven, CT: Yale University Press, 1958).

4. Jeffrey G. Williamson, "Regional Inequality and the Process of National Development: A Description of the Patterns," *Economic Development and Cultural Change* 13, no. 4 (July 1965): part 2, 1–84.

5. Paul Krugman, "Increasing Returns and Economic Geography," *Journal of Political Economy* 99, no. 3 (June 1991): 483–99.

6. The poorer regions of the periphery may feel discriminated against in the context of economic disparities and unequal development, and decide to opt out of the polity in order to be masters of their own economic fate. However, the richer regions of the core may see little benefit in remaining part of the larger nation-state, believing that they

could do quite well by themselves outside the existing political framework, without the burden of supporting the backward periphery.

7. International Monetary Fund (IMF), *International Financial Statistics Yearbook*, 1979, 2000, 2003, 2004.

8. World Development Indicators, available at http://databank.worldbank.org/data/views/variableSelection/selectvariables.aspx?source=world-development-indicators, accessed March 30, 2012.

9. The proposition on economic stagnation is repeated several times by Prabhat Patnaik, *The Retreat to Unfreedom: Essays on the Emerging World Order* (New Delhi: Tulika Books, 2003), 42, 63, 102, 162, 192–93, 195, and 289.

10. World Development Indicators, available at http://databank.worldbank.org/data/views/variableSelection/selectvariables.aspx?source=world-development-indicators, accessed April 13, 2013.

11. Ibid.

12. K. Balakesari, "A Budget Freighted with the Past," *Hindu*, February 27, 2013.

13. Smita Miglani and Arpita Mukherjee, "Logistics Sector in India: Opportunities and Constraints for EU Business," *Journal of Indo-European Business Studies* 1 (November 2011): 87–113.

14. Cited in Arne Melchior, "Globalization, Domestic Market Integration, and the Regional Disparities in India," NUPI Working Paper 780, Norwegian Institute of International Affairs, Oslo, October 2010, 15.

15. Arvind Virmani and Surabhi Mittal, "Domestic Market Integration," Working Paper No. 183, Indian Council for Research on International Economic Relations, New Delhi, 2006.

16. Ibid., 11.

17. Ibid., 17–18, 20–21, 23; emphasis added.

18. Melchior, "Globalization, Domestic Market Integration," 24, 28, 30.

19. Government of India (GoI), *Report of Working Group on Civil Aviation Sector: National Transport Development Policy Committee* (New Delhi: Ministry of Civil Aviation, June 2012), 84.

20. GoI, *Report of Working Group on Civil Aviation Sector*, chap. 8.

21. Ibid.

22. Ibid., 55.

23. GoI, *Tenth Five Year Plan, 2002–2007* (New Delhi: Planning Commission, 2002), vol. 2, 854.

24. Food and Agriculture Organization (FAO), "Towards an Indian Common Market: Removal of Restrictions on Internal Trade in Agricultural Commodities," submitted to the National Commission on Farmers, Ministry of Agriculture, Government of India, New Delhi, December 2005; available at www.fao.org/docrep/010/ai566e/ai566e00.htm.

25. See Durga Das Basu, *Introduction to the Constitution of India*, 13th ed. (New Delhi: Prentice-Hall of India, 1991), 315; and H. M. Seervai, *Constitutional Law of India: A Critical Commentary*, 3rd ed. (Bombay: N. M. Tripathi, 1984), vol. 2, 2155–56.

26. GoI, *Tenth Five Year Plan*, vol. 2, 855.

27. Interview with a senior official, Department of Consumer Affairs, New Delhi, November 4, 2010.

28. National Institute of Public Finance and Policy, *Reform of Domestic Trade Taxes in India: Issues and Options: Report of a Study Team* (New Delhi: NIPFP, 1994), 1.

29. FAO, "Towards an Indian Common Market," 29–30.

30. Ravindra H. Dholakia, "Testing for Trickle-Down or Polarization—Evidence from India," in Pennsylvania Economic Association, *Proceedings: Annual Conference, June 3–5, 2010* (Grove City, PA: Grove City College, 2011), 50–56.

31. This account of the studies draws on ibid.

32. Utsav Kumar and Arvind Subramanian, "Growth in India's States in the First Decade of the 21st Century: Four Facts," *Economic and Political Weekly* 47, no. 3 (January 21, 2012): 48–57.

33. Swati Raju, "Growth across States in the 2000s: Evidence of Convergence," *Economic and Political Weekly* 47, no. 23 (June 9, 2012): 76–79.

34. Dholakia, "Testing for Trickle-Down or Polarization," 53.

35. Catriona Purfield, "Mind the Gap—Is Economic Growth in India Leaving Some States Behind?" IMF Working Paper WP/06/103, International Monetary Fund, Washington, DC, 2006, 5.

36. Behind this elevation lies a story of rapid growth in industry, which as a percentage of gross state domestic product (GSDP) grew from 20.33 percent in 2000–2001 to 35.8 percent in 2010–11; see the website of Directorate of Economics and Statistics, Government of Uttarakhand; available at http://des.uk.gov.in/.

37. Santhosh Mehrotra and Ankita Gandhi, "India's Human Development in the 2000s: Towards Social Inclusion," *Economic and Political Weekly* 47, no. 14 (April 7, 2012): 59–64. The authors note: "These [Bimarou] states have over time shown tremendous improvement in their HDI [Human Development Index] and its component indices over time, leading to a convergence in HDI across states. The coefficient of variation of the HDI for states in 2000 was 0.313 and this had fallen sharply to 0.235 in 2008."

Chapter 8

INVESTMENT AND INTEGRATION

Polarization versus Diffusion

ECONOMIC integration is a function of the flows of goods and services, capital, and labor, and of the nature of economic linkages that promote or constrain such flows through networks of trade, investment, and migration. Chapter 7 deals with the impact of globalization and economic liberalization on trade as an integrative factor; chapter 10 discusses migration. This chapter is concerned with investment, which has to do with the deployment of capital in the production of goods and services together with the supply chains that go with it. In investigating investment's role in integration, the chapter focuses on industry, particularly after liberalization.

The radical critics posit that globalization and economic liberalization have the deleterious consequence of "deindustrialization" (besides economic stagnation), which ultimately leads to economic segmentation and disintegration. These critics further hold that, besides deindustrialization, globalization would result in polarization rather than diffusion of industry among the regions, with some regions advancing industrially—particularly in coastal areas, which are closer to the world economy—while others suffer decline.

How does the prognosis on deindustrialization and polarization hold up against the empirical evidence? In response to this basic question, the present chapter is divided into three sections. The first section examines the issue of deindustrialization, and rejects this proposition in relation to India. The second section reviews several studies on industrial location among the states, the conclusions of which support the polarization thesis. Finally, the third section offers an analysis of more-recent empirical data on such location during the period of growth acceleration, and concludes that the evidence favors diffusion rather than polarization.

THE ISSUE OF DEINDUSTRIALIZATION

Has economic liberalization led to deindustrialization? Deindustrialization would mean the hollowing out of existing industry built during the era of socialism and economic planning. Such deindustrialization could take place through general economic decline, which in actual fact did not occur in the two decades after economic liberalization in 1991. Rather, the economy has grown at an accelerated pace after liberalization, particularly during the second decade after liberalization. In addition, there has been little privatization of public sector industry, banking, or insurance.

Deindustrialization could also take place through the existing industry being overwhelmed by a flood of cheaper imports "from the world economy," which more recently is often equivalent to "from China." No doubt, imports have increased, and that is in addition to India perennially facing the problem of severe imbalance in its merchandise current account. However, as with the general economy, so with industry—including manufacturing—growth has been the order of the day! At least, that had been so until the aftermath of the global economic crisis emergent in 2008 began to impact India.

Regardless, since economic liberalization, industry has seen growth faster than in the 1980s, which was already a period that marked a break with the preceding decade and a half of dismal performance, often referred to as structural retrogression or industrial stagnation.[1] The annual rates of growth for industry and manufacturing, as shown in table 8.1, make this point abundantly clear. As the table makes evident, after the decline of the crisis years of 1991 and 1992, industry saw a sharp revival during the period 1993 to 1996. However, the industrial growth rate again declined in the subsequent five years from 1997 to 2001, perhaps the result of contractionary policies adopted to counter inflationary expectations in order to forestall consequent electoral losses for the ruling party. Additionally, the actual defeat of the Congress Party in the 1996 general elections and the subsequent political instability, besides the economic sanctions against India's nuclear tests in 1998, affected the investment climate adversely.

It was not until 2002 that industrial recovery began, followed by growth acceleration that lasted until 2010. What is remarkable about the acceleration during this period is that in its rate and temporal length it was unprecedented in India's entire postindependence history. To be sure, this performance cannot all be facilely ascribed to globalization or liberalization. It would be simplistic to attribute such performance to any single factor, including the contemporaneous global boom.[2] At the same time, it is undeniable that the growth acceleration occurred in the postliberalization period. Would the boom in the world economy have delivered a stimulus to growth in an autarkic economy? It is doubtful. It remains to be seen, however, what shape industrial recovery is likely to take after the severe downturn in 2011 and 2012, and whether India can return to the higher growth path.

Over the longer period of two decades after economic liberalization from 1992 to 2011, industry grew at the rate of 7.0 percent, and manufacturing at 7.5 percent (see table 8.1). There are, no doubt, variations in the growth rates during

Table 8.1. Share in GDP and Growth Rate of Different Sectors (%)

	Agriculture		*Industry*		*Manufacturing*		*Services*	
Year	*Share*	*Growth*	*Share*	*Growth*	*Share*	*Growth*	*Share*	*Growth*
1980	35.4	12.9	24.3	5.2	16.2	0.2	39.9	4.6
1981	34.1	4.6	25.1	8.0	16.3	8.2	40.4	5.2
1982	32.9	−0.3	25.2	1.4	15.9	3.3	41.5	7.1
1983	33.5	10.1	25.2	7.9	16.1	10.2	40.8	5.7
1984	32.2	1.6	25.6	4.1	16.1	4.2	41.8	6.1
Average	33.6	5.8	25.1	5.3	16.1	5.2	40.9	5.7
1985	30.9	0.3	25.7	4.4	16.0	3.2	43.1	7.7
1986	29.7	−0.4	25.9	5.8	15.8	5.5	44.1	7.6
1987	29.2	−1.6	25.9	5.6	15.9	5.6	44.6	6.4
1988	30.2	15.6	25.8	9.1	15.7	8.5	43.7	6.9
1989	29.0	1.2	26.5	8.3	16.4	8.8	44.2	8.9
Average	29.8	3.0	25.9	6.6	15.9	6.5	43.9	7.5
1990 Crisis	29.0	4.0	26.5	7.3	16.2	4.8	44.2	5.2
1991 Crisis	29.4	−2.0	25.4	0.3	15.2	−2.4	45.0	4.7
Average	29.2	1.0	25.9	3.8	15.7	1.2	44.6	4.9
1992	28.7	6.7	25.8	3.2	15.4	3.1	45.2	5.7
1993	28.7	3.3	25.5	5.5	15.3	8.6	45.6	7.4
1994	28.3	4.7	26.4	9.2	16.2	10.8	45.0	5.8
1995	26.3	−0.7	27.4	11.3	17.3	15.5	46.1	10.1
1996	27.1	9.9	26.6	6.4	16.9	9.5	46.0	7.5
Average	27.8	4.8	26.3	7.1	16.2	9.5	45.6	7.3
1997	25.9	−2.6	26.4	4.0	15.8	0.1	47.5	8.9
1998	25.8	6.3	25.7	4.1	15.0	3.1	48.3	8.3
1999	24.6	2.7	25.4	6.0	14.7	5.4	50.0	11.2
2000	23.1	0.0	26.1	6.0	15.4	7.3	50.8	5.4
2001	23.0	6.0	25.2	2.6	14.7	2.3	51.8	6.9
Average	24.5	2.5	25.8	4.5	15.1	3.6	49.7	8.1
2002	20.7	−6.6	26.2	7.2	14.9	6.9	53.0	7.0
2003	20.8	9.0	26.0	7.3	14.9	6.3	53.2	8.1
2004	19.0	0.2	27.9	9.8	15.3	7.4	53.0	8.1
2005	18.8	5.1	28.1	9.7	15.4	10.1	53.1	10.9
2006	18.3	4.2	28.8	12.2	16.1	14.3	52.9	10.1
Average	19.5	2.4	27.4	9.2	15.3	9.0	53.0	8.8
2007	18.3	5.8	29.0	9.7	16.0	10.3	52.7	10.3
2008	17.8	0.1	28.3	4.4	15.4	4.3	53.9	10.0
2009	17.7	0.8	27.8	9.2	15.1	11.3	54.5	10.5
2010	18.0	7.9	27.6	9.2	14.9	9.7	54.4	9.8
2011	17.5	3.6	26.7	3.5	14.4	2.7	55.7	8.2
Average	17.9	3.6	27.9	7.2	15.2	7.7	54.2	9.8

Source: World Development Indicators, http://databank.worldbank.org/data/views/variableSelection/selectvariables.aspx?source=world-development-indicators, accessed April 22, 2013. Note that there was a major drought in 1979, which made for negative growth rates in agriculture and industry (including manufacturing). The better growth rates in 1980 and 1981 are largely a function of the postdrought recovery.

this period, but taken as a whole, it is unequaled by any comparable period of such length since independence. The growth in industry was, in turn, a reflection of a major rise in investment, which was matched by a similar rise in savings. In the first decade of the twenty-first century, India seemed to be getting close to investment and savings rates of the East Asian "tiger" economies (see table 8.2). During the first twelve years after liberalization, the investment rate had remained largely in the mid-twenties; only in 2004–5 did it rise to 32.5 percent; subsequently, it remained in the mid-thirties, reaching the peak of 38 percent in 2007–8.

The vast transformation wrought in the industrial scene as a result of higher growth over the postliberalization period can be seen in the change in the value added in industry (and manufacturing) from \$68.6 billion in constant 2000 U.S. dollars (and \$37.8 billion) in 1992 to \$116.86 billion (\$68.6 billion) in 2001 and then to \$256.6 billion (and \$151.9 billion) in 2011.[3] As part of this change, there was a virtual explosion in the number of new firms registered (table 8.3), and in the number of factories and of workers employed (table 8.4). It was this record of growth that boosted national self-confidence and also gave birth to a new generation of youth with high expectations. If steel is a key indicator of the industrial capabilities of a country, it is significant that the production of finished steel expanded from 13.5 million tonnes in 1990–91 to 66.01 million tonnes in 2010–11; meanwhile, with 72 million tonnes of production of crude steel in 2011, India

Table 8.2. Gross Domestic Capital Formation and Gross Domestic Savings (as % of GDP)

	Gross Domestic Capital Formation				*Gross Domestic Savings*			
	Public Sector	*Private Sector*	*Valuables*	*Total*	*Private Household Sector*	*Corporate Sector*	*Public Sector*	*Total*
1980–81	9.2	8.9	—	18.0	12.1	1.6	4.1	17.8
1990–91	10.6	14.3	—	24.9	18.5	2.6	1.8	22.9
1994–95	9.7	13.5	—	23.2	17.9	3.4	2.3	23.6
2000–2001	7.2	16.4	0.7	24.2	21.4	3.7	−1.3	23.8
2004–5	7.4	23.8	1.3	32.5	23.6	6.6	2.3	32.4
2005–6	7.9	25.2	1.1	34.3	23.5	7.5	2.4	33.4
2006–7	8.3	26.4	1.2	35.9	23.2	7.9	3.6	34.6
2007–8	8.9	28.1	1.1	38.0	22.4	9.4	5.0	36.8
2008–9	9.4	24.8	1.3	35.5	23.6	7.4	1.0	32.0
2009–10	9.2	25.4	1.8	36.3	25.2	8.4	0.2	33.7
2010–11	8.4	26.5	2.1	37.0	23.5	7.9	2.6	34.0

Source: GoI, *Economic Survey 2012–13*, A.10–A.11. The term "household" should not be taken literally; it is essentially a residual category and includes what is left over after the "organized" (state and private corporate) sector has been accounted for. It encompasses individuals and all nongovernment and noncorporate enterprises and organizations.

Table 8.3. Number of Government and Nongovernment Companies (Limited by Shares)

Year (March 31)	Number of Companies			Year (March 31)	Number of Companies		
	Gov't.	*Nongov't.*	*Total*		*Gov't.*	*Nongov't.*	*Total*
1957	74	29,283	29,357	1985	980	108,329	109,309
1960	125	26,772	26,897	1990	1,160	200,968	202,128
1965	183	26,038	26,221	1995	1,199	352,093	353,292
1970	282	28,727	29,009	2000	1,245	541,189	542,434
1975	573	40,007	40,580	2005	1,328	678,321	679,649
1980	825	55,668	56,493	2010	1,642	834,218	835,860

Source: "Companies at Work in India (1957 to 2011)," available at www.indiastat.com, accessed July 12, 2012.

Table 8.4. Number of Registered Factories and Number of Factory Workers

Year	*Factories*	*Workers*	*Year*	*Factories*	*Workers*
1974–75	64,224	4,762,295	1994–95	123,010	6,970,116
1980–81	96,502	6,066,042	2000–2001	131,268	6,135,238
1984–85	100,328	6,091,409	2004–5	136,353	6,592,298
1990–91	110,179	6,307,143	2009–10	158,877	9,158,295

Source: "Annual Survey of Industries," available at www.indiastat.com, accessed July 12, 2012. The data are drawn from the Annual Survey of Industries and are for manufacturing in the organized sector and exclude the unorganized sector.

emerged as the fourth-largest producer in the world after China, Japan, and the United States. Similarly, if the automotive industry symbolizes the industrial maturity of a country, the advance made by this industry in India is striking. Whereas in 1990–91, the country produced 0.22 million cars, the number in 2010–11 was 2.5 million; for the broader category of motor vehicles, the Organization Internationale des Constructeurs d'Automobiles (International Organization of Motor Vehicle Manufacturers, or OICA) ranks India with a production of 3.9 million units in 2011 at number 6 in the world (after China, the United States, Japan, Germany, and South Korea).[4] A similar story of growth and advance can perhaps be told of several other sectors.

In the presence of the data presented here on the growth of industry in the postliberalization period, it would be hard to sustain the argument that globalization or liberalization generates deindustrialization. On the evidence available, an argument to the contrary carries greater robustness. Yet, gratifying as the industrial growth may have been relative to India's earlier performance, the glass has been seen as only half empty even before the economic downturn in 2011 and 2012 created an atmosphere of gloom and doom. The fundamental reason for dissatisfaction with the industrial performance over the postliberalization period is both a substantive and a comparative one. The stark fact that emerges from looking at the data on the share of different sectors in India's GDP is the patent lack of structural change with respect to industry relative to the rest of the economy. As a share of GDP, industry (and manufacturing) can be seen as having been basically stagnant, for it has never transcended 29.0 percent (17.3 percent), while the average for the postliberalization period from 1992 to 2011 has been 26.9 percent (15.5 percent), as is evident in table 8.1. It is not so much that industry and manufacturing have not grown in absolute terms. They have done so and at higher rates, but there has been little structural change evident with respect to them.

The structural change in India's economy is really represented not by industry but by services (see table 8.1), which can be regarded as the driver of India's growth, while the poster boy of the postliberalization growth story has been information technology (IT). Interestingly, some now use the term "deindustrialization" to refer not to the decimation of local industry—as used to be the case in discussions about the impact of colonialism on India's handicraft textile production—but rather to the declining share of industry and manufacturing in the national economy because of the relatively higher growth of services.[5]

Apart from the substantive reason for dissatisfaction on account of the lack of structural change in favor of industry and manufacturing, another unstated reason for discontent over this performance is that, in comparative terms, India has fallen so far behind China in this respect. As against India's performance, the share of industry in China's GDP in 2008 and 2010 was 47.4 and 46.7 percent while that of manufacturing was 32.7 and 29.6 percent.[6] The relative disparity in performance has serious geopolitical implications, which add to the dissatisfaction. But beyond that, the consequences of the lack of structural change in favor of industry are also far-reaching in terms of employment and modernization, since such lack of structural change is seen as having prevented the transfer of relatively unskilled surplus labor from the rural areas to industry. However, India's inadequate response in industry could hardly be attributed to globalization; after all, China turned itself into the world's workshop by integrating itself more fully and enthusiastically into the world economy and by reorganizing policy and its internal economy to that end. In contrast, India was not only a reluctant liberalizer but also a limited one.

LIBERALIZATION'S IMPACT ON INDUSTRIAL LOCATION AMONG THE STATES

Even if economic liberalization has not been a barrier to continued industrial growth, it does not necessarily follow that such growth has barred economic segmentation. If some regions, especially, for example, those linked to world markets through their location on India's coasts, make rapid advance in industry while other regions stagnate or even decline industrially, it would certainly promote or accentuate economic segmentation. Has economic liberalization contributed to polarization or diffusion, to divergence or convergence, and to increased or decreased disparities among the states in the area of industry?

Though studies on disparities among the states with respect to industry alone do not rival in number those relating to per capita income and other indicators, there are several that are specifically addressed to the issue of the impact of liberalization on disparities in industry. Three of these contributions are briefly reviewed here in the hope that cumulatively they will enhance our understanding of the different dimensions of interstate disparities relating to industry. The refrain of these studies is the widening of industrial disparities among the states in the wake of liberalization.

Subrahmanian: Liberalization's Failure to Reverse Divergence

The first of these four studies is by the economist K. K. Subrahmanian, which proceeds on the plausible assumption that the turn to promarket economic reforms in place of "the command planning regime" means that increasingly "industrial location will gravitate to already industrialized regions" and thus lead to "the concentration of investment and employment in the industrially advanced states, and the widening of inter-regional divergence of development."[7] Interestingly, Subrahmanian is not unaware that the era of command planning was no particularly shining model of interstate equality and acknowledges "the persistence of inequality across India" despite decades of planning.

In order to determine the impact of liberalization, Subrahmanian works out *industrial growth rates* of the major states on the basis of data on the manufacturing component of Net State Domestic Product (NSDP) for two subperiods—with 1980–81 to 1989–90 representing the prereform era and 1990–91 to 1999–2000 the postreform era—and then applies convergence tests to industrial income (value added). This demarcation of the dividing line between the two eras seems, however, to prejudge the issue against reform since it allocates the crisis years of 1990 to 1992—precisely a result of policies in the prereform era—to the postreform era. In any case, if one adds a year or two or more to the crisis years for policy change and transition to the new economic regime, barely five years would be left for the postreform period in Subrahmanian's database to test the impact of reform, a period not particularly long enough for testing the effects of liberalization.

Regardless, Subrahmanian finds that the average industrial growth of the low-income states in the postreform period of his definition was much lower (2.65 percent as against the prereform figure of 6.37 percent) than that of the middle-income states (6.11 percent) and the high-income states (6.91 percent). From this finding, he infers that "inter-state inequality in the levels of industrial development *continued to persist*." Interestingly, he does not allude to the empirical fact, or its significance, that the growth rates of the high-income states dropped from 9.97 percent to 6.91 percent after reform. However, he finds no major change to have occurred in state rankings after liberalization. Subrahmanian seems more tentative and muted in his interpretation of the econometrics of his convergence tests than he is in his final conclusions. Thus, in relation to the standard deviation for the two groups of low-income states and high-income states (having assessed the middle-income group to have been stable), he finds that "there are *no signs of a decreasing trend*, implying thereby the lack of sigma convergence.... This is *suggestive* of the increasing divergence in industrial growth between high and low income states after the introduction of market-friendly reforms." Similarly, he finds that there is no evidence of beta convergence and suggests that "the industrially backward states *have not been able to catch up* with the advanced regions in such a way that the regional differentiation in industrial development is significantly reduced during the post-reform era" (emphasis added).

In his conclusions, however, Subrahmanian is more emphatic about having found "empirical evidence on the increasing disparities in industrial development between the low income and high income states during the post-reform period." Further, he holds that the convergence tests "confirmed the tendency towards divergence in the growth rates and levels of the industrial sector in backward states, thereby increasing inter-state disparities during the post-reform period." He finds the continuing disparities disturbing since "whatever be the reason, the persistence of disparities in development and income across states in India has the potential of unleashing centrifugal forces, increasing social and political tensions and even breaking up the federal character and unity of the nation." On the basis of the evidence of about half a decade, Subrahmanian urges that government intervene to correct market failures. While he acknowledges that "the industrial sector has performed well during the post-reform period," he maintains that "the evidence is less supportive of a growth miracle" of the East Asian pattern.

Chakravorty and Lall: The New Economic Geography and Political Economy

In a sophisticated, map-laden study that is situated in the theoretical literature on industrial location, particularly that of the New Economic Geography, and favors Myrdal's proposition on *backwash effects*, Sanjoy Chakravorty and Somik V. Lall seek to determine the impact of economic liberalization on industrial location in India. For them, liberalization marks a decisive break with earlier economic policy in that "the state moves away from industrial ownership, and therefore location decisions" by giving freedom to private industry to enter all industries and by foregoing egalitarian policies. They regard liberalization as constituting "a watershed for the political economy and the economic geography of growth in India." Its significance lies in the fact that the logic of the private sector, which replaces the state in industrial ownership, is different from that of the state; private capital is profit oriented and will go to the "leading industrial regions, coasts, and metropolises, and away from socialist governments."[8] They are skeptical about the possibilities of decentralization of industry from the privileged regions to the lagging areas.

Chakravorty and Lall place their overall analysis of postreform industrial location against a broader summary view of the entire postindependence period, which they see as falling into two distinct phases, the first up to 1980 and the second from the mid-1980s onward. The first phase demonstrates "industrial decentralization and declining regional inequality" and the second "increasing regional inequality." Notwithstanding this temporal differentiation, they underline the decline of the eastern region over the entire period "in income terms and in the share of industrial investment"; in particular, "Bihar, long the poorest state continued to do poorly, and West Bengal, once the most prosperous state declined to below average levels. In fact, whatever declines in regional inequality took place in earlier decades can be attributed to industrial decline in the east."[9] What this pregnant statement really points out is that the seemingly desirable outcome of greater equality of the first phase—in contrast to the alleged postliberalization increase in disparities—did not issue out of some special virtue of state ownership in the planning era, but was perhaps mostly the outcome of stagnation (of per capita incomes) or decline (of particular well-off states because of policies in thrall to state ownership).

In examining the effects of India's structural reforms on industrial location, Chakravorty and Lall rely on the center's Annual Survey of Industries (ASI) data for the indicators of *fixed capital, employment, and net value added*, and also on new *industrial investment* data from the private sector database at the Center for Monitoring Indian Economy (CMIE). These data pertain to *organized manufacturing*, and exclude the *unorganized* sector. The authors divide the data between prereform and postreform. An important temporal limitation is immediately apparent; their study is based on a limited time frame insofar as reform's impact is concerned. Even though the study does not explicitly specify the end time point for the ASI data, internal evidence in the study indicates that 1994–95 is the last year for such data.[10] The CMIE data cover the period from 1992 to 1997. The end time point thus seems to be too close to reform to offer authoritative assessments about the impact of reform; for that matter, it is equally too close to the economic crisis, which provoked the reform, to sufficiently differentiate the effects of the reform from those of the crisis.

While the Chakravorty-Lall study is quite insightful, its data on the state level are not particularly enlightening, nor are the conclusions based on them. After having delved at considerable length into location theory and after pointing out liberalization's watershed nature, the authors do not deign to connect their results at the state level to any theory or to liberalization. Their conclusions remain essentially descriptive, not explanatory, with their overall summary on new postreform industrial investment being: "At the state level, it is easy to identify the states that have improved their positions significantly: Gujarat, Orissa, Karnataka, and Assam (from all four meta regions), and their opposite numbers, the states whose positions have worsened significantly: Maharashtra, Haryana, Delhi, Uttar Pradesh, Andhra Pradesh, Kerala, and West Bengal (again from all four meta regions). Among these, Maharashtra is clearly the most affected (though it is necessary to point out again that it is still a leading investment magnet) with losses in all sectors."[11] The authors advance no substantial claim with respect to total new industrial investment in these two collections of states. They do, however, offer an interesting finding that private investments and central government investments are differently oriented; private capital favors the coasts and the western and southern states (while neglecting Bihar, the eastern part of Uttar Pradesh, and Assam), whereas central government investments seem to be directed to the eastern region.[12]

Papola, Maurya, and Jena: Variant Patterns in Convergence and Divergence

Situating itself in the literature on "cumulative causation," the contribution by T. S. Papola, Nitu Maurya, and Narendra Jena aims to examine the issue of convergence and divergence in relation to the Indian experience.[13] As a quantitative study, it is quite ambitious in terms of the time periods and political units covered. With regard to temporal coverage, it includes the decade before economic liberalization and two decades after it, thus covering "the period of reform" during the 1990s, as well as "the period of growth acceleration" during the first decade of the 2000s. With respect to political units, it is at first glance very comprehensive, covering thirty-five political jurisdictions, divided into major states (fourteen), new states (three), northeastern states (eight), and union territories and other states (ten). However, this spatial comprehensiveness is somewhat misleading, since in determining issues of convergence and divergence, it focuses only on the fourteen major states, thus ignoring the new states of Chhattisgarh, Jharkhand, and Uttarakhand, which have substantial populations varying from 10 million to 33 million each in 2011. In so doing, the study would seem to have missed out on valuable insights. Basically, the study relies on data from the Central Statistical Office (CSO) for the *share of manufacturing*—both registered and nonregistered—in Gross State Domestic Product (GSDP) of the different states and also for the growth rates of such manufacturing.

Insofar as the *share* of manufacturing of the states in their respective GSDPs is concerned, the study looks at them at four different time points (1980–81, 1990–91, 2000–2001, and 2008–9), and finds that "the overall disparity in the degree of industrialization seems to have declined."[14] This would seem to suggest that there has been greater diffusion of industry to the less industrially advanced states, demonstrating a tendency toward convergence among the states.

However, with respect to *growth rates* of the manufacturing segment of GSDP among the states, the study underlines a different result, stating that these rates "seem to show a tendency towards divergence over the longer period." This conclusion masks some internal variation, however, for it immediately maintains that the: "coefficient of variation among growth rates of different states was 33 per cent during 1981–91, it declined to 28 percent during 1990–91/2000–01; but increased to 36 per cent during 2000–01/2008–09." This finding would seem to suggest not much change over the long haul. Significantly, the study goes on to say: "Also, while better industrialized states grew slower than less industrialized during 1981–91, the reverse seems to have happened in recent decades. Correlation between initial level of industrialization and growth rate was negative during 1981–91 (–0.317), it turned out positive and significant during 1991–01 (0.484) and 2001–09 (0.601). Thus, it appears that the trend towards a decline in differences in the level of industrialization among states observed in earlier years has been reversed in the post-reform period."[15] In this manner, the study favors divergence as the conclusion in the period after economic liberalization.

MORE ON LIBERALIZATION'S IMPACT ON INDUSTRIAL LOCATION

This section offers more-recent data on industrial location and a further analysis of the diffusion versus polarization issue. The analysis is similar to the preceding three studies in that the major question for examination is the same insofar as it investigates liberalization's impact on industrial location (however, with the splitting up of some of the states, several new political units have been added to this analysis). Like the previous studies, this analysis ranks the different states and comments on the position of different regions.

The analysis is, however, different from Subrahmanian's and Papola, Maurya, and Jena's in that it is not based on NSDP or GSDP data. Instead, it employs ASI data, which Chakravorty and Lall also do but, unlike them, it uses only the indicator of *Net Value Added (NVA)*. Obviously, the ASI itself regards this particular indicator as especially significant since it presents all its data on each of the states for different categories only after first ranking them according to their share of the total NVA for India. The ASI data cover only the *registered* or *organized* sector of manufacturing, which, however, constitutes about 70 percent of all manufacturing.[16]

The data are presented in tabular form in a rather simple and transparent manner, which makes it easy for anyone to check the validity or reliability of the generalizations made here against the original data; only the annual raw data for the eleven-year average of growth rates for the twenty states are not offered here because it would be cumbersome to do so. At some places, the discussion is supplemented by information from regression analysis; the data in the tables are all that is necessary for replicating the regressions. The basic intent of the analysis is not simply to substantiate a theoretical claim but also to discuss the various configurations among India's many constituent states in order to more concretely advance our understanding of comparative industrial location in India step-by-step.

In three decisive respects, the analysis presented here is markedly distinctive from any of the studies reviewed earlier. First, unlike those studies, part of the present analysis is based on *per capita figures* by taking account of population. The analysis starts out with the states ranked according to their share of India's total NVA, but it additionally takes into consideration the NVA per capita of states. The latter procedure rests on the belief that a comparison of the states with regard to industrial location that fails to take into account the element of population size of a state will not give a fully accurate picture of the shape of its industrialization. The Indian states differ radically in population because of differences in area and density of population. Comparing states on the basis of NVA alone can lead to a bias in favor of large-population states: a state may appear to be more industrialized simply because it happens to be larger in area or population density. Consequently, *NVA per capita* of states has been added as an additional research instrument. While the NVA value, share, or rank indicates the relative economic or industrial power of the different states, the NVA per capita speaks to the level of industrialization of the states. NVA share and NVA per capita may be close in their significance for some states, but perhaps not for others.

Second, the present analysis is distinctive in that it attempts a more systematic comparison of the regions. Third, it is particularly distinctive in that it is focused more on the first decade of the twenty-first century rather than on the 1990s ("the period of reform"). It starts out with data on 1999–2000 and ends with data on 2009–10. In short, it covers largely "the period of growth acceleration," which the first two of the three previously discussed studies could not have done, precisely because temporally they preceded the arrival of acceleration. Therefore, the differences in the conclusions of this analysis relative to the other studies can perhaps be regarded as arising principally from the different period investigated here as well as from incorporating into the study the three new states created in 2000. Looked at differently, the conclusions can legitimately be considered as applying only to the particular period studied.

A mere decade of growth acceleration is too short a period to reverse the inherited configuration of many decades among the states; perhaps even two or three decades of such acceleration would not suffice. There is little wonder, therefore, that our statistical analysis shows a high correlation between the beginning point in 1999–2000 (Time 1) and the end point in 2009–10 (Time 2) over the period with respect to both NVA shares (R = 0.964) and NVA share rankings (R = 0.869) (see table 8.5). However, some changes are bound to occur over time, so we should expect some shifts in the extent of industrialization among the states. Relying on visual examination and statistical analysis of data, this study

Table 8.5. Correlation Coefficients for NVA among States, 1999–2000 and 2009–2010

Regression	*R*
NVA Share % 1999–2000 and NVA Share % 2009–10	0.96405
NVA Rank 1999–2000 and NVA Rank 2009–10	0.86917
NVA Share % 1999–2000 and NVA Growth Rates	0.35504
NVA Per Capita 1999–2000 and NVA Growth Rates	0.43381
NVA Share % 1999–2000 and NVA Per Capita 1999–2000	0.71503
NVA Per Capita 1999–2000 and NVA Per Capita 2009–10	0.56807
NVA Per Capita 1999–2000 Rank and NVA Per Capita 2009–10 Rank	0.67969
NVA Per Capita 2009–10 and NVA Share % 2009–10	0.58450

Note: All correlations are significant at the 5 percent level.

identifies the extent of such shifts, based on measures related to NVA and NVA per capita.

Comparing States on the Basis of NVA in 1999–2000

This section examines the condition of industrial location in 1999–2000, which it takes as the beginning point for the discussion (especially since three new states were created in 2000 by splitting up the states of Bihar, Madhya Pradesh, and Uttar Pradesh). Table 8.6 shows the different states of India ranked by their *share in total NVA* (column 5) in organized manufacturing in 1999–2000. Only those states and union territories (hereafter referred to simply as states) that had a population of more than 10 million in 2011 are included in the table.

It is apparent that the two states of Maharashtra and Gujarat, ranking 1 and 2 and together constituting the western region, are India's industrial powerhouse. Maharashtra alone, with more than one-fifth of India's total NVA (22.32 percent), is undoubtedly without a peer, since Gujarat is a distant second with 12.44 percent (that is, almost half of what Maharashtra has).

Table 8.6 also makes manifest the rise of the southern region since the three southern states of Tamil Nadu (9.55 percent), Andhra Pradesh (5.88 percent), and Karnataka (5.39 percent) occupy ranks 3, 5, and 6. The other southern state of Kerala (rank 13), however, seems to be the odd man out in industrial location. At the same time, it is obvious that the three great industrial states of the south together do not match the industrial power of the single state of Maharashtra.

The state of Uttar Pradesh (6.60 percent) from the central region seems like an interloper, forcing its way into the group of the first five states at rank 4 on the sheer strength of having the largest population of any state. If the state were to be split, the more developed western part of the state could perhaps be more appropriately placed with the northern region by virtue of its industrial strength.

There does not seem to be any particularly regional focus to the ranks of the remaining states. The other four states among the top ten, each with less than 5 percent NVA share, include Jharkhand (7) which, as the more industrial part of

Table 8.6. States Ranked by NVA in Industry: 1999–2000

State	*NVA 1999–2000 Rs. Million*	*Population 2001*	*NVA per Capita 1999–2000 (Rs.)*	*NVA as % of India's NVA 1999–2000*	*Average of Annual NVA Growth Rates 1999–2000 to 2009–10 (%)*
1	2	3	4	5	6
1. Maharashtra	345,877	96,878,627	3.57 (2)	22.32	13.79
2. Gujarat	192,757	50,671,017	3.80 (1)	12.44	16.82
3. Tamil Nadu	147,953	62,405,679	2.37 (5)	9.55	15.47
4. Uttar Pradesh	102,295	166,197,921	0.62 (17)	6.60	11.13
5. Andhra Pradesh	91,104	76,210,007	1.19 (9)	5.88	16.21
6. Karnataka	83,473	52,850,562	1.58 (8)	5.39	14.95
7. Jharkhand	75,087	26,945,829	2.79 (4)	4.85	17.36
8. Haryana	65,015	21,144,564	3.08 (3)	4.19	16.67
9. West Bengal	57,367	80,176,197	0.72 (15)	3.70	10.92
10. Madhya Pradesh	56,371	60,348,023	0.93 (13)	3.64	13.36
11. Punjab	55,938	24,358,999	2.29 (6)	3.61	12.04
12. Rajasthan	53,147	56,507,188	0.94 (12)	3.43	19.72
13. Kerala	36,298	31,841,374	1.14 (10)	2.34	7.28
14. Delhi	29,372	13,850,507	2.12 (7)	1.89	6.10
15. Odisha	26,744	36,804,660	0.73 (14)	1.73	23.14
16. Chhattisgarh	23,616	20,833,803	1.13 (11)	1.52	18.63
17. Assam	16,979	26,655,528	0.64 (16)	1.09	22.27
18. Bihar	10,874	82,998,509	0.13 (20)	0.70	36.68
19. Uttarakhand	5,178	8,489,349	0.61 (18)	0.33	51.66
20. Jammu and Kashmir	2,126	10,143,700	0.21 (19)	0.14	40.34
Coefficient of Variation	1.08208		0.72542		
India	1,549,744	1,028,737,436	1.51	—	14.12

Sources: NVA data from GoI, *Annual Survey of Industries 2009–10* (New Delhi: Central Statistical Office, 2010), and previous years; population data from GoI, *Provisional Population Totals: Paper 1 of 2011 Series 1* (New Delhi: Registrar General and Census Commissioner, India, 2011), 54.

Notes:

1. Only states and union territories with populations above ten million in the 2011 census are included.
2. NVA per capita for 1999–2000 has been calculated on the basis of 2001 population figures.
3. NVA growth rate is the average of the annual growth rates for the eleven years from 1999–2000 to 2009–10 (both years included), taking into account the data for 1998–99 as the base.
4. The NVA growth rates provide a broad indication of the position of the different states. For a more accurate picture, the rates would have to be adjusted for inflation. There are three possible rates for inflation during the period: (i) an average of 3.92 percent, worked out on the basis of index numbers of prices for "'Manufactured Products' Total" for the eleven-year period from 1999–2000 to 2009–10, with 1998–99 as the base, from GoI, *Economic Survey 2011–12*; (ii) an average of 5.49 percent for "Inflation, Consumer Prices" for the calendar years from 1999 to 2009, from World Development Indicators (2012); and (iii) an average of 5.18 percent for "Inflation, GDP Deflator" for the calendar years from 1999 to 2009, from World Development Indicators (2012).
5. Figures in parentheses under column 4 indicate ranks of states with respect to NVA per capita.

Bihar in the eastern region, was split off from that state in 2000; Haryana (8) from the northern region; West Bengal (9), which is the preeminent but now much diminished industrial power of the eastern region; and Madhya Pradesh (10) from the central region. The third group of states in the ranks from 11 to 15 is literally composed of at least one state from each of India's five regions except the western—Punjab (northern), Rajasthan (central), Kerala (southern), Delhi (northern), and Odisha (eastern), in that order. The last group of states in the ranks from 16 to 20—Chhattisgarh (which split off from Madhya Pradesh in 2000), Assam, Bihar, Uttarakhand (which also split off from Uttar Pradesh in 2000), and Jammu and Kashmir—seemingly has little industrial power; Bihar with its large and fast-growing population seems particularly deficient industrially. That, then, is the picture that emerges from state rankings based on the share of each state in the nation's NVA in 1999–2000.

Taking Account of NVA per Capita in 1999–2000

A comparison of the states on the basis of *NVA per capita* for each state—rather than just the share in the all-India NVA—tells a somewhat different story and offers some surprises. As is made evident by table 8.6, column 4—which shows per capita NVA for the different states in 1999–2000 on the basis of their population in the 2001 census—high rank based on a state's share in India's total NVA does not necessarily mean that the state as such is really more industrialized than a lower-ranking state. For example, Gujarat (rank 1 in per capita NVA) was more industrialized on a per capita basis in 1999–2000 than Maharashtra (rank 2), which contradicts the long-standing image of Maharashtra as the most industrialized state. Particularly noteworthy are the states of Haryana (rank 3) in the northern region and Jharkhand (rank 4) in the eastern region, which were both more industrialized in per capita terms than any of the southern states.

In terms of NVA per capita, while Tamil Nadu (rank 5) still stands out among the states of the southern region, the other states of the region are now clustered together considerably lower, with Karnataka having moved to rank 8 and Andhra Pradesh to rank 9, even as Kerala moved up to rank 10. Surprisingly, in per capita terms, Kerala does not seem as deprived industrially as it is often portrayed to be; note that Papola, Maurya, and Jena refer to Kerala as "the least industrialized state."[17] Turning from the southern region to the northern region, Punjab (rank 6) and Delhi (rank 7) demonstrate a significant level of industrialization and show that industry is more diffused than what a focus on NVA share would lead us to believe. Given that Haryana is at rank 3, the northern region is patently not just an agricultural hinterland; however, in 1999–2000, Uttarakhand (rank 18) and Jammu and Kashmir (rank 19) do hold back the region as a whole.

The table confirms the picture of the eastern region as particularly deprived industrially: Odisha (rank 14), West Bengal (rank 15)—which fell from rank 9 in NVA share—Assam (rank 16), and Bihar at the very bottom (rank 20); only

Jharkhand at rank 4 is among the upper-ranking states. The central region does somewhat better, but not much. Interestingly, Uttar Pradesh as India's most populous state, which was among the top five states in terms of share in total NVA, drops down drastically to rank 17 to belong in the bottom five states in per capita NVA. The other states in the region are, however, clustered together at around the middle—Chhattisgarh (rank 11), Rajasthan (rank 12), and Madhya Pradesh (rank 13).

The preceding rank analyses based on NVA share and NVA per capita also show that the ranks of some states do not change substantially between using the ranking for NVA share or for NVA per capita: some states come across as relatively more industrialized, while others remain as relatively less industrialized on both rankings. Therefore, the correlation between the NVA share and NVA per capita rankings is fairly high at 0.715 for the year 1999–2000 (see table 8.5)—but at the same time, it is not 1, suggesting that some ranks do shift between the two measures.

Change during Growth Acceleration of NVA

So far, the analysis here has provided a view that is *static* in nature since it simply describes the situation with respect to industrial location in 1999–2000. We now turn to the *dynamic* aspect of industrial location and examine change, if any, in the situation during the eleven years from 1999–2000 to 2009–10. It bears particular mention here that the period as a whole was one of high growth in NVA. The all-India growth rate for NVA was 14.12 percent (table 8.6, column 6) during the period, while inflation was at a rather modest level of 4 or 5 percent (see table 8.6, note 4). Accordingly, in most cases, states experienced considerable industrial growth even when they may have suffered loss in rank relative to other states. Except for Delhi, Jharkhand, Kerala, and Bihar, most states saw growth rates of more than 100 percent in NVA per capita between 1999–2000 and 2009–10, half of them more than 200 percent, and seven of them close to or above 300 percent. Regardless of whether it resulted in convergence or divergence, the period of growth acceleration made for expansion of industry in most states.

For an appraisal of change in industrial location, reliance here is placed on table 8.6, column 6, which provides the average of annual growth rates for NVA during the period from 1999–2000 to 2009–10 (both years included). What is particularly striking about the data in column 6 is that the growth rates of the lower-ranking states (bottom ten) are broadly higher than those of the higher-ranking states (top ten). Note, in particular, that except for three instances (Punjab, Kerala, and Delhi), every single state among the bottom ten ranking states has a higher growth rate than that of any of the top ten ranking states. Especially noteworthy is the fact that the bottom five states have distinctly higher growth rates than those of the top five states. This would indicate a tendency toward some *convergence and diffusion, not polarization*. Simply put, given the higher growth rates of the lower-ranking states relative to the upper-ranking states, there is no basis to contend, at the very least, that liberalization generated a tendency toward polarization. This finding ought to make it difficult to suggest that liberalization has somehow barred diffusion at the level of the states, at least in terms of growth of NVA in industry. Nor would it be possible to maintain that only the coastal states feature higher growth rates.

Regression analysis confirms this understanding, since there exists a fairly weak correlation between the NVA shares and NVA growth rates of the states during the period from 1999–2000 to 2009–10 (R = 0.355) (see table 8.5). In other words, states that had high NVA shares did not necessarily demonstrate higher growth rates, while states with low NVA shares tended to do better, thereby indicating a process of diffusion. This finding is confirmed by that from the comparison with regard to NVA per capita.

Change among the States with Respect to NVA Share. Because of the smaller inherited industrial base of the lower-ranking states, the relatively more rapid growth among them did not radically disturb the older rankings. There was diffusion, but not sufficient enough to result in any radical change in their rankings in 2009–10 on the basis of state *shares in total NVA* (see table 8.7). That said, however, it is significant that the data do not indicate an increasing tendency toward polarization, given the disparity in growth rates between the upper- and lower-ranking states in favor of the latter. Moreover, the high correlation between Time 1 and Time 2 in state shares in NVA or state rankings in NVA share did not prevent some states from going against the trend. The outstanding example of this phenomenon is Uttarakhand, which increased its NVA share ninefold from 0.33 percent to 2.99 percent, even as it changed its rank from 19 near the bottom to rank 10 among the upper-ranking states. Uttarakhand is certainly the major surprise of table 8.7. The state's example suggests that it is possible for some states to improve their standing through appropriate policy. Interestingly, Uttarakhand's rise in terms of industrial location is rather broad-based; the state demonstrates high growth of its economy in general and also the highest increase among the states (44.5 percent) in the Human Development Index between 1999–2000 and 2007–8.[18]

Meanwhile, it is noteworthy that the variant growth rates in NVA share made for some change in the ranks of a few of the other states as well. The hinterland state of Rajasthan moved from the group of lower-ranking states to that of the upper-ranking states, jumping from rank 12 to rank 8, directly above West Bengal, while Odisha moved from rank 15 to rank 13. In contrast, some states fell in rank, too. Jharkhand fell steeply from rank 7 to rank 12; Punjab also dropped from rank 11 to rank 14, Uttar Pradesh from rank 4 to rank 6, and Delhi from rank 14 to rank 18 (perhaps because of change in environmental regulations requiring removal of polluting industries from the city).

Table 8.7. States Ranked by NVA in Industry: 2009–2010

State	*NVA 2009–10 Rs. Million*	*Population 2011*	*NVA per Capita 2009–10 (Rs.)*	*NVA as % of India's NVA 2009–10*	*Average of Annual NVA Growth Rates 1999–2000 to 2009–10 (%)*
1	2	3	4	5	6
1. Maharashtra	1,178,724	112,372,972	10.49 (4)	19.91	13.79
2. Gujarat	900,280	60,383,628	14.91 (2)	15.20	16.82
3. Tamil Nadu	591,431	72,138,958	8.19 (5)	9.99	15.47
4. Andhra Pradesh	392,098	84,665,533	4.63 (9)	6.62	16.21
5. Karnataka	366,999	61,130,704	6.00 (6)	6.19	14.95
6. Uttar Pradesh	309,766	199,581,477	1.55 (19)	5.23	11.13
7. Haryana	279,745	25,353,081	11.03 (3)	4.73	16.67
8. Rajasthan	202,777	68,621,012	2.96 (12)	3.43	19.72
9. West Bengal	193,196	91,347,736	2.12 (15)	3.26	10.92
10. Uttarakhand	177,187	10,116,752	17.51 (1)	2.99	51.66
11. Madhya Pradesh	153,575	72,597,565	2.12 (16)	2.59	13.36
12. Jharkhand	151,029	32,966,238	4.58 (10)	2.55	17.36
13. Odisha	147,997	41,947,358	3.53 (11)	2.49	23.14
14. Punjab	147,361	27,704,236	5.32 (7)	2.49	12.04
15. Chhattisgarh	132,806	25,540,196	5.19 (8)	2.24	18.63
16. Kerala	71,973	33,387,677	2.16 (14)	1.22	7.28
17. Assam	50,621	31,169,272	1.62 (18)	0.86	22.27
18. Delhi	37,807	16,753,235	2.26 (13)	0.64	6.10
19. Jammu and Kashmir	26,306	12,548,926	2.09 (17)	0.44	40.34
20. Bihar	23,213	103,804,637	0.22 (20)	0.39	36.68
Coefficient of Variation	0.94897		0.90872		
India	5,921,138	1,210,193,422	4.89	—	14.12

Sources: NVA data from GoI, *Annual Survey of Industries 2009–10* (New Delhi: Central Statistical Office, 2010), and previous years; population data from GoI, *Provisional Population Totals: Paper 1 of 2011 Series 1* (New Delhi: Registrar General and Census Commissioner, India, 2011), 54.

Notes:

1. Only states and union territories with population above ten million in the 2011 census are included.
2. NVA per capita for 2009–10 has been calculated on the basis of 2011 population figures.
3. NVA growth rate is the average of the annual growth rates for the eleven years from 1999–2000 to 2009–10 (both years included), taking into account the data for 1998–99 as the base.
4. The NVA growth rates provide a broad indication of the position of the different states. For a more accurate picture, the rates would have to be adjusted for inflation. There are three possible rates for inflation during the period: (i) an average of 3.92 percent, worked out on the basis of index numbers of prices for "'Manufactured Products' Total" for the eleven-year period from 1999–2000 to 2009–10, with 1998–99 as the base, from GoI, *Economic Survey 2011–12*; (ii) an average of 5.49 percent for "Inflation, Consumer Prices" for the calendar years from 1999 to 2009, from World Development Indicators (2012); and (iii) an average of 5.18 percent for "Inflation, GDP Deflator" for the calendar years from 1999 to 2009, from World Development Indicators (2012).
5. Figures in parentheses under column 4 indicate ranks of states with respect to NVA per capita.

A focus on the first five ranks in 2009–10 in terms of share in NVA makes it obvious that Maharashtra still stands out at rank 1. At the same time, with its share of total NVA now reduced to 19.91 percent from the earlier 22.32 percent, its industrial luster has dimmed somewhat. On the other hand, Gujarat (rank 2) has sharply augmented its industrial prowess and, with its share of NVA having climbed from 12.44 percent to 15.20 percent, it is now snapping at the heels of Maharashtra. In a sense, while Maharashtra is still industrially preeminent, it has lost ground in relative terms.

Remarkably significant is the consolidation of the southern states in industry, consistent with popular perception; the three states of Tamil Nadu (rank 3), Andhra Pradesh (rank 4), and Karnataka (rank 5) come directly after Gujarat and now occupy the next three ranks consecutively in a cluster; they have pushed Uttar Pradesh down from the earlier rank 4 to rank 6. Unlike 1999–2000, the three southern states put together are now industrially more powerful than Maharashtra, even though the margin of advantage of the first two combined (that is, Tamil Nadu and Andhra Pradesh) over Gujarat has come down somewhat because of Gujarat's greater stride in the meantime.

Change among the States with Respect to NVA Per Capita. The high correlation that was seen regarding change among the states in NVA shares is not manifest with regard to change between Time 1 and Time 2 in NVA per capita of states. There is only a moderate correlation with respect to the latter ($R=0.568$). That finding suggests the presence of significant changes in NVA per capita among the states during the decade of growth acceleration. In line with its performance with respect to NVA share, but far more dramatically, Uttarakhand rose from rank 18 to the very top in NVA per capita. The states of Chhattisgarh and Odisha showed significant rise, ascending from ranks 11 and 14 to ranks 8 and 11, respectively. However, several states demonstrated stability in their ranking (Haryana, Tamil Nadu, Andhra Pradesh, Rajasthan, West Bengal, and Bihar). Jharkhand and Delhi witnessed the most striking fall, from ranks 4 and 7 to ranks 10 and 13, respectively, followed by Kerala and Madhya Pradesh from ranks 10 and 13 to ranks 14 and 16, respectively. The remaining states showed change in the order of only one or two ranks. As with NVA per capita, so with NVA per capita ranks—the correlation coefficient is only moderate between Time 1 and Time 2 ($R=0.679$).

Similarly, there is only a weak correlation between NVA per capita of states in 1999–2000 and NVA growth rates ($R=0.433$). At the same time, NVA per capita in 1999–2000 is only moderately correlated ($R=0.568$) with NVA per capita in 2009–10. This finding suggests that, because of some significant changes in NVA per capita between the two time points, states did not move entirely in tandem with their standing at Time 1 with respect to NVA per capita. However, while change by way of diffusion is palpable overall, there is also substantial continuity in some other respects.

Comparing Regions

In order to compare the regions more directly, the data on the states in tables 8.5 and 8.6 have been restructured by regions on the basis of *NVA per capita* (see tables 8.8 and 8.9). The twenty states have been divided into five regions—northern, central, eastern, western, and southern. If one were to proceed only on the basis of a region's *share in India's NVA*, whether for 1999–2000 or 2009–10, then the ranking among the regions would perhaps be more or less consistent with the popular understanding of how the different regions stack up industrially. That ranking likely would be: the western region on top (with a share of 34.76 percent in 1999–2000 and 35.11 percent in 2009–10), followed by the southern (23.16 percent and 24.02 percent), the central (15.19 percent and 13.49 percent), the eastern (12.07 percent and 9.55 percent), and then, a little more ambiguously, the northern region (10.16 percent and 11.29 percent) (see tables 8.8 and 8.9, column 5). Perhaps the northern region at the bottom in the matter of share in NVA may seem appropriate in view of its image as being primarily an agricultural producer. But absolute share in NVA does not necessarily translate into an accurate picture of a particular state's or region's level of industrialization, since population intervenes to modify the situation.

Understandably, then, a significantly different picture emerges when *NVA per capita* is taken into account. The western region is still on top (with NVA per capita being Rs. 3.65 in 1999–2000 and Rs. 12.03 in 2009–10). But, surprisingly, it is followed by the northern (Rs. 2.02 and Rs. 7.23) and then the southern (Rs. 1.61 and Rs. 5.66) regions, while the central region (Rs. 0.78 and Rs. 2.18) and the eastern region (Rs. 0.74 and Rs. 1.88), quite close in their respective profiles, are at the bottom (see table 8.10, columns 5 and 6). The oft-projected picture of the western and southern regions, with all their constituent states being coastal states, as perhaps the only two regions to have advanced industrially after economic liberalization does not seem to be entirely accurate and is in need of revision since the northern region, too, is significantly ahead of the southern region, at least in NVA per capita terms. The level of industrialization of the northern region in per capita terms to a certain extent represents economic diffusion and convergence since it goes against the traditional (perhaps outdated) image of the western and eastern regions to have largely been the locus of India's industry, to which the southern region has subsequently been added. However, it could well be that the current standing of the northern region is of longer duration than what is apparent at the end of either "the period of reform" or "the period of growth acceleration."

The performance of the central and eastern regions, which together contain more than half of the country's population, runs counter, at least at first blush, to any pretensions about substantial diffusion or convergence. Both the regions demonstrate a decline, thus polarization and divergence, in relation to the other regions with respect to both NVA share and per capita NVA. This is obvious

Table 8.8. States Ranked by NVA in Industry (Organized by Region): 1999–2000

State	*NVA 1999–2000 Rs. Million*	*Population 2001*	*NVA per Capita 1999–2000 (Rs.)*	*NVA as % of India's NVA 1999–2000*	*Average of Annual NVA Growth Rates 1999–2000 to 2009–10 (%)*
1	*2*	*3*	*4*	*5*	*6*
1. Maharashtra	345,877	96,878,627	3.57 (2)	22.32	13.79
2. Gujarat	192,757	50,671,017	3.80 (1)	12.44	16.82
Western Region	538,634	147,549,644	3.65	34.76	
8. Haryana	65,015	21,144,564	3.08 (3)	4.19	16.67
11. Punjab	55,938	24,358,999	2.29 (6)	3.61	12.04
14. Delhi	29,372	13,850,507	2.12 (7)	1.89	6.10
19. Uttarakhand	5,178	8,489,349	0.61 (18)	0.33	51.66
20. Jammu and Kashmir	2,126	10,143,700	0.21 (19)	0.14	40.34
Northern Region	157,629	77,987,119	2.02	10.16	
3. Tamil Nadu	147,953	62,405,679	2.37 (5)	9.55	15.47
5. Andhra Pradesh	91,104	76,210,007	1.19 (9)	5.88	16.21
6. Karnataka	83,473	52,850,562	1.58 (8)	5.39	14.95
13. Kerala	36,298	31,841,374	1.14 (10)	2.34	7.28
Southern Region	358,828	223,307,622	1.61	23.16	
4. Uttar Pradesh	102,295	166,197,921	0.62 (17)	6.60	11.13
10. Madhya Pradesh	56,371	60,348,023	0.93 (13)	3.64	13.36
16. Chhattisgarh	23,616	20,833,803	1.13 (11)	1.52	18.63
12. Rajasthan	53,147	56,507,188	0.94 (12)	3.43	19.72
Central Region	235,429	303,886,935	0.78	15.19	
7. Jharkhand	75,087	26,945,829	2.79 (4)	4.85	17.36
9. West Bengal	57,367	80,176,197	0.72 (15)	3.70	10.92
15. Odisha	26,744	36,804,660	0.73 (14)	1.73	23.14
17. Assam	16,979	26,655,528	0.64 (16)	1.09	22.27
18. Bihar	10,874	82,998,509	0.13 (20)	0.70	36.68
Eastern Region	187,051	253,580,723	0.74	12.07	
India	1,549,744	1,028,737,436	1.51	—	14.12

Source: See table 8.6.

from the ratios of each of the two regions to the top region, as shown in columns 3 to 6 of table 8.10. It is understandable that their per capita NVA should appear to be low, since the two regions manifest the highest population growth rates of all the regions (table 8.10, column 2). But even the growth in their shares of NVA has not been strong enough to reduce the distance between them and the other regions. Whereas the ratios for the northern and southern regions for both NVA

Table 8.9. States Ranked by NVA in Industry (Organized by Region): 2009–2010

State	NVA 2009–10 Rs. Million	Population 2011	NVA per Capita 2009–10 (Rs.)	NVA as % of India's NVA 2009–10	Average of Annual NVA Growth Rates 1999–2000 to 2009–10 (%)
1	2	3	4	5	6
1. Maharashtra	1,178,724	112,372,972	10.49 (4)	19.91	13.79
2. Gujarat	900,280	60,383,628	14.91 (2)	15.20	16.82
Western Region	2,079,004	172,756,600	12.03	35.11	
7. Haryana	279,745	25,353,081	11.03 (3)	4.73	16.67
10. Uttarakhand	177,187	10,116,752	17.51 (1)	2.99	51.66
14. Punjab	147,361	27,704,236	5.32 (7)	2.49	12.04
18. Delhi	37,807	16,753,235	2.26 (13)	0.64	6.10
19. Jammu and Kashmir	26,306	12,548,926	2.09 (17)	0.44	40.34
Northern Region	668,406	92,476,230	7.23	11.29	
3. Tamil Nadu	591,431	72,138,958	8.19 (5)	9.99	15.47
4. Andhra Pradesh	392,098	84,665,533	4.63 (9)	6.62	16.21
5. Karnataka	366,999	61,130,704	6.00 (6)	6.19	14.95
16. Kerala	71,973	33,387,677	2.16 (14)	1.22	7.28
Southern Region	1,422,501	251,322,872	5.66	24.02	
6. Uttar Pradesh	309,766	199,581,477	1.55 (19)	5.23	11.13
8. Rajasthan	202,777	68,621,012	2.96 (12)	3.43	19.72
11. Madhya Pradesh	153,575	72,597,565	2.12 (16)	2.59	13.36
15. Chhattisgarh	132,806	25,540,196	5.19 (8)	2.24	18.63
Central Region	798,924	366,340,250	2.18	13.49	
9. West Bengal	193,196	91,347,736	2.12 (15)	3.26	10.92
12. Jharkhand	151,029	32,966,238	4.58 (10)	2.55	17.36
13. Odisha	147,997	41,947,358	3.53 (11)	2.49	23.14
17. Assam	50,621	31,169,272	1.62 (18)	0.86	22.27
20. Bihar	23,213	103,804,637	0.22 (20)	0.39	36.68
Eastern Region	566,056	301,235,241	1.88	9.55	
India	5,921,138	1,210,193,422	4.89	—	14.12

Source: See table 8.7.

share and per capita NVA increased from 1999–2000 to 2009–10, demonstrating thus convergence among the three regions, these ratios suffered a decline—indeed, quite substantially in NVA share—in the case of both the central and eastern regions (see table 8.10).

Some element of ambiguity remains in these results over the issue of diffusion and polarization, however, because of the fact that the constituent states in

Table 8.10. Comparison of Regions on the Basis of Share of NVA and of NVA per Capita

Region	*Population Growth Rate 2001–11*	*Ratio of Region to Top Region in Share of NVA*		*Ratio of Region to Top Region in Per Capita NVA*	
		1999–2000	*2009–10*	*1999–2000*	*2009–10*
1	*2*	*3*	*4*	*5*	*6*
1. Western	1.71	100.00 (34.76)	100.00 (35.11)	100.00 (3.65)	100.00 (12.03)
2. Northern	1.86	29.23 (10.16)	32.16 (11.29)	55.34 (2.02)	60.09 (7.23)
3. Southern	1.25	66.63 (23.16)	68.41 (24.02)	44.11 (1.61)	47.05 (5.66)
4. Central	2.06	43.69 (15.19)	38.42 (13.49)	21.37 (0.78)	18.12 (2.18)
5. Eastern	1.88	34.72 (12.07)	27.20 (9.55)	20.27 (0.74)	15.62 (1.88)

Source: Calculated on the basis of data in tables 8.8 and 8.9. The ratios have been worked out on the basis of the figures in parentheses. The order in which the regions appear is based on the region's per capita NVA.

the central and eastern regions show not only positive but respectable growth, as reflected in their average annual NVA growth rates, with most of the states doing even better than the states of the southern region. Apparently, what pulls the two regions down is the growth performance of three particular but quite populous states—Uttar Pradesh (the most populous), West Bengal, and to some extent, Madhya Pradesh. Surprisingly, however, some of the other populous states in the two regions have done quite well in relation to their NVA growth rates—such as Rajasthan and, particularly astoundingly, Bihar, with the third-highest growth rate after Uttarakhand and Jammu and Kashmir among the states. The performance of these two populous states of Bihar and Rajasthan, as well as the strong performance of some of the other less populous states of these two regions—such as Chhattisgarh, Jharkhand, Odisha, and Assam—patently demonstrates a broad pattern of diffusion and convergence taking place, to which there are, of course, some serious exceptions like those of Uttar Pradesh and West Bengal. In other words, what emerges is a broad pattern of diffusion and convergence, to which Uttar Pradesh and West Bengal are the exceptions; it is but appropriate that exceptions ought not to overshadow the broader pattern.

It is important to bring into the analysis here another factor relating to the internal social structure—rather than that of the global economy or economic liberalization—which tends to wash out some of the positive effects of diffusion of industry under the impetus of growth acceleration as manifest in the higher growth rates in NVA shares of the lower-ranking states. That factor pertains to population growth. It is not insignificant that some of the central states have about the highest population growth rates in percentage terms between 2001 and 2011—Bihar, 25.06; Chhattisgarh, 22.59; Jharkhand, 22.34; Rajasthan, 21.44; Madhya Pradesh, 20.29; and Uttar Pradesh, 20.08. The southern region presents a very different picture in this regard despite being the recipient of some in-migration from the central and eastern regions—Kerala, 4.86; Andhra Pradesh, 11.09; Karnataka, 15.67; and Tamil Nadu, 15.59. The contrast in population planning is to a certain extent a reflection of performance in governance. Furthermore, if population growth is one factor that considerably dissolves the impact of industrial diffusion, there is also another domestic factor that runs counter to diffusion itself—and that pertains to the attitudes and policies of the governing elites in some states. Such elites cannot carry out anti-industry policies and simultaneously expect industrial advance to take place or expect their grievances about discrimination to be taken seriously.

CVs on Convergence and Divergence

Beyond the general analysis here, comparisons of the degree of diffusion between Time 1 and Time 2 based on NVA share and NVA per capita values also can be based on compact statistical measures. One of these measures is standard deviation across periods. However, this measure is very often affected by shifts in the mean or average values of NVA and NVA per capita over the period. A measure that adjusts for such shifts in the mean over the period is provided by the coefficient of variation (CV), which divides the standard deviation during a period by the mean over the period. A higher value of CV indicates an increase in divergence, while a lower one indicates a decrease in divergence. Using this measure enables us to judge whether divergence or convergence has occurred over time.

The CV for the absolute value of NVA (Rs. million) of the states fell from 1.082 in 1999–2000 (see table 8.6, column 2) to 0.948 in 2009–10 (see table 8.7, column 2), thus indicating a fall in the disparity among the states between Time 1 and Time 2, although it is difficult to judge whether a decrease to this extent is really significant. However, this decrease in disparity is not reflected in the CV with respect to NVA per capita of the states; the CV for NVA per capita among the states rose from 0.725 in 1999–2000 (table 8.6, column 4) to 0.908 in 2009–10 (table 8.7, column 4), thus indicating a rise in divergence during the period. It would be difficult to speak with any certainty on the reasons for this anomaly between absolute value of NVA and NVA per capita among the states, but one reason for it is likely to be differences in the population growth rates among the various states.

SUMMARY AND CONCLUSION

In the ongoing debate about the impact of globalization and economic liberalization on economic integration, this chapter looks more closely with empirical data at the industrial sector as an area of investment. It investigates two particular aspects of the position of the critics on this issue; one aspect relates to the argument that liberalization would lead to deindustrialization, while the other pertains to liberalization likely making for polarization rather than diffusion of industry among the states.

With regard to the first aspect, the data on industrial growth and on the associated factors of investment and savings, and also on the expansion in the number of new companies founded and the number of new factories opened, all testify to the continued growth of industry and even its acceleration during the second decade of liberalization, at least until 2010. Such data clearly demonstrate that any notion of the occurrence of deindustrialization in India after liberalization is decidedly a myth. To be sure, India's industrial performance may not have been adequate either in comparative terms relative to its competitors or in terms of its own needs, but the data do not support the view that there has been either industrial stagnation or deindustrialization.

The other aspect—polarization as against diffusion—was studied in two different ways. First, several earlier postliberalization studies were reviewed. These studies tended to support the polarization thesis, with the coastal states seen as benefiting at the cost of the hinterland. The review, however, pointed out some of the weaknesses in their argument. This should not occasion any surprise, since almost all endeavors in the social sciences, including the present one, have some weakness or another.

Second, a new analysis on the basis of recent ASI data on net value added (NVA) in industry was offered for the period of accelerated growth, based on NVA shares and NVA per capita for both states and regions. Much of the postliberalization period covered in the analysis here was marked by acceleration in economic and industrial growth. Almost all *states* partook of this growth. However, they partook in varying measure. While there was considerable continuity in the ranking among the states, some change nonetheless occurred in the relative ranks of the states between 1999–2000 and 2009–10.

Broadly, the growth of industry during the period demonstrates some measure of diffusion and convergence in a mere single decade; certainly, the data do not demonstrate polarization. Such diffusion and convergence are concretely evident in the fact that: (1) most of the states that ranked in the lower half of the states in 1999–2000 in terms of their share in total NVA demonstrated better growth rates than those in the upper half; and, as a result, (2) some states could make substantial change from their ranking in 1999–2000 to that in 2009–10, such as Uttarakhand and Rajasthan, even as others were pulled down considerably (Jharkhand and Punjab). In addition, diffusion is obvious in: (3) the rise of the states of the southern region; and (4) the spread of industry beyond the coastal states, as manifest in the case of several of the northern region states. However, this measure of diffusion in the matter of a mere single decade understandably has not been sufficient to make radical change in the inherited industrial hierarchy among the states.

Perhaps there seems to be greater stability in the rankings of the *regions*, but even here there is evidence of diffusion. For example, the two middle regions (northern and southern) have moved closer to the performance of the top western region. However, the distance between the top region and the bottom two regions (central and eastern) has somewhat widened. Still, most of the constituent states of the latter two regions have done quite well by way of growth performance, indeed, better than the bulk of the states in the higher-ranking regions. However, these two regions seem to have been held back in the convergence process by the performance of three very populous states—especially Uttar Pradesh and West Bengal and, to some extent, Madhya Pradesh. It seems governance is the key to such performance; perhaps Uttar Pradesh is too large a political unit to be administered effectively while West Bengal has been lacking in policy that encourages entrepreneurship.

In his econometric study of the issue of trickling-down versus polarization among the states in India, Dholakia examined the GSDP of twenty-five states during a twenty-seven-year period, dividing the states into rich and poor on the basis of their per capita incomes relative to the Indian average. Employing the Granger Causality test, he found that economic advance in the richer states had a positive effect on the poorer states by way of spurring growth, and concluded that his study offered clear support for "the hypothesis of spread or trickle-down effect rather than the backwash or polarization effect."[19] The present study is, by and large, in accord with Dholakia's conclusion, even though its methodology is simpler, covers a fewer number of states, and restricts itself only to NVA in organized industry and a shorter period of time. Overall, the evidence supports a broad pattern of diffusion and convergence among the states to which there are some exceptions.

NOTES

1. See S. L. Shetty, "Structural Retrogression in the Indian Economy since the Mid-Sixties," *Economic and Political Weekly* 13, nos. 6/7 (February 1978): 185–244; and Isher Judge Ahluwalia, *Industrial Growth in India: Stagnation since the Mid-Sixties* (Delhi: Oxford University Press, 1985).

2. In a persuasive and nuanced argument, Dr. Nagaraj argues that the high growth period from 2003 to 2008, rather than representing any growth acceleration owing to liberalization, was an exceptional debt-led episode that was driven by an unusual expansion in world trade and serviced by both domestic savings and huge foreign capital inflows. See R. Nagaraj, "India's Dream Run, 2003–08: Understanding the Boom and Its Aftermath," *Economic and Political Weekly* 48, no. 20 (May 18, 2013): 39–51.

3. World Development Indicators, available at http://databank.worldbank.org/data/views/variableSelection/selectvariables.aspx?source=world-development-indicators, accessed April 22, 2013.

4. Government of India (GoI), *Economic Survey 2011–12*, A32, available at http://indiabudget.nic.in/es2011-12; GoI, "An Overview of Steel Sector" (New Delhi: Ministry of Steel, 2012), available at http://steel.gov.in/overview.htm; Organization Internationale

des Constructeurs d'Automobiles (International Organization of Motor Vehicle Manufacturers, or OICA), "World Motor Vehicle Production by Countries," available at http://oica.net.

5. See Surajit Mazumdar, "Industry and Services in Growth and Structural Change in India: Some Unexplored Features," Working Paper 2010/02, Institute for Studies in Industrial Development, New Delhi, January 2010.

6. World Development Indicators, available at http://databank.worldbank.org/data/views/variableSelection/selectvariables.aspx?source=world-development-indicators, accessed April 22, 2013.

7. K. K. Subrahmanian, "Inter-Regional Dimension of Industrial Growth," in B. A. Prakash, *The Indian Economy since Independence* (New Delhi: Pearson, 2009), 361–72.

8. Sanjoy Chakravorty and Somik V. Lall, *Made in India: The Economic Geography and Political Economy of Industrialization* (New Delhi: Oxford University Press, 2007), 22, 26, 28, 76.

9. Ibid., 33.

10. Ibid., 45, table 2.4.

11. Ibid., 52.

12. Ibid., 93.

13. T. S. Papola, Nitu Maurya, and Narendra Jena, "Inter-Regional Disparities in Industrial Growth and Structure," Occasional Paper Series 2011/4, Institute for Studies in Industrial Development, New Delhi, 2011.

14. Ibid., 9, 75.

15. Ibid., 15.

16. Ibid., 20–24.

17. Papola, Maurya, and Jena, "Inter-Regional Disparities," 7.

18. GoI, *Twelfth Five Year Plan (2012–2017): Faster, More Inclusive and Sustainable Growth* (New Delhi: Sage, 2013), vol. 2, 310; available at http://planningcommission.nic.in.

19. Ravindra H. Dholakia, "Testing for Trickle-Down or Polarization—Evidence from India," in Pennsylvania Economic Association, *Proceedings: Annual Conference, June 3–5, 2010* (Grove City, PA: Grove City College, 2011), 53.

Chapter 9

ARE WE ALL VAISHYAS NOW?

The Indian Capitalist Class as an Integrative Factor

THIS chapter goes beyond looking at the flows of capital (investment) as an element in economic integration to examine the providers of capital, that is, the capitalist or entrepreneurial class. It discusses the diffusion of entrepreneurship in *social* terms as distinguished from that in *spatial* terms (covered in chapter 8). The capitalist class in contemporary India is the object of high praise for starting and expanding industry and particularly for launching India on a course of high growth after economic liberalization. It is also, however, the object of trenchant criticism for its failure to effectively push India's industrialization and for having merely installed a corrupt and exploitative system of crony capitalism.[1] The present chapter sidesteps this controversial aspect and remains focused on the issue of economic integration, treating the capitalist class as a factor in that process. The chapter is divided into several sections that discuss: (1) the origins of the modern capitalist class; (2) the social composition of the class at independence; (3) the process of transformation of local business into national business; (4) concentration and competition in the capitalist class; (5) the social composition of the contemporary capitalist class; and (6) the direct and indirect contribution of the capitalist class to economic integration. Basically, the conclusion is that the capitalist class is an important factor that strengthens economic integration.

THE ONTOGENY OF THE MODERN CAPITALIST CLASS IN INDIA

The omens for the development of a modern capitalist class in India were not quite propitious after the British conquest. Besides the constraints of "a predominantly pre-capitalist agrarian structure" and "the dominance of foreign (mainly

British) capital over most of the 'modern' sector" of its colonial economy,[2] there were the serious obstacles flowing from the country's pervasive linguistic and ethnic diversity and the rigidity of its social system. But the situation was not entirely without some positive factors.

The top two castes in the ideal Hindu social hierarchy have been the priestly or intellectual caste of the Brahmins and the warrior and administrative caste of the Kshatriyas, who were both regarded as twice-born. The merchant caste of the Vaishyas, next in the social hierarchy, also was viewed as twice-born, but its position was marked by some ambiguity. On the one hand, "business was not considered a particularly honorable vocation," while the Vaishyas were considered inferior to the upper castes;[3] in addition, "a strong undercurrent of an anti-business ideology has been a continuing element all through the long history of India."[4] On the other hand, "no indignity was attached to their occupations which in Hindu tradition were religiously neutral."[5]

The birth of the modern capitalist class of indigenous provenance in India took place perforce under colonial rule. To a considerable degree, it also grew in opposition to colonialism and its commercial ally, the expatriate British business community. However, in its opposition to colonialism and its support of nationalism, the domestic capitalist class had to exercise caution and prudence for fear of injury to its economic interests at the hands of the colonial masters.[6] Given the racism of the time and the hostility of the colonial rulers and business expatriates to Indian business, the development of an indigenous capitalist class in India has been a source of some marvel for observers. As historian Claude Markovits underlined, "in no other colonial country was there a capitalist class comparable in size and wealth to the Indian capitalist class . . . the birth of a modern industry in the context of colonial India, despite all its limitations and shortcomings, represented a remarkable and perhaps unique feat of entrepreneurship."[7]

This tribute notwithstanding, right until independence and for some time even after that, British capital while in retreat reigned supreme over the Indian economy. Markovits himself provided data on the top fifty-seven business groups in 1939, ranked on the basis of the value of paid-up share capital.[8] British domination is patent; thirty-seven of the groups were British, while only nineteen were Indian, and one was Swedish. Significantly, the British firms were mostly clustered in the top two-thirds of the list, while the Indian firms, barring a few, were concentrated in the bottom third. Most British groups (twenty-four) were based in Calcutta, while the Indian firms were mostly located in western India (ten in Bombay and three in Ahmedabad).

The modern Indian capitalist class emerged in the nineteenth century. If one takes a long historical view, it would demonstrate that the capitalist class in India, whatever its alleged limitations, has seen a vast process of diffusion from small beginnings over the long stretch of history since then, even as the period has been marked by strong continuities. The origins of the class lie in the mid-1830s, when the East India Company's monopoly over trade ended. At that time, some of the enterprising Indian traders—especially Parsis (Zoroastrians)—who had migrated from the Gujarat region to Bombay City and had been assisting the British in their trading activities, joined in the China trade in opium and cotton on their own account. As such trade saw a major expansion in the following two decades, some of these traders experienced considerable capital accumulation. One of the Parsi businessmen started the first cotton textile mill in Bombay in 1854. The launching of that one mill in that particular place can be regarded as the beginning of modern industry in India; thus, it was Indians, not foreigners, who took the initiative.

Inspired by this bold example, other Indians followed with more textile mills; soon, Bombay and Ahmedabad became the two renowned centers of textile production in India. The textile industry then spread to other locations as well. By 1892, there were 127 textile mills in India (employing 100,000 workers). Most of these mills, except those in Cawnpore and Madras, were the handiwork of Indians, not British expatriates, by way of conceptualization, finance, and management.[9] Significantly, the rise of the textile industry in India was accomplished in the face of resistance from British textile interests when they became aware of the fact that the natives could establish and profitably run textile factories. This resistance manifested itself in such interests successfully lobbying the colonial government to enact policies on labor and customs duties that adversely affected local industry.

The pioneers in the industrial effort in western India had largely been members of the Parsi community, whose role in the introduction of industry in India is inestimable. They were uniquely qualified to undertake this role. As they moved down to the city of Bombay from Gujarat, they proved particularly adept at quickly adapting themselves to the new colonial dispensation and soon became the most westernized community in India, while the British, in turn, found them to be closest to them in their own ethos. The Parsis were generally perceived to be "socially closer to the ruling race"; indeed, they could in modern-day parlance be said to have been regarded by the British as honorary whites.[10] As such, the Parsis became a natural intermediary between the colonial rulers and the local population, including business. Their contribution to India's economy over time has been enormous, both as pioneers of industry and in setting high ethical standards in business. This is best symbolized by the heroic figure of Jamsetji Nusserwanji Tata (1839–1904), a true visionary, who vastly diversified the House of the Tatas, venturing into steel production, and launched it on its path to becoming a colossal industrial conglomerate that to this day stands at the summit of corporate business in India.

Meanwhile, in the eastern region at Calcutta (now Kolkata), Scottish enterprise led to the setting up of the first jute mill in 1855; other Scotsmen followed with more jute mills, mining, and tea plantations, making the British the dominant force in the economy of the eastern region, and therefore in India as a whole. Thus, it was in Bombay and Calcutta as two relatively isolated commercial centers constituting two lonely industrial poles across the vast expanse of an otherwise overwhelmingly rural India that the foundations of modern industry in the subcontinent were laid. About a century and a half later, it is apparent that the growth and diffusion of industry from those two centers has made India one of the top ten industrial powers of the world, underlining the massive and diversified industrial complex that has been created within the country.[11] At the same time, however, there is no denying the serious limitations of the Indian achievement, especially when compared to the East Asian tigers.

Much of the growth of the indigenous capitalist and industrialist class prior to independence occurred during and between the two world wars, when India was largely delinked from the British economy. Huge wartime profits led to the launching of new industrial enterprises and takeovers of British companies, even as they earned the class an ugly image of being exploiters. The expansion of the capitalist class also made for sociological change among the class. After World War I, local business became more self-conscious of itself as a class and began to organize itself on an all-India basis to articulate its demands to the colonial authorities for tariff protection and also to firm up its nexus with the rising nationalist movement. The widening of the modern capitalist class also engendered changes in its social composition, none more remarkable than the entry and rapid rise of Marwari businessmen. The term Marwari does not connote a homogeneous group; rather, it refers to many subcastes belonging to the larger merchant *bania* caste in the Vaishya order, but one that is distinctive for having originated in the inhospitable desert region of Marwar.

Perhaps because of the harsh nature of its desert environment, the Marwar region has been witness over time to waves of out-migration from among its traditional money-lending and trading community to various parts of India in search of economic opportunity. In this manner, the region has unintentionally provided a core element in India's economic integration, even if sometimes at the cost of local resentment. One such wave of out-migration occurred in the second half of the nineteenth century, particularly to the seat of the imperial government and British economic power in Calcutta, and more generally to the eastern region. Given its humble origins and meager material assets at the beginning, the community ought to have elicited universal admiration for its indisputably monumental achievement in advancing business and industry in India and building several industrial empires. Instead, it has often evoked awe and derision (and, of course, jealousy) among the intelligentsia and upper castes.

In due course, after many migrations to diverse parts of the subcontinent, Marwari businessmen became transformed into a pan-Indian capitalist community. If Jamsetji Tata from the Parsi community is the iconic figure of business in India during the nineteenth century, then Ghanshyam Das Birla (1894–1983) from the Marwari community is certainly one in the twentieth century. Coming from a family of humble origins, he led "the transition of the community from trade to industry" and became "the Tatas' most formidable rival for supremacy in the Indian business world" and eventually "the most dominant voice of the Indian business."[12] He played a particularly important role in the pan-Indian organization of the Indian business community as a defense against British expatriate interests, in supporting the nationalist movement and in serving as a go-between for the colonial regime and the nationalist movement. Medha M. Kudaisya refers to him as "one of the greatest Indians of the twentieth century."[13]

Despite its support to the nationalist movement, business was to be deeply disappointed with the turn of events after independence. While the capitalist class no doubt saw expansion and diversification after independence, independent India severely limited its opportunities because the new leadership preempted a large part of the industrial arena for the public sector because of its socialistic inclinations. It was only after the mid-1980s, especially after 1991, that business began to be regarded as a potential driver of economic growth. Meanwhile, as the economy slowly expanded under the socialist regime, new business groups emerged even as others saw decline. The most spectacular of the new groups was Ambani, founded by Dhirubhai Ambani, a Gujarati of humble origins, belonging to the bania caste in Gujarat. Dhirubhai's emergence "easily dwarfs all other post-independence entrants in the world of Indian business. . . . His rise, without question, is the single most momentous development in the business history of free India. . . . Never before had an Indian business house, starting virtually from dust, risen so high within such a short time."[14] By 2001, his group had emerged as the largest business group in India.[15] The unparalleled meteoric rise of Ambani in independent India makes him truly the iconic figure of Indian business for the second half of the twentieth century, comparable to J. N. Tata and G. D. Birla. Parsi, Marwari, and Gujarati bania thus provide a pithy summation of the key business communities that dominated the indigenous advance of industry prior to independence.

The rise of Ambani from the state of Gujarat and its bania community is a reflection of the ethos of the state and its people, which favors the market and active participation in it. As with the Parsis—whose original home in India is also Gujarat—and the Marwaris, there is a sociological explanation for it. That explanation lies in Gujarat's location: its vast coastline has exposed it to foreign trade for many centuries.

ENTRENCHMENT AND EXPANSION IN SOCIAL COMPOSITION

A long-standing image, owing perhaps to the pioneering work of the economist D. R. Gadgil, has been that the contemporary Indian business class is basically populated by the trading, money-lending, and banking occupational communities from traditional India prior to colonialism. Besides the microscopic minority group of the Parsis, most other business groups are regarded as having emerged from such communities. Preeminent among the latter are the Marwari and Gujarati banias, who come under the umbrella of the Vaishya order in the Hindu caste hierarchy.

These traditional communities in commerce ("the bazaar") were, besides the Parsis, the first to avail of modern business opportunities that opened up under colonial rule, first as traders and intermediaries and then as industrialists, apparently utilizing their historical accumulation of both physical and human capital in business.[16] It is emblematic of this transformation from traditional to modern business that the three heroes of modern business in three successive periods of India's recent economic history—J. N. Tata, G. D. Birla, and Dhirubhai Ambani—were from the Parsi, Marwari bania, and Gujarati bania communities, respectively, and that the industrial houses they built still stand many decades later almost head-to-head at the peak of Indian business. The formidable position of these communities in modern business runs like a common thread through any listing of the top business groups even today. In that sense, the modern business class in India can be said to represent simply the transmutation of traditional society's commercial castes into the industrial conglomerates of contemporary society.

It is understandable that the Parsis and the Marwari and Gujarati banias would be in the vanguard of Indian business groups. The Parsis flourished under colonialism since many among them were already engaged in trading and other important economic activities, even as they found much in their economic and social ethos to be compatible with that of the colonizers. For their part, the Marwaris and Gujaratis were, in greater or smaller measure, already accustomed to travel and migration over a wide geographic area and to establishing trading and banking networks in India. The prominence and predominance of these and other traditional mercantile communities in the world of contemporary business, therefore, should not be surprising.

However, given the vast changes in the industrial landscape of the country over the last century and a half, particularly after independence, it would seem far-fetched to take the earlier patterns of the social composition of modern business to have been frozen for all time. Change, but not necessarily revolutionary change, would seem to be pervasive in business. The social pattern in India traditionally has been that of a palimpsest, where there is no overthrow or complete displacement of what exists, but the adding of additional layers onto it over time. Gradualism and accommodation have been more characteristic of Indian social change. In the process, while some business houses—particularly the preeminent ones—have adapted and continued to benefit from their first-mover advantage, many others instead have declined or were reduced to irrelevancy, and still others have been born, have risen, and were added onto the previous ones.

It is the particular merit of the fascinating, well-researched, award-winning book of Harish Damodaran that it debunks the earlier understanding of the social composition of modern Indian business and industry that focuses on traditional business communities.[17] Damodaran sees three different routes to entry into modern business in India. The first of these, *from bazaar to factory*, is, of course, the one that reflects the customary understanding of the transformation of traditional mercantile communities into modern industrialists, such as the Marwaris and Gujaratis.

The second route that he delineates, *from office to factory*, represents a change, however, from the customary understanding of the origins of the modern Indian business class insofar as it underlines the entry into business of the higher priestly or administrative castes, such as the Brahmins and Kshatriyas. Apparently, groups or individuals from these scribal castes took to modern English education and became administrators or joined the professions, and then from that vantage point, they or their progeny made the transition to business and industry. However, this is not entirely a postindependence phenomenon. It already may have been present earlier. Regardless, the burden of the following discussion is that the presence of the scribal castes is very much evident as early as the beginning of the 1950s, that is, soon after independence.

The eminent postindependence critic of economic concentration, R. K. Hazari, provided a listing of the top twenty business groups (not companies, but conglomerate groups) in India for 1951 and 1958 (see table 9.1). The table highlights several things about the state of business in India within four years of independence. First, there is the marked displacement of the once seemingly impregnable British expatriate business by Indian business soon after independence. The process had begun even before independence arrived, as expatriate firms felt uncertain about their future while Indian business groups were eager to buy them out. The end of colonialism thus proved fatal for the expatriates. After a long struggle, Indian capital had finally triumphed. By 1951, there were really only two expatriate groups left among the top twenty groups—Bird Heilger at rank 5 and Andrew Yule at rank 7; and even these two groups vanished in the next few decades.

Second, while the Tatas are at the top among all the groups in this table—as they had been even in 1939—the once dominant economic power of the Parsi community had suffered relative decline since there is only one other Parsi group in the list of twenty—Shapoorji, at rank 18. Third, the table makes abundantly obvious the predominance of the bania caste among the various business communities, since seven business groups belonged to that caste; what is more, they are clustered mostly among the top two-thirds of the list. Most prominent among them were the Marwari banias—with the Birlas at rank 2 and the others at ranks 6, 8, and 10; another Marwari bania at rank 4 was a follower of the Jain religion. Gujarati banias from the Jain religion also had a fair representation among the bania group (ranks 11, 13, and 20). The discussion to this point simply confirms the popular understanding of Indian business being overstocked by the traditional trading communities. However, the list reveals some other dimensions that go beyond this popular understanding.

Fourth, there are five groups among the twenty listed that fit the description of the second route *from office to factory* taken by the scribal castes; two of them

Table 9.1. Top Twenty Business Groups by Gross Capital Stock in 1951 and 1958

Group	Caste and Provincial Origin	Group	Caste and Provincial Origin
1. Tata	Parsi	11. Kasturbhai	Bania, Jain, Gujarati
2. Birla	Bania, Marwari	12. Mafatlal	Patel (farmer), Gujarati
3. Martin Burn	Bengali Brahmin/ British	13. Walchand	Bania, Jain, Gujarati
4. Dalmia Sahu Jain	Bania, Jain, Marwari	14. Ramakrishna	Kamma (farmer), from Andhra Pradesh
5. Bird Heilger	British	15. Indra Singh	Sikh Jat (farmer), from Punjab
6. Bangur	Bania, Marwari	16. Mahindra	Khatri, from Punjab
7. Andrew Yule	British	17. Seshayee	Brahmin, in Tamilnadu
8. Shri Ram	Bania, "sociologically" Marwari	18. Shapoorji	Parsi
9. Thapar	Khatri, from Punjab	19. Kirloskar	Brahmin (Maharashtra)
10. J. K. [Singhania]	Bania, "sociologically" Marwari	20. Khatau	Bhatia, from Kutch in Gujarat

Source: R. K. Hazari, *The Structure of the Corporate Private Sector: A Study of Concentration, Ownership and Control* (London: Asia Publishing, 1966), 17, 25.

Notes: The groups are ranked for 1958, but the list is the same for 1951 though the ranking is different for some of the groups. With respect to the groups at ranks 8 and 10, Hazari states that they "trace their original 'native places' to areas that may be sociologically described as Marwari homelands," even though the areas are outside Marwar or even Rajasthan, such as Haryana, Delhi, and western Uttar Pradesh. As for rank 3, the majority interest is Bengali Brahmin. Khatau, at rank 20, is presumed here to be Bania.

are Punjabi Khatris (ranks 9 and 16), while three are Brahmins—one each from Maharashtra (rank 19), Tamil Nadu (rank 17), and West Bengal (rank 3). That is not all, however. Fifth, there are three groups that fit another category that Damodaran offers, *from farm to factory*, that is, farmers who accumulated wealth and took to business, often preceded by advance in education. This category is represented by a business group from Gujarat (rank 12), Andhra Pradesh (rank 14), and Punjab (Jat Sikh, at rank 15). Looked at another way, the table shows that a little more than half of the groups (11 out of 20) are Hindu by religion, while one-fifth of them are Jains (three Gujaratis and one Marwari), two are Parsis, and one is Sikh. There is no Muslim group, however, perhaps because any likely candidate for the list shifted to Pakistan. Besides the Marwaris (five in number), there are four Gujaratis (three Bania Jains and one from a farming background). Punjab is represented by three business groups (two Hindu Khatris and one Jat Sikh), and West Bengal by one, if the Marwari and British expatriate groups based in Calcutta are excluded from consideration. There may be some limits to the significance of the list, however, since it pertains to a time of political and economic upheaval and confusion following the end of colonialism and the partition, and it remains to be seen if the pattern of diversity evident here has been sustained;

certainly, some of the groups vanished before long, such as Indra Singh and Seshayee, and many others declined.

Nonetheless, the picture that emerges from examining the list of the top twenty business groups at independence is one of business that was somewhat more diversified than earlier thought, and it does not fit the stereotypical image of business in India being populated solely by Marwaris and Gujaratis, though the latter two groups undoubtedly had plenty more than their share. Business was not confined simply to Marwaris and Gujaratis; it was open to others who wanted to seize the opportunity. Of course, in the subsequent decades as the economy advanced, more groups joined, and not a few of these came from the scribal and farmer castes. However, entry was one thing and reaching the top altogether was another, though quite a few did. As the field got increasingly more crowded, competition got tougher and reaching the top became much more arduous. Interestingly, meanwhile, the scribal castes found another route to the top of the economic ladder, which is touched on here only briefly.

While business at the top at independence was more diversified than popularly believed, at the same time, the popular stereotype had some basis in fact since Marwari and Gujarati banias along with the Parsis held a disproportionate share of such business. But Marwari and Gujarati dominance in business radically diverged sociologically from the caste background of the bulk of the political leadership that succeeded to state power after independence, which was largely drawn from the scribal or intellectual upper castes of Brahmins and Kshatriyas. These were precisely the castes that had eagerly taken to English education and, becoming thus transformed into the new middle class, had led the nationalist struggle against colonial rule; interestingly, Nehru himself came from a Brahmin family. He may have been a socialist out of ideological conviction, but the new middle class, at the time primarily composed of the scribal castes, also followed him and after independence came to man all the strategic positions in the political system, the academia, and the professions. Regardless of whether or not socialism is, indeed, the ideology of the intellectuals—that is, a legitimizing set of ideas that serves to mask their real will to power—the new middle class came to control all the levers of not only political but also economic power during the heyday of socialism in India from the mid-1950s to the mid-1990s. Apart from the economic power derived from the system of licensing and controls over the private sector, this class directly controlled the principal means of production in the form of the public sector in addition to banking and insurance.

The public sector has continued to provide economic power to the new middle class, since little privatization took place after economic liberalization. It has also enabled the same class to enter the private sector as advisers to corporate groups or as entrepreneurs after retirement. However, the process of diffusion of economic power to castes other than the traditional business communities has not stopped with these largely urbanized higher castes.

The really innovative contribution by Damodaran, building on the work of anthropologists and sociologists, is about the already-mentioned third route, *from farm to factory*. In this route, landowning or peasant groups from the intermediate caste of the Shudras (officially, Other Backward Classes), who are not regarded as twice-born, have made a transition from agriculture to modern business—whether through accumulation of surplus capital from advances in agriculture by way of irrigation and the Green Revolution or through acquisition of modern education—either as individual entrepreneurs or by joining together in cooperatives. It is noteworthy that Damodaran finds this phenomenon limited to the states of the southern and western regions and does not see much movement on the part of similar groups in other regions of India. He ascribes this distinctiveness of the south and west to a "Vaishya vacuum," that is, the absence of a dominant Vaishya presence, whether in numbers or in status. In contrast, the caste order in the other regions has been more in accord with the classical type, particularly with the Marwari diaspora having already shot ahead under colonial rule, with the result that farming communities of the intermediate castes there continue to suffer from a business deficit.

Significantly, even in the southern and western regions, the industrial advance among different communities has yet to trickle down in any significant manner to the Dalit community, that is, the group of former untouchables. Damodaran does discuss the rise of the Nadars and Ezhavas in Tamil Nadu, but he also underlines the ambiguity of their social status by alluding to their position "as belonging to the highest division of the lowest classes or the lowest of the middle classes."[18] Still, state patronage has been enabling for Dalits to enter business, even if for now only small and medium business. This would represent, then, a fourth route, *from state patronage to factory*. The factors behind the extension of state patronage to the Dalits for business have varied: ideological conviction about compensatory discrimination for historically disadvantaged groups, recognition of the power of numbers under democracy, and the actual acquisition of power by Dalits on the basis of political mobilization. Dalits are not the only group to avail of state patronage for advancement in business; other better-placed caste groups or individual business houses have also utilized it. Apropos of this route, it is noteworthy that the rise of the intermediate castes in business in the southern and western regions was not a stand-alone phenomenon, but was part and parcel of a wider social and political mobilization of the intermediate castes for social reform, economic benefits, and acquisition of political power.

Reservations for Dalits in educational institutions, government bureaucracies and public sector enterprises, and elected legislatures—more or less in proportion to their share in the population—were instrumental in the creation of a middle class among the Dalits over two or three generations. In due course, this middle class went on to demand a share in the expanding business of the country and to support the creation of a Dalit entrepreneurial class. As a start, it pressed for "supplier diversity," a mechanism under which the state would favor Dalits in extending contracts for the supply of goods and services to the government and the public sector, perhaps also even requiring the private sector to do so. This demand was articulated in the Bhopal Declaration in 2002 by Dalit intellectuals.[19]

Since economic liberalization, an increasing number of Dalit entrepreneurs have emerged, and there is now even a Dalit Indian Chamber of Commerce and Industry (DICCI). In July 2011, the *Economic Times* ran a series of interesting articles on the rise of Dalit entrepreneurs, mostly from western India. While not many of these entrepreneurs meet the criterion of an annual turnover of Rs. 1 billion that Damodaran used for coverage in his 2008 book, one particular enterprise stands out for being in a highly sophisticated field—DAS Offshore Engineering, with an annual turnover of Rs. 1.3 billion and 4,500 employees. Its owner, Ashok Khade, is the son of a cobbler who built the enterprise by dint of his own Herculean efforts.[20] Southern India provides another example of Dalit enterprise of even larger proportions with a turnover of Rs. 7.5 billion in 2011–12 and the only such enterprise to be listed on the stock exchange—Visaka Industries Limited, headquartered in Secunderabad, Andhra Pradesh. This enterprise is the second-largest manufacturer of fiber cement sheets, and has seven factories in six different states. Unlike the previous entrepreneur, however, the career path of the founder of Visaka, G. Vivekanand, is very different. The son of a former minister in the central government, Vivekanand went to an elite public school and obtained an MBBS (bachelor of medicine, bachelor of surgery) degree from Osmania University, having benefited perhaps from the reservations policy.[21] Interestingly, some of the strongest expressions about the glories of capitalism from the oppressed have come from Dalit representatives.[22]

The market with competition as its hallmark is a dynamic and expansive social institution; social change is an inherent part of it, with some business groups rising and others falling. Over time, it is evident in the case of India that there has been an expansion of industry in which new castes and social groups have entered the world of business and escaped the occupational and social rigidities of the traditional caste system, no doubt at times with the assistance of the state. Even though he emphasizes the southern and western regions as the home of such "inclusive capitalism," Damodaran nonetheless underlines: "The central point conveyed is that capitalism in India has evolved a long way since Independence and today is fairly well diversified not just in terms of production profile (spanning a whole range of industries) but also social base. Capital is not the privileged bastion of a few mercantile castes the way it was; its base has expanded to incorporate a wide spectrum of communities."[23]

There is no reason to assume that this process is likely to stop with the particular regions or with the particular castes and classes that have already entered business any more than it did in the past, provided an open and receptive environment for the functioning of the market is sustained.

FROM LOCAL TO REGION TO NATION: THE DYNAMICS OF BUSINESS GROWTH

To some extent, Damodaran's proposition on the entry of rural intermediate castes into the world of modern business and industry had been presaged by another economist, Sanjaya Baru, but the latter also had brought forward a different dimension that has an important bearing on the issue of economic segmentation and integration.[24] Baru had observed that the transformation of intermediate caste peasants into agricultural capitalists in the 1960s and 1970s and further into urban capitalists in the 1980s was linked in a mutually supportive way with the rise of regional or state political parties. As rising urban capitalists in the states, these first-generation entrepreneurs in the regions found themselves to be at a disadvantage during the "license and permit raj" in the competition with the already established business houses belonging to the pan-Indian capitalist class. Consequently, regional business used the leverage of the regional political parties to put pressure on the national government in order to obtain the necessary licenses and permits for starting and expanding enterprises.

In particular, Baru pointed out how in the case of Andhra Pradesh the rise of the Kamma peasant caste in business was intertwined with the political advance of the Telugu Desam Party (TDP) to that party's ascension to power in the state, and to its increasing influence at the national level, which in turn served the interests of regional business.[25] Baru commented: "That this process is intrinsically linked to the rise of regional politics in states like Andhra Pradesh has been widely commented upon. It is not an accident that the Telugu Desam Party is dominated by Kammas and its chief financiers, as well as key leaders, remain Kamma businessmen." He further demonstrated that his analysis of Andhra Pradesh had applicability to Gujarat, Maharashtra, and Tamil Nadu, and also to Karnataka, Haryana, and Punjab. Baru believed that a situation of conflict existed between the national big business with urban origins and "the new generation of businessmen we call 'regional' [who] have agrarian origins and rural roots," the emergence of which was related to agrarian change, which has been unevenly spread across India under the Green Revolution, however. He further held that, while the national big business, which earlier had supported the nationalist movement, identified itself with the national government, regional business tended to identify itself with regional parties and invested in them in order "to gain market leverage over national big business."[26]

While there is considerable merit in Baru's analysis, perhaps it is time-bound in the sense that it describes economic-political change at a given point in time. For example, with the postliberalization dismantlement of much of the system of controls, regional business does not need the leverage of pressure from the state government to obtain licenses to establish industry in most areas of business. Moreover, state governments may no longer necessarily want to discriminate against national big business, because most state governments are in competition with each other to attract capital, any capital, since economic advance of a state is important to getting reelected. More important, any conflict between a regional firm and a national firm is likely to be a contingent, not a generalized, phenomenon. For, at the beginning, all business is essentially local. When the first textile mill in Mumbai or the first jute mill in Calcutta was founded, it was a local phenomenon. It was only after a long time that business groups with a national scope came into being and it took even longer to develop a pan-Indian business identity. Well into the twentieth century, Indian business was basically confined to particular regions and business consciousness was largely regional. It is only after World War I that business began to organize itself on a national basis since it saw itself in conflict with colonial rule and expatriate business. This effort became manifest in the organization of the Federation of Indian Chambers of Commerce and Industry (FICCI) in 1927, but it is worth recalling that it required some doing to bring regional businesses to a common platform.[27]

Over time, business groups may graduate from the local to the state, to the regional, and to the national level (and some even to the international level). Expansion is natural and inherent in the market and capitalism, but accomplishment depends on competence and opportunity. What was regional yesterday may become national today, no longer remaining merely regional, and it may indeed become global tomorrow. The process of expansion of business from the region to the nation is illustrated by the following few brief case studies, to begin with from the very state of Andhra Pradesh, which formed the starting point for both Damodaran and Baru on the rise of regional business. Those among the peasantry in Andhra Pradesh, who came into affluence because of advances in irrigation by the 1930s, diversified into money lending and trading, helped in this endeavor by the "Vaishya vacuum." What propelled them into investing in nontraditional lines of business was the Great Depression. They then took to agroprocessing, construction, public contracts, transport, and moviemaking. The next generation also took to professional education.

As Damodaran comments in relation to one agricultural community: "At the beginning of the 1980s the Kammas had penetrated a range of industries from sugar, tobacco, and rice milling to government contracts, transport, textiles, ferroalloys, and cinema. This transformation for a primarily agriculture-based community had come within a matter of fifty years."[28] The industrial thrust among its members received a tremendous boost during the 1980s as a result of huge public sector projects in steel manufacturing, power production, and canal and road construction, all of which opened up opportunities for the growth of entrepreneurship in the state. Many construction magnates grew from this investment boom, some of whom then diversified into industry. The growth in economic power, meanwhile, fueled political ambition, which found expression in the new Telugu Desam Party. For Damodaran, "there is no doubt that the party's coming into power has coincided with a resurgence of Kamma capital. And unlike the past, this has been powered not by the old landlord class but by educated folk of relatively humble farming background."[29] The transformation of farmers into industrialists was not limited to the Kammas, however; it also encompassed other farming communities such as the Reddys and Rajus.

The growth of industrial entrepreneurship may have developed within the boundaries of a single state in which state-level political parties may or may not have been involved in a mutually supportive way, even as the whole process was boosted by massive national investments in industry and infrastructure. But once triggered, it did not remain confined within the boundaries of the state. As they rose, business groups expanded beyond the state, with their business vision advancing to encompass the larger nation and, indeed, the world beyond. Some of these groups in due course joined the big league of Indian business. In turn, the larger business community accommodated regional business at the national level, and the market thus advanced India's economic integration, rather than its economic segmentation. The market is a dynamic social system in which firms rise and fall; it is not a static system. Regional firms can and do rise to the national and international level, in the process persuading others of the possibilities of emulation, even as they stand as a reminder that the system at the national level is not a closed but open one. The following illustrative cases demonstrate the national reach achieved by daring individual entrepreneurs, regarded at one time merely as emerging regional players, perhaps resentful of and opposed to the established national business.

GVK

"Today's big Reddy houses are all products of the last few decades," says Damodaran.[30] One of the more prominent of these is certainly GVK, named after its founder and chairman, Gunapati Venkata Krishna Reddy.[31] Reddy was born and grew up in a village in the Nellore District of Andhra Pradesh, ostensibly of affluent parents, who sent him to college in the state capital of Hyderabad for his BA in economics. At age twenty-one, prior to his graduation, a division of family business brought him as his share part of the contract work for building the Nagarjuna Sagar Dam. Prospering as a contractor, Reddy diversified into industry, pioneering the production of prelaminated particleboards through starting Novopan Industries in 1979, and later launching backward vertical integration with GVK Petrochemicals. After a decade of business in the United States, he returned to India in 1992, persuaded by the state's chief minister, also a Reddy. Then, the shift in economic policy to liberalization gave him his big break. He entered the power generation business, and leaped from one successful venture to another, which soon extended across India. By 2012, GVK had become an infrastructure conglomerate with an investment of some US$3.3 billion and a workforce of 32,000; its interests encompassed energy, resources, airports, roads and ports, hotels, and scientific research. What is noteworthy about GVK is the national, and even international, reach of its projects in various sectors, extending across many states. This is true of the energy sector, as it is of the resources, road-building, and hospitality sectors.

What really shot GVK into public prominence, however, has been its private public partnership (PPP) role in the modernization and management of the airport at Mumbai (Bombay) and the building and running of a new greenfield airport at Bengaluru (Bangalore). Airport building has taken it abroad as well. Under a memorandum of understanding with the government of Indonesia, GVK is planning the development of two airports at Bali and Yogyakarta. From what has been described here, it is obvious that coming out of Andhra Pradesh, GVK's vision and reach now extends across India and beyond. GVK is not alone in this regard, however.

GMR

GMR is a strong competitor and rival to GVK as another infrastructure giant from Andhra Pradesh, even though this business group, now headquartered in Bangalore, originates not in one of the state's peasant castes but in the traditional mercantile community of the Komati Chettys (Arya Vaishyas).[32] The firm is called GMR after its founder and chairman, Grandhi Mallikarjuna Rao, a mechanical engineer, who was born in the small town of Rajam in Srikakulam District in Andhra Pradesh. A first-generation entrepreneur, Rao's accomplishments are legendary, for which he has won numerous awards that would be the envy of any national-level businessman. Rao's self-confessed heroes are Dhirubhai Ambani in asset building and humility, Ratan Tata in institution building, and Warren Buffett and Bill Gates in giving back to society.

Founded in 1978, GMR is similar in its profile to GVK, with a workforce of 17,000 and investments in energy, roads, urban infrastructure, and airports—again, extending across many states. Interestingly, GMR also owns a major cricket team in the national capital—in an effort "to earn the reputation of a young and vibrant organization" and to better "connect with the citizens of Delhi." What catapulted the GMR group to national recognition is its joint venture with the Airports Authority of India—in which it has a majority interest (54 percent)—for the restructuring, modernization, and management of Delhi's international airport.

GMR regards the airport project as an iconic achievement, in effect lifting the airport from the number 106 position among the world's airports to number 2, with its chairman claiming in 2012 to have "brought pride to India . . . brought pride to the country. . . . The best part of the last two years was that we got 30 awards. Today, we are the second best airport in the world. Thirty-two countries came here to see how we built the airport. This is very good for the country. It becomes a brand for the country. . . . We have shown to the world that yes, Indians can also build and operate. It has given a brand name to the community."[33] Of course, with acclaim have also come charges about excessive profit making and heartbreaks in dealing with government regulators. The Delhi airport is not GMR's only aviation venture. In another joint venture in which it has majority control (63 percent), it built and operates the airport in Hyderabad in Andhra Pradesh. Further, going abroad in this sector, it has developed and operates one airport in Istanbul, Turkey. Expanding the business across India and to the world has brought attitudinal change, as well. When GMR's chairman was asked if he, as already the owner of the cricket team Delhi Daredevils, would also buy another team, the Deccan Chargers, he responded: "I belong to Delhi now. Either I am a Bangalorean or a Delhiite now."[34]

Dr. Reddy's Laboratories

It is not in infrastructure alone that firms from Andhra Pradesh have shown their luster. They have shone in the area of pharmaceuticals, too. To begin with, Damodaran comments: "Pharmaceuticals is a sector that has produced an avalanche of new-generation Kamma entrepreneurs from the 1980s." However, it is Dr. Reddy's Laboratories (DRL) that radiates in this sector, emerging as one of the top three pharmaceutical companies in India. In 2012, its revenue earnings crossed the US$2 billion mark, the overwhelming part of which (82 percent) came from outside India: North America, 45 percent; Russia and the Commonwealth of Independent States, 19 percent; Europe, 12 percent; and the rest of the world, 6 percent; India's share in the revenues was 18 percent.[35] DRL proved itself to be the fastest-growing Indian pharmaceutical firm, for it reached this landmark by doubling its revenues within four years. Considering all this, it is hard to believe that it was not until as late as 1984, with barely Rs. 2.5 million as capital outlay, that Dr. Kallam Anji Reddy—a chemical engineer who had worked with the public sector enterprise Indian Drugs and Pharmaceuticals Limited in Hyderabad from 1969 to 1975—founded DRL, of which he remained chairman until his death in 2013.

In 2001, DRL was additionally listed on the New York Stock Exchange. Today, DRL has six plants approved by the Food and Drug Administration (FDA) in India and one FDA-approved plant each in Mexico and the United Kingdom for the manufacture of drugs. While most of its manufacturing and research and development facilities are located in Hyderabad, the reach of its products is India-wide. Particularly interesting is its endeavor to see that its medicines are accessible in the rural areas.[36]

Some Other Businesses

DRL is not the only example in the medical field from Andhra Pradesh of having transformed itself from a regional business to a national enterprise with a global reach. One could cite many others, an important one being the Apollo Hospitals Group, founded by Dr. Prathap C. Reddy, which as "the largest healthcare service provider in Asia and the third largest in the world," owns or manages more than forty hospitals, with more than eight thousand beds, across India and in other parts of Asia and Africa.[37] Nor are such examples by any means confined to Andhra Pradesh or to Karnataka and Tamil Nadu.

Though they are not from the farming community, Ranbaxy (as also Escorts and Apollo Tyres) from Delhi and Hero Cycles from the Punjab are other outstanding examples of firms starting from scratch but seizing the opportunity to make it big; in the process, they have driven home the point that firms can start locally and then become national. Ranbaxy is an excellent illustration of a Punjabi Khatri Sikh, Bhai Mohan Singh, taking over a small-scale drug distribution firm and raising it to the status of India's top pharmaceutical manufacturer specializing in the production of generic drugs, based on reverse engineering on the strength of its own research and development facilities. By 2005, its sales were more than US$1 billion, with three-fourths of them in the overseas market, including 29 percent in the United States. The firm proved to be too attractive, however, for Japan's Daiichi Sankyo Company to resist taking it over in 2008.[38] Similarly, the four Munjal brothers from the Hindu Khatri community in Ludhiana, Punjab, emerged out of the ashes of the partition of the subcontinent to start making cycle components on a small scale. They then went on to establish Hero Bicycles in 1956, as a minor operation to make twenty-five bicycles a day. Under the leadership of Dayanand Munjal, the firm was transformed to make 18,500 bicycles a day by 2000, taking about half of India's market; in 1986, it had already entered the Guinness book as the largest manufacturer of bicycles in the world, a record that it has maintained since. From 1984 to 2010, the Munjals also had a joint venture with Honda, which facilitated their making it big in the world of motorbikes; the successor, Hero MotoCorp, claims to be the world's largest producer of two-wheelers; with two plants in Haryana and one in Uttarakhand, it has the capacity to produce three million motorbikes.[39]

The foregoing discussion reinforces the point of how the expansion of industry since independence, if not earlier, has broadened the social base of business in India beyond the traditional business communities to incorporate new caste groups beyond the twice-born. At the same time, it demonstrates how the dynamic of expansion of industry and market is enabling economic and national integration, with enterprises beginning on a small scale and expanding beyond the region to national and even international scale. Business groups may find it instrumental to emphasize regional identities when they are newly emergent, but "as the capital accumulation process intensifies, the lines between the national and regional bourgeoisies are progressively blurred."[40] In the course of this process, the capitalist class has assumed a pan-Indian form; what the traditional communities began now extends beyond them, encompassing many new groups, even if there is not—and, perhaps, never can be—equal representation in business any more than it is in other sectors, such as the army. Different sections of the population bring different talents and specializations to the economic process;

what is essential is not equal representation but that the system remains open to all who have the talent and the capacity to advance in it.

CONCENTRATION AND COMPETITION IN THE CAPITALIST CLASS

Business concentration was an issue in India even before independence. Moreover, super profits, black market operations, and resort to unethical practices during World War II did not particularly endear business to the public. After independence, as business expanded, the attacks mounted against business concentration became more vociferous in Indian politics, especially during the 1960s, and the government responded by setting up inquiry commissions and committees. The Monopolies Inquiry Commission summed up the popular posture on business:

> In the eyes of the common man in India concentrated economic power is wholly evil. The great disparity of wealth and income between the small section of the people possessing such power and the vast majority that constitute the remainder is by itself sufficient to explain this attitude. The dislike for concentration of economic power is turned into hatred by the abysmal poverty in which millions of our countrymen live and die. . . . This antipathy for big business is aggravated by belief not infrequently held that the big businessmen are responsible for all their misfortune.[41]

Given the turbulent politics of the time, the reports of this and other government bodies had consequential results of government enacting policies that restricted expansion by existing business houses. In addition, the government cut the wings of big business by nationalizing the major banks, the coal industry, and a large segment of the textile industry. In brief, the 1970s saw what an authoritative work characterizes as "a relentless attack on private enterprise by the Indira Gandhi government."[42] The actual negative experience with the antibusiness policies in slowing down industrial growth, however, led to the relaxation of some of the restrictions in the 1980s and then to economic liberalization in the 1990s. Business concentration and its impact on competition has nonetheless remained a lively topic in research, the focus not on individual companies as such, but on family-owned business groups that, in the fashion of the Japanese zaibatsu of old, are business conglomerates controlling a large number of companies through various mechanisms.

A major issue in such research concerns the extent to which there is stickiness at the top of the hierarchy of the business houses, particularly with the loosening of government controls after liberalization, with such dominance and entrenchment of big business presumably blocking off competition and closing down the doors to new entrants. The principal mode of analysis has been to examine changes in the rankings of the top twenty or fifty business houses over time. Not unexpectedly, there is some disagreement among the researchers, but there is also some common ground.

In 2005, Tarun Khanna and Krishna G. Palepu made a long-term comparison of the top fifty business groups at three points in time, about thirty years apart—1939, 1969, and 1997—and concluded that the modern history of India's corporate sector demonstrated that, while there has been "a persistence of concentrated ownership at the aggregate level," there also has been "a significant lack of persistence of dominance at the individual business group level" since the latter has been marked by "a considerable turnover in ranks." This conclusion was unaffected by taking into account the withdrawal of expatriate groups after independence. Actually, the authors showed that "the turnover in the ranks of Indian groups is greater in the second thirty-year window than in the first." Whereas thirty-two of the fifty top groups in the 1969 list were not present in the 1939 list, forty-three of the fifty top groups in the 1999 list were not present in the 1969 list.[43] In this interpretation, then, India's capitalist system is an open one, there are limits to entrenchment, and competition is manifest.

Two years later, J. Dennis Rajakumar and John S. Henley offered another analysis of the configuration among a smaller number of twenty big business groups under three different economic regimes—(1) 1951–69, industrial licensing under Nehru; (2) 1970–90, licensing and controls on monopolies under Indira Gandhi and Rajiv Gandhi; and (3) 1991–2001, economic liberalization. They found that, paradoxically, the top twenty business groups saw growth under the first regime when "the licensing regime was arguably at its most restrictive." However, the combination of even stricter licensing and new controls on monopolies under the second regime arrested such growth. Still, while some business groups experienced a decline in growth after liberalization, the top three groups—Reliance, Tata, and Birla—consolidated their position. Nonetheless, except for these three groups, the rankings among the other groups saw "considerable churning," with some being pushed out of the top twenty while others moved up. Indeed, the authors concluded that liberalization "has been more effective in dispersing economic concentration than microeconomic policy interventions" that had preceded it. Over the longer haul, the authors saw the growth and decline of big business groups as "an evolutionary process," in which "many well-known groups of the 1950s could not survive in the 1960s, and hitherto unranked groups have surged ahead in the 1970s and 1980s. During the 1990s, while the Top-3 very large business groups have increased their market capitalization, new or already existing smaller groups have generally replaced erstwhile dominant groups."[44]

Working with a similar number of business groups, Jayati Sarkar studied the question of concentration persistence at shorter intervals of ten years, each at five different time points: 1969, 1980, 1990, 2000, and 2006. It would seem, however, that she set very high standards for measuring change. Her analysis underlined:

"Apart from the period 1990–2000, when, as might be expected, there was a significant turnover of rankings among the top twenty, with only nine managing to remain in the list while eleven new groups made their entry, in the remaining periods, more than 50 percent of the groups continued to remain in the list." Looked at from another angle, one also could argue that close to 50 percent did not continue to remain on the list. She nonetheless maintained: "While there have been changes in the relative rankings of those that continued during the ten-year periods, some with ranks up, some with ranks down, and some maintaining their positions, there have seldom been dramatic changes in ranking, where ranks have changed by more than five places (up or down) among them." Therefore, for Sarkar, the emergent picture was one of "substantial *persistence* of the identity of business groups."[45] Interestingly, working with about the same data, Dwijendra Tripathi and Jyoti Jumani stressed the enormous extent of change that had occurred: "As many as 11 of the 20 largest business houses of 1968, based on total assets, in the country remained in that list until 1990. Within a pace of just about 15 years after the process of liberalization set in, except the Tatas, Birlas, TVS, and Goenkas, all others of the 1968 list yielded place to new entrants, some of which did not even exist or at best had an insignificant existence in 1968."[46]

A compelling recent contribution by R. Nagaraj, an eminent economist generally sympathetic to the left, sheds authoritative light on whether liberalization had increased concentration and thereby decreased competition, as many suggested. Employing multiple modes of quantitative analysis—the share of the top one hundred private firms in the private corporate sector in value added, net worth, and assets at five-year intervals beginning with 1990; the share of the top fifty business houses in value added of the private sector; and the mobility of firms among the top one hundred firms—he offered the terse but incisive conclusion that "despite the rapid growth of the private corporate sector, economic concentration of power of large firms or top business has, in fact, not gone up after the reforms. While the share of the private corporate sector in the domestic output has increased marginally, competition within the corporate sector has also increased. Further, considerable mobility of firms within the top 100 firms is discernible, indicating perhaps greater contestability in industrial markets."[47] In short, while there is undoubtedly persistence at the very top—in a way, a testimony to the flexibility and adaptability of the top business houses over the generations—the system as such is open for entry by others, and demonstrably so. This empirical position differs significantly from the one taken by Atul Kohli, which maintains that there is "very little evidence to suggest that the level of concentration among India's private business groups has declined; if anything, evidence on capital stock and sales suggests that concentration has increased."[48] Further testimony is offered below on the revisionist position advanced here.

THE SOCIAL COMPOSITION OF THE CONTEMPORARY CAPITALIST CLASS

Chapter 8 notes the explosion in the number of registered nongovernment companies from some 200,000 in 1990 to nearly 835,000 in 2010. It would be interesting to find out the social background of the founders of all these companies, but that would be a formidable undertaking. Still, it is possible to get some idea as to what extent, if at all, the changes adumbrated earlier by way of the broadening of the capitalist class at its base have percolated up to its higher ranks.

That task is approached here by an analysis of the top sixty business groups. Even though it is a larger number than used before by analysts, still there can be only very modest expectations of percolation upward by new social groups, for the world of business is fiercely competitive and it is not easy to rise to the top. Many may aspire, but only a few manage to reach the top.[49] The list at table 9.2 of the top sixty nonfinancial private sector business houses, ranked by assets in 2010, is drawn from the Center for Monitoring Indian Economy's (CMIE's) Prowess database. No comparison over time is attempted here since it is hard enough to figure out the social background even of contemporary groups. The analysis that follows is based on fifty-eight of the business groups since the one at number 8 is a professional group, while information on social background is lacking for number 44. The gathering of information on social background and also the differences on categorization are explained in the notes to the table.

Consistent with what has been discussed before, the top three groups in table 9.2—treating numbers 2 and 3 for the moment as one, since each is headed by a brother—represent the Parsi, Gujarati bania, and Marwari bania communities, respectively, which have traditionally dominated the business scene for almost seven decades. The Parsi community now, of course, has only three representatives (numbers 1, 38, and 47), but the Tatas are nonetheless simply an incomparable colossus on India's business scene. The dominance of the other two communities of the Marwari and Gujarati banias pervades throughout the entire list, numbering 21 and 7 (including the one Kutchi Bhatia group at number 46), respectively—adding to twenty-eight groups in all. These three communities of the Parsis, Marwaris, and Gujarati banias can be said to represent the traditional route "from bazaar to factory."

Of course, some other groups also can be added as belonging to this route: the two Muslim Shia Bohra business groups at numbers 16 and 57; the two Hindu bania business groups at numbers 9 and 24; the Komati Chetty business group from Andhra Pradesh at number 14; and the two Nattukottai Chettiar business groups from Tamil Nadu at numbers 25 and 60. Further, one could add to them the two Shikarpuri Sindhi business groups at numbers 13 and 55. All that would make for a hefty—though socially, regionally, and religiously diverse—total of thirty-seven business groups for this particular route, signifying the continuing

Table 9.2. Top Sixty Business Groups in India—2010 (by Assets)

Rank and Name	*No. of Companies*	*Time Founded*	*Assets Rs. (bill.)*	*Social Background*
1. Tata	174	1902	4,328	Parsi
2. Reliance (Mukesh Ambani)	83	1966	3,818	Gujarati Hindu Bania
3. Reliance (Anil Ambani)	49	1966	2,375	Gujarati Hindu Bania
4. Birla, Aditya	64	1920s	1,582	Marwari Bania
5. Essar (Ruia)	46	1969	1,438	Marwari Bania—from Tamil Nadu
6. Om Prakash Jindal	57	1957	1,402	Marwari Bania—from Haryana
7. Vedanta	24	1976	1,351	Marwari Bania [Anil Agarwal]—from Bihar
8. Larsen & Toubro	91	1938	1,164	Professional Group
9. Bharti Telecom	11	1985	1,048	Hindu Bania [Sunil Bharti Mittal]—from Punjab
10. Jaiprakash	19	1979	845	Gaur Brahmin—from Uttar Pradesh
11. Adani	57	1988	702	Gujarati Jain Bania
12. Mahindra & Mahindra	76	1945	640	Punjabi Hindu Khatri
13. Hinduja (Ashok Leyland)	41	1914	623	Shikarpuri Sindhi
14. GMR	68	1978	513	Telugu Komati Chetty, trad. mercantile community
15. Bajaj	32	1926	453	Marwari Bania
16. WIPRO	8	1945	364	Gujarati Muslim Shia, Bohra
17. TVS Iyengar	67	1911	311	Tamil Brahmin, Iyengar
18. UB	22	1857	286	Goud Saraswat Brahmin (Vijay Mallya)
19. RPG Enterprises	43	1979	268	Marwari Bania
20. Videocon	9	1979	263	Marwari Bania [Venugopal Dhoot] from Maharashtra
21. Sterling Infotech	10	1994	249	Mudaliar, agriculturist
22. Lanco	12	1986	239	Andhra Kamma [Lagadapati Rajagopal]
23. Suzlon	13	1995	239	Gujarati Patidar, agriculturist [Tulsi Tanti]
24. Krishna	9	1943	239	Hindu Bania [PK Tayal]
25. Murugappa Chettiar	28	1900	231	Nattukottai Chettiar
26. Piramal Ajay	24	1980s	229	Marwari Bania
27. Future	44	1983	206	Marwari Bania [Kishore Biyani]

(*continued*)

Table 9.2. Top Sixty Business Groups in India—2010 (by Assets) (*continued*)

Rank and Name	*No. of Companies*	*Time Founded*	*Assets Rs. (bill.)*	*Social Background*
28. Birla KK	67	1920s	200	Marwari Bania
29. Nagarjuna	18	1974	189	Telugu Raju, agriculturist [Founder KVK Raju]
30. HCL	14	1975	175	Nadar, backward agricultural community
31. Avantha	22	1929	170	Punjabi Hindu Khatri [Gautam Thapar]
32. Gulabchand Doshi	51	1920	169	Gujarati Jain Bania [Walchand]
33. Birla BK	14	1900s	166	Marwari Bania
34. Hero (Munjals)	14	1956	165	Punjabi Hindu Khatri
35. IVRCL	73	1987	152	Andhra Reddy, agriculturist
36. Welspun	21	1983	149	Marwari Bania [Chairman: BK Goenka]
37. Ruchi	11	1970s	144	Marwari Bania
38. Godrej	33	1897	144	Parsi
39. Torrent	11	1959	142	Gujarati Jain
40. Dr. Reddy's	11	1984	141	Andhra Reddy, agriculturist
41. Amtek	4	1977	138	Punjabi Hindu Khatri [Chairman: Arvind Dham]
42. S. Kumars	14	1986	137	Marwari Jain [Shankarlalji Surajmalji Kasliwal]
43. Zee Telefilms	27	1992	131	Marwari Bania, Haryana; Subhash Chandra [Goenka]
44. Gammon India	43	1922	129	Not available [CMD: Abhijit Rajan]
45. GVK Reddy	16	1979	126	Andhra Reddy, agriculturist
46. GE Shipping	3	1948	124	Kutchi Bhatia, traditional mercantile community
47. Shapoorji Pallonji	60	1865	119	Parsi
48. Sahu Jain (Times of India)	40	1946	116	Marwari Jain
49. Dalmia	43	1930s	108	Marwari, from Rohtak, Haryana
50. Punj Lloyd	9	1985	103	Punjabi Saraswat Brahmin [Chairman Atul Punj]
51. Kalyani (Bharat Forge)	16	1961	103	Lingayat, agriculturist, from Maharashtra

(*continued*)

Table 9.2. Top Sixty Business Groups in India—2010 (by Assets) (*continued*)

Rank and Name	*No. of Companies*	*Time Founded*	*Assets Rs. (bill.)*	*Social Background*
52. Sanmar	34	1962	99	Tamil Brahmin [Dy Chairman: Vijay Sankar]
53. Jubilant Bhartia	13	1959	99	Marwari [Founder: Shyam S. Bhartia]
54. ABG	15	1989	96	Marwari [Chairman: Rishi Agarwal]
55. Raheja Rajan	53	1945	94	Shikarpuri Sindhi
56. Hari Shankar Singhania	20	1918	90	Hindu Bania, "sociologically" Marwari
57. CIPLA	1	1935	89	Gujarati Muslim Shia, Bohra
58. LNJ Bhilwara	14	1960	85	Marwari Bania
59. Ramco [Madras Cements]	12	1965	85	Telugu Raju
60. Chidambaram M.A.	28	1944	85	Nattukottai Chettiar

Sources: Harish Damodaran, *India's New Capitalists: Caste, Business, and Industry in a Modern Nation* (Houndmills, Basingstoke, UK: Palgrave Macmillan, 2008); R. K. Hazari, *Structure of the Corporate Private Sector: A Study of Concentration, Ownership and Control* (London: Asia Publishing, 1966); Raman Mahadevan, "Everyone Is a Vaishya: India's Business Communities, Ever in the Forefront, Now See Their Role Evolving," [Lead Essay/Business Communities] *Outlook India Magazine*, October 1, 2012; Dwijendra Tripathi, *The Oxford History of Indian Business* (New Delhi: Oxford University Press, 2004); Dwijendra Tripathi and Jyoti Jumani, *The Oxford History of Contemporary Indian Business* (New Delhi: Oxford University Press, 2013).

Notes:

1. The data for the list were collected in the following manner: (1) a list of the top sixty nonfinancial, nonrealty, nonforeign business groups in the corporate private sector was compiled from the Center for Monitoring Indian Economy's (CMIE's) Prowess database, ranked by assets in 2010; (2) information on the year of founding of each business group was obtained from Wikipedia or Prowess and it pertains to either the group or its flagship company; (3) information on social background was gleaned from the sources indicated above; and (4) for the dozen or so groups for which such information could not be found, the eminent authority on Indian business communities, Mr. Harish Damodaran of the *Hindu Business Line*, and Dr. T. K. Bhaumik, economic adviser, JK Paper Limited, New Delhi, were approached, and they most kindly and wholeheartedly obliged and furnished all missing information. Where there was conflict in the advice obtained, I have exercised my best possible judgment in the matter.

I am highly indebted to Mr. Damodaran and Dr. Bhaumik for their help, and also to Mr. Vikash Vaibhav (PhD candidate, Indira Gandhi Institute of Development Research, Mumbai) for compiling the original list, and to Professor R. Nagaraj for recommending Mr. Vaibhav.

2. No pejorative connotation is implied in using particular caste terms.
3. Gujarati Bania may refer to either Gujarati Hindu Bania or Gujarati Jain Bania; intermarriage exists between the two groups.
4. Unless otherwise specified, Marwari Bania refers to Marwari Hindu Bania.
5. There is some question whether the description should be Sikh or Hindu for item 41.

enormous impact of tradition on contemporary economy and society and the profound transformation of traditional human capital into modern business.

Certainly, as it holds twenty-one business groups out of sixty, there can be no doubt about the commanding position of the Marwari community among all the communities in the business world. It is ironic, then, that there has been some recent expression of angst over "the drop in the pecking order of Marwaris in India's top business groups" and over the loss of the "feisty and formidable spirit" that had characterized the community in the twentieth century. Such angst on the part of a Marwari industrialist had been provoked by "the rise of a new entrepreneurial class in India which comprises very few Marwaris and consists of primarily Gujaratis, Punjabis and South Indian industrial groups."[50] Given the continued paramount leading position of the Marwaris, such protestation would seem highly exaggerated, and a little too rich. It is true, however, that the contemporary group of business leaders from the Marwari and other similar mercantile communities have undergone change in that they are highly educated, professionally and technically qualified, progressive, and ambitious, belying the traditional image of their progenitors as lacking in education or being steeped in frugality.[51]

Undoubtedly, the Gujaratis have done very well for themselves in business, both at the state level and at the pan-Indian level, particularly if one takes a broader view of the groups from Gujarat, ignoring distinctions of religion and caste. Certainly, the Parsis also can be treated as Gujarati for this purpose, for they originated in Gujarat, too, even though Mumbai has been their home for long. Apart from the Tatas and the Ambanis at numbers 1 to 3, the top twenty business groups include two other Gujarati groups—Adani at number 11 and Wipro under the Muslim house of Azim Premji at number 16. Adani's rise has been spectacular, for the head of the group is a first-generation entrepreneur who entered business only in the 1980s. The broader cluster of Gujarati business groups totals thirteen: Gujarati banias (both Hindu and Jain) numbering six; Parsis, three; Muslim Bohras, two; Kutchi Bhatia, one; and Patidar, one.

Marwari and Gujarati dominance notwithstanding, about the remaining half of the list does represent other communities and, to that extent, reflects change that apparently has occurred on the business scene in relation to the origins of business groups; the word "apparently" is used advisedly because there is no known comparable list this large for an earlier period to use as a quantitative reference point. The most impressive feature of the list after the domination by the Marwari banias (totaling twenty-one) and Gujarati banias (totaling seven)—simultaneously symbolizing the change from the traditional understanding of the regional and community origins of modern business groups—is the large representation of as many as seven business groups from the single state of Andhra Pradesh. This number, of course, includes one business group from the traditional commercial community of Komati Chetty (number 14), but the remarkable fact remains that all the other six are from the three farming communities of

Reddy (numbers 35, 40, and 45), Raju (numbers 29 and 59), and Kamma (number 22), all of which may be said to belong to the Shudra caste. The rise of these Telugu agricultural castes in business, which Damodaran had rightly highlighted in his work, underlines an impressive development in terms of community origins of business groups, signifying as it does the route "from farm to factory."[52] Starting out as small enterprises, these groups over time have certainly acquired national status. Equally, piling up as many as seven business groups in a list of the top sixty is strong testimony to the economic advance made by the state of Andhra Pradesh.

As important as the route "from farm to factory" has been in Andhra Pradesh, it does not seem to have wide applicability in the other regions of India. Two business houses in Tamil Nadu can be flexibly included under this category—the Mudaliar business group at number 21 and the Nadar group at number 30—as can the Lingayat business group in Maharashtra at number 51. Certainly, the Patidar business group in Gujarat at number 23 would belong to the category. However, beyond these, there is no representation from the other states, even in southern India. This observation is, however, consistent with Damodaran's position that this route has not been open to the rural communities of northern India, apparently because of the absence, unlike southern and western India, of the "Vaishya vacuum." In actuality, the route may have considerably more presence in business at large, but it is not yet reflected among the top sixty business groups. Given that context, the achievement of Andhra Pradesh is all the more striking.

Relative to the previous route, the other route "from office to factory," used by the scribal castes of Brahmins and Kshatriyas through taking to modern education, seems to have been more important and perhaps more spread out geographically. Taking the Brahmins first, there are five business groups affiliated with this caste; there are two in Tamil Nadu (numbers 17 and 52), and one each in Uttar Pradesh (number 10), Karnataka (number 18), and Punjab (number 50). (Apart from national and multinational groups, the industrial advance by Tamil Nadu centers on four Tamil business groups that have originated there—the two Brahmin groups just noted, and the two Nattukottai Chettiar business groups at numbers 25 and 60. Only one Tamil group, at number 30, is located outside Tamil Nadu.)

The other striking feature of the list that parallels the achievement of Andhra Pradesh's farming communities pertains to the scribal caste of the Punjabi Hindu Khatris; most members of this community take the term Khatri to be a corruption of Kshatriya, though Muslim conquests and domination of the region may have forced them into trade and agriculture. It is quite impressive that a community that is modest in size has as many as four business groups in the list of India's top sixty business groups (numbers 12, 31, 34, and 41).[53] Indeed, the Khatri representation would have been larger were it not for the fact that the Punjabi Sikh Khatri business group of Ranbaxy decided to sell out the enterprise to a Japanese multinational in 2008. Besides the four Khatris and one Brahmin, it is noteworthy that Punjab has a leading business group at number 9 headed by a

Hindu bania—seven business groups in all. Interestingly, unlike the Tamil groups, four of which have their headquarters in Chennai (with number 30 being located in the National Capital Region), all the Punjabi groups are located outside the Punjab; even the Punjabi Sikh Khatri group in the form of Ranbaxy had been located in New Delhi.

There is one absence in the list that conspicuously stands out. The metropolitan city of Kolkata, the capital of West Bengal, was and is a major commercial center of India and, as such, it has had a lot going for it to develop a local business class, given its highly intelligent and educated elites in the arts and sciences. Unfortunately, it has failed to produce any major industrial group out of its indigenous population since independence. When this issue has been privately raised with numerous academicians, business chambers, bureaucrats, and sundry individuals, the response invariably has been that the people of Bengal are risk averse and prefer government employment to entering business.[54] This may well be true, however, only at the level of big business rather than that of small industries.

Any list of the top sixty business groups can provide only a narrow view of the vast and complex world of business in India. Yet, it is sufficient to show that there has been considerable diffusion of entrepreneurship beyond the Parsis, Marwaris, and Gujaratis. Besides these traditional groups, the world of business in India now encompasses a wide spectrum of India's ethnic communities. Perhaps this pattern may have been visible at independence, too, but given the largely agrarian nature of the economy at the time, it could only have been episodic and unstable in nature. Therefore, with the greater advance in industrialization, one could say with justification: We are all Vaishyas now, though not yet in the same measure. This process of all becoming Vaishyas may well have been facilitated by the larger change in the social and economic milieu. The narrowly defined business community of earlier times may no longer be as critical to capital accumulation as it was in the earlier stages of developing capitalism since other institutions can now substitute for it. Meanwhile, the social diversification in the composition of India's contemporary capitalist class over the years would certainly seem to be a favorable element for India's economic integration.

THE CAPITALIST CLASS AND ECONOMIC INTEGRATION

The capitalist class contributes to India's economic integration in two ways—directly and indirectly. It contributes directly in that it is the ambition of most capitalists, if not all, to expand their business of producing and supplying goods and services on a national scale. We have discussed how businesses that had started on a small scale later expanded to cover the national market as a whole. In this fashion, these business groups have contributed directly to India's economic integration.

Size Matters

Even though, following Gandhi, India has often tended to cherish and foster small-scale industries, it seems that from the perspective of the country's economic integration, it is the contribution of large-scale enterprises that matters more. For it is the big business groups that cover the entire Indian market through their many production plants and supply chains that are spread throughout the country and the manifold distribution centers for their products and services all across India. Take, for instance, the Tata group, which is perhaps the most admired of Indian business groups. It is India's biggest conglomerate with more than one hundred individual companies; it is a multinational operation with a worldwide workforce of 450,000, while nearly 60 percent of its annual revenues of more than $100 billion come from abroad.[55] Within India, its products go to almost every nook and corner of the Indian market. It has operations in literally every part of the country, covering steel, automobiles, trucks, power, information technology, telecommunications, hotels, watches, jewelry, and so forth. Tata is literally a household word in India, with Titan watches as the country's most powerful brand.[56]

Similarly, Reliance has the entire Indian market within its scope. The business house that Dhirubhai Ambani founded now stands split into two groups at numbers 2 and 3 in table 9.2, as the inheritance of two feuding brothers, Mukesh and Anil, after the death of the founder in 2002. That business house was built on the efforts of one man with only a high school education, who started his career as an attendant at a gasoline filling station, then went on to trade in yarn and fabrics in 1958, and later in 1966 set up in a move of backward vertical integration—the founder's hallmark—a small textile mill with seventy workers. From that base, in a blitz of expansion and diversification over the following three and a half decades, the founder made Reliance the third-largest industrial group in the country. Interestingly, if one were to take the two successor groups in combination, their assets are larger than those of the Tatas at number 1. The operations of the two groups extend all across India, with the Mukesh group focused on petrochemicals, refining, oil and gas exploration, and retail, and the Anil group on power, communications, infrastructure, and entertainment. The Mukesh group has manufacturing facilities in the states of Gujarat, Punjab, Maharashtra, and Uttar Pradesh, and offshore gas exploration and production in Andhra Pradesh. The Anil group has an India-wide fiber-optic network, and has about 45,000 ground and rooftop telecommunication towers. As one contribution describes it, the group has "a business presence that extends to over 20,000 towns and 450,000 villages in India, and across the globe."[57]

Again, take the case of the Aditya Birla group, which—after the many splits resulting from the disintegration of the industrial empire after the 1983 death of the eighty-nine-year-old patriarch, G. D. Birla—comes right after the Tatas and the Ambanis in India's business hierarchy. Even though much reduced and now a distant fourth in the hierarchy, it is regarded as having inherited the mantle of the Birla house; however, other remnants of GD's empire are still large enough to be included among the top fifty of India's business groups (numbers 28 and 33, table 9.2). The Aditya Birla group is an industrial conglomerate and a multinational, too, having operations in thirty-six countries with a worldwide workforce of 136,000 employees; indeed, the late Aditya Birla pioneered taking business abroad long before liberalization, persuaded to do so by the difficulty of doing business in India. As owner of Hindalco-Novelis, the group is the world's largest aluminum roller; it is also its largest producer of viscose staple fiber and carbon black. More than 50 percent of the group's revenues come from abroad.

Again, like Tata and Ambani, the Birla group is a household name. Within India, it has interests in metals (aluminum and copper), textiles, chemicals, cement, fashion, telecommunications, and insurance. Even though, at rank 4, it is much smaller than the previous three business groups, the broad reach of its operations in India's economic geography is made abundantly evident by the location of its numerous production plants. Its twelve cement plants are located in Andhra Pradesh, Chhattisgarh, Gujarat, Karnataka, Madhya Pradesh, Maharashtra, and Rajasthan; the garments plant is in Karnataka; the three carbon black plants are situated in Maharashtra, Tamil Nadu, and Uttar Pradesh; and the three textile plants are located in Gujarat, Madhya Pradesh, and West Bengal. The group's three fertilizer plants are situated in Gujarat, Uttar Pradesh, and West Bengal; its two chemical plants are in Gujarat and Madhya Pradesh; and the four fiber and pulp plants are based in Gujarat, Karnataka, and Madhya Pradesh. Its two aluminum and the associated power plants are in Odisha and Uttar Pradesh, with the one in the latter state being the group's flagship; the copper plant is in Gujarat; the seven bauxite and coal mines are in Chhattisgarh, Jharkhand, Karnataka, Maharashtra, and Odisha; and the seven aluminum products plants are located in Andhra Pradesh, Dadra and Nagar Haveli, Kerala, Maharashtra, and West Bengal.[58]

Even though they may not be as diversified as the Tatas, Ambanis, and Birlas, there are many other groups, too, like Bajaj (number 15) and Hero (number 34), the products of which—such as Bajaj or Hero motorbikes, or Bajaj three-wheelers and Hero bicycles—are marketed throughout the length and breadth of the country. The same is the case with Bharti Telecom (number 9, table 9.2), whose flagship Bharti Airtel is, besides being the world's third-largest telecommunications company, India's largest cellular service provider.[59] With some business houses, pan-Indian networks are built into the very nature of their business; thus, Bharti Airtel has an all-India cellular network, while Reliance has a fiber-optic network across the country. Reliance also has plans for building a gas pipeline network.[60] Besides, there are a large number of fast-moving consumer goods (FMCG) companies who see India as a single market and make the development of a wholesales network across India a part of their corporate strategy. Moreover, business houses support two great unifying social institutions in India—cricket and the Bollywood movie industry—through investment and sponsorships.

It is thus in the course of producing and supplying goods and services across the country that India's large business houses directly contribute to its economic integration. No doubt, being in business, they do it for the purpose of private profit but, as Adam Smith counterintuitively discerned in a different context, the invisible hand of the market serves to strengthen India's economic integration. Further, because the making of profits by these business groups depends on the continued economic unity of the country, the class of big capitalists of the country has a vested interest in its economic and national integration. As one executive of an industry association privately explained at length in Mumbai:

> Business has a very distinctive role in keeping this country's economy together. In fact, you have big business houses—Tata, Birla, Reliance—they have their business branches all over the country, right from Kashmir to Kanyakumari, from Gujarat to Assam. These sorts of activities are doing far more to promote national integration than what politicians would have achieved by their speeches and actions. So, this country owes a great deal to the entrepreneurial class.
>
> If there is one factor that keeps this country together it is the common vested economic interest. It is the common economic interest that will see that this country remained as one. Common interests have now become far too firmly entrenched all over the country. There will be, for example, many senior businessmen from Maharashtra who will be having huge investments in Assam, Punjab, the South, Kerala or Tamil Nadu. These people will exert all their influence over the government that under no condition the unity of the country is jeopardized. It is obvious that they want the country to remain united, otherwise why would they put in so much investment. There is a vested interest in ensuring that this country will always remain one and that it won't disintegrate in a rapidly changing world.[61]

The Role of Peak Business Associations

The capitalist class serves to promote India's economic integration not only through being directly in the business of supplying goods and services but also indirectly by organizing itself at an all-India level to press for the interests of business. For historical and other reasons, business at the all-India level is organized into three peak associations. They are peak business associations in that they stand at the peak of a pyramid of regional business associations, which in turn are based on local associations and individual companies. In a sense, each is an association of associations.

British expatriate companies in India were the first ones to organize the Associated Chambers of Commerce and Industry (Assocham) in 1920. As domestic business groups—some of them sympathetic to the nationalist movement—felt their interests threatened by the organization of Assocham, they established the FICCI in 1927 under the leadership of G. D. Birla. It was no mean feat to organize the federation, given the diversity of the country in terms of language, religion, region and level of development, the Indian proclivity to factionalism, and the hostility of the expatriate community.[62] After independence, the FICCI emerged as the preeminent business association, while Assocham saw a decline. The third peak association, the Confederation of Indian Industry (CII), has long historical roots in the engineering industry of the eastern region, but its most recent incarnation as an industry-wide, pan-Indian organization was founded in 1992. Its rise reflected "the rise of new elements within the sector but also a change in the convictions and interests of private industry with a new outlook coming to the forefront, different from the traditional outlook of Indian industry."[63] Despite the differences that may have underlain their separate formation, there are no hard-and-fast lines to differentiate them today in their positions on economic issues. They are all strong supporters of globalization, liberalization, and advancement of manufacturing in the country.

The relevance of these associations to India's economic integration lies in two important areas. First, they make for the organization of the capitalist class on an all-India basis. Their annual and special meetings bring together businessmen from all over the country, where they learn about national issues, hear government leaders and officials, and exchange views among themselves. Each association rotates the appointments of its officials, such as the president and members of the executive committee among the different regions. The very comprehensive nature of organization of the peak associations and the exchange of information among their members is a contributory factor in economic integration. In the specific case of the CII, a senior official privately pointed out:

> For one thing, we are a pan-Indian body, this is our central office [in New Delhi], we have 65 offices, which means that we are actually present in every state. There are certain values and systems and policy thrusts that we believe in from a national point of view. That being so, we do follow those across the country, which gives us a way, I believe, to transmit the thought processes across the different regions, across policymakers in different parts of the country, which in some ways is also aimed at integrating.[64]

Second, some of the policies that the peak associations have strongly pushed for with the government have a vital bearing on India's economic integration. In recent years, these associations have been powerful supporters of the value added tax (VAT) and the goods and services tax (GST); they have also been strong advocates for the abolition of octroi (entry tax) and also of the Agricultural Produce Marketing Committees, which constrain the free flow of agricultural goods. As one senior CII official explained privately in December 2012:

> We believe in the philosophy of the free market, therefore in turn we believe in economic integration. We believe there needs to be a unified market. Just as much as we have faith in the free market, we respect the institutions that we created to enable fiscal federalism, but we do not believe that that mechanism should be [used] for dividing the market. We are the strongest votary of GST. It [GST] is the first step to unify India, which is not a common market yet. We believe in the principles of market and we believe in the principles of social justice and empowerment, and these can only happen when there is a more integrated society. I tell you, we believe in a unified market, the GST—which is the first step for unifying the market. If you put it all together, this will aid in the integration of India, not dividing it.[65]

SUMMARY AND CONCLUSION

Anybody who keeps abreast of the daily news about India cannot help but be aware of the constant din about the major corruption scandals that have implicated business groups with respect to, among other things, allocation of telecommunications licenses, land acquisitions, and mining. It is difficult to escape the conclusion about the existence of crony capitalism from this pervasiveness of corruption and the insatiable hunger for profiteering. However, it is difficult to pinpoint the basic cause of this predicament. Does the fault lie with the system of politics that requires political parties to collect—or perhaps, more accurately, extort—funds from business, or does it lie with the nature of the business class, where individual business groups aim to extract special favors from decision makers through bribery in order to beat their competitors? Probably, both factors are at work. Many hope, however, that perhaps there are enough self-correcting mechanisms in the Indian system to overcome this predicament in the course of time.

There is, however, a different and less sinister aspect to Indian business, on which this study has attempted to shed light through an examination of the contribution of the business class to India's economic integration. First and foremost, that contribution lies in the capitalist class in India not being a closed system, but one that is open to entry not only by new business groups from a narrow circle of social strata but also by new business groups from across India's vast social diversity. A historical examination of the Indian business class reveals that in a still-ongoing process, it has over a period of time consistently expanded from a narrow social base to encompass increasingly more groups across the stratification system, from the highest to the lowest. There has thus been diffusion of business among India's various communities. In that sense, it is possible to aver that we are all Vaishyas now, even though not yet in the same measure.

Besides, by its very nature, business has tended to advance India's economic integration, both directly and indirectly. It has done so directly by individual business groups supplying goods and services across the entire nation and pushing to expand their productive processes to national scale by setting up operations in different parts of the country. Further, business has aided economic integration indirectly by organizing itself on a pan-Indian basis and advocating policy measures, such as the GST, that would truly transform India into a common market.

NOTES

1. For a reasoned position on the state-business alliance, see Atul Kohli, *Poverty amid Plenty in New India* (Cambridge: Cambridge University Press, 2012), chap. 1.

2. Claude Markovits, *The Indian Business and Nationalist Politics, 1931–1939: The Indigenous Capitalist Class and the Rise of the Congress Party* (Cambridge: Cambridge University Press, 1985), 2.

3. Harish Damodaran, *India's New Capitalists: Caste, Business, and Industry in a Modern Nation* (Houndmills, Basingstoke, UK: Palgrave Macmillan, 2008), 2.

4. Dwijendra Tripathi and Jyoti Jumani, *The Oxford History of Contemporary Indian Business* (New Delhi: Oxford University Press, 2013), 205.

5. Markovits, *Indian Business and Nationalist Politics*, 2–3.

6. Dwijendra Tripathi, *The Oxford History of Indian Business* (New Delhi: Oxford University Press, 2004); Markovits, *Indian Business and Nationalist Politics.*

7. Markovits, *Indian Business and Nationalist Politics*, 5, 19.

8. Ibid., 192–93.

9. Tripathi, *Oxford History of Indian Business*, 112, 116.

10. Ibid., 262.

11. In 2010, the United Nations Industrial Development Organization (UNIDO) ranked India at number 9 (China at 2 and Brazil at 10); see UNIDO, Press Release, March 18, 2010, available at www.unido.org.

12. Trpathi, *Oxford History of Indian Business*, 166, 180, 182.

13. Medha M. Kudaisya, *The Life and Times of G. D. Birla* (New Delhi: Oxford University Press, 2003), 395.

14. Tripathi, *Oxford History of Indian Business*, 300–302.

15. Tripathi and Jumani, *Oxford History of Contemporary Indian Business*, 169.

16. See Tripathi, *Oxford History of Indian Business*; Medha M. Kudaisya, ed., *The Oxford India Anthology of Business History* (New Delhi: Oxford University Press, 2011); Markovits, *Indian Business and Nationalist Politics.*

17. Damodaran, *India's New Capitalists*, chaps. 1 and 10.

18. Ibid., 176.

19. See D. Shyam Babu, "India's Liberalization and the Dalits," Asia Programme Working Paper, Royal Institute of International Affairs, Chatham House, London, 2004; and Sudha Pai, *Developmental State and the Dalit Question in Madhya Pradesh: Congress Response* (New Delhi: Routledge, 2012), chap. 3.

20. Kruttika Nadig, "Ashok Khade: Man Who Built Most Sought-After Offshore Fabrication Company DAS Offshore," *Economic Times*, July 21, 2011; available at http://articles.economictimes.indiatimes.com/2011-07-21/news/29798122_1_blanc-pens-mont-blanc-ssc-exam.

21. Personal communication from Harish Damodaran, June 12, 2013; and Visaka Industries website, available at http://www.visaka.biz.

22. See the interview with DICCI chairman Milind Kamble and his mentor Chandra Bhan Prasad, by Shekhar Gupta, "Walk the Talk: Capitalism Is Changing Caste Much Faster than Any Human Being, Dalits Should Look at Capitalism as a Crusader against Caste," *Indian Express*, June 11, 2013; available at www.indian express.com.

23. Damodaran, *India's New Capitalists*, 312.

24. Sanjaya Baru, "Economic Policy and the Development of Capitalism in India: The Role of Regional Capitalists and Political Parties," in *Transforming India: Social and Political Dynamics of Democracy*, ed. Francine R. Frankel, Zoya Hassan, Rajeev Bhargava, and Balveer Arora (New Delhi: Oxford University Press, 2000), 207–30.

25. For a brief discussion of Telugu Desam Party (TDP) leader Chandrababu Naidu's role in attracting aid and investment to Andhra Pradesh, see Jason A. Kirk, *India and the World Bank: The Politics of Aid and Influence* (London: Anthem Press, 2010), 63–72.

26. Baru, "Economic Policy," 219, 223.

27. Kudaisya, *Life and Times of G. D. Birla*, 112–41; Markovits, *Indian Business and Nationalist Politics*, 35–40, 149; Tripathi, *Oxford History of Indian Business*, 200.

28. Damodaran, *India's New Capitalists*, 105.

29. Ibid., 108–9.

30. Ibid., 114.

31. The account on GVK is based on G. V. Krishna Reddy, "Only Trust and Confidence Will Help Achieve Your Goal," *Outlook Business*, August 18, 2012, available at www.business.outlookindia.com; Sekhar Seshan, "Grabbing the Big Chance," *Business India*, August 19, 2012, 74–78, available at www.businessindiagroup.com; and GVK's website, available at www.gvk.com.

32. The account on GMR is based on the GMR website, available at www.gmrgroup.in, accessed October 25, 2012; G. M. Rao, "We Are an Airport Company, Not a Real Estate Company" [Walk the Talk on NDTV 24x7 with the Indian Express Editor-in-Chief Shekhar Gupta], *Indian Express*, August 7, 2012, available at www.indianexpress.com; Ashwini Phadnis, Mamuni Das, and Shishir Sinha, "What Undue Favors? Airport Bidding Went through 9 Levels" [Interview with G. M. Rao, founder chairman, GMR Group], *Hindu Business Line*, September 8, 2012, available at www.thehindubusinessline.com; Kausik Datta, "Crunch Time for GMR Infrastructure as Regulatory Surprises May Weigh on Revenues," *Economic Times*, September 4, 2012, available at www.economictimes.com; and Cuckoo Paul, "G. M. Rao: Build, Operate, and Be Damned," *Forbes India*, June 21, 2011, available at www.forbes.com/2011/06/21/forbes-india-grandhi-mallikarjun-rao-shattered-dreams.html.

33. Rao, "We Are an Airport Company." Perhaps the statement needs to be more nuanced; in 2012, the World Airport Awards certainly ranked the Delhi International Airport at number 1 among the World's Most Improved Airports, but only at number 9 in the 20–30 million passenger airport category and only at number 62 globally among the World's Best Airports; available at www.worldairportawards.com.

34. Phadnis, Das, and Sinha, "What Undue Favors?"

35. Dr. Reddy's Laboratories, *Annual Report 2011–12: Life, Research, Hope*, 5–6; available at www.drreddys.com/investors/annual-reports.html.

36. Dr. Reddy's Laboratories, *Annual Report 2011–12*, 15.

37. Wikipedia offers a short history of the business group and lists the various companies and projects under it; see http://en.wikipedia.org/wiki/Apollo_Hospitals.

38. Wikipedia provides a discussion of the status of the organization and the changes in its ownership; see http://en.wikipedia.org/wiki/Ranbaxy.

39. Gita Piramal, Sudeep Budhiraja, and Sumantra Ghoshal, "Hero Honda Motors: A Web of Relationships," in *World Class in India: A Casebook of Companies in Transformation* (New Delhi: Penguin, 2001), 101–49, 553–86; available at www.herocycles.com/about.php and www.heromotocorp.com; and http://en.wikipedia.org/wiki/Hero_MotoCorp, accessed May 6, 2013.

40. Damodaran, *India's New Capitalists*, 317.

41. Government of India (GoI), *Report of the Monopolies Inquiry Commission* (New Delhi: Government of India Press, 1965), 135.

42. Tripathi and Jumani, *Oxford History of Contemporary Indian Business*, 224.

43. Tarun Khanna and Krishna G. Palepu, "The Evolution of Concentrated Ownership in India: Broad Patterns and a History of the Indian Software Industry," in *A History of Corporate Government around the World*, ed. Randall K. Morck (Chicago: University of Chicago Press, 2005), 283–324.

44. J. Dennis Rajakumar and John S. Henley, "Growth and Persistence of Large Business Groups in India," *Journal of Comparative International Management* 10, no. 1 (2007): 3–22.

45. Jayati Sarkar, "Business Groups in India," in *The Oxford Handbook of Business Groups*, ed. James R. Lincoln, Takashi Hikino, and Asli M. Colpan (Oxford: Oxford University of Press, 2010), 294–322; emphasis in the original.

46. Tripathi and Jumani, *Oxford History of Contemporary Indian Business*, 178.

47. R. Nagaraj, "Trends and Patterns in Industrial Growth: A Review of Evidence and Explanations," a paper sponsored by the Indian Council of Social Science Research, Indira Gandhi Institute of Development Research, Mumbai, June 21, 2012.

48. Kohli, *Poverty amid Plenty*, 46.

49. For instance, there are no Dalit representatives in the list of the top sixty business houses, yet there is the claim that 10 percent of the micro, small, and medium enterprises (MSMEs) are owned by Dalits, that is, about 164,000. See Gupta, "Walk the Talk."

50. Harsh Goenka, "Marwari Businesses at Crossroads," *Economic Times*, November 15, 2012; available at http:economictimes.indiatimes.com.

51. Tripathi and Jumani, *Oxford History of Contemporary Indian Business*, 218, 235.

52. Damodaran, *India's New Capitalists*, chap. 4.

53. Punjab's total population in 2011 was 27.7 million; Hindus were 37 percent of the population, and the Khatris are one caste among many; see http://en.wikipedia.org/wiki/Punjab_India.

54. Even when specifically invited to contradict this stereotypical view, the interviewees stuck to it; several interviews in Kolkata in November 2012.

55. A massive amount of information on the Tata group is available at its website at www.tata.com, accessed May 21, 2013.

56. Tripathi and Jumani, *Oxford History of Contemporary Indian Business*, 124.

57. A discussion of the various businesses of the two Ambani groups appears in Wikipedia at http://en.wikipedia.org/wiki/Reliance_Industries and http://en.wikipedia.org/wiki/Anil_Dhirubhai_Ambani_Group.

58. Information on plant locations is from UltraTech Cement Limited, *Annual Report 2011–2012*; Aditya Birla Nuvo Limited, *Annual Report 2011–2012*; and Hindalco Industries Limited, *Annual Report 2010–2011*.

59. See "Bharti Airtel," available at http://en.wikipedia.org/wiki/Bharti_Airtel.

60. Interview at the Federation of Indian Chambers of Commerce and Industry (FICCI), New Delhi, November 22, 2010.

61. Interview, Mumbai, November 16, 2012.

62. On the history of the FICCI, see Stanley A. Kochanek, *Business and Politics in India* (Berkeley: University of California Press, 1974), chaps. 7 and 8; and H. Venkatasubbiah, *Enterprise and Economic Change: 50 Years of FICCI* (New Delhi: Vikas, 1977).

63. Jorgen Dige Pedersen, *Globalization, Development and the State: The Performance of India and Brazil since 1990* (Houndmills, Basingstoke, Hampshire, UK: Palgrave Macmillan, 2008), 135.

64. Interview at the Confederation of Indian Industry (CII) in New Delhi, December 6, 2012.

65. Interview at the CII in New Delhi, December 6, 2012.

Chapter 10

MIGRATION AND INTEGRATION

IN the understanding of the critics, globalization and economic liberalization would result in the "backwash effects" of increased spatial and social polarization, which would then strain economic and national integration. Indeed, this critique extends specifically to the area of migration. In a broadside against globalization and "neo-liberalism," one of India's major experts on migration and urbanization, Amitabh Kundu, underlines:

> The process of globalization has led to weakening of institutions like family, community, common property resources etc.... Migration which brought about redistribution of population from poorer to developed regions and helped them in finding a survival strategy is yet another institution which has come under strain. Despite increase in regional imbalances, Indian population has become somewhat *immobile* due to emerging socio-political factors. This poses a major challenge for the development strategy, currently being pursued in the country. The policy of unbalanced development, if continued despite this ominous trend, can have *serious negative implications* ... it would be dangerous to follow the strategy of unbalanced development or leave the spatial structure of development to be determined by forces of global and national market.[1]

The examination earlier in this study of the impact of India's policy of economic liberalization in the areas of trade and investment has made apparent that, instead of polarization, these areas manifest "spread effects" by way of economic diffusion and the tendency toward convergence. It remains to be seen whether such a tendency toward economic diffusion and convergence extends to the area of domestic migration. In investigating the issue, this chapter looks at several aspects: the positions of the supporters and opponents of economic liberalization in relation to migration; long-term trends in migration in India; economic and social factors in migration; interstate migration after economic liberalization; and the spread effects of interstate migration. The story with regard to migration is in line with the earlier stance on economic liberalization having a positive integrative impact.

THE NEGATIVE AND POSITIVE CONSEQUENCES OF LIBERALIZATION FOR MIGRATION

It is interesting that both supporters and opponents of economic liberalization had thought this policy shift would lead to increased migration.[2] The supporters felt that liberalization would accelerate economic growth, which would then intensify the "pull" factors in migration because of the greater economic opportunities that enhanced growth rates would generate in specific locations. This assumption rested on the fundamental economic proposition since Adam Smith in the eighteenth century that economic growth results in widening the market, which leads to greater division of labor and that, in turn, makes for greater economic integration because of the accompanying economic and social complementarities. In other words, higher growth would transform the nodal points of investment in urban or potentially urban areas into a magnet that would pull in migrants from villages or towns to meet their increased requirements for labor. In contrast, the opponents of liberalization believed that it would undoubtedly result in higher migration of labor but that its cause would be the "push" factors resulting from the increased immiserization of the population, particularly in the rural areas, resulting from the economic stagnation and deindustrialization allegedly inherent in liberalization.[3] The outcome, in their view, would be "distress migration" from the rural areas that would flood the urban areas with indigent migrants, thus merely transferring poverty from the rural to the urban areas. In turn, such migration would strain national integration when it involves crossing regional boundaries by labor from outside the region.

It would seem, however, that the likely relationship between economic liberalization and migration is not such a straightforward one; instead, it may well be more complex. On the one hand, even if liberalization does result, as its supporters assume, in accelerated economic growth, it may not necessarily contribute much by way of employment opportunities since such growth in the era of technologically advanced globalization may be highly capital-intensive and may offer only "jobless growth." On the other hand, it is not an unreasonable assumption that, if economic liberalization promotes higher standards of living in rural areas—either directly through economic growth or indirectly through welfare programs that accelerated growth may financially facilitate—it may not necessarily make for distress migration from the rural areas. Besides, to some extent, migration may have extraeconomic causes, such as ethnic conflict.

In view of these various considerations, it is appropriate to look at the evidence. There are two basic sources of evidence that analysts have relied on in their work on India's migration patterns: decennial census data and the results of surveys undertaken every five years by India's National Sample Survey Office (NSSO). The two sources differ somewhat in their definition of what constitutes migration—for example, the NSSO requires a minimum stay away from the last place of residence for a person to be regarded as a migrant—and also on details about the reasons for migration. Comparable data on migration in the census reports on the basis of last place of residence are available for 1971, 1981, 1991, and 2001. Since migration is not a priority for the census organization, by 2013, it had not released migration data from the 2011 census; the latest of the National Sample Surveys (NSSs) is for 2007–8.

LONG-TERM TRENDS IN MIGRATION

Has economic liberalization been a factor in the trends in migration? On the basis of census data up to 2001, Amitabh Kundu and Lopamudra Ray Saraswati maintain that "the percentage of lifetime migrants by their *place of birth* (persons born at a place other than that of enumeration) to the total population can be noted to have gone down from 30.8 in 1961 to 29.3 in 2001, which questions the proposition that Indians have become more mobile over time." Even as they find that "the figure has gone up during the 1990s," they repeat that "the trend appears similar for migrants by *place of last residence* (persons residing elsewhere or other than the place of enumeration)" and go on to discern "for males, a secular decline" and "a corresponding decline . . . for women as well" in migration.[4] This assessment does not seem to be tenable, however.

Regardless of whether or not liberalization actually has been a causal factor, the decade after its inauguration saw a reversal of the earlier turn to a decline in the share of domestic migrants in the total population. As such, liberalization can be said to be a phenomenon that is associated with *increase*—not decline—in the rate of migration, enhancing linkages between different parts of the economy in the process. No doubt, the share of migrants in the total population—on the basis of the last place of residence having been different from that at the time of the census enumeration—had declined from 29.1 percent in 1971 and 30.3 percent in 1981 to 26.9 percent in 1991. However, it is abundantly manifest that at least during its first phase of "the period of economic reform" in the 1990s, economic liberalization saw a jump in the share from 26.9 percent in 1991 to 30.1 percent in 2001 (see table 10.1). The significant reversal of the decline in migration in general is evident as well in the share of interstate migrants in total population; whereas the latter share had declined to 3.2 percent in 1991 from around 3.5 percent in 1971 and 1981, it increased to 3.7 percent in 2001. The increase in interstate migration is particularly striking in the case of males, whose share increased from 2.7 percent in 1991 to 3.4 percent in 2001. It would not be correct,

Table 10.1. Domestic Migrants by Change of Place of Last Residence in Population Census, 1971–2001

	Share of Total Population (%)				*Size (million)*
	1971	*1981*	*1991*	*2001*	*2001*
Total Migrants	29.1	30.3	26.9	30.1	309.4
Interstate Migrants	3.4	3.5	3.2	3.7	41.2
Male Migrants	17.5	17.2	14.7	17.0	90.7
Interstate Migrants	3.4	3.3	2.7	3.4	19.1
Female Migrants	41.7	44.3	40.8	44.1	218.7
Interstate Migrants	3.5	3.8	3.7	4.1	22.1

Source: Adapted from Amitabh Kundu and Lopamudra Ray Saraswati, "Migration and Exclusionary Urbanization in India," *Economic and Political Weekly* 47, nos. 26–27 (June 20, 2012): 219–27, table 1; adapted with permission.

therefore, to generalize about a long-term decline in migration. Even if there was such a trend apparent earlier, it seems to have been interrupted and reversed by liberalization. Of course, it is not possible to offer a definitive statement on the impact of liberalization during its second phase of "the period of growth acceleration" in the first decade of the 2000s since the migration data from the 2011 census are not yet available.

Even within the limits of the current availability of census data, the advance in migration subsequent to liberalization emerges in a more stark fashion if one examines the *growth rates* with respect to particular types of migration over the different census periods. Whereas the growth rate with respect to all migrants was 27.0 percent during the period 1971–81, it dropped to the low figure of 9.8 percent during 1981–91—that is, during the decade prior to liberalization—but then it jumped to the high figure of 34.7 percent during "the period of reform" in 1991–2001. Particularly striking is the growth rate with respect to interstate migration, which made a big leap to 53.6 percent during the period 1991–2001 (compared to 28.1 percent and 11.7 percent for 1971–81 and 1981–91, respectively).[5] The huge increase in interstate migration can be better appreciated by taking notice of the jump in interstate migrants from 26.7 million in 1991 to 41 million in 2001 (table 10.2).

Although census data do not enlighten us on migration trends during "the period of growth acceleration," NSS data fill the gap to some extent. Table 10.3 documents the trends over several NSS rounds since 1983. It is obvious that, even though the table does not cover the entire first decade of the 2000s, it does not show any reversal during the growth acceleration period of the trend witnessed in the reform period. Clearly, the record with respect to female migrants and all migrants in the rural and urban areas shows that, except for the break at around the time of the launching of liberalization, their share in migration has been

Table 10.2. Types of Migrants by Last Residence, 1991 and 2001

Type of Migrants	Size (million)		Share of Total Migrants (%)	
	2001	1991	2001	1991
1	2	3	4	5
Intradistrict	192.3	140.4	61.5	60.5
Interdistrict	74.3	58.9	23.8	25.4
Interstate	41.0	26.7	13.1	11.6
International	5.1	5.9	1.6	2.5
All Migrants	312.7	232.1	100.0	100.0
Population	1,028.7	846.3	—	—

Source: GoI, *Census of India 2001: Data Highlights: Migration Tables* (New Delhi: Registrar General and Census Commissioner, n.d.), 13; available at www.censusindia.gov.in. The table excludes Jammu and Kashmir; elsewhere at p. 3, the census authority gives the figure for total migrants by last residence in 2001 as 314.5 million.

Table 10.3. Trends in Share of Migrants (per 100 Persons) in Rural and Urban Areas

Round	Rural			Urban		
	Male	Female	Total	Male	Female	Total
64th (2007–8)	5.4	47.7	26.1	25.9	45.6	35.4
55th (1999–2000)	6.9	42.6	24.4	25.7	41.8	33.4
49th (1993)	6.5	40.1	22.8	23.9	38.2	30.7
43rd (1987–88)	7.4	39.8	23.2	26.8	39.6	32.9
38th (1983)	7.2	35.1	20.9	27.0	36.6	31.6

Source: GoI, *Migration in India 2007–08: NSS 64th Round (July 2007–June 2008)* (New Delhi: National Sample Survey Office, 2010), 23; available at http://mospi.nic.in/Mospi_New/upload/533_final.pdf.

consistently rising. Even with respect to male migrants in urban areas, the trend of the rise in their share has not been reversed after liberalization. To be sure, there is a slight fall in the share of male migrants in rural areas, but that is to be expected in an economy where the share of agriculture in GDP has seen a considerable fall; rural areas are more the source of migration, not the destination. Interestingly, the NSSO's own take on the longer-term trends is that of a rise in migration; it holds that "in both the rural and urban areas, migration rates have been gradually increasing during the period 1983 to 2007–8, except for a marginal fall in migration rate in NSS 49th round."[6]

In light of all the data currently available for the period after 1991, it would thus seem erroneous to subscribe to the narrative of a continuous decline in migration in general or of interstate migration in particular.

Apropos of the data on migrants, it is noteworthy that there is a considerable consensus among scholars that both the census counts and the NSSO surveys underestimate the actual extent of migration, insofar as they do not take into account temporary, seasonal, or circulatory migrants, especially those in remote areas. At the conclusion of Priya Deshingkar's study of all households in six villages in Andhra Pradesh and Madhya Pradesh during several years in the first decade of the 2000s, she forthrightly asserts: "Both the empirical findings and the secondary material reviewed in this paper show that migration is higher in remote rural areas and, within those areas, among the chronically poor, who in this case are the SCs [scheduled castes] and STs [scheduled tribes]. An important finding was that permanent migration constituted a small proportion of total movements for work and that circular migration was the most important form of mobility. This demonstrates powerfully the inadequacy of official statistics in capturing the mobility of the poor."[7]

The NSS of 2007–8 did offer separate information on "short-term migrants," that is, migrants who, while not having changed their usual place of residence, were away from their village or town for thirty days or more, but not more than six months, in the preceding 365 days for the purpose of employment or search for employment. However, the survey came to the conclusion that only "a very small proportion" of the population was involved in short-term migration, amounting to just 1.7 percent in the rural areas and less than 0.5 percent in the urban areas. Interestingly, such migration was largely characteristic of the male population, but it was still no more than 2.8 percent.[8] This assessment is not likely to satisfy the critics on underestimation.[9]

ECONOMIC AND SOCIAL FACTORS IN MIGRATION

Although there may be many factors that propel people to migrate, fundamentally, the data demonstrate that migration is profoundly driven by economics. As Kala Seetharam Sridhar, A. Venugopala Reddy, and Pavan Srinath argue, "migration should be seen as an equilibrating response to disequilibrium existing in the economy. As long as there are gaps in rural-urban employment opportunities caused by urban bias there will be migration."[10] Support for this proposition is evident both in terms of (1) the position occupied by migrants in the society's economic structure, and (2) the reasons offered by migrants themselves for having migrated. There is a major caveat to this proposition, however, in that it largely applies primarily to male migrants. It is obvious from table 10.1 that female migrants (218.7 million in 2001) far outnumber male migrants (90.7 million); they are almost two and a half times the number of male migrants. The unfortunate

Table 10.4. Share of Migrants (per 100 Persons) in Each Monthly per Capita Expenditure (MPCE) Decile Class during 2007–2008

MPCE Decile Class	*Rural*			*Urban*		
	Male	*Female*	*Total*	*Male*	*Female*	*Total*
0–10	2.6	38.8	20.9	9.6	35.7	22.9
10–20	3.1	42.3	22.7	14.2	41.4	27.7
20–30	3.4	43.7	23.5	16.0	41.2	28.4
30–40	3.4	44.5	23.7	17.5	42.9	29.8
40–50	3.7	47.2	25.0	23.8	45.5	34.2
50–60	4.5	48.2	25.7	26.7	47.8	36.8
60–70	4.1	48.1	25.2	30.1	47.8	38.5
70–80	5.3	52.2	27.9	34.7	50.0	41.9
80–90	7.0	54.0	29.4	37.3	50.1	43.2
90–100	16.6	59.2	36.6	46.2	55.5	50.5
All Classes	5.4	47.7	26.1	25.9	45.6	35.4

Source: GoI, *Migration in India 2007–08: NSS 64th Round (July 2007–June 2008)* (New Delhi: National Sample Survey Office, 2010), 25.

fact, however, is that most female migrants are not independent agents in their decision on migration. Their superior numbers, especially in the rural areas, are considerably (but not entirely, since society is patently undergoing significant change, especially during the period after liberalization) a reflection of the sociological—perhaps, ultimately, economic—act of dependency on males through marriage or economic support. The disproportionately large numbers of female migrants are primarily explained by the social custom that mandates over much of India, particularly in the north, that females be married some distance away from their ancestral village; in addition, female minors, like male minors, migrate with the breadwinner of the household, who is usually a male.

Table 10.4 on the migration patterns among different migrant groups classified into deciles on the basis of the migrant's monthly per capita expenditure (MPCE) supports the argument that migration is a function of the migrant's position in the society's economic structure. By and large, it is obvious that the higher the economic status, the greater the tendency to migrate, particularly pronounced among urban males; contrastingly, the lower the economic status, the lesser the tendency to migrate. The table shows that the share of migrants in each of the first seven decile classes among *rural males* was less than 5 percent, but it gradually rose above that level in the eighth and ninth decile classes, and then suddenly, in the last decile class, it reached the comparatively high figure of 16.6 percent. In the case of males in *urban* areas, the share of migrants started out relatively higher at about 10 percent in the first decile class and then rose consistently, at times considerably, reaching the figure of 46.2 percent in the last decile class. Similar tendencies characterize female migrants, though their level of migration is much higher than that of male migration. The configuration resulting from MPCE decile classes seems to be more or less replicated in the area of literacy.

The pattern of acceleration in the rate of migration being associated with a rise in the economic hierarchy has been interpreted to be indicative of the absence of distress migration in India. Kundu argued in 2007:

> Poverty is not the key factor behind seasonal migration in urban areas. Indeed, this mobility is not very high among the poor when compared to middle class households. The bottom 40% of the population account for only 29% of the total seasonal migrants. . . . Migration rates for SCs and STs are around 20.4% in rural areas in 1999–2000. The rate for the remaining segment of the population is about 25%. Among women, too, the migration rate for the non-backward classes is marginally above that of the others. One would infer that poverty and immiserization, often linked with SC, ST and other backward castes, have not led to massive push factor migration.[11]

While migration thus may not be a function of poverty and immiserization, it certainly would not seem to be an inclusive process, since the wealthier groups are its principal beneficiaries.

However, the view about poverty and immiserization not being a factor in migration has been contested by others who have conducted local-level studies. In taking an equally strong but opposed position on the basis of her intensive multiyear study of half a dozen villages in two states, Deshingkar concludes that short-term migration of various kinds from remote villages is fairly high among the chronically poor and it is a survival strategy driven by poverty.[12] Interestingly, the data in the NSS of 2007–8 on the share of *short-term migrants* among the various decile classes in the population demonstrated a configuration that is the reverse of the one on regular migrants (see table 10.5). More broadly, Arjan de Haan underlines the macro-micro paradox in migration: "On the one hand, national-level data highlight that migration is selective with opportunities biased against the poorer, a process that might be reinforced with technological change. On the other hand, micro studies often show very high rates of migration amongst poorest and socially marginalized groups, and over-representation of migrants—including bonded and child labor, with Adivasis and Dalits over-represented—amongst the bottom layer of the working class. Much of the latter may go unrecorded, which may add to their vulnerability."[13]

Regardless, it is obvious that economics dominates the migration process. That is certainly true in relation to regular migration, where the process is overall associated with the economic structure of society. Even the socially based female predominance numerically in migration is in the ultimate analysis rooted in economic dependency. At the same time, short-term migration is economic by definition in official surveys since it is linked to the sole objective of employment or search for employment, while scholarly microlevel studies underline its role as a survival strategy for the chronically poor. Thus, both pull and push factors

Table 10.5. Share of Short-Term Migrants (per 100 Persons) in Each MPCE Decile Class during 2007–2008

MPCE Decile Class	Rural			Urban		
	Male	*Female*	*Total*	*Male*	*Female*	*Total*
0–10	4.5	1.0	2.7	1.0	0.1	0.5
10–20	3.9	0.9	2.4	1.1	0.1	0.6
20–30	3.7	0.7	2.2	0.9	0.2	0.5
30–40	3.2	0.5	1.8	0.6	0.1	0.4
40–50	3.2	0.6	1.9	0.5	0.1	0.3
50–60	2.6	0.4	1.6	0.4	0.1	0.3
60–70	2.1	0.3	1.2	0.6	0.2	0.4
70–80	2.2	0.3	1.3	0.6	0.1	0.4
80–90	1.6	0.3	0.9	0.5	0.1	0.3
90–100	1.4	0.2	0.8	0.3	0.1	0.2
All Classes	2.8	0.5	1.7	0.6	0.1	0.4

Source: GoI, *Migration in India 2007–08: NSS 64th Round (July 2007–June 2008)* (New Delhi: National Sample Survey Office, 2010), 93. A short-term migrant is defined as one who stayed away from home for thirty days or more, but not more than six months for purposes of employment or search for employment.

have been at work—pull for those higher up in the economic hierarchy and push for those at the bottom. For the better off, migration is an aspirational act; for the poor, it is a survival strategy. As with most other things, there is a class dimension to migration.

The view of migration as economic in nature is further reinforced by the motivation ascribed to the act of migration by the migrants themselves. Data on reasons offered by migrants for migration are available for much of the period since economic liberalization in three NSSs (1993, 1999–2000, and 2007–8). It is noteworthy that there is a drastic disparity between male and female migrants in their reasons for having migrated. To take *male* migrants first, the predominance of economics among the reasons for migration stands out even as this predominance has increased quite significantly during the period since liberalization. In 1993, 41.5 percent of urban male migrants had migrated for employment-related reasons; subsequently, the percentage increased to 51.9 in 1999–2000 and 55.7 in 2007–8 (see table 10.6). In other words, liberalization seems to have had a decisive economic impact on the aspirations of male migrants. Interestingly, the trend for employment-motivated migration is inversely related to that for the migration of urban male dependents who have moved with migrating parents (or an earning member of the household). In the case of *rural* male migrants, although a preponderant number migrated for employment-related reasons in 1993 (47.7 percent), there was subsequently a sharp decline in that preponderance (27.0 percent and 25.2 percent in 1999–2000 and 2007–8, respectively). It is as if liberalization

Table 10.6. Distribution of Different Types of Migrants (%) by Broad Reasons for Migration

	Migrants in Rural Areas		*Migrants in Urban Areas*	
Reason	*Male*	*Female*	*Male*	*Female*
49th NSS Round (1993)				
Employment related	47.7	8.3	41.5	4.9
Studies	4.1	1.1	18.0	7.0
Marriage	2.3	61.6	0.9	31.7
Migration by parents/earner	20.8	23.7	28.3	49.5
Other reasons	25.1	5.3	11.3	6.9
55th NSS Round (1999–2000)				
Employment related	30.3	1.0	51.9	3.0
Studies	5.3	0.4	6.2	1.3
Marriage	9.4	88.8	1.6	58.5
Migration by parents/earner	26.0	6.3	27.0	31.0
Other reasons	29.0	3.5	13.3	6.2
64th NSS Round (2007–8)				
Employment related	28.6	0.7	55.7	2.7
Studies	10.7	0.5	6.8	2.2
Marriage	9.4	91.2	1.4	60.8
Migration by parents/earner	22.1	4.4	25.2	29.4
Other reasons	29.2	3.2	10.9	4.9

Source: GoI, *Migration in India 2007–08: NSS 64th Round (July 2007–June 2008)* (New Delhi: National Sample Survey Office, 2010), 33.

has made the urban areas the centerpiece of attraction for male migrants; in contrast, the rural areas are of declining importance in this respect.

The centrality of the urban areas as a relative beacon impelling males to migrate there emerges from another perspective, as well. Table 10.7, based on the NSS of 2007–8, divides domestic migrants into four rural-urban streams and specifies the reason for migration within each stream. A very high percentage of males in the "rural to urban" stream (60.9 percent) and "urban to urban" stream (48.2 percent) had migrated for employment-related reasons, compared to "rural to rural" and "urban to rural" streams (29.1 percent and 28.8 percent, respectively). By contrast, employment-related reasons were almost a nonexistent consideration in the case of female migrants, regardless of whether rural or urban areas were the destination; instead, marriage was the sole impulse for migration, particularly where rural areas were involved. Even though employment does not figure to any significant degree in the reasons for female migration, it has been suggested that "labor force participation after migration increases steeply" for women.[14]

If the act of migration is profoundly economic, at least in relation to males, have the migrants been vindicated in their expectations in this regard? The data would seem to suggest a qualified response in the affirmative, but not an

Table 10.7. Share of Domestic Migrants (%) by Reason for Migration in Different Rural–Urban Streams, 2007–2008

	Male				*Female*			
Reason	*RR*	*UR*	*RU*	*UU*	*RR*	*UR*	*RU*	*UU*
Employment related	29.1	28.8	60.9	48.2	0.5	2.0	2.6	2.7
Studies	10.5	12.5	7.8	5.3	0.5	1.2	2.5	1.9
Marriage	12.2	2.1	1.6	1.2	92.6	74.2	62.8	58.5
Migration by parents/earner	23.7	18.4	22.8	28.9	3.6	15.4	28.2	31.1
Other reasons	24.4	38.2	6.9	16.4	2.9	7.3	4.0	5.7

Source: Tabulated from GoI, *Migration in India 2007–08: NSS 64th Round (July 2007–June 2008)* (New Delhi: National Sample Survey Office, 2010), 34.

Notes:

1. RR = Rural to Rural; UR = Urban to Rural; RU = Rural to Urban; and UU = Urban to Urban.
2. "Employment related" includes: in search of employment; in search of better employment; business; take up employment or better employment; transfer of service or contract; proximity to place of work.
3. "Other reasons" includes: acquisition of own house or apartment; housing problems; health care; postretirement.

overwhelming one. Migration assures no El Dorado, but it certainly has, by and large, made for a decided improvement in the life of migrants compared to their condition prior to moving. Testimony to this effect is provided by Kundu and Saraswati, who have constructed an interesting table (replicated here as table 10.8) based on unit-level data from the 1999–2000 and 2007–8 NSSs with respect to the employment status of *male* migrants aged fifteen to fifty-nine, divided into different migration streams along the rural-urban dimension.

Table 10.8 demonstrates visible improvement in most respects after migration in the 1999–2000 survey, which was done at the end of the period of economic reform, and also (perhaps slightly more) in the 2007–8 survey, which took place in the middle of the period of growth acceleration. Of special note, particularly where the destination is urban, is the reduction in the incidence of unemployment and in the "not in the labor force" category and, contrarily, the increase in the incidence of regular employees. While the incidence of self-employment rose, it may not have been of much satisfaction to migrants in most cases because of its largely poor and uncertain nature. The position of casual labor, however, did not show much improvement.

Kundu and Saraswati express considerable satisfaction at the rise in the share of regular employees, at the decline of the unemployed among migrants after migration (particularly when migrants had moved from rural to urban areas), and at the decline in the share of the unemployed and of those not in the labor force. They comment: "All this suggests that the adult males are able to improve their economic conditions through migration. There is no evidence of strong distress factors behind RU [rural-urban] migrants, driving them out of their place of origin or keeping them in distress in the labor market even after the mi-

Table 10.8. Share of Adult Male Migrants (%) in Different Rural–Urban Streams by Employment Status

	1999–2000 Survey					*2007–8 Survey*				
Principal Activity	*RR*	*UR*	*RU*	*UU*	*Total*	*RR*	*UR*	*RU*	*UU*	*Total*
Current Status										
Self-employed	32.9	33.7	26.1	22.4	28.1	31.2	32.3	27.2	23.4	27.6
Regular employee	21.1	26.2	44.7	52.2	37.3	21.0	25.8	45.2	53.3	39.7
Casual labor	31.8	23.5	13.7	6.4	18.6	31.1	16.2	13.1	4.9	15.7
Unemployed	1.7	5.5	1.9	3.1	2.5	1.6	2.6	1.7	2.3	1.9
Not in labor force	12.5	11.1	13.5	15.9	13.5	15.1	23.1	12.9	16.1	15.1
Status before Migration										
Self-employed	20.3	12.7	21.6	13.1	18.3	20.4	13.6	20.9	14.8	18.6
Regular employee	11.6	31.6	11.9	36.2	19.4	10.2	29.1	10.7	34.4	18.2
Casual labor	29.2	23.6	15.7	6.6	18.5	28.0	20.6	18.2	4.9	17.4
Unemployed	5.3	3.8	14.2	7.6	8.8	6.4	2.8	19.1	9.9	12.2
Not in labor force	33.6	28.4	36.6	36.4	34.8	35.0	33.9	31.1	36.1	33.5

Source: Amitabh Kundu and Lopamudra Ray Saraswati, "Migration and Exclusionary Urbanization in India," *Economic and Political Weekly* 47, nos. 26–27 (June 20, 2012): 219–27, table 6; reprinted with permission.

Notes: RR = Rural to Rural; UR = Urban to Rural; RU = Rural to Urban; and UU = Urban to Urban. Only male migrants aged fifteen to fifty-nine have been taken into account.

gration. Migration decisions have a positive and significant impact on livelihood patterns."[15] This comment is noteworthy in light of the fact that, ostensibly, Kundu is generally a strong critic of economic liberalization.

Even when analysts have been critical of official agencies for underestimating the extent of migration or for not adequately providing social protection to migrants, at the same time, they have nonetheless stressed the beneficial aspects of migration in alleviating poverty and of improving life conditions.[16] Deshingkar, for example, who had underlined the poverty-driven nature of migration on the basis of her study of remote villages, thus emphasizes:

> In remote villages, migration involved all but the poorest (disabled, old and sick) and the richest households. . . . The broad base of migration has resulted in its benefits accruing to a large number of households, challenging the notion that migration benefits only a privileged few with the right contacts, assets and education. Circular migration earnings account for a higher proportion of household income among the lower castes and tribes, namely SC, BC [backward classes] and ST (in households with one person working outside the village). Migration is critical to managing risk and smoothing consumption for a majority of chronically poor households living in remote rural areas. . . .
>
> For those who have few assets, education or social networks, migration provides a way of coping and survival, providing income for consumption and

> paying off debt . . . sending areas benefit from migration first through an improvement in the lives of households with migrants and over time through knock-on effects on the entire village, through improved agricultural productivity and more economic activity.[17]

The last point in this citation is testimony to the correctness of John Kenneth Galbraith's observation a long time ago that the act of migration is beneficial not only to the migrants themselves and their families but also to the communities they leave behind and to the communities they settle in (by meeting the needs of employers or consumers).[18] Economic liberalization has not diminished but rather enhanced all these aspects.

INTERSTATE MIGRATION AFTER ECONOMIC LIBERALIZATION

From the perspective of economic integration, it is interstate migration that is of special importance, even though intrastate migration forms the predominant part of migration in India. Such migration, also referred to as long-distance migration in contrast with the short-distance migration of the intrastate variety, is an important mechanism that contributes to some level of equalization between economically backward and economically advanced states through benefiting the individuals that migrate and their households back home that receive funds from them.

Table 10.1 shows that in 2001, there were 41.2 million interstate migrants (out of a total of 309.4 million migrants). Interstate migration of this magnitude undoubtedly constitutes a massive social phenomenon, since its scale is larger than the total population of more than a hundred countries, including Kenya, Poland, Algeria, Canada, Uganda, Iraq, and Morocco (all of which are in the 30 to 40 million range). Interstate migration in India has had the highest growth rate (53.6 percent) during the first decade of economic liberalization (corresponding to the period covered by the 2001 census) compared to the other main types of migration, such as intradistrict, interdistrict, and international. Interestingly, it is migration to urban areas, whether from rural areas (39.3 percent) or from other urban areas (27.4 percent), that dominates the interstate migration scene and underlines the city's role as a magnet.[19]

Three issues seem relevant in the analysis of interstate migration: (1) which states are the sources of interstate migration, and which the destinations; (2) what has been the impact of economic liberalization on trends in interstate migration; and (3) has interstate migration after liberalization made for convergence or divergence among the states? Existing data place limits in answering these questions fully since the census results for the 2001–11 period are not yet available. Consequently, the discussion below relies primarily on the data from the 2001 census and

Table 10.9. Net Migration Rates for Major States: Census 1991 and 2001

	1981–91 (millions)			*1991–2001 (millions)*				
State	*In-Migrants*	*Out-Migrants*	*Net Migrants*	*In-Migrants*	*Out-Migrants*	*Net Migrants*	*Net Migration Rate*	*Population Growth Rate (%)*
Andhra Pradesh				0.42	0.64	−0.21	−0.3	26.90
Assam				0.12	0.28	−0.15	−0.7	18.92
Bihar	0.32	1.23	−0.86	0.46	2.24	−1.72	−2.7	28.62
Jharkhand				0.50	0.62	−0.11	−0.5	23.36
Delhi	1.54	0.28	1.31	2.17	0.46	1.76	18.7	47.02
Gujarat	0.70	0.31	0.41	1.13	0.45	0.69	1.7	22.66
Haryana	0.69	0.56	0.15	1.23	0.59	0.67	4.1	28.43
Karnataka				0.88	0.77	0.13	0.3	17.51
Kerala				0.24	0.43	−0.17	−0.6	9.43
Madhya Pradesh				0.82	0.84	−0.02	−0.0	24.26
Chhattisgarh				0.34	0.45	−0.10	−0.6	18.27
Maharashtra	1.61	0.77	0.87	3.23	0.89	2.38	3.0	22.73
Orissa				0.23	0.44	−0.21	−0.7	16.25
Punjab				0.81	0.50	0.34	1.7	20.10
Rajasthan				0.72	0.99	−0.26	−0.6	28.41
Tamil Nadu				0.27	0.67	−0.38	−0.7	11.72
Uttar Pradesh	0.73	2.46	−1.67	1.08	3.81	−2.69	−2.0	25.85
Uttarakhand				0.35	0.35	0.03	0.4	20.41
West Bengal				0.73	0.73	0.25	0.4	17.77

Source: Tabulated from data in GoI, *Census of India 2001: Data Highlights, Migration Tables* (New Delhi: Registrar General and Census Commissioner, n.d.), 6, 14.

Notes: This source provides only selective information for a few states for 1981–91. The table is based on "migrants by last residence (duration 0–9 years)." Figures for in-migrants are only for in-migrants from other states, while the figures for net migrants are worked out after also incorporating the figures for in-migrants from other countries. "Net migration rate" represents the contribution of net migration to the population growth of the state during the period 1991–2001; thus, for example, "of the 47.0% growth in population in Delhi between 1991–2001, migration constituted 18.7%" (ibid., 15).

Table 10.10. Rate of Net Interstate (Inter-census) *Male* Migration, 1961–2001

	Total Net Male Migrants (%)					*Urban Net Male Migrants (%)*				
State	*1961*	*1971*	*1981*	*1991*	*2001*	*1961*	*1971*	*1981*	*1991*	*2001*
Andhra Pradesh	−0.7	−0.3	−0.2	−0.1	−0.3	−2.5	−0.9	−0.8	−0.3	−0.1
Assam	2.4	1.1	–	0.1	−0.5	7.7	3.5	–	0.5	−0.6
Bihar	−2.4	−1.4	−1.2	−1.3	−2.5	−15.9	−6.6	−6.2	−6.7	−2.4
Gujarat	0.0	0.4	0.6	1.1	1.9	−1.1	0.7	1.2	2.2	4.3
Haryana	–	0.7	0.9	1.0	3.3	–	−3.2	1.0	2.2	7.6
Karnataka	1.3	0.4	0.2	0.3	0.4	1.6	−0.1	0.4	0.9	2.2
Kerala	−2.6	−1.8	−1.3	−0.8	−0.6	−15.0	−10.6	−7.8	−3.6	−1.3
Madhya Pradesh	2.0	−0.9	0.3	0.6	−0.2	7.9	−2.7	1.6	1.8	1.5
Maharashtra	2.9	1.9	2.2	1.3	3.0	9.1	5.9	5.1	3.1	6.2
Orissa	−0.8	0.2	0.2	−0.3	−0.8	−7.7	1.8	0.3	−1.7	0.2
Punjab	−1.9	−1.7	0.2	0.3	1.8	−6.7	−3.7	0.7	0.4	4.6
Rajasthan	−1.7	−0.9	−0.5	−0.5	−0.6	−8.5	−4.6	−2.5	−1.9	0.3
Tamil Nadu	−1.2	−0.3	−0.7	−0.7	−0.7	−2.3	−0.1	−0.9	−1.2	−0.4
Uttar Pradesh	−2.0	−1.6	−1.8	−1.4	−1.9	−12.2	−9.3	−8.5	−6.2	−1.1
West Bengal	4.1	1.5	0.7	0.3	−0.1	11.6	3.8	2.1	0.8	0.6

Source: Adapted from Amitabh Kundu and Lopamudra Ray Saraswati, "Migration and Exclusionary Urbanization in India," *Economic and Political Weekly* 47, nos. 26–27 (June 20, 2012): 219–27, table 2; adapted with permission.

Note: The rate of net migration equals in-migrants minus out-migrants, and the division of the result by the relevant population.

on secondary works; as evident, the census of 2001 covers only about half the period—the phase of reform—since the launching of liberalization.

Drawing on the official report on the census of 2001, table 10.9 provides data on in-migrants and out-migrants for the major states. These data pertain to interstate migrants during the period since the previous census.[20] Table 10.10, drawn from the secondary work of Kundu and Saraswati, enables us to take a longer view on *male* migrants during the period from 1961 to 2001 in most, but not all, the major states.

Destination States

Broadly, although interstate migration is a phenomenon that affects all the states of India, it is primarily north India that has been the scene of major migratory action, at least until the 2001 census. Turning to in-migration first, table 10.9 shows that the major destination states of *net* interstate migrants (in-migrants minus out-migrants) during the census period 1991–2001 are: (1) Maharashtra, 2.38 million;

(2) Delhi, 1.8 million; (3) Gujarat, 0.69 million; (4) Haryana, 0.67 million; and (5) Punjab, 0.34 million. These are obviously large numbers for states to absorb during a ten-year period, and it is little wonder that some states, particularly Maharashtra, have at times witnessed antimigrant "sons of the soil" movements. Particularly striking is the growth in the numbers of net in-migrants to this handful of states during the ten-year period of 1991–2001 compared to the numbers for the 1981–91 period, selective information for which is provided in table 10.9. The growth for four of the states was: (1) Haryana, 343.0 percent; (2) Maharashtra, 172.8 percent; (3) Gujarat, 68.4 percent; and (4) Delhi, 35.1 percent.[21]

The previous paragraph makes it abundantly apparent that a virtual explosion in the number of net in-migrants occurred during the first decade of economic liberalization (1991–2001) compared to the previous decade (1981–91). Since migration is a profoundly economic process, it could not be sheer coincidence that this explosion in net in-migration to these traditional destination states coincides with the period of reform. Whether this level of migration has continued into the period of growth acceleration during the first decade of the 2000s can be determined only after the release of data on migration for the 2011 census. It may well be that growth acceleration simply sustained the pace of migration growth to these states, that it may have even sped up the process further, or that it may have merely facilitated consolidation of the earlier burst of expansion. Regardless, it is noteworthy meanwhile that interstate migration is no longer confined to the metropolitan cities such as Delhi, Kolkata, and Mumbai. Rather, with the economic diffusion following economic liberalization, interstate migration now extends to other large cities such as Bengaluru in Karnataka, Chennai in Tamil Nadu, Hyderabad in Andhra Pradesh, Jaipur in Rajasthan, Pune in Maharashtra, and other such major urban centers.[22]

The challenge in terms of absorption of in-migrants would seem to vary for the destination states. However, it cannot be simply read off from the number of total in-migrants or net in-migrants, where Maharashtra is undoubtedly ahead of all the other states. Prima facie, Delhi and Haryana would seem to face the more serious challenge—particularly Delhi, with its small territory, a mere 1,483 sq km—given the smaller relative population size of each in 1991, which served as the base for absorption of the in-migrants. The population of Delhi and Haryana in 1991 was 9.4 million and 16.4 million, respectively, as against that of Maharashtra's 78.9 million; Gujarat and Punjab had a population of 41.3 million and 20.2 million, respectively. Interestingly, Delhi state's chief minister Sheila Dikshit has referred to the culture of Delhi as having become transformed into "Bihari culture."[23]

A similar disparity in migration-induced challenges in the destination states emerges when the net migration rate is considered; that rate indicates the percentage contribution of net migration into the state to the state's decadal population growth. Delhi had the highest net migration rate of all the states in 2001 at 18.7 percent, distantly followed by Haryana at 4.1 percent, and only then

Maharashtra at 3.0 percent, with Gujarat and Punjab both having a rate of only 1.7 percent. Yet, it is Maharashtra, India's second-largest state in population, which often gives the appearance of being the epicenter of hostility toward interstate migration in the form of the militant political movement headed by the Shiv Sena. Perhaps the problem arises from the fact that until recently it has been Mumbai, the political capital of the state and the financial and commercial capital of the nation, which has been the star destination for migrants from all over India. In addition, the state of Maharashtra has a high degree of internal economic disparities, and Mumbai and now other urban centers like Pune are attractive destinations for rural migrants from within the state; this phenomenon sets intrastate migrants in opposition to in-migrants from other states and makes the former receptive to the political appeal of the Shiv Sena. In most other states—barring the special case of the much-fragmented northeastern region—while there may be resentment against migrants, there are no major organized political movements against them. Though social tensions of various kinds are pervasive across India, it would be premature and mistaken to single out interstate migration as a major cause of social conflict.

To a considerable extent, the destination states represent one side of the line that separates the economically more advanced states from the less advanced or backward states of India. Since migration comes from economic rationality, it stands to reason that people would move from low-income states to high-income states unless deterred by other social and economic constraints.[24] Because the more advanced states were the first ones to take advantage of economic liberalization, it is no surprise that migrants headed in their direction after liberalization. However, not all advanced states are net importers of migrants. For example, all the southern states are among the more advanced states, but except for Karnataka, they are themselves net—though not high—exporters of migrants, including Tamil Nadu, the most advanced among them. Even the key destination states are themselves sources of out-migration; thus, Maharashtra and Gujarat both export migrants to each other; indeed, the former is at times a net exporter to the latter.[25] Similarly, Tamil Nadu and Kerala as well as Karnataka and Tamil Nadu have significant levels of exchange of migrants.

Source States

There are two key source states in interstate migration: Uttar Pradesh and Bihar, belonging to what are often characterized as the backward states and, more pejoratively, as the *bimaru* states. The quantitative dimensions of out-migration from these two states over the 1991–2001 period are enormous; their scale is comparable to the in-migration of Maharashtra and Delhi; indeed, the former two states are the mirror image of the latter two. Uttar Pradesh, often referred to as simply UP, is a mammoth state, and so is the scale of its out-migration. Remarkably, the single largest figure in the entirety of table 10.9 is for out-migrants from that one state—3.81 million—with these migrants spread far and wide among the other states, with Delhi and Maharashtra likely their largest destination states, followed by Madhya Pradesh and Haryana.[26] At the same time, UP received large numbers of in-migrants amounting to more than a million, perhaps the largest number among them from Bihar. Because of the immense size of its population and its high population growth rate, the 2.69 million net out-migrants made for a net migration rate of a mere –2.0 percent.

Bihar is an equally huge exporter of migrants, second only to UP, whose key destinations are also Delhi and Maharashtra. During the period 1991–2001, Bihar sent out 2.24 million migrants and received less than half a million; again, because of its large population and its higher growth rate, Bihar's net migration rate was only –2.7 percent. It is primarily migrants from the two states of UP and Bihar that have been the focus of antimigrant resentment in the destination states, particularly Maharashtra. Compared to these source and destination states, the contribution of the other states to migration has been marginal both in terms of in-migration and out-migration, at least according to the data from the 2001 census.

The situation has been changing, however, and the migration data from the 2011 census may throw up some surprises. Both anecdotal and impressionistic evidence indicates that states like Tamilnadu and Kerala—indeed, all the states in the southern region—have become increasingly attractive for migrants, including those from faraway northeastern India.[27] A government study sees demographic change occurring in Kerala as a result of the migration into the state of new migrants, along with the large outflow of its own citizens to West Asia and elsewhere and a lower fertility rate.[28] Migrants from northeastern India are particularly visible in the hospitality industry, where they are apparently preferred because of their fair color. The church in Kerala, given the state's large Christian population, has provided a vantage point for the Christian community in northeastern India to gain entry into Kerala.[29]

Impressionistic evidence indicates that there is a large body of opinion in the southern region that perceives the north in the same light that the developed countries see the underdeveloped world—poor, backward, illiterate, unhygienic, and fractious. It was not always thus; this perception has occurred with the backdrop of the recent economic rise of the south, particularly after the launching of liberalization. When there are robberies in Tamil Nadu, for example, they are often blamed on in-migrants from Bihar and UP. However, there is no active opposition to in-migration as such, since these states themselves, as long time net exporters of migrants, have been beneficiaries of out-migration and also because, with the rise in relative prosperity and education, the local population is no longer much attracted to the low-paying occupations in which the migrants are concentrated, such as road building, work at the brick kilns, or security services.[30]

Longer-Term Trends in Interstate Migration

Although it can be maintained that there are long-term roots to the contemporary configuration of source and destination states, some changes are nonetheless evident. Table 10.10, which replicates, in part, the table developed by Kundu and Saraswati from census data, provides information on several major states with respect to the rate of net interstate intercensus *male* migration, both total and urban (rural is excluded here), during the period from 1961 to 2001. The interstate migration rate had been worked out by the authors by taking the figure for the number of male in-migrants for each state, then subtracting from it the figure for male out-migrants, and finally dividing the result by the state's male population.[31] The table is ideal in discerning trends over half a century, while its focus on male migrants facilitates analysis of economic trends since it excludes female migrants, whose movement is primarily driven by marriage considerations. It is not comprehensive, however, since it does not include the important destination state of Delhi.

Table 10.10 confirms the earlier assessment that the decade after economic liberalization marks a break in interstate migration trends not only with the previous 1981–91 decade but also, by and large, with the earlier decades. Barring a few exceptions, the figures for the rates of total net male migrants in the states are higher in 2001 than in 1991. Why this change should have occurred is not easily explicable, since it is often maintained that the decade of the 1990s did not mark a radical break from the previous decade with respect to the rate of economic growth.[32] Interestingly, even the data on indicators of social stability, such as riots, robberies, and industrial disputes, show a downward trend after 1980 or thereabouts.[33]

Perhaps, the data on social stability do not adequately capture the impact of the multiple political and economic crises that marked the decade of the 1980s.[34] Maybe the economic and social environment stemming from this concatenation of crises was not conducive to migration despite the assumed economic growth breakthrough of the 1980s. It is probably the élan of economic change that liberalization promised, the expectations of economic and political renewal after liberalization, and the manifest rapid capacity expansion, at least until the mid-1990s, which propelled the reversal of the earlier trend of decline in migration.[35]

With respect to the destination states, table 10.10 confirms the earlier status of Maharashtra, Haryana, Punjab, and Gujarat as the dominant recipients of migrants (Delhi is not included in the table). However, the table also intimates that the urban areas are the primary focus of in-migration in these states, since the rate of urban in-migration is invariably two or more times that for the total. At the same time, Maharashtra shows a long history of being a prime destination, indeed a history that far predates independence and stretches back to the days of the founding of the British Empire in India. K. C. Zachariah, who studied interstate migration during the first three decades of the twentieth century, underlined that "Bombay was a predominantly in-migrating zone and gained population by migration through the 30-year period."[36] While Maharashtra has been consistently an important importer of male migrants, it was a much more attractive destination in the first decade of economic planning (1951–61); it saw some decline in the subsequent three decades, until there was a reversal of that trend—and a remarkable one at that—during the first decade of liberalization. The earlier prominent position of in-migration with respect to Maharashtra, the subsequent declining trend, and then the trend reversal are especially marked in the case of urban migrants.

Haryana did not emerge as a separate state until 1966, but since its origin has displayed a rising trend in receiving total male migrants, which reached its peak in 2001; its import of manpower is particularly noteworthy in the urban areas, where its net migration rate in 2001 is, indeed, higher than that of Maharashtra. Punjab presents a dichotomous picture, in which the first two decades mark it as a source state and the next three as a destination state; the state has a long history of emigration, not just to the rest of India but also to the world.

Gujarat has shown a persistent rising trend of in-migration since at least 1971. West Bengal does not stand out particularly as a destination state, but that belies its status as a paramount magnet in the past. With its major city of Calcutta (now Kolkata) as the seat of the British Empire in India and the home of India's jute, tea, and engineering industries, Bengal was the principal importer of manpower from the rest of the subcontinent. However, the shifting of the imperial capital to Delhi in 1911, the partition of Bengal in 1905, and the rise of Bombay (now Mumbai) as a rival industrial center started a process of relative economic decline that has been unrelenting. As a consequence, "an eastward movement gave way to a westward movement" in interstate migration during the first three decades of the twentieth century.[37] Subsequently, the aftermath of the partition of 1947, continual social and political conflict in the state, and economic mismanagement by the state government precluded economic renewal.

Ironically, then, rather than being something that ought to be viewed negatively, in-migration seems to stand profoundly as an indicator of a state's economic dynamism as long as it remains within some reasonable limits that prevent it from overwhelming the local population. In-migration underlines the advanced economic status of a state, while out-migration points to the underdeveloped nature of its economy. Gujarat provides a neat illustration of economic advance resulting in the state's transformation from a source state to a destination state in interstate migration.

Uttar Pradesh and Bihar, as relatively backward states economically, have long been regions marked by heavy out-migration, and this status, too, goes back to the days of the British Empire. One economist attributed the perpetual status of UP, and by extension Bihar, as major sources of interstate migration to a combination of economic and social factors: "Population pressure was probably not a significant factor during this period [1901–31]. . . . Migration is contagious, and a tradition of migration once established continues to operate unless serious obstacles arise. Economic opportunities elsewhere probably influenced the direction of movement if not the volume, but it is also likely that the long established tradition of out-migration gave the would-be migrants the necessary contacts in the area of destination and was therefore an important factor in the continuation of migration even in the periods of heavy 'natural decrease' of population."[38]

The perpetual export of manpower, however, has not been particularly helpful in pulling these states up economically. To be fair, the total net male out-migration from the two states has been on a decline over the long haul, except for the spurt in 2001; barring 2001, the decline story also is true with respect to *rural* net male out-migration (not shown in the table) and, especially, for urban net male out-migration. It can only be a matter of speculation at this time whether the MGNREGA (Mahatma Gandhi National Rural Employment Guarantee Act) program, launched in 2006, will lead to slowing down out-migration from the rural areas of these two states.[39] For now, these states, despite commendable growth in recent years, continue to remain at or near the bottom among the major states in per capita income and development.

It is noteworthy that, like UP and Bihar, the states of south India, with the exception of Karnataka, have consistently been net exporters of manpower, particularly in the earlier decades after independence and especially from their urban areas. Remarkably, the heavy out-migration from Kerala, relative to its own population, has been comparable in scale to that of Bihar. At the same time, through better economic and social management, all the southern states have developed to the rank of the more advanced in India. The current status of the other states is rather ambiguous, not standing out as either a major source or a major destination. Rajasthan, however, is notable for reducing its out-migration as it has advanced economically in recent years. Orissa, too, has reduced its out-migration. While not particularly developed economically, Madhya Pradesh has been more a destination than a source state.

THE SPREAD EFFECTS OF INTERSTATE MIGRATION

In a situation where there are serious interstate economic disparities, interstate migration functions as a balancing mechanism between the economically advanced states and the less advanced ones. Its immediate consequence is to reduce population pressure and the level of unemployment in the source state that would otherwise exist if it were not for the out-migration from the state. In this manner, out-migration tends to work toward some degree of economic convergence between source and destination states.

A more direct effect of out-migration in aiding both economic relief and economic advance in the source state is through remittances of funds by out-migrants to their families in the home state. Huge income transfers are involved through such financial remittances. Although there are no data available separately for remittances made specifically by interstate migrants, some appreciation of the consequent income transfers can be gained from the information that the NSS of 2007–8 provides on remittances by Indian migrants in general, that is, intrastate and interstate migrants, as well as emigrants to foreign countries. To avoid unnecessary complexity, the discussion here focuses on male migrants only.

To begin with, the NSS of 2007–8 found that, while about 80 percent of male migrants in India and 95 percent of the male emigrants abroad were economically active, 55 percent of the migrants in India and a much higher proportion among those abroad (78 percent) sent remittances to their households. While both migrants in India and those who were abroad remitted money home five times in a year, there was a huge disproportion in the amounts that the two sets of out-migrants had remitted during the preceding 365 days, with each of the remitters from the former set sending Rs. 15,000 and from the latter Rs. 57,000.[40] Note that the per capita net state domestic product (NSDP) of the two primary source states in 2007–8 at current prices was Rs. 16,436 for UP and Rs. 11,074 for Bihar, while India's per capita income was Rs. 33,283.[41]

Given these figures, it would be difficult to disagree with the assessment that the remittances "play a vital role in improving the livelihoods of the households." Some 95 percent of the recipient households have used the remittances for consumption expenditure, primarily for food, education, and health care, and also for paying down debt and improvement of housing.[42] In this manner, through the consequent financial transfers, interstate migration can be said to have brought some degree of convergence in living standards between the source and destination states, which would not have occurred in the absence of the remittances. In a larger sense, too, the remittances by millions of interstate migrants must have added billions of rupees to the economies of the source states, and thus, with their consequent multiplier effects, contributed in some measure to economic convergence between the source and destination states.

More precision to this assessment is provided by a quantitative study by Veena Jha, one of a few of its kind that employs regression analysis to directly and specifically address the question of convergence through migration. Jha is particularly focused on determining the influence of high growth on the effects of interstate migration during the first decade of the 2000s. Using NSS data, she examines two relationships during the period of high growth: (1) the effect of out-migration on asset formation in the source state as a result of remittances; and, more important, (2) the impact on convergence of state incomes. Her regression analysis leads her to conclude that "the rate of out-migration has a positive effect on asset formation in the state of origin, thus showing positive effects on poverty." Indeed, the greater the distance of state income from the national average, the greater was the level of asset formation.[43] On the convergence hypothesis, again, her regression analyses demonstrate

> the strong presence of convergence both in terms of absolute values and in the standardized variable. The difference in the per capita product from the national average decreases with increasing out-migration rates. Moreover, the higher the initial levels of poverty the higher is the convergence, where poverty is used as the control variable. This result does indicate that while higher poverty rates are associated with higher difference between the state and the national average domestic product, interstate migration acts as an intermediating variable leading to convergence in the state domestic product per capita to the national average.[44]

Jha supplemented her quantitative analysis based on NSS data with her own questionnaire-based survey of five hundred migrants, predominantly male, in five states: Andhra Pradesh, Delhi, Karnataka, Punjab, and Uttarakhand. The results from her survey were basically along the lines of her conclusions from the NSS-based quantitative study on asset building. Unlike earlier studies, her survey results underlined that remittances were addressed to asset building rather than debt repayment. She also found that an overwhelming number of migrants (80 percent), having seen a 50–200 percent rise in their incomes, emphatically did not intend to return to their villages apart from brief visits; in other words, their transition from rural to urban areas was irreversible.[45] The remaining 20 percent were largely temporary migrants.

SUMMARY

The critics of globalization have viewed this social process negatively, not only in general but also specifically in the case of migration. They have seen it as leading to economic segmentation and to economic, indeed national, disintegration. This study has examined the data on migration in India, including interstate migration, not only since the country opened itself to globalization with the launching of economic liberalization in 1991, but also during a longer period. The data do not support the contentions of the critics.

Economic liberalization is shown to have marked a reversal of the earlier trend of decline in migration, instead demonstrating a rise in migration, at least during the phase of reform in the 1990s. Moreover, the work of analysts at the local level shows that the official data on migration underestimate the level of migration. While official data point to pull factors at work in migration since it has been driven by the upper part of the economic hierarchy, microlevel studies underline the push factors insofar as it is the chronically poor who are compelled to undertake migration as a survival strategy—albeit as temporary, seasonal, or circulatory migrants.

While globalization wields no magic wand to make poverty and underdevelopment quickly vanish and to replace them overnight with prosperity and development, the data do demonstrate results that are positive in terms of both poverty alleviation and reduction of disparities between the advanced and backward states, thus adding to economic convergence rather than divergence among the states. That is a contribution to economic integration, not economic segmentation, as the critics have posited.

NOTES

1. Amitabh Kundu, "Migration and Urbanization in India in the Context of Poverty Alleviation," paper presented at the International Conference on Policy Perspectives on Growth, Economic Structures and Poverty Reduction, Beijing, China, June 7–9, 2007, 23; emphasis added; available at www.networkideas.org/ideasact/jun07/Beijing_Conference_07/Amitabh_Kundu.pdf.

2. Amitabh Kundu, "Trends and Structure of Employment in the 1990s: Implications for Urban Growth," *Economic and Political Weekly* 32, no. 24 (June 14, 1997): 1399–1405. See also R. B. Bhagat, "Internal Migration in India: Are the Underclass More Mobile?" in *Migration, Identity and Conflict: India Migration Report 2011*, ed. S. Irudaya Rajan (New Delhi: Routledge, 2011), 6.

3. Analysts of migration trends often employ the binary categories of push-and-pull factors as an explanatory device; see, for example, Bhagat, "Internal Migration in India," 7–8. For a summary review of the theoretical and empirical literature on the issue, see Kala Seetharam Sridhar, A. Venugopala Reddy, and Pavan Srinath, "Is It Push or Pull? Recent Evidence from Migration in India," Final Report 10-04, paper submitted on 10th Round Regional Research Competition of South Asia Network of Economic Research Institutes (SANEI), June 2010, 1–5, 6–12; available at http://saneinetwork.net/Files/10_04___K_S_Sridhar.pdf.

4. Amitabh Kundu and Lopamudra Ray Saraswati, "Migration and Exclusionary Urbanization in India," *Economic and Political Weekly* 47, nos. 26–27 (June 20, 2012): 220; emphasis added. It is obvious from an earlier citation that this proposition about the decline in migration is linked with a strong critique of globalization and "neo-liberalism." See Kundu, "Migration and Urbanization," 23.

5. Bhagat, "Internal Migration in India," 7–24, table 2.3.

6. Government of India (GoI), *Migration in India 2007–08: NSS 64th Round (July 2007–June 2008)* (New Delhi: National Sample Survey Office [NSSO], 2010), 23.

7. Priya Deshingkar, "Migration, Remote Rural Areas and Chronic Poverty in India," ODI Working Paper 323, Overseas Development Institute, London, 2010, 27. On the official underestimation of migration, see also Priya Deshingkar and Shaheen Akter, "Migration and Human Development in India," Research Paper 2009/13, UNDP Human Development Reports, United Nations Development Programme, New York, 2009, 2–5; Arjan de Haan, "Inclusive Growth? Labor Migration and Poverty in India," ISS Working Paper No. 513, Institute of Social Studies, The Hague, 2011, 19; R. B. Bhagat and Soumya Mohanty, "Emerging Pattern of Urbanization and the Contribution of Migration in Urban Growth in India," *Asian Population Studies* 5, no. 1 (March 2009): 5–20; Kunal Keshri and R. B. Bhagat, "Temporary and Seasonal Migration: Regional Pattern, Characteristics and Associated Factors," *Economic & Political Weekly* 47, no. 4 (January 28, 2012): 81–88;

Ravi Srivastava and S. K. Sasikumar, "An Overview of Migration in India, Its Impacts and Key Issues," paper for Regional Conference on Migration, Development and Pro-Poor Policy Choices in Asia, Department for International Development, London, 2003; and Jayati Ghosh, "The New Reality," *Frontline* 29, no. 18 (September 21, 2012): 30–32.

8. GoI, *Migration in India 2007–08*, 93.

9. The discourse on underestimation of migration has a parallel with respect to underestimation of urbanization. For a forceful argument in favor of the level of urbanization being considerably higher than what is presented in official statistics, especially in terms of the urbanization of rural areas instead of the traditional pattern of the transfer of populations from the villages to the cities, see Eric Denis, Partha Mukhopadhyay, and Marie-Helene Zerah, "Subaltern Urbanization in India," *Economic and Political Weekly* 47, no. 30 (July 28, 2012): 52–62.

10. Sridhar, Reddy, and Srinath, "Is It Push or Pull?" 9.

11. Cited in Deshingkar, "Migration, Remote Rural Areas," 5; see also Kundu, "Migration and Urbanization."

12. Deshingkar, "Migration, Remote Rural Areas," 27. See also Srivastava and Sasikumar, "An Overview of Migration," 3–4.

13. de Haan, "Inclusive Growth?" 14.

14. Ibid., 15.

15. Kundu and Saraswati, "Migration and Exclusionary Urbanization," 223.

16. Ram B. Bhagat, "Migrants' (Denied) Right to the City," in United Nations Educational, Scientific and Cultural Organization, *Urban Policies and the Right to the City in India: Rights, Responsibilities and Citizenship* (New Delhi: UNESCO, 2011), 39–47; and Srivastava and Sasikumar, "An Overview of Migration," 7–8.

17. Deshingkar, "Migration, Remote Rural Areas," 27.

18. John Kenneth Galbraith, *The Nature of Mass Poverty* (Cambridge, MA: Harvard University Press, 1979).

19. Bhagat, "Internal Migration in India," 7–24, table 2.4.

20. GoI, *Census of India 2001: Data Highlights, Migration Tables* (New Delhi: Registrar General and Census Commissioner, n.d.), 6, 14.

21. Ibid., 6.

22. Veena Jha, "Trickle Down Effects of Inter State Migration in a Period of High Growth in the Indian Economy," CSGR Working Paper 253/08, Center for the Study of Globalization and Regionalization, University of Warwick, Coventry, UK, 2008.

23. Rakesh Sinha, "All Over, Police Is under the State Government" [Sheila Dikshit], *Indian Express*, February 17, 2013.

24. More systematically, Bhagat developed a correlation matrix for interstate migration and per capita income along with other social indicators, which demonstrated that "per capita income is very strongly correlated with in-migration rate and also moderately with out-migration rate." See Bhagat, "Internal Migration in India," 18.

25. Tim Dyson and Pravin Visaria, "Migration and Urbanization: Retrospect and Prospects," in *Twenty-First Century in India: Population, Economy, Human Development, and the Environment*, ed. Tim Dyson, Robert Cassen, and Leela Visaria (Oxford: Oxford University Press, 2004), 108–29. Note also the observation that "Gujarat is the only state

to which Maharashtra lost a substantial number of people during 1991–2001"; see Bhagat and Mohanty, "Emerging Pattern of Urbanization," 5–20.

26. GoI, *Migration in India 1999–2000: NSS 55th Round (July 1999–June 2000)* (New Delhi: NSSO, 2001), 41, table 4.1. Note also the recent trend of greater international emigration from Uttar Pradesh (UP), "now surpassing Kerala in total numbers"; see de Haan, "Inclusive Growth?" 12.

27. The upheaval and exodus among migrants from the northeast in 2012—which was caused because of the scare spread through social media networking about possible antimigrant violence against them by sectarian elements—paradoxically underlined the large-scale presence of such in-migrants in the southern states, which had developed unobtrusively during the previous years. See the cover story "Behind the Exodus," *Frontline* 29, no. 18 (September 21, 2012).

28. Shaju Philip, "A Youthful, Migrant Workforce Takes Root in an Ageing Kerala," *Indian Express*, February 21, 2013; available at www.indianexpress.com.

29. Note the more general comment by Srivastava and Sasikumar, "An Overview of Migration," 6: "The church also plays an active and more benign role in bringing potential employers and employees together."

30. Some of these comments are based on discussions with the faculty members of the Madras School of Economics in Chennai and the Center for Development Studies in Thiruvananthapuram, conversations with informants, and personal observation during visits in 2011.

31. Professor Amitabh Kundu, personal communication, February 16, 2013.

32. Dani Rodrik and Arvind Subramanian, "From 'Hindu Growth' to Productivity Surge: The Mystery of the Indian Growth Transition," IMF Working Paper 04/77, International Monetary Fund, Washington, DC, 2004.

33. See Baldev Raj Nayar, "Social Stability in India under Globalization and Liberalization," *India Review* 6, no. 3 (July–September 2007): 133–64.

34. These crises included: the unprecedented drought in 1979–80, the threat to national unity by the insurgency in the Punjab during the 1980s, the assassination of Prime Minister Indira Gandhi in 1984 as a consequence of that insurgency, the riots and killings in Delhi following the assassination, four years of monsoon failures during the mid-1980s, another unprecedented drought in 1987–88, political conflict within the government of Rajiv Gandhi and the dismissal of Defense Minister V. P. Singh—who went on to establish a new opposition party and launch a major anticorruption movement against the government—the failure of the Congress Party to obtain a majority in the 1989 elections, the 1990 crisis in the Persian Gulf and the consequent massive Indian airlift of expatriates from West Asia, Operation Desert Storm, and finally the enormous economic crisis that confronted India literally with the threat of financial insolvency, compelling it to submit to a structural adjustment program.

35. Bhagat, too, relates the decline in migration to economic crisis, which he sees as having prevailed not only during the 1981–91 period but also during the 1971–81 period; similarly, he attributes the reversal of the decline to postliberalization economic recovery, emphasizing: "There is no doubt that the interstate mobility has considerably increased during 1991–2001 coinciding with India's economic liberalization program initiated in 1991"; see Bhagat, "Internal Migration in India," 12, 14.

36. K. C. Zachariah, *A Historical Study of Internal Migration in the Indian Sub-Continent, 1901–1931* (Bombay: Asia Publishing, 1964), 211.

37. Ibid., 200.

38. Ibid.

39. Relying on anecdotal evidence, some suggest that the Mahatma Gandhi National Rural Employment Guarantee Act (MGNREGA) "has indeed stemmed migration. Contractors have had to raise wages in cities to attract workers from the surrounding countryside. Even states like Bihar are sending fewer agricultural workers to work in Punjab and elsewhere." See Sridhar, Reddy, and Srinath, "Is It Push or Pull?" 49.

40. GoI, *Migration in India 2007–08*, 103–7.

41. GoI, "Central Statistics Office: National Account: Press Releases and Statements: State Domestic Product and Other Aggregates: Statement: Per Capita Net State Domestic Product at Current Prices" (New Delhi: Ministry of Statistics and Program Implementation, 2013); available at http://mospi.nic.in/mospi_new/upload/statewise_sdp1999_2000_9sep10.pdf, accessed February 21, 2013.

42. GoI, *Migration in India 2007–08*, 103, 112–13.

43. Jha, "Trickle Down Effects of Inter State Migration."

44. Ibid.

45. This finding runs counter to de Haan's position that "migration by and large remains circular rather than constituting the classic rural-urban transition." See de Haan, "Inclusive Growth?" 11.

IV
SUMMING UP

Chapter 11

CONCLUSION

GLOBALIZATION has been the reigning economic phenomenon since about the last quarter of the twentieth century, signifying the sharper and continued integration of the world economy. As such, it has been the target of a wide range of criticisms—among them, that it leads to economic destabilization, stagnation, deindustrialization, inequality, and regional disparities. All these themes have received considerable treatment in the substantial literature on globalization. The present study chose one particular part of the general critique of globalization for empirical examination, which asserts that it tends to lead to economic segmentation—the opposite of economic integration—and then to economic and, indeed, national disintegration. In itself, this assertion of the critics of globalization is not novel, since dependency theorists had earlier forcefully argued that international integration leads to national disintegration. Taking an agnostic view of overly general statements about the pitfalls of globalization, this study took recourse to examining the issue empirically through an inquiry into the single case of India after economic liberalization.

There is a serious lacuna in the critique that is noteworthy—and that has to do with the absence of the state as an active and dynamic agent with responsibility for the integration and adaptation of the society of which it is a part (of course, intentionally or not, incompetent states may aid forces of disintegration). Perhaps this lacuna springs from a tacit assumption that the state is epiphenomenal and merely represents market or economic forces. However, it is widely accepted that, while they interact and influence each other, the state and market are two separate social institutions with their separate logics. Even if it is conceded that the state has only "relative autonomy," such autonomy can be critical to outcomes; it is, indeed, the strategic position of the state that it compels those who seek to change the nature of the economy to first achieve or seize control of the state. Therefore, the role of the state cannot be left out of account in inquiring about the impact of globalization by way of economic segmentation and what it means for economic integration.

While the market has its separate sphere and separate logic, it is not an entirely independent social force but one that is regulated by the state. Moreover, the market, too, need not be taken as one-sided in having only adverse consequences for economic integration ("backwash effects"), for it may also have beneficial results ("spread effects"). Only empirical examination can reveal whether or not the effects have been beneficial. Consequently, both state and market are relevant in examining the impact of economic liberalization on India's economic integration. Besides state and market, history is also of relevance, for the impact of globalization on economic integration did not start on a clean state only after liberalization's inauguration. Thus, history, state, and market are all important to an empirical inquiry.

HISTORY

Ignoring the condition of the economy and polity before India opened to globalization through economic liberalization is likely to set up unrealistic standards in measuring the impact of globalization on economic integration. Things were not quite idyllic prior to globalization under the socialist or dirigiste regime, since poverty, inequality, economic stagnation, frequent economic crises, and interstate disparities as economic and social ills prevailed at that time, perhaps in greater measure than ever seen since. Indeed, India had to open up to globalization precisely because of the economic stagnation that had become the dominant feature of the earlier socialist regime, at least in the decade and a half from around 1965 to 1980, which was marked by frequent economic crises. Such stagnation had negative consequences not only for the country's national security but also for poverty alleviation and living standards. Perhaps it also may be related to the contemporaneous political turmoil and institutional decay from the mid-1960s onward, as witnessed in massive agitations, the splintering of the political party system, the regionalization of politics, and the fragmentation of the country's potential common market—all of this very evident in the decades *prior to* economic liberalization.

It is also instructive to note that threats to national integration existed long before globalization. National integration had been under assault from many sides since independence, and it is significant that Selig Harrison's book, *India: The Most Dangerous Decades*, which dealt with precisely the issue of India's possible breakup, was published as early as 1960. Also, V. S. Naipaul's *India: A Million Mutinies Now* was published in 1990, a year before economic liberalization was launched. The causes of the threats lay in India's domestic social structure of immense diversity and economic stagnation under socialism, not globalization.

STATE

Despite the institutional deterioration that the state had suffered during the decades prior to economic liberalization, the state has continued to play an important role as the guardian of India's economic integration. This study examined that role in three key areas: economic planning, change and adaptation in fiscal federalism, and reform of the indirect taxation system.

Despite economic liberalization, the Planning Commission continues to be an important institution for the coordination of economic planning at the center and in the states. It was retained because India's decision makers felt strongly that it was essential to India's economic advance and interests. True, the role of planning has diminished somewhat because of the turn to the market, but it is still substantial and significant. After economic liberalization, investment has become largely a function of the market. However, the public sector constitutes a huge part of India's economic life, and the Planning Commission has the responsibility for designing the outlays for that large sector, which is spread all across India. More significant, the commission has become the locus of pushing forward the state's new additional focus on "inclusiveness" or "inclusive growth," which places greater emphasis on welfare. Importantly, the commission continues to give a national cast to its planning endeavor through its coordination of state plans that fit into a larger economic vision for the country as a whole. Moreover, the National Development Council maintains its traditional function of bringing together the decision makers at the center and in the states to discuss issues related to planning. In these various respects, the Planning Commission as a state institution performs a constructive and crucial role in India's economic and national integration. Economic liberalization has modified that role, but it has not overthrown it.

The presence of the state as a dynamic actor is also evident in the area of fiscal federalism. The prevailing challenges in fiscal federalism preceded economic liberalization and were, in a sense, instrumental in making India turn to economic reform in 1991. In the ultimate analysis, these challenges boiled down to the perennial economic problem of scarcity—too few funds, too many demands. The compulsions of politics under a democracy at the center and in the states, in the face of limited revenues, have strained the center's finances, as reflected in persistently high fiscal deficits. The challenges have come to assume a more severe form due to the greater assertiveness on the part of the states and the weakening of the center because of coalition governments, in which regional parties sometimes have veto power.

Even in its weakened condition, however, the center has been creative in overseeing the transformation of the role of the Finance Commission to assure the financial health of the republic, to the extent possible within a democratic system, by pushing forward the aim of fiscal consolidation on a pan-Indian scale. This is strictly a postliberalization phenomenon. Equally, the endeavors of the Finance Commission have led to the rationalization and modernization of both the system of vertical devolution of fiscal transfers from the center to the states and that of horizontal distribution of fiscal transfers among the states. Through adroitly managing the challenges in fiscal federalism, the Finance Commission as an integrative institution has contributed to economic integration in considerable measure. Interestingly, while the center is often the target of criticism for not being generous enough toward the states in fiscal transfers, the remarkable fact is that India stands out among the world's federations in providing the highest share of nationwide revenues to its constituent states. However, fiscal stress remains an ever-present threat since fiscal populism is a constant temptation in a democratic system.

Indirect taxation is an area where, ironically, contrary to the predictions of the critics, globalization has been influential in persuading the state's decision makers to undertake reform that is "nationalizing" rather than segmenting in its effects. The stimulus for reform in this area lies in the requirement of efficiency since the national economy is now exposed to heightened competition in the world economy as a result of economic liberalization. Surprisingly, the center was enormously successful in persuading all the states to move to a value added tax (VAT) system in place of the multiple tax systems with their cascading levies that had prevailed among the various states prior to the opening to globalization. That success then emboldened the center and the states to undertake an even more ambitious endeavor to institute a comprehensive goods and services tax (GST) system.

However, it has been harder to achieve a full consensus between the center and the states on the various issues implicated in the proposed shift to the GST since a lot is at stake for both the center and the states. Remarkably, the impediments to reaching consensus are not external at all, but domestic. These have to do with the fragmentation of the national party system, the regionalization of politics, and the compulsion to forge coalitions in the formation of government at the center since the 1990s. Still, there is considerable momentum in the GST's favor. If and when the GST is implemented, it will make a formidable contribution to transforming India into a single common market—a truly monumental step in economic integration, provided other interstate barriers are also removed. The reform process relating to indirect taxation is an instructive case of how, on the one hand, globalization can have the unintended consequence of advancing economic and national integration and, on the other hand, how the state is not a passive object before international economic forces but a dynamic subject that acts to further economic integration in the face of challenges from the world economy.

It is apparent that the activities of the state in all three areas of economic planning, fiscal federalism, and reform of the indirect taxation system have endeavored to aid economic integration and to overcome its challenges.

MARKET

The critics of globalization often see the market—and, indeed, capitalism—as economically segmenting and disintegrating. In actual fact, the market incorporates both segmenting and integrating tendencies, even though analysts differ over which set predominates in what situations. Perhaps the balance of opinion would maintain that over the longer term, the market tends to integrate. This study has examined the integrative role of the market in India in the three areas that correspond to flows of goods and services, capital, and labor—that is, trade, investment, and migration—which serve as linkage mechanisms in economic integration.

With regard to trade, it is noteworthy first and foremost that it has seen a huge expansion. That expansion follows naturally from the fact that, contrary to the prognoses of economic stagnation posited by the critics of globalization, the economy has seen sustained growth after liberalization. Indeed, it saw outstanding growth acceleration for half a dozen years during liberalization's second decade, which was simply unprecedented in India's history in terms of its high rate and duration. Incidentally, some analysts demonstrate that growth acceleration has effects similar to autarky in promoting economic integration. In that sense, globalization and liberalization have aided integration. In constant U.S. dollars, India's economy expanded between three and a half and four times during the two decades from 1991 to 2011; the average growth rate of GDP from 1992 to 2002 was a healthy 5.8 percent and a remarkable 8.2 percent in the eight years from 2003 to 2010. To be sure, the Indian economy suffered a setback with the severe slowdown in 2011, but it would be hasty to make a couple of years of slower growth the basis for discrediting the entire growth record since liberalization. However, expectations meanwhile have risen steeply and what was believed to be a high growth rate in the preliberalization era is no longer considered satisfactory. More legitimate would be the criticism that, in its eagerness to step up the growth rate—either for geopolitical reasons or from considerations of electoral gains through measures of fiscal populism that higher growth would facilitate—the state has not been careful enough in adequately regulating hot money inflows.

To a certain extent, the increase in trade has been aided by some growth in physical infrastructure, though it is well established that inadequate infrastructure—for which the responsibility rests with the state—is a serious constraint on India's growth and integration. In the absence of separate data on domestic trade, it is difficult to discern whether the rise in domestic trade is a mere reflection of the expansion of foreign trade after the opening to globalization or whether it has domestic sources as well. Using civil aviation as a proxy for trade, this study demonstrates that the increase in internal trade has been generated by national economic expansion beyond its relationship to external trade. As such, the increase in trade after the opening to globalization has aided the country's economic integration rather than segmentation. Moreover, as documented in chapter 7 of this study, an analysis by Arvind Virmani and Surabhi Mittal—who specifically assessed the impact of liberalization on domestic market integration by comparing prices of commodities over time across different regional markets in India—established the strengthening of integration. No doubt, there are some serious impediments to trade integration in the country, but they often originate with the state rather than the market, primarily by way of poor infrastructure, the imposition of restrictions on interstate and intercity movement of commodities, and the levying of fiscal demands on such movement, thus inhibiting economic integration. Change in state policy with respect to these weaknesses is essential.

If there is increased economic integration through trade—as well as through other linkages, such as investment and migration—then the presumption would be that it ought to aid in the transmission of growth impulses across regions. Using sophisticated econometrics methodology, Ravindra H. Dholakia had earlier demonstrated—as discussed in chapter 7—that growth *diffusion* rather than *polarization* was manifest between the group of upper-income states and the group of lower-income states. A methodologically simpler treatment of the issue undertaken in this study with data on economic growth rates in the Indian states during the period 1985–2011 confirms that position, showing that growth acceleration has made for greater growth diffusion to the lower-income states. During 2000–2010, high growth in the upper-income states has been accompanied by high growth among the lower-income states, even though not always at the same pace. The evidence in favor of diffusion is thus quite robust. In addition, the accelerated growth rate of the economy has made for an accelerated rate of poverty reduction, far greater than anything seen before economic liberalization. In short, openness to the world economy has aided economic growth, the diffusion of such growth, and economic integration.

A weakness in this respect, however, is the increase in inequalities, which tend to diminish national solidarity. However, the second decade after liberalization has been noteworthy for the huge investments—in some eyes, excessive and fiscally imprudent—in the welfare of the underprivileged. In this regard, the state has modified the traditional efficiency-based understanding of economic liberalization by incorporating "inclusiveness" and thus attenuating inequality.

In investigating the linkage mechanism of investment, this study has focused on industry and industrial location. Regarding industry, the prognosis on deindustrialization offered by the critics seems simply untenable in light of the industrial growth manifest in the postliberalization period. No doubt, there is considerable dissatisfaction with India's industrial performance both in comparison with other Asian powers and in terms of India's own needs. The fault for this performance lies with the state for neglecting not only infrastructure but also the development of a comprehensive industrial policy (including foreign exchange policy) for pushing industry. The state could have been more assertive in working out such a policy earlier and, while there has been some change in this regard more recently, implementation is key. Regardless of the failure with respect to this in the past, it would be far-fetched to claim that there has been either deindustrialization or industrial stagnation.

Similarly, in relation to industrial location, an examination of the decade of growth acceleration demonstrated higher growth rates in net value added (NVA) among the lower-NVA states than among the upper-NVA states. That fact makes manifest the considerable diffusion of industrial growth to the lesser-industrialized states. Certainly, it would be difficult to maintain, as popular and scholarly discourse often does, that industrial growth has been limited to the coastal states. Seemingly, observers have failed to adequately take into account the industrial advance in the northern region. The inherent dynamism of the market seems to be advancing economic integration by expanding the scope of industry across the states, even if not at a rate that would satisfy the lower-NVA states. As ought to be expected, a single decade of higher growth rates among the lower-NVA states is not sufficient to radically alter the inherited industrial hierarchy among the states; besides, several of the lower-NVA states have experienced much higher population growth rates than the upper-NVA states, a fact that tends to adversely affect their status in industrialization on a per capita basis. Broadly, industrial performance among the states testifies to a general pattern of industrial growth and diffusion, to which there are a few exceptions.

This study extended the investigation of the linkage mechanism of investment to examine change with respect to the social composition of the providers of capital, that is, the capitalist class, to determine if it is still limited to the traditional business communities, as popular thought assumes. The evidence from the top sixty business groups in 2010 demonstrates that the capitalist class now encompasses a far wider spectrum of strata from India's social hierarchy than previously thought, although the traditional business communities do have a disproportionate share. Overall, there can be little doubt that the market, as a system that is inherently expansive and constantly expanding, has broadened the scope of the capitalist class to include groups that, until a few decades ago, were restricted only to agriculture.

Investigating only the top fifty or sixty business groups does not, however, provide an adequate picture of the changing social composition of the capitalist class as a whole, since room at the top is limited and the competition is fiercely intense. What is quite illustrative and impressive, however, is the emergence of business entrepreneurs even from among the Dalits as the oppressed section of the population; interestingly, the Dalits are now in the forefront of those who outspokenly sing the praises of capitalism in India. The domestic capitalist class has thus advanced economic integration by demonstrating that it is not closed, but open to entry from across the vast social diversity of India. It has advanced integration, too, by economically knitting India together into a single national market through the production and supply of goods and services across the country, and also through organizing itself into pan-Indian peak associations, which explicitly and energetically support policies (such as the GST and the common market) for the strengthening of India as a single economic entity.

Migration is the third of the linkage mechanisms in economic integration that has been examined in this study, since it serves to equalize economic opportunity to a certain extent between the more prosperous and the less prosperous areas and states. Interestingly, the first decade after economic liberalization, that is, 1991–2001 (data on migration are not yet available for the second decade, that is, 2001–11), saw a reversal of the earlier trend of decline in the migration rate, as if signifying that migration is a function of higher economic growth. Considering that massive numbers running into many millions are involved in interstate migration, one can only be impressed by the largely inconspicuous but still pervasive nature of the process, notwithstanding occasional eruptions of protests, sometimes accompanied by violence (that tend to attract greater media attention). Interstate migration has enabled many of the poor to escape poverty and many of the more well-off to avail of better opportunities elsewhere; both aspects contribute to the reduction of disparities between the advanced and backward areas and states and, in so doing, contribute to economic integration.

SUMMING UP

This empirical study of the issue of economic segmentation and integration under the impact of globalization and economic liberalization reveals a picture quite different from that offered by the critics of globalization in their critique of that social process. A succinct summary of the contrast between the critique and the empirical findings would suggest that instead of economic stagnation, there has been economic growth and growth acceleration, as well as an unprecedented fall in poverty accompanying the latter; instead of deindustrialization, there has been industrial growth; and instead of economic segmentation, there has been considerable strengthening of linkage mechanisms through trade expansion, diffusion of industry spatially, and an increase in interstate migration. As an expansive and dynamic social institution, the market has been instrumental in these various ways in strengthening economic integration, especially with the enhancement of its role after economic liberalization. It may well be that the beneficial results of globalization have been contingent on an economic boom in the world economy, but in the absence of liberalization, the Indian economy would not have been able to take advantage of them.

Besides the market, the state also has helped in the process of economic integration through continuing with economic planning (even though in its indicative rather than comprehensive form), especially in light of its new emphasis on inclusive growth. The state has, in addition, advanced economic integration through reforming fiscal federalism to emphasize fiscal consolidation on a pan-Indian scale, and also by pushing the cause of the common market by bringing about the implementation of VAT in the states and by further pressing for the introduction of the GST. Paradoxically, fiscal consolidation and the common market have been a response to the pressures of globalization for economic efficiency; in that sense, globalization has been integration-enabling rather than integration-fracturing. Nevertheless, some difficulties in pushing forward with the common market have emerged, not from globalization, but from India's own political structure with the weakening of the center because of the fragmentation of the party system, the regionalization of politics, and the dependence on coalitions. The state can further advance the cause of economic integration, however, by improving the condition of the nation's economic and social infrastructure and by removing controls on the movement of commodities across state boundaries.

On the negative side, social inequality has increased, with the top groups having benefited more from economic growth, but there still has been an impressive decline in poverty and the globalization-enabled state has instituted massive subsidies and income transfers to the poor, so that in effect it is possible to say that, while the rich have gotten richer, the poor have not gotten poorer. In addition, the size of those in the middle-income group as a percentage of the population has increased.

At first blush, it seems foolhardy to highlight some of the beneficial aspects of globalization given the enormous turmoil in the world economy, including the emerging economies and India, following the financial meltdown in 2008. However, the ethic of the social sciences dictates that the results of empirical investigation take priority over general and sweeping statements. Regardless, globalization is no panacea; it offers both benefits—much beyond those of any other economic system known to humans—and costs through exposure to external shocks and volatilities. As a stage in societal evolution, globalization is an existential fact of life and is indeed inescapable, as the experience of the Soviet bloc and China illustrates. What is required, therefore, is not avoidance of globalization but strategic engagement with it in which the relative costs and benefits are constantly weighed in an effort to minimize the former and maximize the latter by an appropriately reformed and capable state.

BIBLIOGRAPHY

Acharya, Shankar. "My Friend Amaresh." In *Public Economics: Theory and Policy—Essays in Honor of Amaresh Bagchi*, edited by M. Govinda Rao and Mihir Rakshit, 326–29. New Delhi: Sage, and NIPFP, 2011.

Ahluwalia, Isher Judge. *Industrial Growth in India: Stagnation since the Mid-Sixties.* Delhi: Oxford University Press, 1985.

Alesina, Alberto, and Enrico Spolaore. "On the Number and Size of Nations." *Quarterly Journal of Economics* 112, no. 4 (November 1997): 1027–56.

Alesina, Alberto, Enrico Spolaore, and Romain Wacziarg. "Economic Integration and Political Disintegration." *American Economic Review* 90, no. 3 (December 2000): 1276–96.

Amin, Samir. *Accumulation on a World Scale: A Critique of the Theory of Underdevelopment.* New York: Monthly Review Press, 1974.

Ash, Robert F., and Y. Y. Kueh. "Economic Integration within Greater China: Trade and Investment Flows between China, Hong Kong and Taiwan." *China Quarterly*, no. 136 (1993): 711–45.

Austin, Granville. *The Indian Constitution: Cornerstone of a Nation.* Oxford: Clarendon Press, 1966.

Babu, D. Shyam. "India's Liberalization and the Dalits." Asia Program Working Paper, Royal Institute of International Affairs, Chatham House, London, 2004.

Bagchi, Amaresh. "Evaluating India's Fiscal Federalism: Some Reflections on Past Half Century." In *Fiscal Federalism in India,* edited by P. K. Chaubey, 86–103. New Delhi: Deep and Deep, 2003.

———. "'Rethinking Federalism': An Overview of the Current Debates with Some Reflections in the Indian Context." In *Development, Poverty, and Fiscal Policy: Decentralization of Institutions*, edited by M. Govinda Rao, 224–52. New Delhi: Oxford University Press, 2002.

———. "Role of Planning and the Planning Commission: Case for a Review." *Economic and Political Weekly* 42, no. 44 (November 3, 2007): 92–100.

———. "Symposium on Report of Twelfth Finance Commission: Introduction and Overview." *Economic and Political Weekly* 40, no. 31 (July 30, 2005): 3388–95.

Bagchi, Amaresh, and Pinaki Chakraborty. "Towards a Rational System of Center-State Revenue Transfers in India: An Exploration." In *The Dynamics of Fiscal*

Federalism: Challenges before the Twelfth Finance Commission, edited by G. C. Srivastava, 15–44. New Delhi: Taxmann, 2004.

Bagchi, Amiya Kumar. *Colonialism and Indian Economy*. New Delhi: Oxford University Press, 2010.

———. *Private Investment in India, 1900–1939*. Cambridge: Cambridge University Press, 1972.

Balakrishnan, Pulapre. *Economic Growth in India: History and Prospect*. New Delhi: Oxford University Press, 2010.

Baru, Sanjaya. "Economic Policy and the Development of Capitalism in India: The Role of Regional Capitalists and Political Parties." In *Transforming India: Social and Political Dynamics of Democracy*, edited by Francine R. Frankel, Zoya Hassan, Rajeev Bhargava, and Balveer Arora, 207–30. New Delhi: Oxford University Press, 2000.

Basu, Durga Das. *Introduction to the Constitution of India*. 13th ed. New Delhi: Prentice-Hall of India, 1991.

Basu, Partha Pratim. "The CPI (M) and Globalization: Anatomy of Ambivalence." In *Facing Globality: Politics of Resistance, Relocation, and Reinvention in India*, edited by Bhupinder Brar and Pampa Mukherjee, 180–200. New Delhi: Oxford University Press, 2012.

Bhagat, R. B. "Internal Migration in India: Are the Underclass More Mobile?" In *Migration, Identity and Conflict: India Migration Report 2011*, edited by S. Irudaya Rajan, 7–24. New Delhi: Routledge, 2011.

Bhagat, Ram B. "Migrants' (Denied) Right to the City." In *Urban Policies and the Right to the City in India: Rights, Responsibilities and Citizenship*, edited by Marina Faetanini, 39–47. New Delhi: UNESCO, 2011.

Bhagat, R. B., and Soumya Mohanty. "Emerging Pattern of Urbanization and the Contribution of Migration in Urban Growth in India." *Asian Population Studies* 5, no. 1 (March 2009): 5–20.

Bhagwati, Jagdish. *In Defense of Globalization*. New York: Oxford University Press, 2004.

Bhagwati, Jagdish N., and Padma Desai. *India: Planning for Industrialization*. London: Oxford University Press, 1970.

Bhattacharya, Mohit. "The Mind of the Founding Fathers." In *Federalism in India: Origins and Development*, edited by Nirmal Mukarji and Balveer Arora, 87–104. New Delhi: Vikas, 1992.

Bhaya, Hiten, ed. *Indian Planning: Search for Change*. New Delhi: Asian Institute of Transport Development, 1997.

Bolton, Patrick, and Gerard Roland. "The Breakup of Nations: A Political Economy Analysis." *Quarterly Journal of Economics* 112, no. 4 (November 1997): 1057–90.

Bose, Prasenjit, ed. *Maoism: A Critique from the Left*. New Delhi: LeftWord Books, 2010.

Chakravarty, Sukhamoy. *Development Planning: The Indian Experience*. Oxford: Clarendon Press, 1987.

Chakravorty, Sanjoy, and Somik V. Lall. *Made in India: The Economic Geography and Political Economy of Industrialization*. New Delhi: Oxford University Press, 2007.

Chandhoke, Neera. "Globality, State, and Collective Imagination: The Indian Experience." In *Facing Globality: Politics of Resistance, Relocation, and Reinvention in India*, edited by Bhupinder Brar and Pampa Mukherjee, 94–110. New Delhi: Oxford University Press, 2012.

———. "Putting Civil Society in Its Place." *Economic and Political Weekly* 44, no. 7 (February 14, 2009): 12–16.

Chang, Ha-Joon. *Globalization, Economic Development and the Role of the State*. London: Zed Books, 2003.

Chatterjee, Partha. *The Nation and Its Fragments: Colonial and Postcolonial Histories*. Princeton, NJ: Princeton University Press, 1993.

Chaubey, P. K., ed. *Fiscal Federalism in India*. New Delhi: Deep and Deep, 2003.

Chelliah, Raja J. *Towards Sustainable Growth: Essays in Fiscal and Financial Sector Reforms in India*. Delhi: Oxford University Press, 1996.

Chelliah, Raja J., M. Govinda Rao, and Tapas Kumar Sen. "Issues before Tenth Finance Commission." *Economic and Political Weekly* 27, no. 47 (November 21, 1992): 2539–50.

Chen, Yu, Fung Kwan, and Guang-Zhen Sun. "Economic Integration and Development of the Chinese Economy: An Introduction." *Journal of the Asia Pacific Economy* 15, no. 4 (November 2010): 337–40.

Communist Party of India. "CPI Election Manifesto." Available at www.communistparty.in/.

———. "Political Resolution, XX Congress." Available at www.communistparty.in/.

Communist Party of India (Maoist). Central Committee, "Political Resolution" (Draft, September 2004). Available at www.bannedthought.net.

———. Central Committee (Provisional), "Party Program" (September 21, 2004). Available at www.bannedthought.net.

Communist Party of India (Marxist). *Documents of the 20th Congress of the Communist Party of India (Marxist) (Kozhikode, Kerala, April 4–9, 2012)*. New Delhi: CPI (M), 1912.

———. *Manifesto for the 15th Lok Sabha Elections, 2009*. New Delhi: CPI (M), 2009. Available at www.cpim.org/.

———. "Political Resolution Adopted at the XIX Congress of the Communist Party of India (Marxist), March 29 to April 3, 2008, Coimbatore." Available at www.cpim.org/.

Damodaran, Harish. *India's New Capitalists: Caste, Business, and Industry in a Modern Nation*. Houndmills, Basingstoke, UK: Palgrave Macmillan, 2008.

Dandekar, V. M. "Planning: What and How." In *Indian Planning: Search for Change*, edited by Hiten Bhaya, 119–52. New Delhi: Asian Institute of Transport Development, 1997.

de Haan, Arjan. "Inclusive Growth? Labor Migration and Poverty in India." ISS Working Paper 513, The Hague, Institute of Social Studies, 2011.

Denis, Eric, Partha Mukhopadhyay, and Marie-Helene Zerah. "Subaltern Urbanization in India." *Economic and Political Weekly* 47, no. 30 (July 28, 2012): 52–62.

Deshingkar, Priya. "Migration, Remote Rural Areas and Chronic Poverty in India." ODI Working Paper No. 323, Overseas Development Institute, London, 2010.

Deshingkar, Priya, and Shaheen Akter. "Migration and Human Development in India." Research Paper 2009/13, Human Development Reports, United Nations Development Programme, New York, 2009. Available at http://hdr.undp.org/en/reports/global/hdr2009/papers/HDRP_2009_13.pdf.

Dholakia, Ravindra H. "Testing for Trickle-Down or Polarization—Evidence from India." In Pennsylvania Economic Association, *Proceedings: Annual Conference, June 3–5, 2010*, 50–56. Grove City, PA: Grove City College, 2011.

Dr. Reddy's Laboratories. *Annual Report 2011–12: Life, Research, Hope*. Available at www.drreddys.com/investors/annual-reports.html.

Dyson, Tim, and Pravin Visaria. "Migration and Urbanization: Retrospect and Prospects." In *Twenty-First Century in India: Population, Economy, Human Development, and the Environment*, edited by Tim Dyson, Robert Cassen, and Leela Visaria, 108–29. Oxford: Oxford University Press, 2004.

Economic Times. "ET 500." October 2010.

Empowered Committee of State Finance Ministers. *First Discussion Paper on Goods and Services Tax in India*. New Delhi: Ministry of Finance, November 10, 2009. Available at http://finmin.nic.in.

———. *A White Paper on State-Level Value Added Tax*. New Delhi, January 17, 2005. Available at www.tinxsys.com.

Evans, Peter B., Dietrich Rueschemeyer, and Theda Skocpol, eds. *Bringing the State Back In*. Cambridge: Cambridge University Press, 1985.

Food and Agriculture Organization. "Towards an Indian Common Market: Removal of Restrictions on Internal Trade in Agricultural Commodities." Submitted to the National Commission on Farmers, Ministry of Agriculture, Government of India, New Delhi, December 2005. Available at www.fao.org/docrep/010/ai566e/ai566e00.htm.

Frank, Andre Gunder. *Dependent Accumulation and Underdevelopment*. New York: Monthly Review Press, 1979.

Gadgil, D. R. *Planning and Economic Policy in India*. Poona, India: Gokhale Institute of Politics and Economics, 1961.

Gae, R. S. "Administrative Relations between the Union and the States." In *Political System in India: Volume 4*, edited by Verinder Grover, 384–423. New Delhi: Deep and Deep, 1989.

Galbraith, John Kenneth. *The Nature of Mass Poverty*. Cambridge, MA: Harvard University Press, 1979.

Garrett, Geoffrey, and Jonathan Rodden. "Globalization and Fiscal Decentralization." In *Governance in a Global Economy: Political Authority in Transition*, edited by Miles Kahler and David A. Lake, 87–109. Princeton, NJ: Princeton University Press, 2003.

Ghosh, Jayati. "Economic Globalization, Cultural Identity and Social Conflict." In *India in the Age of Globalization: Contemporary Discourses and Texts*, edited by Suman Gupta, Tapan Basu, and Subarno Chattarji, 1–33. New Delhi: Nehru Memorial Museum and Library, 2004.

———. "The New Reality." *Frontline* 29, no. 18 (September 21, 2012): 30–32.

Gilpin, Robert. *The Political Economy of International Relations*. Princeton, NJ: Princeton University Press, 1987.

Goenka, Harsh. "Marwari Businesses at Crossroads." *Economic Times*, November 15, 2012. Available at http://economictimes.indiatimes.com.

Government of India. *Census of India 2001: Data Highlights, Migration Tables*. New Delhi: Registrar General and Census Commissioner, n.d.

———. *Economic Survey*. Annual.

———. *Eighth Five Year Plan (1992–1997)*. New Delhi: Planning Commission, 1992. Available at http://planningcommission.nic.in.

———. *Eleventh Five Year Plan (2007–2012): Inclusive Growth.* New Delhi: Oxford University Press, 2008. Available at http://planningcommission.nic.in.

———. *Final Report of the Expert Group on Taxation of Services.* Typescript. Ministry of Finance, Department of Revenue, 2001.

———. *Finance Ministers' Budget Speeches, 1947 to 1996.* New Delhi: Lok Sabha Secretariat, 1996.

———. *Migration in India 1999–2000: NSS 55th Round (July 1999–June 2000).* New Delhi: National Sample Survey Office, 2001.

———. *Migration in India 2007–2008: NSS 64th Round (July 2007–June 2008).* New Delhi: National Sample Survey Office, 2010.

———. "Press Note on Poverty Estimates, 2011–12." New Delhi: Planning Commission, July 2013.

———. *Provisional Population Totals: Paper 1 of 2011 Series 1.* New Delhi: Registrar General and Census Commissioner, India, 2011. Available at www.censusindia.gov.in.

———. *Public Enterprises Survey 1989–1990.* New Delhi: Bureau of Public Enterprises, 1991.

———. *Public Enterprises Survey 2009–2010.* New Delhi: Department of Public Enterprises, 2011.

———. *Report of the Advisory Group on Tax Policy and Tax Administration for the Tenth Plan.* New Delhi: Planning Commission, May 2001. Available at http://planning commission.nic.in.

———. *Report of the Eleventh Finance Commission (for 2000–2005).* New Delhi: June 2000.

———. *Report of the Eleventh Finance Commission on the Additional Term of Reference (for 2000–2005).* New Delhi: August 2000.

———. *Report of the High Level Expert Committee on Efficient Management of Public Expenditure.* New Delhi: Planning Commission, July 2011.

———. *Report of the Monopolies Inquiry Commission.* New Delhi: Government of India Press, 1965.

———. *Report of the Task Force on Implementation of the Fiscal Responsibility and Budget Management Act, 2003.* New Delhi: Ministry of Finance, July 2004. Available at http://finmin.nic.in.

———. *Report of the Twelfth Finance Commission (2005–10).* New Delhi: November 2004.

———. *Report of Working Group on Civil Aviation Sector: National Transport Development Policy Committee.* New Delhi: Ministry of Civil Aviation, June 2012.

———. "Scenarios: Shaping India's Future." New Delhi: Planning Commission, 2012. Available at http://planningcommission.nic.in/reports/genrep/scenarios_v10712.pdf.

———. *Second Five Year Plan.* New Delhi: Planning Commission, 1956. Available at http://planningcommission.nic.in.

———. *Seventh Five Year Plan (1985–1990).* New Delhi: Planning Commission, 1985. Available at http://planningcommission.nic.in.

———. *Task Force Report on Indirect Taxes: Final Report on Indirect Taxes.* New Delhi: Ministry of Finance, 2002.

———. Tenth Finance Commission. *Report for 1995–2000.* New Delhi: 1994.

———. *Tenth Five Year Plan 2002–2007.* New Delhi: Planning Commission, 2002. Available at http://planningcommission.nic.in.

———. Thirteenth Finance Commission. *Report of the Task Force on Goods and Services Tax*. New Delhi: December 15, 2009. Available at http://fincomindia.nic.in.

———. Thirteenth Finance Commission, 2010–2015. *Volume I: Report*. New Delhi: December 2009.

———. *Towards Faster and More Inclusive Growth: An Approach to the 11th Five Year Plan*. New Delhi: Planning Commission, 2006.

———. *Twelfth Five Year Plan (2012–2017): Faster, More Inclusive and Sustainable Growth*. New Delhi: Sage, 2013. Available at http://planningcommission.nic.in.

Government of India, Tax Reforms Committee. *Final Report: Part I*. New Delhi: Ministry of Finance, August 1992.

———. *Final Report: Part II*. New Delhi: Ministry of Finance, 1993.

———. *Interim Report*. New Delhi: Ministry of Finance, 1991.

Guhan, S. "Report of Tenth Finance Commission." *Economic and Political Weekly* 30, no. 16 (April 22, 1995): 877–86.

Gupta, Shekhar. "Walk the Talk: Capitalism Is Changing Caste Much Faster than Any Human Being, Dalits Should Look at Capitalism as a Crusader against Caste." *Indian Express*, June 11, 2013. Available at www.indian express.com.

Gupta, S. P. *Planning and Development in India*. New Delhi: Allied Publishers, 1989.

Hanson, A. H. *The Process of Planning: A Study of India's Five-Year Plans, 1950–1964*. London: Oxford University Press, 1966.

Hazari, R. K. *The Structure of the Corporate Private Sector: A Study of Concentration, Ownership and Control*. London: Asia Publishing, 1966.

Herd, Richard, and Willi Leibfritz. "Fiscal Policy in India: Past Reforms and Future Challenges." Working Paper No. 595, Economics Department, Organization for Economic Cooperation and Development, Paris, 2008.

Hindu Business Line. "Plan for Change." Editorial, April 25, 2011.

Hirschman, Albert O. *The Strategy of Economic Development*. New Haven, CT: Yale University Press, 1958.

Indian Institute of Public Opinion. *Quarterly of Public Opinion* 124–25 (July–December 1988).

Indian National Congress. *Lok Sabha Election: Manifesto of the Indian National Congress*. New Delhi: INC, 2009.

Iyer, P. Vaidyanathan. "A Four-Year Plan?" *Indian Express*, January 5, 2010.

Jain R. B. "Federalism in India: Emerging Pattern and Public Policy." In *Political System in India: Volume 4*, edited by Verinder Grover, 440–55. New Delhi: Deep and Deep, 1989.

Jenkins, Rob. *Democratic Politics and Economic Reform in India*. Cambridge: Cambridge University Press, 1999.

Jha, Veena. "Trickle Down Effects of Inter State Migration in a Period of High Growth in the Indian Economy." CSGR Working Paper 253/08, Center for the Study of Globalization and Regionalization, University of Warwick, Coventry, UK, 2008.

Kahl, Colin H. *States, Scarcity and Civil Strife in the Developing World*. Princeton, NJ: Princeton University Press, 2006.

Keshri, Kunal, and R. B. Bhagat. "Temporary and Seasonal Migration: Regional Pattern, Characteristics and Associated Factors." *Economic & Political Weekly* 47, no. 4 (January 28, 2012): 81–88.

Khanna, Tarun, and Krishna G. Palepu. "The Evolution of Concentrated Ownership in India: Broad Patterns and a History of the Indian Software Industry." In *A History of Corporate Government around the World*, edited by Randall K. Morck, 283–324. Chicago: University of Chicago Press, 2005.

Khera, Reetika, ed. *The Battle for Employment Guarantee*. New Delhi: Oxford University Press, 2011.

Kirk, Jason A. *India and the World Bank: The Politics of Aid and Influence*. London: Anthem Press, 2010.

Kochanek, Stanley A. *Business and Politics in India*. Berkeley: University of California Press, 1974.

Kohli, Atul. *Poverty amid Plenty in New India*. Cambridge: Cambridge University Press, 2012.

———. *State-Directed Development: Political Power and Industrialization in the Global Periphery*. Cambridge: Cambridge University Press, 2004.

Krishnaswamy, K. S., I. S. Gulati, and A. Vaidyanathan. "Economic Aspects of Federalism in India." In *Federalism in India: Origins and Development*, edited by Nirmal Mukarji and Balveer Arora, 180–212. New Delhi: Vikas, 1992.

Krugman, Paul. "Increasing Returns and Economic Geography." *Journal of Political Economy* 99, no. 3 (June 1991): 483–99.

Kudaisya, Medha M. *The Life and Times of G. D. Birla*. New Delhi: Oxford University Press, 2003.

———, ed. *The Oxford India Anthology of Business History*. New Delhi: Oxford University Press, 2011.

Kumar, Dharma, ed. *The Cambridge Economic History of India*. Cambridge: Cambridge University Press, 1983.

Kumar, Pradeep. *Studies in Indian Federalism*. New Delhi: Deep and Deep, 1988.

Kumar, Utsav, and Arvind Subramanian. "Growth in India's States in the First Decade of the 21st Century: Four Facts." *Economic and Political Weekly* 47, no. 3 (January 21, 2012): 48–57.

Kundu, Amitabh. "Migration and Urbanization in India in the Context of Poverty Alleviation." Paper presented at the International Conference on Policy Perspectives on Growth, Economic Structures and Poverty Reduction, Beijing, China, June 7–9, 2007. Available at www.networkideas.org/ideasact/jun07/Beijing_Conference_07/Amitabh_Kundu.pdf.

———. "Trends and Structure of Employment in the 1990s: Implications for Urban Growth." *Economic and Political Weekly* 32, no. 24 (June 14, 1997): 1399–405.

Kundu, Amitabh, and Lopamudra Ray Saraswati. "Migration and Exclusionary Urbanization in India." *Economic and Political Weekly* 47, nos. 26–27 (June 20, 2012): 219–27.

Maddison, Angus. *Class Structure and Economic Growth: India and Pakistan since the Moghuls*. London: George Allen and Unwin, 1971.

———. "Why and When Did the West Get Rich?" In *Globalization and Politics in India*, edited by Baldev Raj Nayar, 76–89. New Delhi: Oxford University Press, 2007.

Mahadevan, Raman. "Everyone Is a Vaishya: India's Business Communities, Ever in the Forefront, Now See Their Role Evolving." *Outlook India*, October 1, 2012.

Maira, Arun. "A New Vision for Planning: 15th Dr. Rajendra Prasad Memorial Lecture, New Delhi, 9th December 2011." Typescript, New Delhi, 2011.

Malik, Ashok. "The BJP, the RSS Family, and Globalization in India." In *Globalization and Politics in India*, edited by Baldev Raj Nayar, 288–306. New Delhi: Oxford University Press, 2007.

Markovits, Claude. *The Indian Business and Nationalist Politics, 1931–1939: The Indigenous Capitalist Class and the Rise of the Congress Party*. Cambridge: Cambridge University Press, 1985.

———. *Merchants, Traders, Entrepreneurs: Indian Business in the Colonial Era*. Houndmills, Basingstoke, Hampshire, UK: Palgrave Macmillan, 2008.

Marx, Karl, and Frederick Engels. *Manifesto of the Communist Party*. Moscow: Progress, 1975.

Mazumdar, Surajit. "Industry and Services in Growth and Structural Change in India: Some Unexplored Features." Working Paper 2010/02, Institute for Studies in Industrial Development, New Delhi, January 2010.

Mehrotra , Santosh, and Ankita Gandhi. "India's Human Development in the 2000s: Towards Social Inclusion." *Economic and Political Weekly* 47, no. 14 (April 7, 2012): 59–64.

Mehta, Uday S. "Constitutionalism." In *The Oxford Companion to Politics in India*, edited by Niraja Gopal Jayal and Pratap Bhanu Mehta, 14–27. New Delhi: Oxford University Press, 2012.

Melchior, Arne. "Globalization, Domestic Market Integration, and the Regional Disparities in India." NUPI Working Paper 780, Norwegian Institute of International Affairs, Oslo, October 2010.

Migdal, Joel. *Strong Societies and Weak States: State-Society Relations and State Capabilities in the Third World*. Princeton, NJ: Princeton University Press, 1988.

Miglani, Smita, and Arpita Mukherjee. "Logistics Sector in India: Opportunities and Constraints for EU Business." *Journal of Indo-European Business Studies* 1 (November 2011): 87–113.

Mukhopadhyay, Debes. "Center-State Financial Relations in India: An Account of Major Debates." In *Fiscal Federalism in India*, edited by P. K. Chaubey, 55–68. New Delhi: Deep and Deep, 2003.

Myrdal, Gunnar. *Asian Drama: An Inquiry into the Poverty of Nations*. New York: Twentieth Fund, 1968.

———. *Rich Lands and Poor Lands: The Road to World Prosperity*. New York: Harper and Row, 1957.

Nadig, Kruttika. "Ashok Khade: Man Who Built Most Sought-After Offshore Fabrication Company DAS Offshore." *Economic Times*, July 21, 2011. Available at http://articles.economictimes.indiatimes.com/2011-07-21/news/29798122_1_blanc-pens-mont-blanc-ssc-exam.

Nagaraj, R. "India's Dream Run, 2003–08: Understanding the Boom and Its Aftermath." *Economic and Political Weekly* 48, no. 20 (May 18, 2013): 39–51.

———. "Trends and Patterns in Industrial Growth: A Review of Evidence and Explanations." Paper sponsored by the Indian Council of Social Science Research, Indira Gandhi Institute of Development Research, Mumbai, June 21, 2012.

National Institute of Public Finance and Policy. *Reform of Domestic Trade Taxes in India: Issues and Options: Report of a Study Team*. New Delhi: NIPFP, 1994.

Nayar, Baldev Raj. "BJP's Economic Nationalism in Theory and Practice." In *India and the Politics of Developing Countries: Essays in Memory of Myron Weiner*, edited by Ashutosh Varshney, 227–55. New Delhi: Sage, 2004.

———. "Economic Planning as an Integrative Mechanism in India: Changes and Challenges after Economic Liberalization." *India Review* 11, no. 4 (October–December 2012): 226–58.

———. *The Geopolitics of Globalization*. New Delhi: Oxford University Press, 2005.

———. *Globalization and India's Fiscal Federalism: Finance Commission's Adaptation to New Challenges*. Monograph 20/2012, Madras School of Economics, Chennai, India, March 2012.

———. *Globalization and Nationalism: The Changing Balance in India's Economic Policy, 1950–2000*. New Delhi: Sage, 2001.

———. "Globalization, the State, and India's Halting March to Common Market: The Political Economy of Tax Reform under Federalism." *India Review* 10, no. 3 (July–September 2011): 201–45.

———. *India's Globalization: Evaluating the Economic Consequences*. Washington, DC: East-West Center, 2006.

———. *India's Mixed Economy: The Role of Ideology and Interest in Its Development*. Bombay: Popular Prakashan, 1989.

———. *The Modernization Imperative and Indian Planning*. New Delhi: Vikas, 1972.

———. *The Myth of the Shrinking State: Globalization and the State in India*. New Delhi: Oxford University Press, 2009.

———. "Political Mainsprings of Economic Planning in the New Nations: The Modernization Imperative versus Social Mobilization." *Comparative Politics* 6, no. 3 (April 1974): 341–66.

———. "Social Stability in India under Globalization and Liberalization." *India Review* 6, no. 3 (July–September 2007): 133–64.

———. "When Did the 'Hindu' Rate of Growth End?" *Economic and Political Weekly* 41, no. 19 (May 13, 2006): 1885–90.

———, ed. *Globalization and Politics in India*. New Delhi: Oxford University Press, 2007.

Nehru, Jawaharlal. *The Discovery of India*. New York: John Day, 1946.

Nielsen, Klaus. "Indicative Planning." In *The New Palgrave Dictionary of Economics* (2008). Available at www. dictionaryofeconomics.com.

Nove, Alec. "Planned Economy." In *The New Palgrave: A Dictionary of Economics*, vol. 3, edited by John Eatwell, Murray Milgate, and Peter Newman, 879–85. London: Macmillan, 1987.

Pai, Sudha. *Developmental State and the Dalit Question in Madhya Pradesh: Congress Response*. New Delhi: Routledge, 2012.

Palma, Gabriel. "Dependency: A Formal Theory of Underdevelopment or a Methodology for the Analysis of Concrete Situations?" *World Development* 6 (July–December 1978): 881–922.

Panagariya, Arvind. "Growth and Reforms during 1980s and 1990s." *Economic and Political Weekly* 39, no. 25 (June 19, 2004): 2581–94.

———. *India: The Emerging Giant*. New York: Oxford University Press, 2008.

Papola, T. S., Nitu Maurya, and Narendra Jena. "Inter-Regional Disparities in Industrial Growth and Structure." Occasional Paper Series 2011/4, Institute for Studies in Industrial Development, New Delhi, 2011.

Parikh, Kirit S. "The Role of Planning." *Business Standard*, July 21, 2007.

Patnaik, Prabhat. *The Retreat to Unfreedom: Essays on the Emerging World Order*. New Delhi: Tulika Books, 2003.

Pedersen, Jorgen Dige. *Globalization, Development and the State: The Performance of India and Brazil since 1990*. Houndmills, Basingstoke, Hampshire, UK: Palgrave Macmillan, 2008.

Philip, Shaju. "A Youthful, Migrant Workforce Takes Root in an Ageing Kerala." *Indian Express*, February 21, 2013. Available at www.indianexpress.com.

Piramal, Gita, Sudeep Budhiraja, and Sumantra Ghoshal. "Hero Honda Motors: A Web of Relationships." In *World Class in India: A Casebook of Companies in Transformation*, edited by Sumantra Ghoshal, Gita Piramal, and Sudeep Budhiraja, 553–86. New Delhi: Penguin, 2001.

Polanyi, Karl. *The Great Transformation*. New York: Rinehart, 1957.

Purfield, Catriona. "Mind the Gap: Is Economic Growth in India Leaving Some States Behind?" IMF Working Paper WP/06/103, International Monetary Fund, Washington, DC, 2006.

Pylee, M. V. *Constitutional Government in India*. Bombay: Asia Publishing, 1965.

Rajakumar, J. Dennis, and John S. Henley. "Growth and Persistence of Large Business Groups in India." *Journal of Comparative International Management* 10, no. 1 (2007): 3–22.

Raju, Swati. "Growth across States in the 2000s: Evidence of Convergence." *Economic and Political Weekly* 47, no. 23 (June 9, 2012): 76–79.

Rangachari, A. "Role and Relevance of Planning Commission." *Hindu*, September 18, 2011. Available at www.thehindu.com.

Rangarajan, C., and D. K. Srivastava. *Federalism and Fiscal Transfers in India*. New Delhi: Oxford University Press, 2011.

Rao, G. M. "We Are an Airport Company, Not a Real Estate Company" [Walk the Talk on NDTV 24x7 with the *Indian Express* Editor-in-Chief Shekhar Gupta]. *Indian Express*, August 7, 2012. Available at www.indianexpress.com.

Rao, M. Govinda. "India: Intergovernmental Fiscal Relations in a Planned Economy." In *Fiscal Decentralization in Developing Countries*, edited by Richard M. Bird and Francois Vaillancourt, 78–114. Cambridge: Cambridge University Press, 1998.

———. "Tax System Reform in India: Achievements and Challenges Ahead." Paper prepared for the International Symposium on Tax Policy and Reform in Asian Countries, Hitotsubhashi University, Tokyo, Japan, July 1–2, 2005. Available at www.econ.hit-u.ac.jp/~kokyo/sympojuly05/papers/Tax%20System%20Reform-Tokyo(india)2.pdf.

———. "Think TIN, Not Just GST." *Business Standard*, March 21, 2010. Available at www.business-standard.com.

———. "The 13th Finance Commission's Report: Conundrum in Conditionalities." *Economic and Political Weekly* 45, no. 48 (November 27, 2010): 46–55.

Rao, M. Govinda, and R. Kavita Rao. "Trends and Issues in Tax Policy and Reform in India." In *The India Policy Forum 2005–06*, edited by Arvind Panagariya and Suman Bery, 55–122. New Delhi: Sage, 2006.

Rao, M. Govinda, and Nirvikar Singh. *The Political Economy of Federalism*. New Delhi: Oxford University Press, 2005.

Reddy, G. V. Krishna. "Only Trust and Confidence Will Help Achieve Your Goal." *Outlook Business*, August 18, 2012. Available at www.business.outlookindia.com.

Rodrik, Dani. *The Globalization Paradox: Democracy and the Future of the World Economy*. New York: W. W. Norton, 2011.

———. *Has Globalization Gone Too Far?* Washington, DC: Institute for International Economics, 1997.

Rodrik, Dani, and Arvind Subramanian. "From 'Hindu Growth' to Productivity Surge: The Mystery of the Indian Growth Transition." IMF Working Paper 04/77, International Monetary Fund, Washington, DC, 2004.

Rosecrance, Richard N., Etel Solingen, and Arthur A. Stein. "Globalization and Its Effects: Introduction and Overview." In *No More States? Globalization, National Self-Determination, and Terrorism*, edited by Richard N. Rosecrance and Arthur A. Stein, 3–21. Lanham, MD: Rowman and Littlefield, 2006.

Rothermund, Dietmar. *An Economic History of India: From Pre-Colonial Times to 1991*. London: Routledge, 1993.

Roy, Tirthankar. *The Economic History of India, 1857–1947*. New Delhi: Oxford University Press, 2000.

Sapir, Andre. "European Integration at the Crossroads: A Review Essay on the 50th Anniversary of Bela Balassa's *Theory of Economic Integration*." *Journal of Economic Literature* 49, no. 4 (2011): 1200–29.

Sarkar, Jayati. "Business Groups in India." In *The Oxford Handbook of Business Groups*, edited by James R. Lincoln, Takashi Hikino, and Asli M. Colpan, 294–322. Oxford: Oxford University Press, 2010.

Sarkar, Sumit. *Modern India, 1885–1947*. Delhi: Macmillan, 1983.

Sarkaria Commission. *Sarkaria Commission and Its Recommendations*. Available at http://interstatecouncil.nic.in/CHAPTERX.pdf.

Seervai, H. M. *Constitutional Law of India: A Critical Commentary*. 3rd ed. Bombay: N. M. Tripathi, 1984.

Seshan, Sekhar. "Grabbing the Big Chance." *Business India*, August 19, 2012, 74–78. Available at www.businessindiagroup.com.

Shetty, S. L. "Structural Retrogression in the Indian Economy since the Mid-Sixties." *Economic and Political Weekly* 13, nos. 6–7 (February 1978): 185–244.

Shome, Parthasarathi. "India: Resource Mobilization through Taxation." In *A Sustainable Fiscal Policy for India: An International Perspective*, edited by Peter S. Heller and M. Govinda Rao, 189–215. New Delhi: Oxford University Press, 2006.

Singh, Bhawani. "Federalism and State Autonomy in India: The Paradigm and the Paradox." In *Political System in India: Volume 4*, edited by Verinder Grover, 97–107. New Delhi: Deep and Deep, 1989.

Singh, Manmohan. "Commanding Heights." PBS Interview, 2000. Available at www.pbs.org/wgbh/commandingheights/shared/minitext/int_manmohansingh.html.

———. "PM's Key-Note Address at the India-Today Conclave." New Delhi, March 18, 2011. Available at http://pmindia.nic.in/.

Sinha, Rakesh. "All Over, Police Is under the State Government" [Sheila Dikshit]. *Indian Express*, February 17, 2013.

Sinha, Yashwant. *Confessions of a Swadeshi Reformer.* New Delhi: Penguin/Viking, 2007.

Sridhar, Seetharam A., Venugopala Reddy, and Pavan Srinath. "Is It Push or Pull? Recent Evidence from Migration in India." Final Report 10-04; paper submitted on 10th Round Regional Research Competition of SANEI, South Asia Network of Economic Research Institutes, June 2010. Available at http://saneinetwork.net/Files/10_04___K_S_Sridhar.pdf.

Sridharan, E., ed. *Coalition Politics and Democratic Consolidation in Asia.* New Delhi: Oxford University Press, 2012.

Srinivasan, T. N. "The Costs of Hesitant and Reluctant Globalization: India." *Indian Economic Review* 38, no. 2 (2003): 131–55.

———. *Growth, Sustainability, and Economic Reforms.* New Delhi: Oxford University Press, 2011.

Srivastava, D. K. "Vertical Sharing and Horizontal Distribution of Resources: The Equity and Efficiency Trade-Off." *Economic and Political Weekly* 45, no. 48 (November 27, 2010): 64–70.

Srivastava, D. K., and Bhujanga C. Rao. "Fiscal Relations between the Center and the States: Dependence of States on Devolution of Funds." In GoI, *Commission on Center–State Relations: Supplementary Volume-II: Research Studies*, 1–78. New Delhi: Commission on Center–State Relations, March 2010.

Srivastava, Ravi, and S. K. Sasikumar. "An Overview of Migration in India, Its Impacts and Key Issues." Paper for Regional Conference on Migration, Development and Pro-Poor Policy Choices in Asia, Department for International Development, London, 2003.

Streeten, Paul. "Paradoxes of Globalization." In *New Thinking in Macroeconomics: Social, Institutional, and Environmental Perspectives*, edited by Jonathan M. Harris and Neva R. Goodwin, 53–78. Cheltenham, UK: Edward Elgar, 2003.

Subrahmanian, K. K. "Inter-regional Dimension of Industrial Growth." In *The Indian Economy since Independence*, edited by B. A. Prakash, 361–72. New Delhi: Pearson, 2009.

Sunkel, Osvaldo. "Capitalismo transnacional y desintegracion nacional en la America Latina." *Trimestre Economico* 63, no. 250 (April–June 1996): 525–85.

Tilly, Charles. "Reflections on the History of European State-Making." In *The Formation of National States in Western Europe*, edited by Charles Tilly, 3–85. Princeton, NJ: Princeton University Press, 1975.

Tripathi, Dwijendra. *The Oxford History of Indian Business.* New Delhi: Oxford University Press, 2004.

Tripathi, Dwijendra, and Jyoti Jumani. *The Oxford History of Contemporary Indian Business*. New Delhi: Oxford University Press, 2013.

Tyler, William G., and J. Peter Wogart. "Economic Dependence and Marginalization: Some Empirical Evidence." *Journal of Inter-American Studies and World Affairs* 15, no. 1 (1973): 36–45.

Venkatasubbiah, H. *Enterprise and Economic Change: 50 Years of FICCI*. New Delhi: Vikas, 1977.

Virmani, Arvind. "India's Economic Growth: From Socialist Rate of Growth to Bharatiya Rate of Growth." Working Paper 122, Indian Council for Research on International Economic Relations, New Delhi, 2004.

Virmani, Arvind, and Surabhi Mittal. "Domestic Market Integration." Working Paper 183, Indian Council for Research on International Economic Relations, New Delhi, 2006.

Wallerstein, Immanuel. *World-Systems Analysis: An Introduction*. Durham, NC: Duke University Press, 2004.

Weiss, Linda, ed. *States in the Global Economy: Bringing Domestic Institutions Back In*. New York: Cambridge University Press, 2003.

Wiarda, Howard J. "Rethinking Political Development: A Look Backward over Thirty Years, and a Look Ahead." *Studies in Comparative International Development* 24, no. 4 (Winter 1989–90): 65–82.

Williamson, Jeffrey G. "Regional Inequality and the Process of National Development: A Description of the Patterns." *Economic Development and Cultural Change* 13, no. 4 (July 1965): part 2, 1–84.

Wolf, Martin. *Why Globalization Works*. New Haven, CT: Yale University Press, 2004.

Zachariah, K. C. *A Historical Study of Internal Migration in the Indian Sub-continent, 1901–1931*. Bombay: Asia Publishing, 1964.

INDEX